POWDER KEG IN
THE MIDDLE EAST

POWDER KEG IN THE MIDDLE EAST

The Struggle for Gulf Security

Edited by
Geoffrey Kemp and Janice Gross Stein

AMERICAN ASSOCIATION FOR
THE ADVANCEMENT OF SCIENCE
and
ROWMAN & LITTLEFIELD PUBLISHERS, INC.

ROWMAN & LITTLEFIELD PUBLISHERS, INC.

Published in the United States of America
by Rowman & Littlefield Publishers, Inc.
4720 Boston Way, Lanham, Maryland 20706

3 Henrietta Street
London WC2E 8LU, England

British Cataloging in Publication Information Available

Library of Congress Cataloging-in-Publication Data

Powder keg in the Middle East : the struggle for Gulf security / edited by Geoffrey
Kemp and Janice Gross Stein.
p. cm.
Includes bibliographical references and index.
1. Middle East—Politics and government—1979– I. Kemp, Geoffrey. II. Stein, Janice
Gross.
DS63.1.P683 1995   956.05—dc20 95-4607

ISBN 0–8476–8075-4 (cloth : alk. paper)
ISBN 0–8476–8076-2 (pbk. : alk. paper)

Printed in the United States of America

⊖™ The paper used in this publication meets the minimum requirements of
American National Standard for Information Sciences—Permanence of
Paper for Printed Library Materials, ANSI Z39.48–1964.

Contents

Part III. Key Regional Security Issues: Weapons and Water

Part IV. Security Arrangements and Implications for U.S. Policy

List of Tables and Figures

Introduction

In 1992, the Program on Science and International Security of the American Association for the Advancement of Science organized a study group on "Future Security Arrangements in the Middle East." The steering committee for this project consisted of Thomas Wander, Janice Gross Stein, Geoffrey Kemp, Marvin Miller, Thomas Naff, and William Quandt. Over the next two years, the project convened three international workshops; this volume brings together a selection of the papers presented at these meetings.

The focus of the first workshop was on "Sources of Conflict in the Middle East." This meeting provided a very productive forum for detailed exchanges on the diverse and complex problems of war and peace that beset the Middle East. With this foundation and in view of the formal diplomatic initiatives on Arab-Israeli peace that began with the Madrid Conference in November 1991 and were well underway by the spring of 1993, the next two workshops were focused more narrowly on the problems of the Persian Gulf, an area not presently part of the Middle East peace process.

The Persian Gulf continues to be a region of critical importance to the United States and the industrial world. Its oil and natural gas resources are, if anything, more important today than they were in the 1970s, when the energy crisis emerged as a dominant feature of the international landscape. Despite the allied victory in Desert Storm, the Gulf remains dangerous because the underlying sources of conflict in the region remain unresolved. The present leaders of Iraq and Iran continue to challenge Western interests, and there are growing signs of unrest within each country. In addition, the future stability of key U.S. allies, most notably the Gulf Cooperation Council states, is at risk because of the political and sociological dynamics of the peninsula.

Accordingly, the second workshop focused specifically on "Future Developments in Iran and Iraq: Implications for Regional Security." At this meeting it became clear that while Iran and Iraq are key players in any future Gulf security arrangements, it was not possible to consider future stability in either country without considering the broader context, including the future of the Kurds and the importance of Turkey and the United States as influences on domestic politics in both countries.

Drawing upon a detailed agenda of issues that surfaced in that meeting and the need to examine the practical implications of regional instability, the third workshop in the project focused on "Future Security Arrangements in the Gulf." While the main emphasis was on the implications of regional dynamics for American policy, the impact of Gulf security issues on the concerns and policies of other countries was also discussed in some detail.

Based on the deliberations at all three workshops, this volume adopts a broad mandate for considering future sources of conflict in the Gulf. While military issues and the dynamics of the arms race remain very important in the context of the regional military balance and the dynamics of conflict escalation, it is our belief that the underlying sources of conflict—which drive the arms race—are related to broad-based demographic, technological, cultural, and ideological factors and trends. These embrace issues from water security to religious conflict and population dynamics.

The introductory chapter by Kemp and Stein outlines the breadth of the sources of conflict in the Gulf and points to some of the wild cards that could shock the Gulf in the coming decade. It attempts, on the basis of expert judgment, to assign rough probabilities to anticipated future events. The next section deals primarily with the key regional players, including nonstate actors such as the Kurds. The essays by Bakhash, Chubin, Ozel, McDowell, Salih, and Tripp provide a timely overview of both the general and unique circumstances that face the current leadership in each case. These chapters alone make sober reading and confirm the fragility and instability of the region. Resource and military issues are covered in the chapters by Naff and Miller. Both authors stress that with political will there are practical solutions to the problems posed by water scarcity and the spread of weapons of mass destruction. In the last section, a wide menu of security arrangements to deal with these potential conflicts are discussed by Salame, Quandt, McNaugher, and Hermann. The last three chapters also provide practical advice on how the United States should manage its Gulf policy at a time of dynamic change.

The editors would like to acknowledge the support, advice and practical help they have received from their co-committee members in assuring the speedy editing of papers and the format and focus of the volume. In particular they would like to thank Tom Wander for his leadership of the workshops, Ray Orkwis for his excellent logistical support, and Angela Telesford for providing important administrative support for the meetings. With respect to this volume, Angela Telesford initially and, later, Linn Stanley worked assiduously to bring the papers through their various stages, incorporating edits, typing hard copy, and collating proof copies for the editors. Tom Wander reviewed several chapters, Ray Orkwis produced the publication, and Linda Owens developed the final cover design. David Elwell's copyediting skills honed the authors' various styles into a consistent whole, without homogenizing the contributions. In addition, Janice Stein thanks Gillian Manning and Geoffrey Kemp thanks Jeremy Pressman, Chris Bicknell, and Assia Ivantcheva all of the Carnegie Endowment for International Peace's Middle East Arms Control Project for their work on the volume.

Finally, AAAS and all of the project participants are grateful to the John D. and Catherine T. MacArthur Foundation and the U.S. Institute of Peace for their generous support of this workshop series.

Geoffrey Kemp

Janice Gross Stein
January 1995

Part I.
SOURCES OF CONFLICT
IN THE PERSIAN GULF

1

ENDURING SOURCES OF CONFLICT IN THE PERSIAN GULF REGION: PREDICTING SHOCKS TO THE SYSTEM

Geoffrey Kemp and Janice Gross Stein

The likelihood of major military conflict in the Persian Gulf region depends on both global and regional trends. So long as Persian Gulf oil is of continuing strategic importance to the global community, the stability of the Gulf is intimately connected to the global economic system. Regimes in the Gulf are also sensitive to the political, economic, environmental, demographic, religious, and ideological forces that are bubbling within the region.

Many countries in the region have made remarkable political and economic progress over the past few decades. The standard of living, including the literacy and health of the people in most Gulf countries, has risen to unprecedented heights, and some of the problems, such as water and border disputes, are amenable to economic and political solutions.

Nevertheless, militant religious forces continue to destabilize regional politics, as do local nationalist aspirations, the struggle over political succession in both conservative and radical regimes, high rates of population growth, unequal economic growth, and heavy spending on military capabilities. This chapter looks first at global trends and then at the underlying regional dynamics that set the broad parameters of future conflict. It then examines the interstate sources of regional conflict, the impact of an unstable periphery, ethnic and religious conflicts that transcend borders, and the military dynamics that can fuel violent conflict within the Persian Gulf region. In the conclusion, we map the most dangerous and most likely shocks to the system and examine their implications for conflict management.

The Changing Global System

The global system has undergone dramatic changes since the end of the Cold War; moreover, the process of change is ongoing. Many of the changes have had a positive impact on the Persian Gulf region. The breakup of the Soviet Union and the emerging democracies in Eastern Europe and the former Soviet Union have eliminated the bipolar competition for influence and have reduced the flow of subsidized military equipment to the region. The United States is the sole global superpower, with a preponderance of military force at its disposal and headed by a president pledged to seek cooperation and engagement with the rest of the world rather than unilateralism, isolation, and retreat. Conjointly, a renewed focus on the United Nations and other international organizations as the natural conduits for conflict resolution and the beginnings of a cooperative security paradigm have created new opportunities to ensure the security of like-minded groups of states within the region.

In the world economic system, strong groups have emerged that continue to support efforts to promote free trade. A global communications revolution also makes it increasingly difficult for dictatorships and authoritarian regimes to isolate their people and to restrict their capacity to communicate directly with supporters elsewhere.

However, not all the changes in the global system are conducive to more effective conflict management: the future is still opaque. Russia has not yet established itself as a viable democracy, and it is possible that an authoritarian regime could reemerge. Violent conflicts have erupted around the periphery of the former Soviet Union, and some impinge directly on the Persian Gulf. A vacillating administration in Washington has called into question the United States' commitment to global leadership, and a new Republican-controlled Congress is likely to further weaken the U.S. president. Continuing economic competition between the major economic blocs could lead to deteriorating political relations and new kinds of conflict within the global economic system. The continued proliferation of weapons of mass destruction creates unprecedented challenges to peace globally and within the Persian Gulf.

The Middle East: Population, Resources, and Technology

Within the Middle East there are a number of underlying trends that will have important influences on the regional balance of military and economic power for the indefinite future. The three key variables are population dynamics, the supply of and demand for natural resources, and access to advanced technology.

Population Dynamics

The Middle East, from Egypt to Turkey to Iran, but excluding North Africa, in 1994 had 274,830,643 inhabitants, of which a total of 111,112,318 were living in the Persian Gulf region (see Table 1.1).[1] Arabs form the largest ethnic group, about 50 percent of the population. They are followed by Turks (25 percent), Persians (12 percent), Kurds (7 percent), and Jews (2 percent) (see Table 1.2). Population growth continues at a rapid rate, and experts expect a regional total of 576 million by the year 2025, more than double the current figure. The rate of population growth and the population profile have troubling implications for water use, land use and agricultural production, the distribution of natural resources, and political stability.

Growth in population varies widely within the region. The fertility rates of Oman, Saudi Arabia, and Iraq[2] are among the world's highest, but birthrates are falling in Egypt, Lebanon, and Turkey.[3] In the Persian Gulf region, birth and fertility rates are significantly higher than for other areas in the Middle East, such as Egypt, Turkey, and Lebanon. In Egypt, as well as in all the Arab Mediterranean countries, the rate of population growth has started to decline. In Egypt in 1986, there were 1,928,000 births; five years later the number had decreased by about 10 percent, to 1,754,000 births.[4]

While wealthier countries in the region have brought down their mortality rates, some poorer countries continue to struggle. Thus in Kuwait the infant mortality rate is 12.5 deaths per thousand live births, while Iraq has the highest rate in the Persian Gulf region, 67.1, followed by Iran, 60.2. In Egypt, the infant mortality rate is as high as 76.4.

The richer countries in the Persian Gulf region have significant oil wealth and small populations and have encouraged high fertility rates for political and security reasons. These states have assumed much of the cost of child rearing. In Saudi Arabia, to encourage higher fertility, the government has put restrictions on contraception, including a ban on advertising. In Kuwait, the government encourages fertility by providing

Table 1.1. Persian Gulf region population data.

Country	Population[a] Total No.	Population[a] % Nationals	Population growth rate (%)	Life expectancy at birth (years)	Infant mortality rate[b]	Literacy (%)	Net migration rate[c]	Labor force
Bahrain	585,683	68	2.96	73.51	19	77 (1990 est.)	6.83	140,000[d]
Iran	65,615,474	NA[e]	3.46	65.66	60.2	54 (1990 est.)	0	15,400,000[f]
Iraq	19,889,666	NA	3.73	65.74	67.1	60 (1990 est.)	0.4	4,400,000[g]
Kuwait	1,819,322	39	5.24[h]	74.99	12.5	73 (1990 est.)	23.35	566,000[i]
Oman	1,701,470	73	3.64	67.79	36.7	NA	0	430,000
Qatar	512,779	25	2.56	72.64	21.6	76 (1986 est.)	10.31	104,000[j]
Saudi Arabia	18,196,783	69	3.24	67.91	52.1	62 (1990 est.)	0	5,000,000–6,000,000
United Arab Emirates	2,791,141	24	4.79	72.26	21.7	68 (1980 est.)	23.31	580,000[k]

Source: Central Intelligence Agency, The World Factbook 1994 (Washington, D.C.: Central Intelligence Agency, 1994).

N.B.: Unless otherwise indicated, all the figures are 1994 estimates. Population statistics for any given year vary depending upon the source; here we use Central Intelligence Agency (CIA) data. The International Institute for Strategic Studies (IISS) annual publication *The Military Balance* in its 1994-95 edition (London: IISS, October 1994) gives very similar population numbers. In most cases the IISS figures are within 1 or 2 percent of the CIA estimate. There are a few discrepancies. In the case of Kuwait, the IISS figure of 1.7 million is lower than the CIA's data; in the case of Oman, the IISS 2.0 million figure is lower than the CIA. In the case of Kuwait, the IISS figure of 1.7 million is lower than the CIA's data; in the case of Oman, the IISS 2.0 million figure is considerably higher than the CIA

Table 1.1 (cont.)

data; and the figure of 2.4 million for the United Arab Emirates is again lower than the CIA's estimate. The IISS, unlike the CIA, gives a breakdown of population percentages for nationals, as distinct from expatriates. These percentages are included in the population column and although they may not jibe exactly with the CIA figures given, when considered as approximate readouts of the percentages of expatriates in the various economies, they are surely similar.

Table Notes

[a] Date from IISS, *The Military Balance 1994–1995*.
[b] Number of deaths per thousand live births.
[c] Number of migrants per thousand population.
[d] Forty-two percent of the labor force is Bahraini (1982 estimate).
[e] NA, Not available.
[f] Shortage of skilled labor (1988 estimate).
[g] The figure is from 1982. Also, there was a severe labor shortage, and expatriate labor was about 1.6 million (July 1990) and since then has declined substantially.
[h] This high rate reflects the post-Gulf War return of nationals and expatriates.
[i] The labor force figure is from 1986; 70% of the labor force is non-Kuwaiti (1986 estimate).
[j] Eighty-five percent in the private sector are non-Qatari (1983 estimate).
[k] Eighty percent of the labor force is foreign; the labor force date are from 1986.

Table 1.2. Ethnic and religious divisions in the Persian Gulf region.

Country	Ethnicity	Religions	Languages
Bahrain	Bahraini (63%), Asian (13%), other Arab (10%), Iranian (8%), other (6%)	Shia Muslim (70%), Sunni Muslim (30%)	Arabic, English, Farsi, Urdu
Iran	Persian (51%), Azerbaijani (24%), Gilaki and Mazandarani (8%), Kurd (7%), Arab (3%), Lur (2%), Turkmen (2%), other (3%)	Shia Muslim (95%); Sunni Muslim (4%); Zoroastrian, Jewish, Christian, or Baha'i (1%)	Persian and Persian dialects (58%), Turkic and Turkic dialects (26%), Kurdish (9%), Luri (2%), Arabic (1%), and other (4%)
Iraq	Arab (75–80%), Kurdish (15–20%), Turkoman, Assyrian or other (5%)	Shia Muslim (60–65%), Sunni Muslim (32–37%), Christian or other (3%)	Arabic, Kurdish Assyrian, Armenian
Kuwait	Kuwaiti (45%), other Arab (35%), South Asian (9%), Iranian (4%), other (7%)	Sunni Muslim (45%); Shia Muslim (30%); other Muslim (10%); Christian, Hindu, Parsi and other (15%)	Arabic (official), English (widely spoken)
Oman	Arab, Baluchi, South Asian (Indian, Pakistani, Sri Lankan, or other)	Ibadhi Muslim (75%), Sunni Muslim, Shia Muslim, Hindu	Arabic (official), English, Baluchi, Urdu, Indian dialects
Qatar	Arab (40%), Pakistani (18%), Indian (18%), Iranian (10%), other (14%)	Muslim (85%)	Arabic (official), English (commonly used as a second language)
Saudi Arabia	Arab (90%), Afro-Asian (10%)	Muslim (100%)	Arabic
United Arab Emirates	Emirian (18%), other Arab (23%), South Asian (50%), other expatriates (8%)[1]	Muslim (96%, 16% Shia); Christian, Hindi, or other (4%)	Arabic (official), Persian, English, Hindi, Urdu

Source: Central Intelligence Agency, *The World Factbook 1994* (Washington, D.C.: 1994).

1. Less than 20 percent of the population of the United Arab Emirates are citizens (1982 estimate).

cash for child support, maternity benefits, and housing subsidies to families of government workers.[5]

In the Middle Eastern countries without oil wealth, individual families provide support for their children, and hence they have to "mobilize their work force—including women—in order to assure adequate family income."[6] Egypt, Morocco, and Tunisia were the first to adopt official population programs in the mid-1960s. Iran, Jordan, and Turkey have also implemented policies to lower fertility and have encouraged access to contraception.

Although economic development and fertility rates are correlated, population growth cannot be explained exclusively as a function of economic factors. Israel, a wealthy country by regional standards, encourages fertility among the Jewish population to preserve the Jewish character of the state. The government's social welfare policies encourage the increase of population, although contraceptive information and supplies are distributed as a health measure.

Throughout the region, contraceptive use remains relatively low. Specialists on Islam claim that there is no religious obstacle to the use of contraceptives. Policies toward birth control in the region are a function of how each government interprets cultural and religious tradition. In Iran immediately after the revolution, for example, many conservative leaders declared contraceptives to be a Western weapon used to reduce the number of Muslims and weaken Muslim nations. In 1986, it was estimated that Iran's population had surpassed fifty million. Three years later, Ayatollah Khomeini's government finally endorsed a national birth-control policy. At present, all temporary methods of contraception are legal. Abortion officially remains illegal unless the pregnancy is considered dangerous for the health of the mother. Yet de facto abortion is a frequent practice, and doctors are not usually reprimanded. Though the national birth-control policy has been successful in persuading families to practice family planning, Iran's population is still growing at a very high rate.

Even official government policy can be insufficient to stop robust population growth in the region. Cultural norms, such as early marriage and male attitudes toward family planning, often complicate attempts to limit fertility. Some of these attitudes have started to change, but the past decades of explosive population growth will have implications far into the future. In Egypt, for example, in spite of the fact that the number of women practicing family planning has more than doubled, the number of younger women entering their childbearing years is growing as a result of rapid population growth in the preceding decades. The need to educate the poor, the illiterate, and those living in isolated areas has become pressing.[7]

Literacy also varies greatly by country. Israel has the highest literacy rate in the region, 92 percent (male, 95 percent; female, 89 percent). Literacy in certain Persian Gulf countries—for example, Bahrain (77 percent), Kuwait (73 percent), and Qatar (76 percent)—is quite high as well.

There is wide discrepancy between literacy rates for men and women in the Middle East. In Egypt, the percentage of literate women is 34 percent, while 63 percent of men are literate; in Iran the proportions are 43 percent of women and 64 percent of men; and in Saudi Arabia, they are 48 percent for women and 73 percent of men. Philippe Fargues, a demographer and a director of the Centre d'études et de documentation économique, juridique et sociale in Cairo, asserts that there is a correlation between female illiteracy and fertility rates; better educated women have fewer children. Admission of women into professions and the formal labor markets also affects fertility. The Persian Gulf countries, like most of the Middle East, have strikingly low rates of women in the labor force—5 percent for the Arabian Peninsula as opposed to a 50 percent world average.[8]

While elementary schooling has been made compulsory almost everywhere, it is so recent that it has had little impact on the literacy of adults. The Arab generation born in the beginning of this century was widely illiterate. Schooling was reserved for elites, who in most cases were men. Women entered schools in the middle of the century, but at a much slower pace than men did; as a result, the gender gap became wider, affecting the generation between forty and sixty years of age, which is currently in power.

Apart from gender differences, in the Middle East there is also a discrepancy along local regional lines. In Upper Egypt, for example, adult literacy is less than half that in the Cairo governorate. Also, average life expectancy in Upper Egypt is six years less, and real per capita gross domestic product (GDP) is about 45 percent of that of the capital.[9]

Important asymmetries are present not only in education but also in labor markets. One-third of workers in the Persian Gulf region are still employed in agriculture. In spite of the rising indigenous population, some of the Gulf countries face a shortage of labor (Iraq) or a lack of sufficiently skilled workers (Iran). The population of Kuwait has decreased by 40 percent since August 1990, a decline that has had a negative impact on the economy. The heavy reliance of the smaller Gulf states—Bahrain, Kuwait, Qatar, and the United Arab Emirates (UAE)—on foreign workers hampers sustainable development (see Table 1.1). Abdel Omran and Farzaneh Roudi report that "experts expect continuing growth of population in the Middle East: Nearly all signs point to continued and rapid expansion of the population of the Middle East for the next 30 to 40 years. The centrality of the family in society, young age at marriage, universality of marriage, early childbearing, relatively low educational attainment for women, and low level of female labor force participation, all point to continued high fertility within the region."[10] At present, parts of the Middle East rank second only to Africa in the high rates of their population growth.[11] In the Persian Gulf region, Iran has the largest population: its 65,615,474 exceeds the combined total of Iraq and the Gulf Cooperation Council (GCC) countries of 45,496,844. Although the Iranian government is currently attempting to lower Iran's fertility rate, its population is increasing at a steady rate of 3.46 percent and is projected to reach 105 million by 2010, while the population of Iraq and the GCC states is expected to reach approximately 78 million.[12] The disparity in population has significant implications for the distribution of resources and regional political power.

Iraq will also experience rapid population growth. Forecasts predict a rise from over 18 million in 1992 to over 34 million in 2010. Saudi Arabia should see a similar increase, from 16 million to over 31 million by 2010. The other GCC countries, with populations currently ranging from 512,779 in Qatar to 2,791,141 in the UAE, should also almost double, rising to nearly 13 million in 2010 from 6.5 million today.[13]

The growth in population is exacerbated by the population ratios in many parts of the Middle East. In 1992, approximately 45 percent of the populations of Iran, Iraq, and Saudi Arabia were children under the age of fifteen. In Saudi Arabia, half of the population is under the age of twenty. In the West Bank and Gaza, 50 percent of the population is below the age of fifteen. These ratios are significantly higher than the ratios in developed countries.[14]

Only 4 percent of the region's population is over age sixty-five. The Middle East has a very high ratio of children to working-age adults. The relative youth of society is significantly related to political instability. High numbers of young people without jobs or meaningful careers are likely to become political dissidents and recruits for social movements that promise better opportunities through a change in political regime.

If the growing percentage of young people in the Persian Gulf region is overlaid with their ethnic distribution and if the youth born of foreign parents have little chance of becoming citizens of these countries, then the likelihood of civil turmoil is likely to grow. It should be noted that in 1992, after the destruction of the Ayodhya mosque in India by Hindu nationalists, Pakistanis in the UAE went on a rampage and destroyed several Hindu schools. This was the most serious disruption to the UAE's internal security in many years. UAE officials worry most about such issues when they consider domestic crisis management.

There is a growing body of literature suggesting a strong causal link between the relative youth of a society and its propensity to engage in violence and revolutionary behavior.[15] The combination of high rates of growth in population, increasing pressure on agricultural land and water, and a growing pool of youth that will strain the capacity of existing governments to provide employment and opportunity creates an explosive backdrop for politics in the Persian Gulf.

Economic Problems

Four years after the Gulf War, the region is facing severe economic difficulties. In comparison with their relative affluence before 1990, the Arab Persian Gulf states are now experiencing significant shortfalls of revenues due to the costs of the war and the low world price of oil. Since the legitimacy of the Gulf monarchies depends very much on their capacity to distribute resources to their populations and sustain the extensive services they provide, a shortage of revenues can seriously endanger internal stability and can impair the military capabilities of the Gulf countries, which ultimately rest on their economic power.[16]

All the Persian Gulf economies continue to depend on oil and natural gas as their most important sources of revenue. In Saudi Arabia, oil accounts for about 75 percent of budget revenues, 35 percent of GDP, and almost all of the country's export earnings. In Iran, over 90 percent of export revenues are earnings from oil exports. In Kuwait, oil accounts for nearly half of the GDP and 90 percent of export and government revenues. Even the UAE, which are considered one of the strongest Gulf economies, depend on oil exports and are affected by the weak oil price on the world market.[17]

In most of the Persian Gulf states, sectors of the economies not directly related to oil, such as the mercantile and service sectors and the construction industry, are usually dependent on the oil industry. Both in Saudi Arabia and in Oman, the substantial agricultural sectors are subsidized by the oil industry. Even in Bahrain, where oil reserves are diminishing and the share of oil in the country's GDP is declining, the oil sector still remains very important. In the Gulf countries where the share of oil has fallen below 50 percent of GDP, oil-related revenues from state petrochemical industries and other state industries built with oil money play a significant role.[18] Although diversification has progressed furthest in Bahrain, petroleum production and processing still account for about 80 percent of export receipts, 60 percent of government revenues, and 30 percent of GDP.[19]

The Persian Gulf economies, extraordinarily dependent on the fluctuating price of oil in the world market, have suffered badly due to the currently low prices. If oil prices continue to remain low, the dependence on oil revenues will require the Gulf countries either to expand their production or to reduce production to increase the price. However, some experts doubt that the major oil exporters will be able to embrace a common policy of output freeze, which could result in increased prices. In the past, attempts to control or reduce output have been a significant source of tension among Organization of Petroleum Exporting Countries members in the Persian Gulf region, and, indeed, they contributed to Iraq's invasion of Kuwait in 1990.

The second important characteristic of the economies of the Persian Gulf states is the dominant position of central governments. Governments own the national oil companies, and they are in full control of production and investment decisions. They collect oil revenues, redistribute the capital through the budget, and determine who will profit through spending and regulatory policies. Overall, in the Persian Gulf economies, government policies and spending are critically important, even for the development of the private sector. Government spending, for example, is the engine of the construction industry in the private sector. The role of government in such sectors as banking and finance, which are open to private capital, is still significant.[20]

This dominant position of the governments in the Persian Gulf economies complicates the economic reform that is necessary to increase government revenue. Some of the prescribed measures to deal with economic problems—privatization, reduction of government spending, and imposition of new taxes—carry high political prices for governments today. Saudi Arabia, which has been running a deficit for a decade and has an enormous debt, is trying is to cut government spending, but privatization is unpopular among Saudi citizens accustomed to generous government programs. In Saudi Arabia, as well as in other oil-rich Gulf states, the government has subsidized utilities, goods, and services for decades. Concern about the political consequences of privatization is acute in Saudi Arabia and Oman. Though the Saudi government has approved privatization measures, no significant steps are expected in the next two years.[21]

In Iran, President Rafsanjani has met firm political resistance from conservative Muslim leaders in his efforts to privatize the economy and unify the foreign-exchange rate. In 1994, instead of liberalizing prices, the government enacted a law calling for all bazaar merchants to put price ceilings on their goods.[22] In Kuwait in 1993, the government announced that it is selling its shares in ten state-owned companies and dismantling four others. It also decided to cut its expenditures by 10 percent, thus helping the difficult process of economic recovery.

By 1994, a number of economic experts drew attention to the troubles of the Persian Gulf economies. In Saudi Arabia, according to official government reports, the combined fiscal deficits for 1990 to 1992 were $48 billion, compared with $39 billion in the previous three years. The deficit and the unwillingness of the government to curb expenditure or impose taxes to pay for the Gulf War has led some experts to conclude that the war "made a bad situation worse."[23]

In addition, the Saudi economy relies on about four million foreign workers, who are employed in such sectors as the oil industry and banking. The national product real growth rate for 1993 was 1 percent, the inflation rate was also 1 percent, and the unemployment rate was 6.5 percent (1992 estimate). For the first six months of 1994, the economy grew at under 1 percent, and it is expected to shrink by about 2 percent in 1995.[24]

Iran's growth rate dropped to 3 percent in 1993 from 6 percent in 1992.[25] Although Iran has been trying to attract investment to its new free zones by offering long-term tax, import, and customs duty exemptions, foreign investment is shrinking. The only "success" story was the rescheduling of the payments on Iran's huge debt to its European and Japanese lenders. Nevertheless, Iran continues to face serious payment problems to regional and other creditors (such as Japanese trading houses).[26]

Earnings from oil exports, which had provided 90 percent of Iran's export revenues, have dropped in recent years due to falling oil prices. According to some estimates, Iran's annual revenues dropped 30 percent during 1993 due to declining world oil prices. Iran desperately needs to rebuild its oil fields, because they are currently facing serious production and maintenance problems.[27] Low oil prices are not solely responsible for the country's economic difficulties; economic mismanagement and the impressive amounts spent on arms and nuclear program development have contributed substantially to growing deficits and high inflation.

Strong opposition from conservative Muslim leaders and a lack of adequate social support prevented President Rafsanjani from enacting his program of economic liberalization. In the summer of 1994, when the mosque in Mashhed was bombed, killing twenty-five people, and the riots in Qazvin triggered violent clashes with the police, there was an acute sense of political instability in Iran. Any attempt to free the economy from state control meets vehement political opposition and risks intensifying social and political instability. Nevertheless, without economic reform, the economy is likely to deteriorate further, which in turn will produce further domestic frustration, instability, and political violence.

Iraq suffered economic devastation after the Gulf War, and it is currently operating under UN sanctions. The lifting of the sanctions will present a serious challenge to OPEC's existing "discipline" and price stability. The UN Security Council has repeatedly rejected Iraq's requests to lift the ban on oil exports. When Saddam Hussein moved two Republican Guard units close to the border with Kuwait in October 1994, the United States insisted to the Security Council that this kind of action justified continued imposition of the sanctions. Russia and France argue that the United Nations should begin preliminary steps to lift the embargo now that Iraq has recognized Kuwait and is moving to comply with Security Council resolutions concerning its weapons of mass destruction. The United States and the United Kingdom remain firmly opposed to a lifting of the sanctions so long as Saddam Hussein continues to remain in power.

In 1989, Iraq was pumping 2.8 million barrels of oil per day (b/d) when its quota was 3.1 million b/d. Some observers predict that once Iraq is permitted to sell its oil abroad, its output could eventually rise from a theoretical maximum of 3 million b/d to about 6.5 million b/d, primarily because of the new exploration done by Russian, French, and Italian companies.[28] Iraq's oil minister, Safa Hadi Jawad, said that once the embargo is lifted, his country will start pumping oil at full capacity until it reaches the production levels of Iran. Most Western observers consider such predictions premature. Iraq currently has a provisional quota of 550,000 b/d, and Iran has 3.6 million b/d.[29] Even if Iraq is permitted to export oil, it will not be able to recover its full production ability right away due to poor maintenance of the fields and pipelines.

The economy of Iraq is currently in crisis. Skyrocketing inflation, devastation of the economic infrastructure, lack of basic sanitary conditions, and shortage of food products all testify to acute economic weakness. The decline in economic development started during the eight year Iran-Iraq War, when per capita domestic food production declined by 32 percent between 1980 and 1991. By comparison, between 1965 and 1980, per capita income grew at an annual average of 0.6 percent. Though no current statistics are available, the long war with Iran, the Gulf War, and the embargo resulted in negative economic growth.[30]

The major Persian Gulf economies are all facing severe economic problems. The combination of rapidly expanding populations, limited water resources, and acute financial problems can result in tension among neighbors and increase the possibility of regional conflict. These economic trends are not restricted to the Gulf but rather are characteristic of the broader Middle East region. In its annual report for 1994, the World Bank declared that the growth rates in North Africa and the Middle East continued to decline, falling from an average of 4.3 percent in 1992 to 1.5

percent in 1993. In comparison with the prosperous 1960s and 1970s, the 1980s and the first part of this decade are described as a period of "crisis." The 1994 World Bank report describes "a deteriorating external economic environment—particularly the sharp drop in international oil prices—decreasing efficiency in the use of capital, low levels of private investment and poor export performance."[31] According to the World Bank, in many countries in the region, GDP growth remained below population growth, leading to high and increasing rates of unemployment.[32] Negative economic growth provides a poor context for the diminution of conflict and the construction of cooperative security arrangements.

Conflict over Natural Resources

Water. According to the 1994 World Bank annual report, the Middle East and North Africa are moving toward a "water crisis." Due to rapid population growth and urbanization, the demand for water has reached a point where withdrawal now exceeds replenishment. The report predicts that "by the year 2000, withdrawals in most countries will exceed total fresh water potential. Competing demands from agriculture, industries and municipalities dictate the need for appropriate demand-managing policies, especially in the area of water pricing."[33]

Turkey, Syria, and Iraq all rely on the waters of the Euphrates. Turkey's Grand Anatolia Project, designed to increase hydroelectricity and agricultural irrigation, has generated deep concern in Syria and Iraq,[34] which fear that the Turkish project will reduce their share of the river and give Turkey the power to "shut off" the flow altogether during a conflict or crisis. In fact, in 1990 Turkish president Turgut Ozal threatened to restrict the water flow to Syria over an unrelated political issue; Turkish officials later disavowed the threat.

Turkey also has offered to use water to build trust and confidence in the region. Turkish officials, along with others, have floated proposals to build a "peace pipeline," a water pipeline from Turkey to Syria, Israel, and the other parties to the Arab-Israeli conflict. Water from the pipeline would reduce the centrality of water scarcity in the Arab-Israeli conflict; some hope that the implementation and distribution process itself would also help curb tensions and promote a cooperative approach to resource management.

All the Persian Gulf states use more than one-third of their renewable water supplies on an annual basis. Iran uses only 39 percent and Iraq 43 percent of their renewable supplies. While this is not a catastrophic rate, it does suggest a greater chance of shortages due to growing populations and heavier demand. Several other Gulf countries, however, use 100 percent or more of their annual supplies; they partially depend on water imports, nonrenewable groundwater, or desalination of brackish or salt water. Bahrain and Kuwait both use more than 100 percent of their annual supplies. More significant abusers include Qatar (174 percent), UAE (140 percent), and Saudi Arabia (106).[35] Growing populations will make adequate water supplies even more of a challenge in the future.

The Persian Gulf countries have been the leaders in developing huge agricultural schemes that are not cost-effective. These agricultural subsidies reduce and strain the water supply. Moreover, despite this expensive form of agriculture, these countries have still failed to achieve self-sufficiency, the stated justification for such damaging water policies.[36]

Israel and its neighbors have acute conflicts over water.[37] Israel, Syria, Jordan, and the Palestinians will face severe water shortages in the future. Lebanon has ample water and could, if the political circumstances were right, share some with its neighbors.

Due to the seriousness of regional water problems and the inability of any one party to deal with them independently, water issues must be treated in the Arab-Israeli and Palestinian-Israeli peace processes as part of the land-for-peace debate. The problem can be addressed only through cooperative agreements among Israel, the Palestine National Authority, Jordan, Syria, and Lebanon. Failure to address this problem adequately will undoubtedly lead to increased tensions and possible military confrontation in the future.[38]

The Nile is vital for agricultural production in both Egypt and Sudan. Ninety-seven percent of Egypt's water comes from the Nile, while 95 percent of the Nile waters originate outside Egypt in eight countries of the Nile basin. Over the past fifteen years, Egyptian leaders have stated that an intentional disruption in the flow of the Nile would be a casus belli. Sudan and Egypt signed a water treaty in 1959, but political tensions of late have strained relations between the two states.[39]

Oil and Gas. For the foreseeable future, the industrial powers will remain dependent upon access to Persian Gulf energy and will therefore remain deeply involved in the efforts to assure its security. While the major oil producers of the Gulf already control a large share of the oil market, the distribution of existing oil reserves suggests that they will play an even larger role in the years to come.

Destruction of facilities during the Gulf War, both in Iraq and in Kuwait, makes estimates based on prewar data somewhat less reliable than they otherwise would be. Estimates should therefore be treated with caution. In 1991, three Gulf countries accounted for 23 percent of daily and annual world oil production. Saudi Arabia, Iran, and the UAE produced 5.31 billion barrels of oil, out of a total of 23.44 billion. Because of the Gulf War, Iraq and Kuwait produced negligible amounts in 1991.

Calculations for 1992 based on daily production yield similar results. Saudi Arabia, Iran, and the UAE again led the region, with 24 percent of the world's daily crude oil production. Other, smaller producers included Oman and Qatar. While neither Kuwait nor Iraq returned to 1989 preinvasion levels of production, Kuwait crossed the million barrels per day threshold in 1992.[40]

The Persian Gulf states are in a far stronger position in terms of 1992 proven reserves. Of the total world oil reserves, 55 to 66 percent are located in the Middle East. According to the high estimate, 648 billion barrels of oil are in Saudi Arabia (260 billion), Iraq (100 billion), UAE (98 billion), Kuwait (97 billion) and Iran (93 billion). The world total is only 996 billion barrels. By 2010, some experts predict that the Gulf countries will supply 38 percent of the world total.[41]

While a plurality of world natural gas reserves are controlled by the states of the former Soviet Union, the countries of the Persian Gulf hold the second most significant share. With 13 to 14 percent of world reserves, Iran controls the largest reserves outside of the former Soviet states. Smaller gas reserves, ranging from 2 to 5 percent of global reserves, sit under Qatar, the UAE, Saudi Arabia, and Iraq. As a whole, the Gulf states control 28 to 31 percent of world reserves, compared with 40 to 42 percent in the former Soviet states.

The Gulf War was fought in part over the control of Persian Gulf oil. Iraq's invasion of Kuwait was strongly motivated, in part, by the issue of oil prices and Iraq's acute need for hard currency. Given the importance of oil and gas reserves to the future of the region, the asymmetric distribution of oil and oil revenue can easily create frustration and grievance that can fuel future wars.

One possible scenario of a future energy war is the dispute over the Qatari North Field gas dome. While Iran claims some 30 percent of the dome, Qatar places Iran's share near 5 percent. It is doubtful whether Iran will receive even that much. When the dome comes into production in 1997, it will be an immense revenue source. With ownership rights already in dispute, Iranian military intervention to ameliorate its financial troubles is not unthinkable.[42]

Technology. Access to new technology is an essential ingredient in the efforts of the Persian Gulf region to exploit its natural resources and to develop alternative sources for freshwater. The acute water shortages of the region could be overcome by building new canals, water pipelines, and nuclear desalination plants in key areas. Political stability and large infusions of foreign capital are preconditions, however, for cooperative water projects.

Increasing reliance on capital-intensive high-technology investments, however, increases the vulnerability of the region to devastating damage in the event of war. For, in parallel, new conventional weapons have much greater lethality due to increases in range and dramatic improvements in accuracy. The destruction of Iraq's electric power grid by the coalition in the first days of the Gulf War is a preview of what could happen in future Middle East wars.

An acute shortage of water and disputes over revenue from the strategic resource of oil magnify the fault line of population growth identified above. Population growth increases the pressure for greater access to water and increased revenue from oil. The combination of population dynamics and access to resources and technology sets the broad parameters of conflict into the future. Whether disputes over resources can be managed cooperatively or they flare into violent conflict is in large part a function of the management of the specific conflicts that bedevil the region.

Population growth and resource scarcity increase the pressure on governments and their vulnerability to domestic political opposition. When governments feel pressed and vulnerable, they are more likely to activate latent conflict over long-standing issues.[43] Saddam Hussein was pressed by financial stringency in 1990 and apprehensive about a "unipolar" world. Under those conditions, he activated Iraq's long-standing territorial conflict with Kuwait, and the Persian Gulf exploded into violence.[44] The Middle East—and the Persian Gulf in particular—has an abundance of unresolved disputes and wide asymmetries in the military balance that can lead to instability.

Regional Sources of Conflict

The triggers to violent conflict will arise from ongoing territorial disputes, conflict around the periphery of the region, ethnic and religious disputes, and asymmetries in the regional balance of military power.

Enduring Territorial Disputes

The Persian Gulf. In the Persian Gulf, the Shatt al Arab has a long history as the meeting point of the Arab and Persian worlds. In more recent years, it has served as a vital waterway for Iraqi and Iranian ports and facilitated the export of oil by both countries. After many years of conflict, Iraq, in the 1975 Algiers Communiqué, agreed to a more favorable border definition for Iran in exchange for an end to Iranian support for Iraqi Kurdish rebels. In 1980, Iraq abrogated the agreement and the eight-year Iran-Iraq War commenced; much of the fighting took place in and around the Shatt al Arab. In 1990, two weeks after the Iraqi invasion of Kuwait, Saddam Hussein reversed his position and agreed to accept the 1975 agreement.

Are Iran and Iraq likely to submerge their territorial conflict in order to cooperate against the U.S.-led opposition? While there are undoubtedly some areas where both countries work together, especially in sales of limited quantities of smuggled Iraqi oil, Iran has much to lose if it cooperates with Saddam Hussein. If Saddam is rehabilitated, sanctions will be lifted and Iraq will once more be able to use its revenues to buy weapons and intimidate neighbors.[45]

Iraq has ongoing territorial disputes with Kuwait. The border between Kuwait and Iraq has caused friction between the two nations as far back as 1962 because of Iraq's claim to the whole of Kuwait. Territorial claims over the islands of Bubiyan and Warbah, which occupy a strategic position in front of Umm Qasr, and a dispute over three miles of the border between Iraq and Kuwait brought the two countries to the brink of armed conflict in March 1973. These two disputes figured prominently in Saddam's justification of the invasion of Kuwait in August 1990.[46]

At various times, Iraq has offered Kuwait, for either or both of the islands, an exchange of Iraqi territory, an exchange of freshwater for Kuwait from the Shatt al Arab, or straightforward leasing. Kuwait has refused all these offers. After the Gulf War, the finding of the UN commission that demarcated the border was entirely in Kuwait's favor. Apart from the territory it previously controlled, Kuwait received a greater share of the Rumaila oil field and a sizable portion of the Umm Qasr naval base. Iraq vehemently refused to accept this decision. It was especially opposed to the ruling on Umm Qasr, its only outlet to the sea, its only port, and its only naval base, since the Shatt al Arab has been closed since the Gulf War. Paradoxically, Kuwait has never claimed Umm Qasr, and official Kuwaiti government maps showed the boundary line as south of the port even in mid-1992. The demarcation undoubtedly has reinforced Iraq's sense of grievance and increased the probability of irredentist action in the future. Although Iraq formally recognized the independence of Kuwait in 1994, the recognition was grudgingly given under acute international pressure in the hope that it would lead to the lifting of international sanctions. It seems clear that even if Saddam Hussein is replaced by a more conciliatory leadership, Iraq's antipathy toward Kuwait, grounded now in the issues of borders and access rights, will continue. Iraq will remain a revanchist state until a formal Iraqi-Kuwaiti agreement on borders is openly and freely negotiated.

Iran has a major territorial dispute with the UAE over Abu Musa. Previously, Iran and Sharja, one of the seven emirates of the UAE, had jointly governed the island under a 1971 agreement. Iran, which disputes the current shared sovereignty of the island with Sharja, never denounced the 1971 agreement governing administration or made any additional claim to the island.

The most recent conflict over Abu Musa began in March, 1992, when Iranian forces expelled all foreigners, including UAE citizens. Teachers, engineers in charge of water facilities, and health workers, all of whom provided essential services for the UAE government, were forced out.[47] Iran claims that it acted because the security of the island was at risk, while the UAE contends that the Iranian government is expansionist and seeks to annex the island. The crisis reached a peak on 24 August 1992, when Iranian officials prevented one hundred residents, including UAE citizens, from landing on the island. The GCC, in the Abu Dhabi Declaration, issued on 23 December 1992, rejected the acquisition of territory by force and emphasized UAE sovereignty over Abu Musa and the Tunb Islands.[48]

Despite commercial ties between Iran and the UAE, the conflict over Abu Musa guarantees that bilateral relations will be unstable. In February 1993, the UAE president, Shaykh Zayid bin-Sultan al-Nuhayyan, vowed to regain control of the three disputed Persian Gulf islands. Moreover, he stated that the "development of friendly ties between the two countries hinges on boosting confidence and measures that show Iran's adherence to international law and respect of the UAE sovereignty."[49] In 1994 both the GCC and the Arab league supported the UAE position on the islands, and toward the end of the year the UAE proposed that the matter of ownership be referred to the International Court of Justice. Iran has so far refused to agree to this step toward conflict resolution, and the increasingly bitter dispute continues.

Borders on the Arabian peninsula are widely disputed. Saudi Arabia and Qatar have a long-standing border dispute.[50] Saudi Arabia and Yemen also lack a demarcated border, and both covet the disputed areas partially because of expected oil deposits. Yemen alleges that a 1934 agreement giving the Saudis control of the provinces of Asir, Najran, and Jizan expired in 1992. In addition to periodic reports of border skirmishes, various Yemeni leaders have also alleged over the years that Saudi Arabia has provided arms to factions within Yemen.[51] Several rounds of talks between the two governments have failed to produce an agreement, and the intense fighting between the north and the south in Yemen could exacerbate the dispute. With a population of approximately eleven million and very low per capita income, Yemen has a capacity for creating great instability on the Arabian Peninsula.

The Arab-Israeli Conflict. A lasting peace between Israel and its immediate neighbors will have a profound impact upon the politics of the Persian Gulf and the Arabian Peninsula. The Israeli-Jordanian Peace Treaty, signed in October 1994, has given the peace process a further boost, but serious obstacles still remain between the Palestine National Authority and Israel, as well as between Israel and Syria. If the Palestine Liberation Organization and Israel can reinforce and consolidate the framework agreement they have reached, they will likely accelerate an Israeli-Syrian agreement, which, in turn, would have an immediate and positive impact on the chances for Israel and Lebanon to quickly reach agreements. Progress in the Arab-Israel conflict would ease an agreement on Jerusalem and formal treaties between Israel and the Persian Gulf Arabs.

Under these circumstances, both Iran and Iraq would find it much harder to pursue anti-Israeli and anti-American agendas. The probability of a more stable and cooperative regime in the Middle East would increase, and the likelihood of regional conflict would consequently be reduced. On the other hand, if the Arab-Israeli peace process fails, it would undoubtedly strengthen the forces that are intent on minimizing Western, and especially U.S., influence in the region. Governments with large pools of young unemployed who are dissatisfied with the existing political and economic order would be especially vulnerable to the failure of the internationally sponsored cooperative experiment.

Impact of an Unstable Periphery on the Persian Gulf Region

Leaders in the Persian Gulf states currently look outward to an arc of crisis. They are all threatened by the potential fragmentation of Afghanistan, Iraq, Azerbaijan, or Tajikistan and the spillover effect of more distant regional conflicts from North Africa to the Balkans and the Indian subcontinent. As states in the periphery fragment, refugees flee, carrying ideas, attachment to social movements, and fidelity to Islamic militancy that strike a responsive chord in the Gulf. It is difficult to imagine that the Gulf can remain insulated from the whorl of people, ideas, and organizations that travel across the borders of broken states. Nor does the relationship go only in one direction. States in the region have strong interests and strong commitments in their mutating periphery.

Afghanistan. Since the Najibullah regime fell in April 1992, Afghanistan has been ravaged by civil war and violent conflict among factions of the mujahideen. Iran is not the only regional state with a stake in the war's outcome. Pakistan, Uzbekistan, Tajikistan, and Saudi Arabia also support different factions in the ongoing struggle. The periodic cease-fire agreements have fallen victim to renewed eruptions of hostilities, and this pattern is likely to persist, because as no party has the capability or the authority to consolidate power in the foreseeable future.[52] The growing power of the militantly Islamic mujahideen in Afghanistan affects the domestic politics of Iran and Saudi Arabia.

Tajikistan. With the collapses of the Soviet Union in August 1991 and the Najibullah regime in Afghanistan in April 1992, civil war broke out in Tajikistan in May 1992. Tajikistan lacked both economic resources and a sense of national identity. By September, fighting between the governing Communists and Islamists and other nationalist and democratic opposition forces reached Dushanbe. Uzbekistan and Russia, fearing both Islamic militancy and instability, quickly shored up the Communist leadership. As arms continue to come across the Afghan border to the opposition, refugees stream in the opposite direction. Sporadic attacks from antigovernment militants in Afghanistan continue, despite the continued presence of Russian troops on the border.[53]

The Caucasus. Turkey and Iran are engaged in diplomatic competition in the conflict between Armenia and Azerbaijan, while the fighting edges closer to Iran and hundreds of thousands of refugees have fled the expanding zone of conflict. The proximity of the fighting as well as the flow of refugees creates serious problems for Iran. In August 1993, an Iranian Foreign Ministry statement seriously warned "the Armenian forces for their repeated aggressions" close to Iran's borders.[54]

Iran is deeply concerned about ethnic conflicts, such as that between the Azeris and Armenians over the Nagorno-Karabakh region, that could spill over into Iran's territory and pit its minorities against each other. Iran has balanced a concern for the Azeris, its Shiite but Turkic-speaking neighbors, with an interest in restraining Azeri extremism or a Muslim-Christian conflict.[55]

Georgia has also suffered secessionist movements and civil war. The Abkhazians have battled the Georgian government for independence with considerable success. South Ossetia is a second area where separatist fighters compelled the forces of the Georgian government to retreat. Meanwhile, the Georgians themselves are split between the forces of the current president, Eduard Shevardnadze, and his deposed predecessor, the late Zviad Gamsakhurdia.[56]

The violent confrontation between Russia and the insurgent movement in the Chechnya district in the closing months of 1994 was another indicator of the turmoil and instability that persist in the Caucasus and all along Russia's southern borders. The possibility of protracted conflict in this key strategic area is bound to affect Russia's policies toward both

Turkey and Iran in the coming decade. Furthermore, key oil pipelines from the Caspian Sea run through the Caucasus to the Black Sea, and these disturbances make it more imperative to develop alternative oil routes to the north, through Russia proper, or, alternatively, through Turkey, Iran, or Pakistan. All these alternative routes, however, have different problems, and capital is unlikely to be available in the near term for such risky ventures.

The Balkans. In the ongoing secessionist wars in the territory of the former Yugoslavia, it is the war in Bosnia that resonates in the Middle East and the Persian Gulf region. Bosnia's population is approximately 32 percent Serb, 42 percent Muslim Slav, and 18 percent Croat. Following Croatian and Slovenian independence, the Parliament of Bosnia and Herzegovina authorized a referendum on independence on 29 February 1992, and the United States and the European Union recognized the republic as independent on 7 April 1992. The opposition of Bosnian Serbs spurred violent clashes and civil war. The newly proclaimed Federal Republic of Yugoslavia, consisting only of Serbia and Montenegro, became the principal supplier of arms to the ethnic Serb fighters in Bosnia and Herzegovina.

The United Nations imposed sweeping international sanctions on the former Yugoslavia in an attempt to end the bloodshed in Bosnia. In March 1994, after prolonged fighting, the Bosnian government and the Bosnian Croats signed an agreement for a federation. Although the United Nations deployed thousands of peacekeepers to create safe havens for Muslim populations threatened by Serbian military action and although NATO conducted air strikes against Bosnian Serbs after they failed to stop shelling Gorazde (one of the safe havens), bitter fighting continues in several other regions.[57]

The war in Bosnia has potentially explosive consequences in Europe and in the Middle East, particularly in the Persian Gulf. The most immediate danger is that expanded fighting in the Balkans could eventually draw in Greece and Turkey on opposite sides, as did the conflict over Cyprus. The United States would then face an acute dilemma: under certain circumstances, Washington might be forced to a reevaluate its close military ties to Ankara. Any weakening of the military relationship between the United States and Turkey could threaten the Kurdish enclave in northern Iraq and Turkey's generally supportive position in the Persian Gulf.

Beyond these immediate concerns, the plight of Muslim Bosnians is an important symbolic issue throughout the Middle East. Many leaders and members of the public in the region see the conflict primarily as a struggle between Muslim and Christian forces. They dismiss arguments of feasibility and efficacy and argue strongly that if Christian populations were at risk from Muslim military action, the United States and NATO would have intervened vigorously a long time ago.

Horn of Africa. In Somalia, twenty-one years of one-man rule ended in January 1991 with the flight of General Muhammed Siyad Barrah from the capital. Fighting between rival factions led to 40,000 casualties and, by mid-1992, the civil war, drought, and banditry combined to produce famine that threatened some 1.5 million people with starvation. In July 1992, the secretary-general of the United Nations declared Somalia to be a country without a government, an alarming foretaste of potential anarchy on the periphery of the Persian Gulf region. A multinational relief effort, led by the United States, averted mass starvation and alleviated conditions in the countryside, but did not succeed in creating the architecture for a new political order.

On 21 March 1994, the leaders of the most powerful factions in Somalia agreed in UN-brokered talks to form an interim government, under a plan that leaves the distribution of power in a new government until later. However, sporadic clashes among members of rival Somali clans continue, and the hard political decisions have not yet been faced.[58]

A regime in Somalia hostile to the United States could affect shipping and military passage through the Bab el Mandeb, an important Middle Eastern waterway. The U.S. Navy, for example, would rely on the strait should war break out again in the Middle East. Maritime passage between the waters of the Red Sea and the Gulf of Aden could be hampered if an adversary controlled the littoral on one side. Unimpeded passage through the Bab el Mandeb is important not only to the United States, but also to many Middle Eastern states that ship goods through connecting waterways.

North Africa. In January 1992, the Algerian government, anticipating a near certain and overwhelming victory of Islamist political parties, canceled the second round of national elections. Since then, Algeria has plunged into civil war. Led by the military, the government has battled Islamic militants, with over thirty thousand deaths since the fighting began. Opposition forces have attacked not only the military and security forces, but politicians and foreigners as well.[59] No mediated resolution to the conflict appears likely: either the military government will intensify its repression, creating hundreds of thousands of refugees, or Islamist forces, angered by the failure of Arab governments to support their cause, will prevail. Algeria cannot but be a source of instability, both in Europe and in the Middle East.

Elsewhere in North Africa, Sudan and Egypt continue to accuse each other of meddling in the other's domestic affairs. The Hala'ib triangle is an ongoing dispute between Sudan and Egypt.[60] More ominously, the Egyptian government is involved in a serious battle with Islamic militants at home. The fighting has shrunk Egypt's earnings from its tourist industry, its primary source of hard currency, and created serious pressure on the government of President Hosni Mubarak. After promising a change in leadership, the president recently ran unopposed for a third term and made no important changes in his cabinet. Moderate intellectuals and policy analysts in Egypt are worried by the political paralysis in the government and its single-minded focus on Islamic militants.

The regional balance of power would shift dramatically were Islamists to take power in Egypt. Egypt's pivotal role in promoting a peaceful resolution of the Arab-Israel conflict would likely end, Israel would be seriously alarmed, the Palestine Liberation Organization might be fatally weakened, and Persian Gulf states would be threatened. Iran would welcome another Islamic regime and the opportunity to end its isolation through a new alliance. The political map of the Middle East and the Persian Gulf region would be dramatically altered as Islamist forces were strengthened throughout the region.

Indian Subcontinent. India and Pakistan have fought two wars since they both became independent in the war of 1947 to 1948. The primary bone of contention historically has been the status of the disputed state of Jammu and Kashmir, itself partitioned between India and Pakistan by the 1947–48 war. Since the 1971 war, India and Pakistan have been at peace, albeit an armed, mistrustful, and fragile peace.[61]

In recent years, Iran and Pakistan have often found common ground arising from geographical proximity, mutual opposition to Soviet influence, their Islamic constitutions, and their troubled relations with the United States. Leaders in both states have called for stronger ties and enhanced cooperation on regional issues. Both countries are founding members of the Economic Cooperation Organization, which now includes Central Asian countries. Both have been deeply affected by the protracted conflict in Afghanistan, with refugees and militants creating havoc in their border areas. Though Iran and Pakistan see themselves as mediators in the conflict, their different approaches and allies in Afghanistan have occasionally caused friction. A military alliance, including cooperation on nuclear weapons, between the two has been rumored; India is clearly apprehensive about this possibility.[62]

Good relations with India could be of great benefit to Iran from both a geopolitical and an economic perspective. India, however, remains ambivalent about Iran. On the one hand, a recent annual report to Parliament by the Indian Defense Ministry noted that "Iran stands out conspicuously in terms of rapid military buildup and modernization of its forces with particular emphasis on missile arsenal, air force and force projection capabilities."[64] It was the first time that the defense ministry report included a reference to any state but Pakistan and China. India is worried primarily not about Iran's buildup per se, but about the strategic linkages between Iran and Pakistan. Expanded linkages between Iran and Pakistan suggest not only military cooperation but also an increased degree of influence from Islamic Iranian and Pakistani visionaries over India's Muslims.

On the other hand, Prime Minister P. V. Narasimha Rao's visit to Iran in September 1993 served as a platform for an attempt at cooperation.[64] Both Rao and Rafsanjani spoke of building stronger economic ties and studying ways of enhancing peace and security in the region. During Rao's visit, Iran allegedly reiterated that it considers Kashmir an internal Indian matter, and it publicly denounced terrorism as a means of settling contentious issues—a clear reference to Pakistani intervention in Kashmir. Indian editorials lauded the visit, describing it as a watershed in Indo-Iranian relations.[65] Iran's policies toward India and Pakistan represent a careful attempt at balance to preserve its options. Indian and Pakistani interest in Iran nevertheless attests to its strategic importance to both India and Pakistan and to the interconnections between the conflict in the subcontinent and the Persian Gulf region.

Ethnic and Religious Conflicts

The periphery of the Persian Gulf region is dominated by fragmenting states and violent conflict. Closer to home are ethnic and religious minorities that sometimes cross state borders and can serve as flash points of interstate conflict. The traditional interstate conflicts are paralleled by a long list of exceedingly complex and often violent disputes that transcend national frontiers and have as their root causes deep-seated historical, ethnic, and religious animosities.

Kurds. The Kurdish issue has been of great importance to Turkey since the birth of the modern Turkish state. The Treaty of Sèvres of 1920 prescribed the creation of a weak state from the ruins of the Ottoman Empire and stated that if, within a year, the Kurdish people desired a separate state, and if the Council of the League of Nations approved, it should be created. The treaty quickly became irrelevant because the Turkish nationalists founded a modern and strong Turkish state.

Many Turkish leaders became convinced that the creation of a Kurdish state would inevitably weaken Turkey. The first major challenge to the fledgling Turkish state came from a Kurdish religious leader, who occupied one-third of Kurdish Anatolia. This and two subsequent Kurdish revolts were ruthlessly suppressed by the government. The fact that the three major armed rebellions against the state were led by Kurds and originated in the Kurdish region has firmly established the Kurds in Turkish minds as the originators of the primary challenge to their independent existence.[66]

In a unique conjunction of circumstances, the Kurds in Iraq were given autonomy in northern Iraq at the end of the Gulf War by coalition leaders. Although the current leaders of the Kurds are divided, they are all sensitive to the vulnerability of Kurdistan in northern Iraq. None are now pressing for independence and, on the contrary, constantly reiterate that a solution for the Kurds need not threaten any existing state borders.

Turkey would prefer a unified, democratic Iraq, in large part because the future of the Kurds can best be addressed within the existing borders of an Iraq that is democratic and that respects human rights. Neither Turkey nor any other major power is confident, however, that a democratic regime will emerge as the successor to Saddam, nor do they have a political road map or the leverage to advance this agenda.

The Kurds spill across the frontiers of Turkey, Iran, Iraq, and Syria, complicating relationships among the four. Turkish, Iranian, and Arab dedication to the Kurds is thin, and the Western commitment is uncertain. The coalition commitment to the Kurds at the end of the Gulf War has internationalized the Kurdish question. The future of the Kurds, hostage to the future of Iraq and the successor to Saddam Hussein, will have grave consequences for Turkey, Iran, and Iraq and their relationships. For instance, if the Kurds of northern Iraq eventually establish an independent state because of a collapse of the Baghdad regime, Turkey would face a serious dilemma concerning its own Kurdish population, which is increasingly restless. Similarly, Iran has reason to fear an independent Kurdish state. Iranian leaders openly talk of the Kurdish enclave in northern Iraq as "another Israel" and fear that its success will only whet the appetite of its own Kurds for independence or the right to join their brothers and sisters in Iraq. Clearly, neither Turkey, Iran, Iraq, nor Syria wants to see an independent Kurdistan. Yet if they try to crush a fledgling state with military force, they could face strong opposition from the West, especially if the Kurdish state were seen to be democratic. In these circumstances, a war over the independence of Kurdistan could escalate, creating grave problems for both regional and external powers, especially the United States.

Azeris. About twelve million Azeris live in northern Iran, near the border with independent Azerbaijan.[67] The proximity to Azerbaijan has been a mixed blessing. Conceivably, the external Azeri community could support Azeris within Iran against the central Iranian government. In reality, Azerbaijan is enmeshed in a war with Armenia and has no resources to extend. Iran, already home to the largest refugee population in the world, has received thousands of refugees from the fighting. Iranian Azeris cannot be impressed by Azerbaijan's performance and potential.[68]

Shiites. Iraqi Shiites, numbering some ten or eleven million people, constitute a majority in Iraq. Like several other groups in Iraq, the Shiites are oppressed; their leaders have been arrested and executed by the hundreds. In March 1991, their uprising against Saddam Hussein was brutally crushed. The Iraqi government continues to target the Shiites through its draining and shelling of the southern Iraqi marshlands. The Shiites in Iraq have received little international support. Kuwait and Saudi Arabia are overtly hostile, and even Iran has done little. Most countries fear the fragmentation of Iraq and the possibility of an Iranian-dominated Shiite entity in southern Iraq.

In Saudi Arabia, roughly 2 to 8 percent of the population is Shiite. They live mostly in the Eastern Province, along the Persian Gulf. General discrimination and unfair employment practices against the Shiites are entrenched in Saudi society. Incidents of unexplained sabotage of oil facilities in the early 1980s and periodic disturbances have been attributed to disgruntled Shiites.[69] The Shiites are systematically harassed and denied full religious freedom. Some changes in Saudi policy led to marginal improvements for the Shiites in 1993.

The Shiites in Lebanon are probably the largest single ethnic or religious group in the country. They number at least one million.[70] Hezbollah, a militant Shiite party backed by Iran, continues to battle Israel from southern Lebanon. Future Hezbollah military actions against Israel are partly hostage to Iranian-Syrian relations and to ongoing Syrian negotiations with Israel on the terms of a peace agreement.

Baluchis. There are at least six hundred thousand Baluchis in southeast Iran. Other than the existence in the 1970s of the Baghdad-based Baluch Liberation Front, Baluchi nationalism has been quiescent. The Baluchis are often involved in smuggling across the Afghani and Pakistani borders, despite the presence of Iranian Revolutionary Guards. They are able to do so because of the extraordinary weakness of the Iranian government in the Baluchi-inhabited provinces.[71] In early 1994, scattered attacks and violence rocked Iranian Baluchistan.[72] There are an estimated 4.6 million Baluchis in Pakistan, mostly located in the southwest, near the Iranian border.[73]

Throughout the Persian Gulf states, in the wider region, and on the periphery, ethnic and religious groups that spill across borders are potential sources of instability, conflict, and violence. They become especially important when states are mutating and fragmenting and leaders see opportunities to achieve long-standing objectives. In this context, low-intensity violence can be extraordinarily effective and can trigger wider conflict.

Military Dynamics and Asymmetries

Although force structures in the Middle East and the Persian Gulf region reflect the basic insecurity of the regional states, in some cases local military asymmetries themselves can be treated as independent causes of conflict.

Weapons of Mass Destruction. One of the most contentious asymmetries in the region is in weapons of mass destruction. Unlike the balance of terror between the United States and the Soviet Union, which over the years established a modicum of stability in East-West military relations, nuclear weapons in the Middle East are unlikely to contribute to stability, especially in the Arab-Israeli and Persian Gulf conflicts.

Israel possesses a nuclear capability, and Iran and Iraq are aspiring nuclear powers. World attention has been focused on Iraq's and now Iran's nuclear weapons programs, and they have been under close scrutiny for the past few years. Syria and Egypt possess some chemical capabilities and might under different circumstances look for a nuclear option.

There is widespread belief in Western intelligence circles that Iran has embarked on a covert nuclear weapons program. If this is true, it would represent a new, dangerous threat to the Middle East and the Persian Gulf region. Yet while there is strong evidence that the Iranians are engaged in a modest nuclear research program, the open literature has not identified a known secret facility in Iran that is physically engaged in the process of building components for nuclear weapons.

Iran's nuclear ambitions will undoubtedly be affected by how credible the international community is in persuading Iran that Iraqi nuclear weapons are under permanent international control. Will an Iraqi program reemerge once new leadership comes to power in Baghdad? Iraq may be able to restart its weapons programs covertly once its huge oil revenues are restored.[74]

The main proliferation problem remains Israel's nuclear weapons. Israel, for understandable reasons, wishes to offset the conventional and numerical superiority of Arab forces and possibly those of other Muslim countries, such as Iran. Israel's leaders believe they can do so by sustaining a qualitative edge in weapons technology, particularly in weapons of mass destruction. Yet as long as Israel insists on this capability, other regional powers have no incentive to limit their own nuclear capabilities, and they will develop other means, such as chemical weapons, to offset Israel's capability.

This reinforcing pattern of incentives makes international arms control negotiations extremely difficult. Currently, all parties have accepted the premise that arms control must be secondary to the peace process. However, once significant progress has been achieved, the issue of Israel's nuclear weapons will immediately come to the fore; capping or ultimately reducing Israel's nuclear inventory will become the cornerstone of negotiations.

Control of weapons of mass destruction, however, cannot be achieved absent an elaborate discussion of the conventional military balance, which is of great concern to small countries, such as Israel. While in the short term Israel retains a very significant qualitative edge in conventional weapons over its neighbors, its longer-term advantage is not assured. In theory, Arab forces have access to more money and therefore more technologically advanced weapons systems than does Israel. Should a right-wing government came to power in Israel, for example, and repudiate the agreement with the Palestine Liberation Organization, Israel could be denied access to technologies which Arab countries could buy from several markets. The qualitative and quantitative conventional military balance will, of necessity, be part of any arms control regime. That balance, however, is contested.

Determining what countries should be included in any conventional arms control limitation agreement is itself difficult. Should North Africa be part of an agreement involving Israel? What about Muslim countries beyond the immediate periphery of Israel? Turkey is regarded as a friendly power today and Iran is regarded as an enemy, yet in the past the roles have been somewhat reversed. Developing a formula for negotiating conventional arms-control reductions in the Middle East, whether in the context of the Arab-Israeli conflict or in the Persian Gulf, will be infinitely more complex than anything attempted in Europe when the Treaty on Conventional Forces in Europe was negotiated in the late 1980s.

Similar asymmetries exist in the Persian Gulf region. Iraq, for instance, has always considered that Iran has a built-in quantitative edge, given its large population and its geographic advantages, and has seen technology and qualitative superiority as a way of offsetting this advantage. On the other hand, Saudi Arabia and the other smaller Gulf states see Iraq as a potentially dominant power based on quantitative capabilities. They, in turn, have had to rely on the United States as their guarantor or as the provider of a qualitative military edge.

Perhaps the most difficult questions of military symmetry are force doctrine and philosophy and the willingness to take casualties in warfare. It is well known that Israel, for instance, regards casualty minimization in its own forces and civilian population as a key component of its doctrine, which favors preemptive strategies. On the other hand, preemptive strategies tend to be destabilizing and have led Arabs to develop, on paper, very elaborate systems for launching first strike based on standing armies. Israel relies on a civilian citizen army that requires up to seventy-two hours before mobilization. Hence the trade-off between standing armies and civilian and reserve armies becomes a very important factor in overall discussions of arms limitations.

The Persian Gulf is tightly linked to the Arab-Israel theater through such countries as Iraq and Saudi Arabia, which have a direct interest in both conflicts. Israel, for instance, will never agree to a nuclear or even a conventional arms control agreement with its neighbors if the nuclear potential of Iraq and Iran is not restrained. It is not only nuclear capability in the Gulf that is at issue. The advanced capability in the air of the present Saudi government is not presently worrying to Israel, but would quickly become so were the regime to change.

The problem of arms control and arms limitation throughout the Middle East is so complex, difficult, and intertwined with the political process that no progress is likely until the fundamentals of a solution to the Arab-Israel conflict are in place. Even after peace agreements between Israel and its immediate Arab neighbors are reached, Persian Gulf states will have to join if any arms control regime is to be established.

Industrial Base and Civilian Infrastructure Asymmetries. Despite the growing interest in unconventional weapons and weapons of mass destruction, countries in the Middle East and South Asia continue to spend most of their capital procurement budgets on the acquisition of conventional weapons.[75] While most of the states in the region remain dependent on outside sources for their supply, a number have emphasized domestic development and production capabilities. The greater this capability, the more insulated a country is from outside efforts to restrict the arms race.

Within the Middle East, Israel has the most advanced defense industry. It is not only a major producer and importer of modern conventional weaponry, but also an emerging exporter of military technology to both Southern and Western nations. During 1988, Israel exported $1.47 billion in arms to sixty-one states, and the first half of 1989 saw a 40 percent increase in the sales of Israel Aircraft Industries, 75 percent of which was accounted for by increases in exports.[76] In addition, Israel has a unique strategic and defense cooperation arrangement with the United States that allows for two-way transfers and leasing of military equipment for weapons research and development.[77]

Within the Arab world, Egypt is one of the foremost domestic weapons producers. With twenty-nine arms production companies producing close to $1.5 billion in weapons a year, indigenous arms production is an important component of Egypt's defense, although much of this weaponry is exported to other states in the region.[78] Egypt also engages in licensed production of foreign systems. The most significant development in Egyptian conventional weaponry is the 1987 U.S.-Egyptian agreement on Egypt's licensed production of the state-of-the-art M-1A1 main battle tank.[79]

After the war between Iran and Iraq, both emerged as regional weapons manufacturing centers. Iran's domestic arms industry includes coproduction agreements with China and North Korea. Before the Gulf War, the capability of Iraq's defense industry ranged from the production of all types of small arms and ammunition to the development of upgrades for sophisticated missile systems. Iraqi engineers proved adept at upgrading and modernizing old weaponry. At the First Baghdad International Exhibition for Military Production in 1989, Iraq's minister of industry stated that the government was considering a program to export domestically manufactured arms.[80]

Much of Iraq's military infrastructure, as well as its stockpiles of weapons, was destroyed during the Gulf War. Due to the continuation of sanctions as mandated by Resolution 687 on the transfer of military-related items to Iraq, Baghdad will find it difficult to rebuild its military arms through either purchases or domestic production in the near future.

Other major Arab countries in the region, particularly Libya, Saudi Arabia, and Syria, do not have extensive domestic weapons production capabilities. Both Syria and Libya are dependent on Russia as their main weapons supplier. Syrian exports of Russian-made weapons have, however, made their way to other countries, primarily Lebanon, where thirty thousand Syrian troops are stationed.[81]

Saudi Arabia's indigenous arms production capability is very limited, encompassing only licensed production of small munitions and armored personnel carriers. Its large arms purchases and ability to give financial aid to other countries for military purposes, however, make Saudi Arabia a key player in the Middle East's arms market. Saudi Arabia is increasingly interested in arms deals that include technology transfers and the development of local industry, both civilian and military. Contacts have been made among Saudi Arabia, other GCC nations, and India regarding defense cooperation and training—a considerable departure from the traditional pattern of cooperation with Egypt, Turkey, and Pakistan in the area of technical personnel.[82] Nevertheless, for the foreseeable future, Saudi indigenous production will be limited to relatively simple systems.

The other indigenous weapons-producing giant in the region, alongside Israel, is India. In addition to being one of the world's leading importers of weapons over the last decade, India possesses a sophisticated indigenous defense production capability.[83] India is one of the few states in the Third World capable of acquiring, licensing, and developing state-of-the-art weapons systems. A new Indian proexport policy was announced in February 1989.[84] The Indian government decided to increase exports of its domestically produced weapons to finance imports of high-technology weapons and upgrades.

Pakistan can be expected to continue its conventional arms buildup through imports as well as through local and licensed production of weaponry. Pakistan's defense industry has fourteen branches and is self-sufficient in tank ammunition and artillery. China, in addition to being one of its principal suppliers, is involved in assisting Pakistan's defense industry through joint development projects.[85]

The impact of indigenous productive capability within the Persian Gulf and the wider region is a function of two attributes: its growth and its asymmetries. The growing capability makes some powerful states in the Gulf (for example, Iran) and in the region (for example, Israel and Egypt) less vulnerable to the impact of suppliers' agreements and negotiated arms-control regimes. This asymmetrical capability, however, makes others far less willing to enter into serious arms control agreements that leave intact the asymmetrical capacity to produce weapons that are highly sophisticated. It also reinforces the importance of having good relations with external weapons producers.

Role of External States. The instability of the regional military balance is further compounded by the potential role of external suppliers. So-called maverick states—such as North Korea or possibly Russia in the future under a new, more extreme leadership—pose even more difficult problems. They could upset the balance of power in the short run by providing nuclear technology or very advanced conventional missiles. Maverick states are least likely to enter into binding suppliers' agreements, and they therefore retain the capacity to shift the Mideast balance of power radically.

Terrorist groups, supported from within and outside the region, could also have a dangerous impact on the military balance. Terrorists have the capability to cause enormous damage throughout the region, given the vulnerability of high-value economic targets. Damage and death from the bombing of the World Trade Center, for example, could easily have been far greater. The Persian Gulf region has an equal number of highly lucrative targets that could be subject to terrorist attacks in the future, particularly water desalinization plants and oil production facilities. Ultimately, there is the nightmarish but plausible option of a nuclear terrorist operation.

Political and Military Wild Cards

We have examined the intricate network of interactions among the changing global system; the long-term trends in population, resources, and technology; and enduring sources of conflict within the Persian Gulf region. The changing global system and the demographic and energy profile of the region set the parameters within which enduring sources of conflict can be triggered. Superimposed on this already complex tapestry of interwoven threads is the possibility of political and military shocks to the system that could trigger a rapid escalation to conflict.

The matrix below (Figure 1.1) outlines the "shocks"—both trends and specific events—to the global, regional, and Persian Gulf systems that might occur in the coming decade. We rank their relative danger and probability.

At the global level, the most dangerous development would be an anti-Western coalition that might include Russia under a nationalist government, China, India, and Iran. Each of these countries would be independently antagonistic toward the United States. This kind of coalition would repolarize the Persian Gulf and the Middle East in both military and political terms. While such a coalition would be very dangerous, it is not as likely as disagreements between the United States and Western Europe on Persian Gulf policy; financial and commercial issues are an obvious source of division.

Probably the second most dangerous, and second most likely, global change would be Russia's emergence as a major "spoiler." Even under the most favorable of circumstances, Russia has a very different agenda in the Persian Gulf than does the United States. If a more nationalist government were to come to power in Moscow, a deepening split with Washington would be inevitable. Russia would undoubtedly pursue its independent economic and political agenda with receptive Gulf states. The more nationalist mood in Moscow is likely to strengthen the arguments of those who believe Russia has been too subservient to U.S. interests in the Middle East and thereby denied itself lucrative economic benefits, especially in arms exports to Iran. Vladimir Zhirinovsky,

Figure 1.1. Possible developments in global, regional, and Persian Gulf systems during the next decade.

Level of activity	Changes in order of danger	Changes in order of probability
Global	1. Anti-West coalition (Russia/China/India/Iran, and others)	1. U.S.-Europe split on Persian Gulf policy
	2. Russia as spoiler/arms supplier	2. Russia as spoiler/arms supplier
	3. U.S.-Europe split on Persian Gulf policy	3. Anti-West coalition
Regional	1. Islamicist Egypt	1. Islamicist Algeria
	2. Peace process derailed/terrorism	2. Peace process derailed/terrorism
	3. Unstable Turkey	3. Unstable Turkey
	4. Islamicist Algeria	4. Islamicist Egypt
Persian Gulf	1. Further nuclear proliferation	1. Post-sanctions Iraq
	2. Political upheaval in Saudi Arabia/GCC	2. Upheaval in Iran
	3. Post-sanctions Iraq	3. Upheaval in Saudi Arabia
	4. Upheaval in Iran	4. Further nuclear proliferation

however, sees Iraq, and especially Saddam Hussein, as the natural ally of Russia.[86] Finally, though unlikely, a significant change in U.S. policy toward the Gulf cannot be ruled out. Over this period, greater economic competition among the Middle East oil importers, which increasingly will include Asian countries, could lead to a fundamental challenge to U.S. policy and threaten the close cooperation on security policy that was so evident at the time of the Gulf War.

In the region, the most dangerous change would be the fall of the Mubarak government in Egypt and its replacement by a militantly Islamist regime. Even a military government that embraces important components of the Islamist agenda would challenge U.S. strategy throughout the Middle East, put at risk the Arab-Israeli peace process, and dissuade Israel from making additional concessions in the broader peace process. It would also have a profound effect on U.S. defense policy, which relies so heavily on access through Egyptian strategic straits and on Egypt as a strategic partner to manage serious conflict in the Persian Gulf region. Such a regime change in Egypt would shake the foundations of U.S. post-Gulf War strategy. A related danger would be a derailment of the Arab-Israeli peace process through a change of policy in Israel or fragmentation of the Palestine National Authority and the Palestine Liberation Organization, exacerbated by terrorism.

Yet another danger would be a change in the orientation of the leadership in Turkey. The United States depends very heavily on Turkey for military bases to protect Iraqi Kurds in northern Iraq. Turkish military bases are also important in any defense against an attack on the smaller states in the northern Persian Gulf region. Any change in Turkish-U.S. relations, which might come about as a result of internal upheavals in Turkey or from a disagreement over the conflict in the Balkans, would have very serious implications for Gulf stability.

The most likely regional shock is a militant Islamist government in Algeria. While this is the most probable regional contingency, its effects should not be exaggerated. A change in the Algerian government would pose enormous problems for France and the Mediterranean nations, particularly Tunisia. Nevertheless, an Islamic government in Algeria would confront a bankrupt treasury and economy and would be heavily dependent on Western Europe for assistance and commerce. Such a government would undoubtedly receive some assistance from Iran, but it could not afford to alienate its economic partners in Western Europe. Whether or not the success of militant Islam in Algeria would spread to other North African states, as some suggest, is questionable.

Within the Persian Gulf region itself, the most dangerous contingency would be a nuclearized Iran or Iraq. Open acknowledgement by either that it has acquired nuclear capability would alarm the whole region, create large incentives for other regional states to proliferate, and make impossible any progress toward the control of weapons of mass destruction throughout the region. It would also have major implications for the U.S. commitment to defend Saudi Arabia. As we have argued above, however, evidence is ambiguous about Iran's intention to develop a nuclear capability, and Iraq's acquisition of technology is currently under close international surveillance.

A political upheaval in Saudi Arabia that puts in place an anti-Western regime would also be highly destabilizing. Without Saudi Arabian support, the United States has no base in the Persian Gulf region for projecting power and protecting smaller Gulf states and their oil resources against either Iran or Iraq. The present Saudi regime, however, seems sufficiently resilient to absorb the political currents within the kingdom.

Another dangerous scenario would be adversarial behavior by a postsanctions Iraq, which, even under Saddam Hussein, would have access to greater resources. This is a likely scenario, and planning is already under way for how to manage this kind of challenge. Upheaval in Iran is also quite likely, although—given the weakness of the Iranian regime and the current inability of the Iranian armed forces to project power—the impact would not be as serious as a change in regime in Saudi Arabia.

Conclusion

Our examination of the conflict-generating processes in the Persian Gulf region has identified an intricate network of factors that could provoke violent conflict. Global changes; underlying regional trends in population, resources, and technology; and four regional triggers (enduring territorial disputes, an unstable periphery, ethnic and religious conflict, and asymmetries in the military balance) separately make conflict management in the Gulf difficult. Should political or military shocks occur that have a direct and negative impact on an already combustible region, it is likely that the Gulf will again experience war.

Several caveats are, however, in order. The political and military shocks that we have identified as most destabilizing are also the most unlikely. Those that we consider most probable are shocks that likely could be absorbed by the region if appropriate policies and procedures are in place. In addition, the underlying factors of population growth and conflict over water, energy, and access to technology and their impact on both intra- and interstate conflict can be ameliorated over time if appropriate preventive action is taken. The rate of population growth in Egypt, for example, has now begun to decline. Effective assistance policies can address population growth, both directly and indirectly, through programs that increase female participation in the work force. Within the framework of cooperative security, several plans for water sharing, for improved technology, and for more efficient use of water resources appear to be feasible. In planning for regional security, effective preventive action on population and resources is a critical element.

The triggers to conflict are present and dangerous. Past experience—which may not necessarily be a good guide in a rapidly changing present and future—suggests that each of these triggers alone rarely provokes war. When they overlap and make leaders vulnerable, desperate, and pessimistic that they can address their problems through cooperative security, war becomes an attractive option. Traditional security measures, however, are unlikely to bring about long-term stability. Preventive action to address underlying issues is an essential element of cooperative security in the Persian Gulf region.

The challenge is to put in place quickly as much of the environmental, economic, political, and military architecture of cooperative security as possible in an effort to insulate the region against a lethal combination of resource scarcity and enduring conflict. In sum, it is necessary to strengthen regional shock absorbers to limit the effects of the inevitable shocks to the system in the decade ahead.

Notes

1. All the population data are taken from Central Intelligence Agency, *The World Factbook 1994* (Washington, D.C.: Central Intelligence Agency, 1994).

2. Oman's total fertility rate was estimated in 1994 to be 6.53 children born per woman; Saudi Arabia's, 6.67; and Iraq, 6.71. For comparison, the fertility rate in Egypt is 3.77; Lebanon, 3.39; and Turkey, 3.21. Central Intelligence Agency, *The World Factbook 1994*.

3. Fertility rates and birthrates are two different though closely related population indicators. The birthrate in Oman is 40.38 births per thousand population; in Iran it is 42.43; and in Iraq, 44.11. In contrast to the high birthrates in the Persian Gulf, in Lebanon it is 27.89 per thousand; in Egypt, 28.69; and in Turkey, 25.98. Central Intelligence Agency, *The World Factbook 1994*.

4. Philippe Fargues, "From Demographic Explosion to Social Rapture," *Middle East Report* 190 (September–October 1994): 7.

5. Nazy Roudi, "Population Policies Vary in Middle East," *Population Today*, April 1993, 4.

6. Fargues, "From Demographic Explosion to Social Rapture," 8.

7. Lina Eid, "Population Study Says Mideast Needs 'Attitude' Change," *Washington News*, 1 September 1994.

8. Fargues, "From Demographic Explosion to Social Rapture," 9.

9. UN Development Program, *Human Development Report 1994*, (New York: UN Development Program, 1994), 100.

10. Abdel Omran and Farzaneh Roudi, "The Middle East Population Puzzle," *Population Bulletin* 48, no. 1 (July 1993): 2–39.

11. Eid "Population Study Says Mideast Needs 'Attitude' Change."

12. The Saudi Arabian population figure for 1994 is 18,196,783, up from 16.9 million in 1993. It is projected to rise to 22,069,831 by the year 2000. In Kuwait the population is projected to rise from 1,819,322 to 2,494,451; the population of Iran is projected to reach 78,350,134. U.S. Bureau of the Census, Center for International Research, fax letter, 21 October 1994.

13. The estimates of population doubling refer to the total population, which, in the case of the UAE, includes the 75 percent of the population who are expatriates. Assuming that there is no expulsion of expatriates, by 2010 the population for the UAE could be around 5.6 million, of which well over 4 million would be expatriates. Of these, the majority are from South Asia, adding significantly to the potential for political conflict among expatriate ethnic groups within the emirates.

14. All Persian Gulf demographic figures are taken from "Demographic Data," *Middle East Report*, March–April 1993, 8.

15. See, for instance, Neil W. Chamberlain, *Beyond Malthus: Population and Power* (New York: Basic Books, 1970), 49–54.

16. James Bruce, "Land of Crisis and Upheaval," *Jane's Defence Weekly*, 30 July 1994, 23–35.

17. Central Intelligence Agency, *The World Factbook 1994*, 32.

18. F. Gregory Gause III, *Oil Monarchies: Domestic and Security Challenges in the Arab Gulf States* (New York: Council on Foreign Relations, 1994), 45–46.

19. Central Intelligence Agency, *The World Factbook 1994*, 32.

20. The analysis of the major characteristics of the Gulf economies is based on Gause, *Oil Monarchies*, 44–58.

21. *Middle East Economic Monitor* 4, no. 9 (September 1994): 3–4.

22. Elaine Sciolino, "Iran's Difficulties Lead Some in U.S. to Doubt Threat," *New York Times*, 5 July 1994, A1.

23. Eliahu Kanovsky, lecture at the National Defense Institute conference, "Energy Security in the 21st Century," 10 November 1994.

24. Clay Chandler, "Bentsen Urges Saudis to Make Spending Cuts," *Washington Post*, 6 October 1994, p. D14.

25. Cherif Cordahi, "Middle East-Economy: Declining Growth Rates Hint at Future Crises," *Inter Press Service*, 26 September 1994.

26. Liz Kirkwood, "A Rising Tide in the Gulf," Institutional Investor Inc., July 1993, 93.

27. Sciolino, "Iran's Difficulties Lead Some in U.S. to Doubt Threat," p. A1.

28. Hobart Rowen, "Over the Barrel," *Washington Post*, 13 October 1994, p. A19.

29. Philip Shenon, "OPEC Seeking to Raise Prices by Output Freeze," *New York Times*, 22 November 1994, p. D1.

30. UN Development Program, *Human Development Report 1994*, 42.

31. Cordahi, "Middle East-Economy."

32. Some specialists consider a traditional economic assessment relying on GDP figures to be an insufficient barometer. A new measure, designed to measure socioeconomic development more accurately, is the human development index, which is a composite of three basic components: longevity, measured by life expectancy; knowledge, measured by combination of adult literacy and mean years of schooling; and standard of living, measured by purchasing power. According to the human development index ranking for developing countries, Persian Gulf countries are ranked in the following order, starting with the highest: Kuwait, Qatar, the UAE, Saudi Arabia, Iran, Oman, and Iraq. For ranking of the Gulf countries in the human development index ranking for developing countries, see UN Development Program, "The Human Development Index Revisited," *Human Development Report 1994*, 94.

33. Cordahi, "Middle-East Economy."

34. Historically, there have been other incidents, including a 1974 Iraqi-Syrian controversy over Syria's al-Thawra dam. Peter H. Gleick, "Water and Conflict," *International Security* 18, no. 1 (summer 1993): 88–89.

35. Gleick, "Water and Conflict," 99–100.

36. "Dry Politics," *The Middle East*, February 1994, 5.

37. Geoffrey Kemp, with the assistance of Shelley A. Stahl, *The Control of the Middle East Arms Race* (Washington, D.C.: Carnegie Endowment for International Peace, 1991), 214–215.

38. Ze'ev Schiff, *Security for Peace: Israel's Minimal Security Requirements in Negotiations with the Palestinians* (Washington, D.C.: Washington Institute for Near East Policy, 1989), 22.

39. Gleick, "Water and Conflict," 86.

40. *International Energy Annual 1992* (Washington, D.C.: Energy Information Administration, 1992) p. 6, table 1.

41. Edward R. Fried and Philip H. Trezise, *Oil Security: Retrospect and Prospect* (Washington, D.C.: The Brookings Institution, 1993), 12, 25, 42.

42. Geoffrey Kemp, *Forever Enemies? American Policy and the Islamic Republic of Iran* (Washington, D.C.: Carnegie Endowment for International Peace, 1994), 31, 117.

43. Richard Ned Lebow and Janice Gross Stein, *When Does Deterrence Succeed and How Do We Know?* Monograph Series (Ottawa: Canadian Institute for International Peace and Security, 1990).

44. Janice Gross Stein, "Deterrence and Compellence in the Gulf, 1990–1991: A Failed or Impossible Task," *International Security* 17, no. 2 (autumn 1992): 147–179.

45. Kemp, *Forever Enemies?* 36.

46. Kemp, *The Control of the Middle East Arms Race*, 38.

47. Shahram Chubin, *Iran's National Security Policy: Capabilities, Intentions and Impact* (Washington, D.C.: Carnegie Endowment for International Peace, 1994), 101–102.

48. Kemp, *Forever Enemies?* 120.

49. Ibid., 47–48.

50. Caryle Murphy, "A Small Nation, Qatar Stands Tall by Standing Apart," *Washington Post*, 3 April 1993, p. A22.

51. "Yemeni Minister Arrives in Riyadh with Message for King Fahd," *Agence France Presse*, 30 April 1994, and "Yemen, Saudi Arabia Postpone New Border Talks," *Reuters World Service*, 26 April 1994.

52. Kemp, *Forever Enemies?* 40–42.

53. See Barnett R. Rubin, "The Fragmentation of Tajikistan," *Survival* 35, no. 4 (winter 1993–94): 71–91, and Shahrbanou Tadjbakhsh, "Tajikistan: From Freedom to War," *Current History* 93, no. 582 (April 1994): 173–177.

54. Kemp, *Forever Enemies?* 39–40.

55. Chubin, *Iran's National Security Policy*, 6–7.

56. Richard Clogg, "Turmoil in Transcaucasia," *The World Today* 50, no. 1 (January 1994): 3–5.

57. Robert Famighetti, ed., *World Almanac and Book of Facts 1995* (Mahwah, N.J.: World Almanac, 1994), 52; Samantha Power, *Breakdown in the Balkans: A Chronicle of Events, January 1989 to May 1993* (Washington, D.C.: Carnegie Endowment Special Publication, 1993); "Muslim and Bosnian Croats Give Birth to a New Federation," *New York Times*, 19 March 1994, 4; "U.S. Planes Bomb Serb Positions for a Second Day," *New York Times*, 12 April 1994, p. A1.

58. Famighetti, *World Almanac and Book of Facts 1995*, p. 819 and "Somalia's Faction Leaders Agree to Form an Interim Government," *New York Times*, 22 March 1994, p. A8.

59. "Algerian Militant Base Uncovered in France," *New York Times*, 9 April 1994, p. A10.

60. *Al-ahali* (Cairo), 20 April 1994 in FBIS-NES, 29 April 1994, 21.

61. Kemp, *The Control of the Middle East Arms Race*, 42.

62. For information on Islamic friendship and building stronger ties, see PTV Television Network (Pakistan), 28 August 1993, in FBIS-NES, 31 August 1993, 56–57; Islamic Republic News Agency, 22 March 1993, from Middle East News Network, 25 March 1993; and an article on President Rafsanjani's visit to Pakistan in *Deutsche Press-Agentur*, 8 September 1992. For an article on the Economic Cooperation Organization, see *Jahan-e Eslam*, 14 February 1993, from Middle East News Network, 26 February 1993. For articles on Iran and Pakistan in Afghanistan, see IRIB Television, 6 March 1993 from Middle East News Network, 9 March 1993; *Ettela'at*, 9 February 1993, from Middle East News Network, 26 February 1993; and, for a review of strains caused by Afghanistan, *Interpress*, 1 August 1992. For Indian fears, see Raju Gopalakrishnan, "Pak-Iran Unholy Alliance against India," *News India*, 16 April 1993, 12. Rumors that Iran agreed to underwrite the Pakistani defense budget in exchange for nuclear technology are contained in *The Nation*, 15 April 1993, from Middle East News Network, 20 April 1993.

63. "Indian Defence Ministry Terms Iran a 'Security Threat,'" *These Days*, 14 April 1993, 3.

64. According to the *Times of India*, the "two leaders held wide-ranging discussions on international, regional and bilateral issues of mutual concern." "Close Ties with Iran Mooted," *Times of India*, 21 September 1993.

65. "Better Indo-Iranian Ties," *Indian Express*, 24 September 1993; "Pathbreaking Visit," *The Economic Times*, 24 September 1993; and "Turning Point in Indo-Iranian Ties," *The Independent* (India), n.d.

66. Philip Robins, "The Overlord State: Turkish Policy and the Kurdish Issue," *International Affairs*, 69, no. 4 (1993): 657–676.

67. Some say the figure is closer to 14.3 million (1990). Ted Robert Gurr, *Minorities at Risk* (Washington, D.C.: U.S. Institute of Peace, 1993), 332. The Central Intelligence Agency claims that there are 15.2 million Azeris in Iran. Central Intelligence Agency, *The World Factbook 1993* (Washington, D.C.: Central Intelligence Agency, 1994), 185.

68. Andrew Whitley, "Minorities and the Stateless in Persian Gulf Politics," *Survival*, 35, no. 4 (winter 1993–94): 35.

69. For Iraqi and Saudi Shiites, see Whitley, "Minorities and the Stateless in Persian Gulf Politics," 36–39, 41–42.

70. *Lebanon,* Walden Country Reports (1993) On-Line Service (Saffron Walden, England: Walden Publishing Inc., 1993).

71. Whitley, "Minorities and the Stateless in Persian Gulf Politics," 35. The Central Intelligence Agency claims that there are close to 1.3 million Baluchis in Iran. Central Intelligence Agency, *The World Factbook 1993,* 185.

72. "Martial Law Declared in Sistan Va Baluchestan," *Middle East Intelligence Report,* 10 February 1994.

73. Gurr, *Minorities at Risk,* 332.

74. On Iran and Iraq, see Kemp, *Forever Enemies?* 57–60.

75. See Kemp, *The Control of the Middle East Arms Race,* 86–88.

76. "Israel Defence Export Figures," *Jane's Defence Weekly,* 24 June 1989, 1299, and "Export Boost for IAI," *Jane's Defence Weekly,* 21 October 1989, 887.

77. David B. Ottaway, "Pact Allows U.S. to 'Lend' War Material to Israel," *Washington Post,* 27 September 1989, P. A44.

78. Martin Sieff, "Egypt's Military Posturing Worries Israel," *Washington Times,* 4 April 1988, p. A8.

79. *Reuters* news wire report, cited in *Current News,* Department of Defense, 30 May 1989, 5, and "Plant's Production to Replace U.S.-Built Tanks," Cairo, *Al-Ahram,* 23 January 1990, translated in *FBIS-NES,* 26 January 1990, 7–8.

80. Christopher Foss and Tony Banks, "'Candid' AEW One of Baghdad Show Surprises," *Jane's Defence Weekly,* 13 May 1989, 8.

81. International Institute for Strategic Studies, *The Military Balance 1989–90* (London: International Institute for Strategic Studies, 1989) 115.

82. "Saudi Military Team Visiting Indian Defense Establishments," *Defense and Foreign Affairs Weekly,* 3–9 July 1989, 2.

83. Aaron Karp, "Trade in Conventional Weapons," in *SIPRI Yearbook 1988: World Armaments and Disarmament* (New York: Oxford University Press, 1988), p. 178.

84. "Indian Minister Calls for Manufacture of Export Weapons," *Defense and Foreign Affairs Weekly,* 20–26 February 1989, 3. See also Gregory Copley, "Inevitable India, Inevitable Power," *Defense and Foreign Affairs,* December 1988, 52.

85. Pakistan and China are working together to develop a new main battle tank. "New Sino-Pakistani MBT Project," *International Defense Review,* December 1988, 1553. See also "Pakistan Takes Delivery of First Home-Built Tank and APC," *Defense and Foreign Affairs Weekly,* 2–8 April 1990, 2–3.

86. V. V. Zhirinovsky, *Last Dash to the South,* as translated in FBIS-SOV-022-5, 2 February 1994, p. 38.

2

ETHNIC CONFLICT AND STATE BUILDING IN THE ARAB WORLD

Saad Eddin Ibrahim

All the world's armed conflicts since 1988, with the possible exception of Iraq's invasion of Kuwait, have been over internal ethnic issues. In fact, since 1945, ethnic conflicts have claimed some fifteen million lives, several times those claimed by from interstate wars. At present, ethnic conflicts span three continents. Typical examples are those in Burma and Sri Lanka in Asia; Somalia, Sudan, and Rwanda in Africa; and the former USSR and Yugoslavia in Europe.[1]

With only 8 percent of the world's population, the Arab World and the Middle East have had some 25 percent of all the world's armed conflicts since 1945. Most of these conflicts have been ethnically based. Table 2.1 shows the balance of interstate and interethnic armed conflicts in the region in terms of human and material costs. The Arab-Israeli conflict (some six wars and a continued Palestinian and Lebanese struggle against Israeli occupation), which is considered as the principal one, has claimed some 200,000 lives in forty years. In contrast, during the same period ethnic conflicts have claimed several times as many lives. The casualties of the Lebanese civil war (1975–90) alone matched those of all the Arab-Israeli wars. The Sudanese civil war (on and off since 1956) has claimed at least five times as many lives as all the Arab-Israeli wars. There have been other costly interstate conflicts, but they are, similarly, not comparable to intrastate conflicts in terms of population displacement, material devastation, and financial expenditure.[2]

In the 1990s, armed conflicts in the region likely will be more of the intrastate than of the interstate variety. Militant Islamic activism has added to the ongoing sources of armed civil strife in a score of Arab Middle Eastern countries. Algeria and Egypt are currently two prominent cases in point. Thus, the greatest threats to security of the states in the

Table 2.1. The cost of armed conflicts in the Middle East and North Africa: 1948–93.

Type of conflict	Period	No. of casualties	Estimated cost in billions $U.S. (1991 value)	Estimated population displacement
Interstate conflict				
Arab-Israeli Conflict	1948–1990	200,000	300.0	3,000,000
Iraq-Iran War	1980–1988	600,000	300.0	1,000,000
Persian Gulf War	1990–1991	120,000	650.0	1,000,000
Other interstate conflicts	1945–1991	20,000	50.0	1,000,000
Sub-Total		**940,000**	**1,300.0**	**6,000,000**
Intrastate conflict				
Sudan	1956–1991	900,000	30.0	4,500,000
Iraq	1960–1991	400,000	30.0	1,200,000
Lebanon	1958–1990	180,000	50.0	1,000,000
Yemen	1962–1972	100,000	5.0	500,000
Syria	1975–1985	30,000	0.5	150,000
Morocco (Sahara)	1976–1991	20,000	3.0	100,000
So. Yemen	1986–1987	10,000	0.2	50,000
Somalia	1989–1991	20,000	0.3	200,000
Other intrastate conflicts	1945–1991	30,000	1.0	300,000
Sub-total		**1,690,000**	**120.0**	**8,000,000**
Grand Total (All armed conflicts)		**2,630,000**	**1,420.0**	**14,000,000**

Source: Files of the Arab Data Unit, Ibn Khaldoun Center for Developmental Studies

region are likely to be internal.[3] Manipulation or spillover effects of internal armed conflicts could, of course, lead to interstate conflicts as well. This chapter, however, deals with only one type: ethnically based internal conflicts.

The disproportionate importance of ethnic conflict vis-à-vis interstate conflict is surprising in view of the global sociocultural demographics of the Arab world. When ethnicity is broadly defined to refer to contiguous or coexisting groups differing in race, religion, sect,

Table 2.2. Major ethnic divisions of the Arab world in the early 1990s.

Ethnic division	Population size (in millions)	Percent of population	Countries of concentration
The majority (Arabic-speaking, Muslim, Sunni, Caucasian)	190.0	80.0	In all Arab countries except Lebanon, Iraq, and Bahrain
Lingua-cultural minorities (non-Arab)	32.3	13.7	Morocco, Sudan, Algeria, Iraq
Religious minorities (non-Muslim)	17.9	7.6	Sudan, Eqypt, Lebanon, Israel (occupied territories)
Islamic minorities (non-Sunni)	20.8	8.8	Iraq, Lebanon, Syria, the Persian Gulf
Racial Minorities (non-Semitic, Hamitic, Caucasian)	8.7*	3.7	Sudan

* Also included in lingua-cultural and religious minority divisions

Source: Saad Eddin Ibrahim, Sects, Ethnicity, and Minority Groups in the Arab World (in Arabic) (Cairo: Ibn Khaldoun Center, 1994), 86.

language, culture, or national origin, the Arab world is one of the more ethnically homogeneous areas in the world today.[4]

In 1993, the Arab world had a population of slightly over 236 million. The overwhelming majority (80 percent, or 190 million) share the same ethnic characteristics. Racially, they are a Semitic-Hamitic-Caucasian mix. Religiously, they are Muslims of the Sunni denomination. Culturally and linguistically, they are Arabic-speaking natives. (See Tables 2.3, 2.4, and 2.5 for linguistic and religious breakdowns.) In terms of national origin, they have been rooted for many centuries in the same "Arab Homeland" (extending from Morocco on the Atlantic Ocean to Bahrain in the Persian Gulf). This overwhelming majority grows larger if we add groups each of which differ in only one ethnic variable that is perceived by the group as being a marginal element in the definition of its identity. For example, most Shia Muslims and most Christians living in the Arab world consider their "Arabism" as the primary axis of their identity, superseding their Shiaism or Christianity. For them, the linguistic-cultural variable is the more salient ethnic divide. On this basis the Arab "majority" jumps to over 86 percent of the population in the Arab world.

Table 2.2 shows the major ethnic groupings in the Arab world along four dimensions: cultural-linguistic, religious, denominational, and racial.

Despite the apparent ethnic homogeneity on the pan-Arab level, we observe marked ethnic heterogeneities in several countries: Algeria, Bahrain, Iraq, Lebanon, Mauritania, Morocco, Sudan, Syria, and Yemen. In these nine countries, as many as 35 percent of the population differ from the Arab Muslim Sunni Caucasian majority along one or more of the four ethnic variables of language, religion, sect, or race. It is noted that nearly all nine countries are located at the outer rim of the Arab world, often intersecting a cultural borderland. In all nine countries, there has been some overt form of ethnic tension. In four of them—Iraq, Lebanon, Sudan, and Yemen—such tensions have flared in recent decades into a protracted armed conflict. The unity and the territorial integrity of each have been seriously threatened.[5]

Arab social scientists and political activists have not given ethnic conflict appropriate attention. Marxists, nationalists, and Islamists have tended to ignore the ethnic question or dismiss it as a residual of other problems. The "foreign factor" (for example, imperialists and Zionists) has been offered as a common explanation underlying most ethnic conflicts in the Arab world.[6] Such a factor is not to be dismissed, but a new generation of Arab social scientists is now going far beyond such conspiratorial explanations of ethnic conflicts.[7] The remainder of this chapter reviews these explanations under the following four problematics as they bear on the ethnic question in the Arab world:

- competing loci of identity;
- dilemmas of modern state building;
- socioeconomic cleavages;
- vulnerabilities to external factors.

The four problematics are generally interconnected in all Arab countries, but their interplay is particularly acute in countries with greater ethnic heterogeneity. The disintegration of traditional Islamic polities in the nineteenth century, the final collapse of the Ottoman Empire (1922), and Western colonial designs led to the fragmentation of the Arab world and the embryonic beginnings of modern "territorial states" in the interwar period (1918 to 1939).[8] As these states gained political independence from the 1940s to the 1960s, they inherited fragmented ethnic minorities. The political space was replete with the challenges of forging a national identity, state building, consolidating independence, achieving socioeconomic development, and ensuring reasonable measures of equity. Moreover, these challenges were faced in an international system polarized by the ideological and geopolitical conflict of the Cold War.

The Identity Problematic

Briefly stated, the main competing ideological paradigms in the Arab world since the turn of the century have tended to exclude certain ethnic groups from full-fledged membership in the political community. At present, the Arab intellectual-political space is dominated by Islamic and secular nationalist ideologies. Each has its own locus of political identity.

The Islamists' Vision and Ethnicity

The Islamists, naturally, base the political bond of culture, society, and state on religion. This would automatically exclude non-Muslims from the respective polities of the Arab world—some 18 million people, mostly Christians together with a few hundred thousand Jews (Table 2.3). In its extreme purist form, the exclusion would entail some 21 million non-Sunni Muslims (various Shias and Kharijite sects) as well. Mainstream Islamists would make exclusion partial; they would ban non-Muslims from assuming commanding offices (for example, head of state, governor, or judge).[9] Their rationale is that holders of such offices not only perform temporal roles but also carry out religious duties: leading prayers, implementing the shari'a (Islamic law), and commanding the faithful in the jihad (holy war). The purist Islamists would have non-Muslims excluded completely from any state or governmental role at any level. To them, non-Muslims are to exist as "protected communities" (*ahl zimma*), run their own communal affairs, and pay the *jezia* (a poll tax).[10] So long as they respect the Muslim majority and recognize the sovereignty of the Islamic state, non-Muslim communities are to be treated with respect, compassion, and religious tolerance.

In this vision, all Muslims are considered equal, regardless of their race, culture, or national origin. Accordingly, Kurds (in Iraq and Syria), Berbers (in Algeria and Morocco), and blacks (in Mauritania and Sudan) are not considered "minorities." Together, these Muslim (but non-Arab) groups number over 2 million. This Islamist vision of the "political order" would naturally be welcomed by non-Arab but Muslim members of the community, in which "citizenship" is based on religion. Obviously, in such a polity, non-Muslims in the Arab world feel threatened as well as alienated.

Arab Nationalist Vision

The Arab nationalist vision started to unfold in the last decades of the Ottoman Empire. It emerged as a reaction to both Ottoman despotism and the Young Turks' Tauranic chauvinism. In its pure form, the Arab nationalist vision is predicated on culture and language as the pillars of

Table 2.3. Non-Islamic religious minorities in the Arab world
in the late 1980s.

Non-Islamic religious minorities	Total population of minority group in Arab world*	Important regions of concentration
I. Christian	**12,588,000**	
Greek (Roman) Orthodox	1,900,000	Syria, Lebanon, Jordan, Israel (occupied territories)
Notorious	900,000	Syria, Iraq, Lebanon
Monophisitic	**6,425,000**	
Coptic Orthodox	5,600,000	Egypt, Sudan
Yaccohian (Syrian) Orthodox	225,000	Syria, Lebanon
Armenian Orthodox	600,000	Syria, Lebanon, Jordan, Iraq, Egypt
Catholic	**3,363,000**	
Western Latin	625,000	Sudan, Syria, Lebanon, Israel (occupied territories), Egypt
Greek-Roman	500,000	Lebanon, Syria, Egypt
Syrian	8,000	Lebanon, Syria
Armenian	85,000	Lebanon, Syria
Copt (Roman)	170,000	Egypt, Sudan
Kaldenian	625,000	Iraq, Syria, Lebanon
Maronite	1,150,000	Lebanon, Syria
(Protestant sects)	200,000	Sudan, Lebanon, Syria, Egypt
II. Jewish	**4,700,000**	
Rabbanite Orthodox	4,400,000	Israel (occupied territories)—western countries
Qarite (Karaite)	150,000	Israel (occupied territories)—eastern countries
Samaritan	150,000	Israel

Table 2.3. (cont.)

Non-Islamic religious minorities	Total population of minority group in Arab world*	Important regions of concentration
III. Hetrodox Religious Sector	**4,825,000**	
Sabian	150,000	Iraq
Yazidi	125,000	Iraq
Bohai	50,000	Israel (occupied territories), Iraq
Black Tribal Religions	4,500,000	Sudan
Total Non-Islamic religious minorities	**25,476,000**	

Source: Saad Eddin Ibrahim, *Reflection on the Question of Minorities* (in Arabic) (Cairo: Ibn Khaldoun Center, 1992).

*Most of these numbers are approximations, reached by two methods: the first takes the last official enumeration and adds the percentage of natural increase, which is comparable to the natural increase of the total number of inhabitants in the countries where those groups lived in the years following the last census: the second method averages the maximum and minimum estimations stated in references dealing with the topic, as listed below.

Robert B. Betts, *Christians in the Arab East: A Political Study* (Athens: Layacabettus Press, 1975).

A. W. Homani, *Minorities in the Arab World* (London: Oxford University Press, 1974).

M. O. Beshir, *The Southern Sudan: Background to Conflict* (Khartoum: Khartoum University Press, 2nd impression, 1970).

World Tables (Baltimore, Md.: Johns Hopkins University Press for the World Bank, 1980).

R. D. Maclourin, ed., *The Political Role of Minority Groups in the Middle East* (New York: Praeger, 1979), (appendix B) 268–87.

the political identity of state, society, and citizenship. In this sense, Arab nationalism has been a secular ideology. Accordingly, all native speakers of Arabic, bearers of Arab culture, and those who perceive themselves as "Arabs" would be full-fledged members of the Arab nation, enjoying full rights of citizenship, regardless of race, religion, or sect. The Arab nationalist vision would not recognize non-Arab national or cultural groups living in the Arab Homeland as autonomous communities or independent entities in their own right. However, their individual members would be treated as equal citizens under the law.[11]

Table 2.4. Linguistic minorities in the Arab world at the beginning
of the 1990s.

Minority group*	Total no. in Arab world	Religion of majority	Native country	Important regions of present concentration
Kurd	5,000,000	Muslim	Same as present location	Iraq, Syria
Armenian/ Aramite	1,000,000/ 125,000	Christian	Armenia (Turkey and former Soviet Union)	Lebanon, Syria, Iraq, Egypt
Turkman	125,000	Muslim	Same as present location	Syria, Iraq, Lebanon
Turk	125,000	Muslim	Turkey	Syria, Iraq
Iranian	350,000	Muslim	Iran	Iraq, Persian Gulf countries
Western Jewish	3,500,000	Jewish	Europe-North America, South America	Israel (occupied territories)
Black tribes	5,500,000	Pagan	Same as present location	Israel, So. Egypt
Nubian	500,000	Muslim	Same as present location	No. Sudan
Berber	15,000,000	Muslim	Same as present location	Morocco, Algeria, Tunisia, Libya

* All minority groups in table are of the Hamitic/Semitic races

Source: Saad Eddin Ibrahim, *Reflection on the Question of Minorities* (in Arabic) (Cairo: Ibn Khaldoun Center, 1992).

Most of the numbers above are approximations, estimated or prorated from the following sources:

A. W. Homani, *Minorities in the Arab World* (London: Oxford University Press, 1974).

E. Gellner and C. Micand, eds., *Arabs and Berbers* (London: Duckworth, 1973).

M. O. Beshir, *The Southern Sudan: Background to Conflict* (Khartoum: Khartoum University Press, 2nd impression, 1970).

World Tables (Baltimore, Md.: Johns Hopkins University Press for the World Bank, 1980).

R. D. Maclourin, ed., *The Political Role of Minority Groups in the Middle East* (New York: Praeger, 1979), (appendix B) 268–87.

Table 2.5. Non-Sunni Islamic sects at the beginning of the 1990s.

Non-Sunni Islamic sect	Total population of sect in Arab world*	Century when sect appeared	Important regions of concentration
Ithna 'Ashariyah (Twelvers)	10,000,000	7th–9th	Iraq, Lebanon, Persian Gulf countries
Zaydi	3,500,000	8th	So. Yemen, Arab Peninsula
Isma'iliyah (Seveners)	300,000	8th	Syria, Lebanon, Iraq, Persian Gulf countries
Druze	1,350,000	11th	Syria, Lebanon, Israel (occupied territories)
Alawite	3,000,000	9th	Syria, Lebanon
Abadhi Kharajite	1,500,000	7th	Oman, Algeria, Tunisia
Total	**19,650,000**		

Source: Saad Eddin Ibrahim, *Reflection on the Question of Minorities* (in Arabic) (Cairo: Ibn Khaldoun Center, 1992).

*See table 3 for the methods used to derive these numbers. The following references were used:
A. W. Homani, *Minorities in the Arab World* (London: Oxford University Press, 1974).
Michael Hudson, *Arab Politics: The Search for Legitimacy* (New Haven, Conn.: Yale University Press, 1977).
E. Gellner and C. Micand, eds., *Arabs and Berbers* (London: Duckworth, 1973).
World Tables (Baltimore, Md.: Johns Hopkins University Press for the World Bank, 1980).

Thus, while the Islamists would exclude non-Muslims, the Arab nationalists would exclude non-Arabs from full-fledged membership in the polity; at present (1994), non-Arabs in the Arab world number some 2 million. On the other hand, non-Muslim Arabs would be fully integrated in the Arab nationalists' political community; at present (1994), these amount to some 18 million (mostly Christians).

Naturally, non-Arabs would feel threatened by the Arab nationalist vision. This is particularly the case with sizable non-Arab communities who have national aspirations of their own (for example, the Kurds) or who want to preserve their cultural integrity and language (for example, the Berbers). Also, some non-Muslim communities fear that despite its secular rhetoric, Arab nationalism has Islamic underpinnings. This apprehension is to be found explicitly among the Maronite Christians of Lebanon, and implicitly among the Christian Copts of Egypt.[12]

Thus, each of the competing paradigms of identity in the Arab world would exclude what the other would include in its respective definition of the political community. How modern state builders, in practice, have tried to cope with this dilemma by the subtle evolution of country nationalism referred to as *wataniyya* is discussed below.[13]

The Intractable Question of Identity

The question of identity is one of the most vexing sociopolitical cleavages in the Arab world. It taps cultural, symbolic, and existential notions of the individual and the collective self. Unlike other cleavages (for example, class, occupational, educational, ideological, and political cleavages), ethnic identity and the conflicts it generates are "intrinsically less amenable to compromise than those revolving around material issues."[14]

Both the Islamic and the nationalist visions have failed to take into account subidentities within their own broad primordial frames of reference. Thus, Islamic visionaries have tended to discount sectarian cleavages among fellow Muslims. In the Lebanese civil war (1975–89), Shia and Sunni Muslims killed more of each other than they did Christians. Indeed, Shia Muslims killed more of each other than they did Sunni and Druze Muslims and Christians of all sects. More Christians were killed by other Christians than by Muslims in the Lebanese civil war.[15]

Nor would proponents of the Islamic vision of political identity take much comfort from the fighting among the Afghani Muslim mujahideen, which claimed more Muslim casualties in three years (1990–93) than the ten years (1980–90) of resistance against the Soviet Union and the Soviet-backed regime.[16] Similarly, proponents of the pan-Arab nationalist vision have been seriously discredited by actions of regimes espousing that vision. The quarter-century rivalry between the two Baathist regimes in Iraq and Syria is a dramatic case in point. It happens that the elite of each regime belong to a different religious Muslim minority sect.[17]

Much of the tension in North Yemen (1970–90) and then in unified Yemen (1990-94), which escalated into a full-fledged civil war in mid-1994, has not been without its Muslim sectarian undertones. Despite official denials by all parties to the conflict, the hidden but persistent cleavage has been between the Shia Muslim Zaydies of the north and the Sunni Muslim Shawafi of the south.[18]

Thus, elegant as the two competing visions of identities in the Arab world may be, they have failed in practice to project a coherent or consistent political program. They have failed to deal with subidentities, let alone their interplay with other socioeconomic variables.

Figure 2.1. Orientation of Arab states along religious-secular and country-Arab nation lines.

Religious (Islamic)		Country patriotism (*Wataniyya*)
Saudi Arabia	Morocco	
Persian Gulf States	Tunisia	
Sudan	Algeria	
Morocco	Sudan	
Jordan	Lebanon	
Libya	Saudi Arabia	
Egypt	Persian Gulf States	
Algeria	Egypt	
Yemen	(occupied territories)	
Tunisia	Jordan	
(occupied territories)	Libya	
Iraq	Iraq	
Syria	Syria	
Lebanon	Yemen	Arab
Secular		nationalism (*Qawmiyya*)

The Task of State Building

The modern state-building process in the Arab world is some seven decades old. The earliest state, Egypt (1922), tackled the issue of identity with a compromise. While Egypt's first constitution (1923) was clearly secular, basing full citizenship on birthright, regardless of religion, race, or creed, one article stipulated that "Islam is the state religion." But this was understood, in Egypt and elsewhere in Arab countries with similar constitutions and stipulations, to mean only that the head of state would be a Muslim[19], and that Islamic shari'a would be a source (but not the only one) of legislation.[20] Neither seriously impeded the integration of non-Muslims into the polity.

In practice, nearly every Arab state today has avoided the clear dichotomies of choice—between religious and secular, or national and country (*qawmiyya* and *wataniyya*)—in forging their political-cultural identities. Instead, each Arab state (or regime) has attempted its own reconciliation, with greater emphasis on one particular dimension, but never to the total exclusion of the other. Hence, it is possible to plot the Arab states on the two continua of religious-secular and country (*watan*)-Arab nation (*umma arabiyya*), as Figure 2.1 shows.

The pragmatic reconciliation of secular and religious considerations was not the only issue in forging the identity of the new states. Early state builders also had to contend with reconciling pan-Arab national considerations with those of subnational identities (*qawmmi* versus *qautry*). The leaders of the pan-Arab movement who had rallied around Sherif Hussein of Mecca in the Great Arab Revolt (1916) were frustrated as Britain and France reneged on their promises of Arab independence and unification (as was later revealed by the Sykes-Picot secret agreement). Yet Arab nationalist hopes remained alive. With the independence of one country after another in mid-century, early state builders made another pragmatic choice. In their constitutions or declarations of independence, it was often stipulated that while the country is an "independent sovereign state," it nonetheless remains an integral part of the "Arab Nation" or the "Arab Homeland," waiting for the opportune moment to "reunite with the other Arab parts."[20] The establishment of the League of Arab States in 1945 was a formalization of this compromise. It ensured the separate independence of its member states, but it kept the door open for gradual measures of cooperation, integration, and unification.

Thus, while Arab ideologists debated their competing, sometimes mutually exclusive, visions, practical statesmen and politicians engaged in the "art of the possible." These two compromises were cases in point: They operated reasonably well during the early decades of independence in several Arab countries that adopted "liberal" or quasi-liberal systems of governance—for example, Egypt, Iraq, Jordan, Lebanon, Morocco, and Syria. Where sizable ethnic groups existed, they were accommodated politically under such liberal systems. In some cases (for example, Jordan and Lebanon), ethnic groups were formally or explicitly recognized and allotted a proportional share in elected and ministerial councils. In others (for example, Egypt, Iraq, and Syria), similar though implicit accommodations were practiced. In other words, socioethnic diversity was matched by a political pluralism of one sort or another.

The end of the first liberal experiment in those Arab states during the 1950s and 1960s entailed potential problems for their ethnic communities. The military regimes that took power in many of them adopted militant Arab nationalist ideologies and bold socioeconomic reforms. On both counts, they were bound to alienate this or that ethnic group. In Egypt, for example, Nasser's July 1952 revolution alarmed non-Muslim communities on several grounds. None of the one hundred free officers who staged the revolution was a Christian, although Copts alone (apart from other Christian denominations) represented some 8 percent of the population. Nor were Egypt's Copts particularly enthusiastic about the new regime's Arab nationalist orientation. Worse still were the regime's socialist policies, which in the aggregate targeted the Christians disproportionately, because they were disproportionately represented among the landed bourgeoisie of Egypt. Similar patterns developed elsewhere in the Arab world where military or single-party regimes ruled for several years. In countries with marked ethnic heterogeneity, this lack of political pluralism exacerbated tension. Even when military or single-party regimes attempted to accommodate ethnic groups, such accommodation was often either nominal or arbitrary, depending on the whims of the rulers, leading to further alienation of these groups.[21]

In two extreme cases, ethnic majority rule was replaced by the rule of an ethnic minority. Thus, under the ideological guise of the Arab Baath Socialist Party, an Alawite military regime has ruled the Arab Muslim Sunni majority (65 percent of the population) in Syria since 1970. In Iraq it is members of an Arab Muslim Sunni minority (35 percent of the population) who, since 1968, have dominated all other ethnic groups, including the Shia Muslims, who account for about 45 percent of Iraq's total population.

In Sudan, members of the ruling military elite invariably have come from one Arab Muslim northern province around the capital, Khartoum. Under populist, socialist, and now Islamic guise, the three military coups d'état (of 1958, 1969, and 1989) have been staged by Arab Muslim northern officers. In none of them was there a single southern non-Muslim officer at the start. Later on, a few token southerners were added.

With the exception of Egypt, the alienation of ethnic groups vis-à-vis the ruling military-ideological and single-party regimes has grown into overt unrest. In Algeria, Iraq, Mauritania, Somalia, Sudan, and Syria, it has erupted into violent confrontations of varying degrees during the last three decades. At present, there are protracted armed conflicts in Iraq, Somalia, and Sudan. At times it is not only the legitimacy of the ruling regime which is challenged by this or that ethnic group, but also the legitimacy of the state itself. Thus, the territorial integrity of the Iraq, Somalia, and Sudan is now in serious question. Several decades of a state-building process is giving way to a reverse process of state deconstruction.

The Social Question: Mobilization and Equity

The twin processes of Western penetration and the disintegration of the Ottoman Empire led, among other things, to the breakdown of the traditional organization of ethnic groups in the Arab world. Their residential and occupational patterns have become less segregated. With independence, social mobilization and integration into the societal mainstream were greatly expedited, and their political consciousness was markedly heightened. Modern education, urbanization, expanding means of communication and exposure to the mass media were all instrumental in this respect.[22]

As elsewhere in developing regions, this social mobilization was accompanied or followed by a steady rise in the expectations of ethnic groups in the Arab world. Those expectations included a greater share in power, wealth, and prestige in their newly independent countries. The brief liberal experiment in several Arab states satisfied the demand of ethnic groups for political participation, but not for social justice—specifically, an equitable share in wealth. The early years of military-ideological regimes satisfied ethnic groups or promised to do so, for social equity, through such redistributional measures as land reform, nationalization of foreign and upper class assets, open and free education, the provision of equal opportunities, and the adoption of meritocractic systems of employment. However, as these regimes consolidated their tenure, even the promise of greater equity began to erode for all nonruling groups, including ethnic minorities.

Thus, while political participation has been curtailed and social mobilization has continued unabated, progress in social equity has slowed or halted and relative deprivation has been steadily rising since the 1970s. Such deprivation has been felt more by ethnic groups than by other sectors in society. Consequently, they have been the first and the loudest in expressing their resentment against what by now has become an authoritarian-bureaucratic ruling class, with ideological trappings fading into the background.

Instead of responding to such protests by increasing social equity or reopening the political system for greater participation, most Arab authoritarian-bureaucratic regimes have responded by greater coercion domestically or by military adventures externally. Thus the Syrian regime became embroiled in the Lebanese civil war (since 1975); the Iraqi regime in two Persian Gulf wars (with Iran from 1980 to 1988 and in Kuwait with an international coalition from 1990 to 1991); the Libyan regime, in Chad (1975–88); the Algerian regime, in a proxy war with Morocco in the Sahara (1976–90); the Somali regime, in the Ogden with Ethiopia (1977); and the Mauritanian regime, in series of armed skirmishes with Senegal (1990–91).

Both mounting coercion internally and military adventures externally have increased the share of state budgets allotted to arms purchases and decreased the share allocated to social programs. Thus, social equity has continued to deteriorate further for all nonruling groups, but more so for ethnic minorities, and the ethnic divide in several Arab countries has been intensified by a class divide.[23] The combination of class-ethnic deprivation needed one more factor to erupt into an open armed conflict: a foreign ally.

External Penetration and Ethnicity in the Arab World

Because of its unique strategic location as well as resources, especially oil, the Arab world and the Middle East has been a target of domination by rival foreign powers during the last two centuries. Several structural weaknesses in the Arab world and the Middle East were accentuated by foreigners to enhance their hegemonic designs. The ethnic question has been one of those weaknesses.

As early as the late-eighteenth century, rival Western powers scrambled for clients among various ethnic groups that lived in the provinces of the declining Ottoman Empire, the Sick Man of Europe. This sponsorship was a pretext for possible control when the Sick Man collapsed. A case in point was France's sponsorship of the Christian Maronites, Britain's of the Druze Muslims, and Russia's of the Christian Orthodox—all in one Arab-Ottoman province, Greater Syria (including Mount Lebanon). On the whole, ethnic groups in the Arab world remained reluctant and skeptical of such unsolicited guardianship by foreign powers, but as the corruption and despotism of the ailing Ottoman Empire increased, some groups accepted such guardianship for protection not only against the central authorities but also against real or perceived threats from other ethnic groups at home.

This nineteenth-century pattern of big powers intruding into the Arab world's ethnic politics continued into the twentieth century, first under direct colonial rule of fragmented Arab polities and then after their formal independence. Since World War II, with more independent or new states in the Arab world and the Middle East, several regional actors have also become involved, often by proxy, in one another's ethnic affairs. Notable were Israel (in Iraq, Lebanon, and Sudan), Iran (in Iraq and Lebanon), and Ethiopia (in Sudan).[24] Likewise, at times some Arab states meddled in the ethnic question of neighboring Arab and non-Arab states (for example, Syria in Iraq and Lebanon; Iraq in Iran, Lebanon, and Syria; and Sudan in Ethiopia).[25]

The big-power rivalry during the Cold War (1945–90) added a complicating dimension of ideology to the Arab world's ethnic question. At times, factions of the same ethnic group were as much in conflict with each other as were their external patrons, regional or global. Rarely did the external factor alone trigger serious ethnic conflicts. Indigenous political, socioeconomic, and cultural factors were primarily responsible for such conflicts.

The external factor did intensify, complicate, and extend such conflicts. These protracted armed ethnic conflicts have tended, over time, to create a political economy and a subpolitical culture of their own, far beyond the original issues of the conflict. The civil wars in Lebanon, Iraq, and Sudan are dramatic cases in point. At present (1994), Iraq is de facto divided into three zones. In two of the zones, the north (Kurds) and the south (Shias), the central government in Baghdad exercises only limited control. Only the middle zone (about half of Iraq) has been under the total control of the Iraqi government since its defeat in the Gulf War (1991). The other two zones are now off limits to Iraqi air power by order of the United Nations and the coalition. The Protected Zone in the north has felt sufficiently secure to elect its own Kurdish Parliament in 1992 and has its own government.[26]

Ethnicity, Civil Society, and Democratization

To recapitulate, the ethnic question is one of the most serious challenges facing the Arab world at large, and, in particular, those Arab states with a marked ethnic diversity. The leadership in the nascent system of modern nation-states as well as the Arab intelligentsia have failed to comprehend or address the ethnic problem. Cesarean birth at the hands of colonial midwives brought into existence a number of seriously deformed Arab states. Had the liberal experiment been allowed to continue, or had it been resumed a decade or two after its interruption, much of the early socioeconomic deformities might have been corrected through a genuine process of participation.

Participatory Politics

Participatory political systems have proved to be the most effective modalities of peaceful management of social cleavages in general, and of ethnic conflict in particular. Primordial loyalties are often moderated, reduced, or even eliminated as modern socioeconomic formations (for example, classes and occupational groups) freely evolve and offer members of ethnic groups substitutes or partial alternatives for collective protection and enhancement of legitimate rights and needs. They allow the kind of crisscrossing, modern, associational networks that are captured by the concept of "civil society." In this broad sense, civil society includes political parties, trade unions, professional associations, and other nongovernmental organizations on the community and national levels. Such associational networks have proved to be the sensitive nerves of participatory political systems, even when some of them are avowedly "apolitical."

Participatory politics may contribute to initial political instability or lead to various forms of demagoguery. Rival ethnic leaders may engage in political competition framed in ethnic terms. In a country with a sizable ethnic group concentrated in one province or geographic area, "separatist tendencies" can also develop, once the political system is opened to free expression and free balloting—as has been vividly, and sometimes tragically, witnessed in the former Soviet Union and the former Yugoslavia. While such a right must be conceded in principle, it can result in chaos and violence. But in the longer term, responsible democratic politics is bound to prevail.

Federalism

To avoid the negative consequences of participation, "federalism" and even "confederalism" are attractive options. The flexible and imaginative application of federalism could create a modern functional equivalent of the "millet system" in earlier Muslim empires. Federalism would reconcile the legitimate impulse of Arab states to preserve their territorial integrity with the legitimate right of ethnic groups to preserve their culture, human dignity, and political autonomy.

The legitimate human and political rights of minorities and ethnic groups can hardly be respected unless the rights of the majority are also respected. In fact, as the Lebanese social scientist Antoine Messarra once observed, no political Arab regime has had a serious problem with an ethnic minority without also having a serious problem with the majority in the same country. The Kurds and the southern Sudanese who have long been in rebellion against their central governments have recently come to this conclusion: their problem cannot be resolved without changing the political system to one that is responsive and accountable to both the majority and to ethnic minorities. This proposition has been summed up by the Kurdish national movement in the phrase, "Democracy for all Iraqis, and autonomy for the Kurds." The Sudanese Liberation Army (mostly southerners) has adopted a similar slogan, "Democracy for all of Sudan and federalism for the south."

Despite some serious, protracted armed ethnic conflicts in the Arab world, there are other instances where such conflicts have been well managed or averted through a combination of participatory politics and decentralization or federalism. Of special note here is the case of Berbers in Morocco and Algeria, who constitute roughly 25 to 30 percent in the total population. A cultural-linguistic minority, the Berbers in both countries are like the Arab majority in religion and denomination—that is, Sunni Muslims. The Berbers have been an integral and important part of Maghreb history since the seventh century. They took part in the Arab-Muslim conquest of the Iberian Peninsula and of Saharan and sub-Saharan Africa. In modern times, they were subjected to French colonial rule, resisted its policy of "divide and rule," and struggled valiantly for their countries' independence in the 1950s (Morocco) and 1960s (Algeria). In the decade after independence, Berbers in both countries emphasized their own cultural aspirations as a distinct group. The Moroccan king accommodated those aspirations, but the Algerian Fronte de Liberation Nationale ruling single party rejected any recognition of their distinctiveness. In the 1990s, the Moroccan Berbers are far better integrated into the national politics of their country than are their Algerian counterparts. The threat of Islamic militancy, with its "over Arabization" tendencies, is quickly turning the Algerian Berbers' cultural quest into an equally militant political protest.[27] At this writing, the Algerian state is under severe pressure from both Islamic and Berber militants.[28] Thus, while Morocco is moving toward steady democratization for Arabs and Berbers alike, Algeria is disintegrating under the militancy of some Arab and Berber groups.

Sudan is another illustrative case. In thirty-eight years of independence (1956–94), the country had only ten years of relative calmness between the black south and the Arab-Muslim north (1972–82). Those ten peaceful years were due to the Addis Ababa Agreements, which provided for southern self-rule. When the Numairy military regime reneged on the agreements in 1983 by restoring Khartoum's direct rule and imposed Islamic shari'a on non-Muslims, the south flared up again in an armed insurrection. The situation has not improved, despite the succession of three different regimes since then (1985, 1986, and 1989).[29]

Thus, while Morocco and Algeria represent two comparatively simultaneous test cases of governance and ethnic management, Sudan represents a diachronic test case of such management. The conclusion is stark: societies that are ethnically pluralistic have to be also politically pluralistic if they are to avert violent conflict.

Notes

1. For a recent overview of worldwide ethnic conflicts, see Larry Diamond and Marc F. Plattner, eds., *Nationalism, Ethnic Conflict, and Democracy* (Baltimore and London: The Johns Hopkins University Press, 1994).

2. For details and documentation, see Saad Eddin Ibrahim, *Sects, Ethnicity, and Minority Groups in the Arab World* (in Arabic) (Cairo: Ibn Khaldoun Center for Developmental Studies, 1994), 15–18, 225–90, 323–69, 601–29.

3. Ibrahim, *Sects, Ethnicity, and Minority Groups in the Arab World*, 725–49.

4. See also Diamond and Plattner's definition in *Nationalism, Ethnic Conflict, and Democracy*, p. XVII; Francis Fukuyama, "The End of History," *The National Interest*

16 (summer 1989): 3–18; and Francis Fukuyama, *The End of History and the Last Man* (New York: Free Press, 1992), 201.

5. For a full account of civil armed conflicts in Iraq, Lebanon, and Sudan, see Ibrahim, *Sects, Ethnicity, and Minority Groups*, 225–90, 323–60, 601–29.

6. Ibrahim, *Sects, Ethnicity, and Minority Groups*, 14–15.

7. A full debate has raged among Arab intellectuals over a proposed conference on the *UN Declaration on Minorities' Rights and Peoples of the Arab World and the Middle East* that was to be held in Cairo, May 12 to 14, 1994. The prominent Egyptian writer and journalist M. H. Haikal led the charge against the conference in an article titled "The Copts Are an Integral Part of the National Mass" (*Al-Ahram*, 20 April 1994). Some 240 Arab intellectuals joined the debate between April and September 1994. Two-thirds of the debaters denied the existence of or belittled the minorities issue in the Arab world. See *Civil Society and Democratic Transformation in the Arab World*, April–October 1994.

8. For an account of sociopolitical developments, see Saad Eddin Ibrahim, *The Future of Society and State in the Arab World* (in Arabic) (Amman: The Arab Thought Forum, 1988); Mickael Hudson, *Arab Politics: The Search for Legitimacy* (New Haven: Yale University Press, 1980); and G. Luciani, ed., *The Arab State* (Berkeley: University of California Press, 1990).

9. George Korn, *Variety of Religions and Regimes: A Comparative Sociological and Legal Study* (in Arabic) (Beirut: El Nahar Publishing Center, 1979), 196–261.

10. Joseph Megezil, "Islam and Arab Christianity, Arab Nationalism and Secularism," in *The Seminar of Arab Nationalism and Islam* (in Arabic), 361–84; Constantine Zuraique, in his comment on research by Waguih Kawthrany, "The Christians from the System of Sects to the Modern State," in *The Debate of Arab Christians*, 75; Gamal El Shail, "What Are the Reasons of Susceptibility and What Are Their Ranges?" in the debate on "Minorities in the Arab East and the Attempts of Israel to Use Them" (in Arabic), Amman, 12–15 September 1981.

11. See the proceedings of the Constituent Conference of al Baath Party as they were narrated in Michael Aflaq, *For the Cause of Baath* (in Arabic) (Beirut: El Talia Publishing Center, 1978), part 1, 121. For more information about the Baath's attitude toward minorities, see Mostafa Dandeshly, "Ideology and Political History," *The Arab Socialist Baath Party* part 1 (Beirut: El Talia Publishing Center, 1979), 92–95. Also, see A. Al-Duri, "The Historical Roots of Arab Nationalism," in *Arab Society*, 2d ed., N. Hopkins, and Saad Eddin Ibrahim, eds. (Cairo: American University in Cairo Press, 1985), 20–35.

12. See El Sayed Yassin and others, *Content Analysis of the National Arab Thought* (in Arabic) (Beirut: Center of Arab Unity Studies, 1980), 52.

13. See Sati Al Hosary, *What Is Nationalism?* (in Arabic) (1958; Beirut: Center of Arab Unity Studies, 1985), 175.

14. Diamond and Plattner, *Nationalism, Ethnic Conflict, and Democracy*, p. xviii.

15. Karim Packradoni, "Toward Ethnically Egalitarian Arab Societies" (paper submitted to the conference on the UN Declaration on Minorities' Rights and Peoples of the Arab World and the Middle East, Limassol, Cyprus, 12–14 May 1994).

16. See *1993 Arab Strategic Report* (Cairo: Al-Ahram Center for Political and Strategic Studies, 1994).

17. The Iraqi elite, led by Saddam Hussein's clan since 1968, come from the Arab Sunni Muslim town of Takrit. The Sunni Muslims of Iraq do not exceed 35 percent of Iraq's total population, compared with Arab Shiite Muslims, who constitute 45 percent, and Kurdish Muslims, who constitute 15 percent. The Syrian elite, led by Hafiz al-Assad's clan since 1970s, comes from a small Alawite Shia sect that constitutes no more than 16 percent of Syria's total population (see Tables 2.4 and 2.5).

18. See analyses of recent events in *Civil Society and Democratic Transformation in the Arab World*, April–August 1994.

19. Lebanon, where a constitutional tradition provides that the head of state be a Christian Maronite, is the only exception among Arab states.

20. See constitutional texts and similar documents of Arab countries in Ahmed Sarhal, *Political and Constitutional Systems in Lebanon and the Arab Countries* (in Arabic) (Beirut: El Baath Publishing Center, 1980).

21. Sarhal, *Political and Constitutional Systems*.

22. Ibrahim, *The Future of Society and State*, 400–50.

23. See also Karl W. Deutsch, "Social Mobilization and Political Development" *American Political Science Review* 55, no. 3 (September 1961), 493; and Karl W. Deutsch, *Nationalism amid Social Communication: An Inquiry into the Foundation of Nationality*, 2d ed. (Cambridge, Mass.: MIT Press, 1966); Saad Eddin Ibrahim, *Bridging the Gap Between Decision-Makers and Intellectuals in the Arab World* (in Arabic) (Amman: Arab Thought Forum, 1984), 16–32; Daniel Lerner, *The Passing of Traditional Society: Modernizing the Middle East* (Glencoe, Ill.: The Free Press, 1958); Iliya Harik, "The Ethnic Revolution and Political Integration in the Middle East," *International Journal of Middle East Studies* 3, no. 3 (July 1972): 303, 323; and Bourhan Ghalyoum, *The Sectarian Issue and the Problem of the Minorities* (in Arabic), 1986, pp. 71–79.

24. Ibrahim, *Sects, Ethnicity, and Minority Groups*, 735–40.

25. Ibrahim, *Sects, Ethnicity, and Minority Groups*, 840–60.

26. Ibid.

27. *Minorities Concerns in the Arab World: 1993 Report* (Cairo: Ibn Khaldoun Center for Developmental Studies, 1994), 282–83.

28. "The Berbers Demand a Voice," *Al-Ahram Weekly*, 20 October 1994, p. 5.

29. Ibid.

30. *Minorities Concerns in the Arab World*.

3

ASSESSING ALTERNATIVE FUTURE ARRANGEMENTS FOR REGIONAL SECURITY

Ghassan Salamé

The two issues of security and legitimacy cannot be dissociated, although the first is usually studied by strategic analysts while the latter falls within the domain of political scientists. Regional security very much depends on domestic stability, and stability cannot be ensured without an adequate level of permanent acceptance of the territorial and political status quo by those concerned.

The connection between the three concepts of security, legitimacy, and stability cautions against abstractions such as "Iraq," "Iran," or "Saudi Arabia." I have argued elsewhere that Western analysts are overly interested in the concept of "national interests" and do not pay adequate attention to what I have called *raison de régime* (let alone *raison de famille*), which too often supersedes the better-known *raison d'état* in the rulers' mind and policies.[1] By "raison de régime" I mean political and military calculations which aim at ensuring the political survival of the rulers rather than at the general welfare and future destiny of a given society. A careful study of many "irrational" decisions made by Mideastern rulers would demonstrate that some—if not all—of these decisions are much more rational and much less arbitrary when the survival of the ruler and the regime is the crucial objective. All other objectives are of lesser importance, including some that are elsewhere considered to be "vital national interests." To analyze security from this broader perspective, we need a revised vision of governance, a more critical assessment of political discourse, and a search for sui generis rationality.

The phrase "national interest," used both as an adjective and as a noun, is problematic. The definition of interests presupposes the gradual elucidation of commonly accepted long-term objectives by a community. The permanence of certain policies over a long period of time leads to the assumption that a nation can define long-term national interests, notwithstanding changes in its political regime or fluctuations in its ruling group. Interests are thus defined as beyond politics, as a common heritage of a nation across decades and centuries. These interests are supposed to be "national" in the sense that they are not specific to a certain group within the society.

Although some countries seem to have a concept of national interest, many do not. In newly formed countries, decisions often do not express some national interest. Though they may have a positive effect on the nation as a whole, they are made by a limited number of individuals representing the ruling clan, be it a royal family, a sectarian group, or a single-party clique. When conditions for survival of this ruling group come into conflict with the so-called national interest, it is not uncommon that the former prevail over the latter, in the absence of democratically established processes for accountability—hence the somehow unrealistic flavor in analyses of the Saudi or Iraqi "national interest." I argue that many decisions can be explained less as functions of some presupposed national interest and more as functions of ruling-group survival, which I call raison de régime. This does not mean that the raison d'état is not gradually taking root; it only indicates that this process is far from being complete and that, in certain circumstance, it still looks reversible.

Security in the Persian Gulf: Basic Constraints

Shaping Order in the Gulf: A History of External Intervention

This vulnerability of state entities in all the territories that were once part of the Ottoman or Iranian empires is specifically aggravated in the Persian Gulf by the memory of permanent external intervention in the area's politics. To put it briefly, the sixteenth century was mainly Portuguese (on the borderland) and Ottoman (in the hinterland); the seventeenth, Dutch; and later centuries were mainly British, so that "by the end of World War I, the Gulf had become, to all intents and purposes, a British lake."[2] This long history of external intervention in the Gulf not only protected the interests of the intervening power, it also helped in the consolidation of a number of frail entities—such as Kuwait (in 1899 against Ottoman reassertion of authority, in 1920 against Saudi and Wahhabi invaders, in 1982 against Iraqi claims, and again in 1990 against Iraqi annexation) and Bahrain (in 1871, 1895, and 1905)—and in the reunification of formerly autonomous Ottoman provinces into a single state entity in Iraq in 1921. Sometimes outside powers abetted the disappearance of others, even though they were potentially viable protostates, such as the Qasimi power in the lower gulf and the Khaz'al emirate in present-day southern Iran.

At many crucial junctures, external intervention imposed a regional order that could have been very different were it not for the deployment, and often the use, of force by some distant, non-Persian Gulf power. Threats were sometimes sufficient, as when the Saudi troops invaded Kuwait in 1920: "British planes stationed in the neighborhood of Basra dropped notices on the Wahhabi encampments, warning them against pursuing their aggression against the forces of Kuwait. British warships anchored in Kuwait Bay in plain sight of the Ikhwan and some of their marines landed in Kuwait City. A few cannon balls were enough to warn them that the British wanted them to withdraw. Thus ended the battle of al-Jahra with the Ikhwan's retreat."[3] Sometimes, a massive use of force was necessary for a foreign power to impose the order it deemed favorable to its interests, as when the British navy systematically destroyed Qasimi naval power: "The death knell of the Qawasim was sounded in 1809 when the British launched an expeditionary force against their principal headquarters in Ras al-Khaimah";[4] in 1913 British troops were used to save the ruler of Muscat from the Saudis; in the 1920s, the Royal Air Force stopped by force the Ikhwan incursions into mandatory Iraq; in 1941 British troops were again used to dislodge a pro-Axis government in Iraq; in 1991 the U.S.-led coalition pushed Iraqi troops out of Kuwait. Less visible forms of external intervention were no less effective in shaping important events in the region. The U.S. Central Intelligence Agency, for example, helped topple the Mossadegh government in Iran and bring the shah back to his throne in 1953.

This uninterrupted chain of external intervention is very vivid in the people's (and rulers') memories. It accounts for the cynical reactions among them to the idea of collective security as a possible future security arrangement. It also accounts for some forms of unconditional reliance on the West, or resignation to its superior military power. Citizens in the Persian Gulf compare the effective support of the West for Kuwait with the West's lack of help to the Bosnians, and they conclude that the West defends its interests when it needs to, and allows aggression to go unpunished when these interests are not challenged. The end of the Cold War and the collapse of the USSR have strengthened this widely held view that the United States and the West in general have the capabilities to shape the regional order as they wish. The war for Kuwait had an even larger impact: for these countries' leaders as much as for the man in the street, only Western power could have dislodged Iraq from Kuwait, when local forces were entirely impotent and regional allies were unreliable or insufficiently equipped. It also accounts for the lack of enthusiasm felt in the Gulf for the arrangements proposed in the Damascus Declaration in 1991.

This long heritage of external intervention also has an effect on the definition of security: Security for whom? Security for what? Newcomers to Persian Gulf politics start with the Saddam Hussein phenomenon, and when they dig a bit further, with the Khomeini saga. Regionally, these are only the latest two episodes in a long history in which Western naval powers have tended to protect coastal allies against the hinterland—the Ottomans, the Iranians, the Yemenis (in Aden and its "dependencies"), the Saudis—irrespective of the pro- or anti-Western orientation of the expansionist power. "Britain, primarily interested in the sea route to India, recognized the authority only of those rulers who had jurisdiction over the coastal areas."[5] This protection was extended to the local ruler, and it was his own survival (as much as the interests of the protecting power) that was defended.

External protection was therefore used to quash both local opposition to the ruler and expansionist drives by neighboring regional powers. What was "national" from the perspective of the protector was "clannish" from the perspective of the protected[6]—hence, the complex definition of security. Locally, security is often viewed as being extended to a ruling group rather than to a "nation" (although U.S. support for elections in Kuwait after its liberation in 1991 partly helped dispel this impression). In other words, Western powers, to protect their national (mainly oil) interests in the Persian Gulf, need to convince the ruling regimes that their survival depends on their identification with certain Western policies. But to ensure this is done efficiently, ruling regimes have to convince their own populations that what serves the interests of the rulers serves the interest of all—that it is somehow "national." Failure to make this connection would confirm the centuries-old impression that Western powers promote only their own (and their clients') interests and, more importantly, would push domestic opposition to seek support from regional and anti-Western hegemons.

Iran and Iraq: The Roots of Expansionist Regional Politics

Territorial and political expansionism was not limited, as it is today, to Iran and Iraq. For many centuries, the small emirates were threatened by other powers. Mission-oriented regimes tend to be expansionist in order to legitimize both their authoritarian nature at home and their expansionist policies in regional affairs. For a long time, Saudi Arabia was the typical mission-oriented system: the spread of unitarian Islam (Wahhabism) was the cloak for authoritarianism at home as well as for territorial conquest in and beyond the Arabian Peninsula. Hashemites in both Jordan and Iraq also presented their dynasty as the depository and vehicle of pan-Arab renaissance (Nahda). Healing their European tragedies and recreating their scale have been the two pretexts for Israel's territorial expansionism. Nasserist Egypt became the epitome of a mission-oriented, regionally interventionist regime, calling for Arab unity and national liberation to legitimize its interference in other Arab countries' affairs and sending tens of thousands of troops to Yemen. Of late, Baathist Syria, Gadhafi's Libya, and the FLN in Algeria have all tried, though with little success, to engage in similar expansionism.

Persian Gulf security has generally been negatively affected by the emergence of such mission-oriented regimes. The Wahhabi mission largely explains the present territorial configuration of the Arabian Peninsula. Saudi expansionism, by far the most active for some two centuries, was contained in the twentieth century first by heavy repression (with the Royal Air Force support) of the most extremist elements in Wahhabism from 1928 to 1931 (most notably at the famous Sibila battle in 1929) and then by a complete reversion of Saudi strategy leading to a growing Saudi identification with the territorial status quo as a protective shield for its huge oil riches. More recently, the Gulf has been affected by the emergence both in Iraq and in Iran of mission-oriented regimes: Arab nationalism with Baathist flavor in the former and Islamist with a Shiite undertone in the latter. Baghdad and Tehran have used a wide variety of means (radio propaganda, acts of sabotage, threats, financing of local opposition groups, territorial claims) in order to influence their neighbors' politics and promote their interests.

Mission-oriented regimes generally are not democratically based. It is difficult to imagine that Iran and Iraq would revert to "normal" regional policies without having first progressed to some advanced form of democratization (though admittedly a change toward territorial conservatism took place a half century ago in Saudi Arabia without any kind of democratic opening). Democracies tend not to wage wars against each other, either here or elsewhere, and are, in general, more interested in promoting their populations' welfare. There is a relationship between the adoption of ambitious external missions and the lack of democratic institutions at home. These missions might vary with changes in ideological fashions: Arab nationalism, socialism, Third World antiimperialism, Islamism, and so on. The content of the mission changes, not its function in regional politics; it is a way to express dissatisfaction with the regional order and revisionism, possibly through the use of force.[7] The present weakness of the ideological factor in the shaping of foreign policy in most parts of the world is undisputable; it has, however, only partly affected the Middle East.

At present, it is very difficult to imagine a serious shift toward representative democracy in either one of the two leading countries in the Persian Gulf, though the situation in Iran remains somehow less depressing than that in Iraq. The development of democratic forces is not very encouraging (despite some level of democratic spirit displayed by Iraqi Kurds in the organization of their de facto Western-enforced self-government). In Iraq, democratic forces are unlikely to prevail if and when the present Iraqi regime is toppled. The social fabric is extremely complex, with ethnicity (in the north) running parallel to sectarianism (elsewhere). The sectarianism of the Shiites is not of the same political nature, nor does it constitute the same kind of threat to "national" unity. The Kurds are separatist, whereas the Shiites seek a change in the regime, but not in the territorial configuration of the country. The interference of regional actors (especially Iran and Turkey) and the permanent fear of partition, created seventy years ago from the unification of three distinct Ottoman wilayas, limit the likelihood of a successful process of democratization. In Iran, elections regularly take place, but the human rights record is dismaying, and the political system is not open to all competing forces.

In Iran, the defeat in the war with Iraq, Khomeini's death, and a rather firm U.S. position have brought the Rafsanjani government to a more "realistic" assessment of the limits of Iranian expansionism. The heavy sanctions imposed upon Iraq are gradually compelling the Iraqi leadership to accept—in inspection of arms industries, respect for Kurdish autonomy, and oil production under U.N. supervision—what Baghdad not long ago considered utterly unacceptable. But this pragmatism is very much intertwined with a feeling of defeat: spectacular in the Iraqi case, quite real in the Iranian one. Consequently, revanchism provides fertile political ground for present leaders or their successors. Without a grand *compromesso storico* with its neighbors or permanent deterrence, it is difficult to see any Iraqi leader accepting such a narrow window on the sea or an Iranian leader renouncing Iranian attempts at hegemony in the Persian Gulf. The "pragmatism" that currently exists therefore is likely to be transitory rather than permanent. Any attempt, in Iraq as well as in Iran, to be more assertive in Gulf politics would be favorably received by domestic public opinion. Iraqis generally reproach their leader for failing in his attempt against Kuwait rather than for having tried. In Iran, in many ways, interventionism by the Islamic republic has been a continuation of a policy that started under the shah in the early 1960s, and in any case, Pasdarans are still present in the Gulf islands and waters, and Iran is putting even more pressure on the United Arab Emirates (UAE).

This analysis suggests that a voluntary shift by these leaders from their well-known mission-oriented regional policies and discourse and from their domestic authoritarian practices is unlikely. The critical obstacle is the externally imposed inability to pursue these policies. This has been the pattern for most of the modern history of the Persian Gulf, and there is no reason to expect that a radical alteration of this pattern is likely in the years to come—hence the importance, in any assessment of future security arrangements, of two critical policies. The first is the need within the Gulf Cooperation Council (GCC) countries for policies specifically aimed at strengthening their own domestic legitimacy in the face of permanent challenges originating in Iraq and Iran (and Yemen). The second is the need for containment of these self-appointed missionaries by regional hegemons through permanent pressure from non-Gulf regional and international actors.

The Peculiar Economic Outlook of Iran, Iraq, and Yemen

The Middle East is one of the most asymmetrical regions in terms of regional distribution of per capita wealth. The ratio between Saudi Arabia and Egypt or Kuwait and Yemen is even more unbalanced than the one between the United States and Mexico or between Spain and Morocco. This maldistribution of wealth is aggravated by two cultural factors that were strongly visible during the war for Kuwait. On the one hand, wealth is based on oil—on rent from a natural resource that happens to be located in some countries rather than in others—and not, as is the case elsewhere, on higher productivity, better organization, or more advanced technology. Wealth consequently has a lower political-moral value. It is viewed as an accident of geology rather than an achievement of more advanced, "deserving" societies. On the other hand, the very recent establishment of borders and a common language and religion make many feel that they are somehow entitled to share their neighbors' oil revenues even when they do not legally belong to them. This widespread feeling largely explains the huge disbursements of funds by the oil countries to their impoverished neighbors, less as a form of solidarity than as a device to buy their acquiescence to an evident maldistribution of resources coupled with the less-than-established relevance of freshly demarcated "national" borders.

The war for Kuwait highlighted this explosive mixture of contempt for oil sheikhs and envy at their "undeserved" wealth. Those sentiments echoed across the Middle East, from Pakistan to Morocco, in societies vying for diminishing oil-generated income—even in a milieu like Egypt, where the opposition to Iraqi actions was almost unanimous. The Iraqi defeat momentarily silenced the regionwide call for wealth sharing, but the postwar arrangements do not address the underlying frustration. To the contrary, the huge financial losses by both Iraq and the GCC countries and the unavailability of any funds for regional development, as had been promised by the United States in a moment of enthusiasm during the crisis, have exacerbated this frustration—most notably among those directly disadvantaged by the war's effects, such as the 400,000 Palestinians expelled from Kuwait or the million or so Yemenis expelled from Saudi Arabia.

While Iraq and Iran share with Egypt, Sudan, and Pakistan a large population per square kilometer and technological backwardness, they are also relatively large oil and gas producers. Consequently, they have sufficient resources to extract themselves from a state of dependency on their neighbors' disbursements, but not enough to be able to achieve their publicly stated regional missions. Their oil revenues are enough to build a respectable military machine, but expansion depends on external funds (as shown by Iraq at the end of the Iran-Iraq War). Their oil (and gas) revenues are substantial (potentially enviable for Iraq, with the second OPEC rank in proved oil reserves), but only if military spending is limited can the regimes meet broader social and economic demands. Iraq had enough funds to start a regional war against Iran but inadequate resources to meet the needs of tens of thousands of soldiers thrown back into the civilian economy. High unemployment in 1988 and 1989 accounted in part for Iraqi aggression against Kuwait. Yemen is beginning to earn respectable revenues from its oil at a time when unification has substantially added to its military capability while the border dispute and the mute political tension with Saudi Arabia is latent. The increasingly volatile political situation in Yemen, which exploded into war in the spring of 1994, increases instability and uncertainty.

Reduced military spending in these three countries is critical to the security of the Persian Gulf. Reductions could be achieved in three different ways: by the recognition of upper limits of sustainability by present regimes, as seems to be the case in Iran since mid-1992, when the new contracts for arms were reduced due to evident financial limitations; by sanctions imposed from outside (Iraq); or by the emergence of clearly inward-looking, general welfare-oriented regimes. Unless military spending is reduced, the combination of nondemocratically based, mission-oriented regimes with the availability of substantial oil resources and many unsettled territorial disputes remains a disquieting factor for the GCC regimes. Complicating the attempt to reduce military expenditures, both Iraq and Iran have invested heavily in education and research and have a deep familiarity with a growing level of military technology; they can count, for a long time to come, on thousands of first-class engineers and technicians.

The Special Position of the Small Gulf Countries

The survival of the five small GCC members (Bahrain, Kuwait, Oman, Qatar, and the UAE) has generally depended on external help against the regional hegemonic powers, Iran, Iraq, and Saudi Arabia. It has been convincingly demonstrated, however, that external protection of the smaller entities and the availability of resources in the hands of ruling families have led to local authoritarianism. In general, the issue of survival is so dominant in the minds of the ruling families that they define their security needs first in terms of what they consider the most serious threat: the domestic threat against the state.

The five smaller entities are parties to an additional predicament that is uniquely theirs. On the one hand, their survival as a group obviously depends on a higher level of intra-GCC integration of their forces; on the other, a high level of GCC integration is viewed as a threat to their existence as individual entities. The war for Kuwait has not resolved this dilemma. Quite to the contrary: it has been followed by a serious incident on the Saudi-Qatari border, renewed tension between Qatar and Bahrain, and some tension between Oman and Saudi Arabia as well as between Kuwait and Saudi Arabia. In general, no steps have been made toward standardization of their armaments—not within the GCC as a whole nor even within the UAE armed forces, though the latter has spent billions of dollars on its defense in the past three years. On the other hand, Oman has demarcated its borders with both the UAE and Yemen, a step in the right direction.

This dilemma is a serious constraint on any future arrangement. The smaller entities naturally give preference to their own survival over any other consideration. They consequently tend to favor a high level of fluidity in the Persian Gulf regional subsystem, where they can use their traditional deftness in playing one regional power against the other. Interpreted in this context, Oman's support of the Camp David Accords in the face of opposition from the others; the call by the UAE for reconciliation among Arabs (including Iraq) in order to confront the Iranian challenge; and Qatar's flirtation with Iraq and its allying itself with Iran after the Khafus incident, supporting the northerners in the recent inter-Yemeni war, and pioneering the establishment of normal relations with Israel are intelligible. A fluid subsystem is not what the Saudis would prefer, nor is it the best framework for a "dual containment" U.S. policy. Any future security arrangement that does not address this deeply rooted fear of the small five would be strongly opposed by them. Militating against their individual fears for their survival is the reality of Iraqi and Iranian expansionism.

The Oil Factor

Though rarely mentioned in official utterances during the war for Kuwait, oil is a crucial factor in any assessment of the region's future security. It is obvious that a region where half of the world's proved oil reserves are located must be organically different in its security problems from any other region in the South. Beyond this obvious truism, how does oil shape regional security problems?

- As discussed above, oil is unevenly distributed, leading to the maldistribution of wealth along lines that do not parallel to the distribution of strength.

- Oil is at the origin of many border disputes, complicating the sometimes already sensitive relations between such neighbors as Qatar and Bahrain, the UAE and Oman, the UAE and Saudi Arabia, Saudi Arabia and Yemen, Kuwait and Iraq, and even Iraq and Iran.

- Oil revenues can either moderate or aggravate conflict. In the Iraqi Kurdish situation, control of Kirkuk is an important source of contention, but in Saudi Arabia, the fact that all provinces take advantage of the Eastern Province's riches helps to integrate Saudi society and cement the country's unity. Oil therefore has contradictory implications for stability: it allows some regimes to "buy" peace by their large disbursements both domestically and regionally, but it also triggers an appetite for more disbursements and hence leads to all kinds of pressures on the wealthiest countries.

- Oil triggers two forms of international involvement. Control of the Persian Gulf area has been instrumental in consolidating the territorial status quo in the face of regional hegemonic powers. Oil in the Gulf area has also triggered forms of international competition among industrialized countries for Gulf markets. In international politics in the Gulf, oil therefore inspires cooperation and competition among the Western importing countries. There are also reasons to believe that attempts by the United States to establish a long-term, preeminent, strategic posture in the Gulf are also related to its attempts to use its influence in the Gulf as a counterweight in dealing with currently or soon-to-be oil-importing countries, such as Japan, India, and China. Oil therefore has ambivalent consequences for domestic, regional, and international stability.

Oil is an ambiguous factor in the security equation: it triggers higher levels of regional expansionism and international interventionism, but oil revenues can also play a moderating role in many regional conflicts and encourage "national" integration at home. The strategic significance of oil in the Persian Gulf will change radically if and when it ceases to be a strategic resource in the world economy. Since oil discoveries are *grosso modo* contemporary and intimately linked to the emergence of the modern state, the end of the oil era will necessarily affect the territorial status quo. But this development is beyond the foreseeable future.[8]

Types of Future Security Arrangements

Arrangements Based on Collective Security

Tripolar Regional Collective Security (Iran-Iraq-Gulf Cooperation Council). One precondition for an Iran-Iraq-GCC tripolar collective-securitysystem model of course would be an integration of GCC capabilities. Moving beyond their military projects, the GCC countries have declared an interest in full economic integration before 1999. This is probably unrealistic. Some countries with little oil, such as Oman and Bahrain, would not easily remove their tariffs, and there is little to be traded among these six countries. Militarily, the smaller entities' obsession with their independence is another obstacle. On paper, a mixture of GCC integrated forces and a higher level of military technology could partially compensate for much greater Iranian and Iraqi manpower so that some balance among these three poles is established and a collective security system of peers becomes possible. Military analysts are, however, quite pessimistic about the ability of GCC countries to increase their integration and, at the same time, to acquire the capacity to operate modern weaponry. Manpower will remain scarce as long as these countries continue to fear national armies as sources of coups that have ended monarchical rule in most of the Middle East.

A tripolar collective-security regime also depends on the rehabilitation of Iraq within the Persian Gulf. This is unlikely to happen. Iraq is generally viewed as a revanchist power, and its revanchism is seen as Iraqi, rather than Baathist or Saddamist. Kuwaiti behavior since the cease-fire has encouraged revanchism: the issue of the border demarcation and the biased attitude of UVSCOM toward Kuwait led many Iraqi opposition groups to express their condemnation of Kuwait.

The integration of Iran into such a system is also difficult. Relations between Iran and the smaller GCC countries have clearly improved in the past few years, but Iran's relations with Bahrain—where a Shiite majority of the population is a worry to the ruling Khalifas—are shaky, and they are tense with the UAE because of the question of the islands. The Saudi leadership does not appear to trust Iran's offer of a rapprochement because of historical and sectarian differences and persistent pressure during the hajj season.

A collective security system is not necessarily organized among allies, among similar powers, or among equals and peers. It does require that each actor have an interest in the stability of the others, notwithstanding differences in political orientation or domestic organization. Even with such an enlarged definition, collective security remains a very distant possibility in the Persian Gulf. It presupposes a leap in imagination and courage and a radical alteration in the dominant political culture. Both are not likely in the near future.

Riparians' Collective Security: The Club of Eight

A riparian collective security system in the region also would require the reintegration of both Iraq and Iran and the independence of each of the six GCC members in defining their regional security needs. Iran has been the strongest proponent of a riparian arrangement, which, insofar as it excludes nonriparian states from the arrangement, would make it easier for the Iranian superiority to prevail, would reduce the likelihood of an anti-Iranian, Saudi-led GCC common front, and would diminish the Arab-Persian cleavage that hinders Iranian attempts at hegemony. It would be a local version of the Conference on Security and Cooperation in Europe (CSCE), where big and small, notwithstanding their differences and inequalities, agree on the common defense of the territorial status quo and on a peaceful resolution of their disputes. For all these reasons, such an arrangement would be unacceptable to the Saudis, though some smaller emirates might find it attractive, since it would establish at least a formal parity between large and small countries and give the smaller entities a wider margin of maneuver to play one hegemon against the other.

What kind of common interests do these eight have in common, beside questions of oil pricing or the defense of the environment? Like the tripolar scenario, a riparian arrangement seems unrealistic: the imbalance in power, the maldistribution of wealth, and the expansionist tendencies in Iran and Iraq make it quite unlikely. Would the United States find it attractive? Probably not, since it would reduce the U.S. role and put the GCC under much heavier pressures from its neighbors. Many in the Persian Gulf are deeply skeptical of U.S. intentions. It is widely believed that if Saddam is still in power and if the Iranians buy all the weapons they have ordered in the past few years, it is because the United States has tacitly consented, thanks to some U.S. complacency aimed to keep the GCC governments fearful of both Iran and Iraq and therefore subservient to its wishes.

Regional Balance of Power

Arab-Iranian Balance. An Arab-Iranian balance of power is the model that Iraq tried to impose between 1980 and 1990. It posits the existence of two nationalisms facing each other across the Persian Gulf: the Iranian, which is embodied in one specific state, the post-1924 Iran, and another much more elusive in the Arab world. This division is considered the principal divide in the Gulf.

It would be easy, in light of the war for Kuwait and its effects, to discount this cleavage. Many had written the obituary of Arab nationalism long before this crisis erupted. Arab nationalism has been the victim of many challenges: its crude manipulation by some (Iraq, Libya, Syria), its replacement by Islamism as the main ideological current in opposition circles, and its discounting in practical politics and in the Arab-Israeli conflict, where Arab countries are coming to the peace table individually, not as a group.

Despite this triple retreat of Arab nationalism, when discussing the future, one should not entirely discount the Arab-Iranian cleavage, at least because in Persian Gulf politics it more or less overlaps with another important cleavage: the Sunni-Shiite divide. This overlap in cleavages suggests that when Iran becomes more assertive, identification with Arabism intensifies. Arab nationalism remains a latent but potent political force that can be mobilized, as it was during the Iran-Iraq War.

Iran-Iraq Balance without the Gulf Cooperation Council. Another concept of security would exclude the GCC from the relationship between Iran and Iraq and preclude the stationing of foreign forces on the territory of GCC countries. Such a security arrangement would be consistent with a hostile relationship between the two large Persian Gulf countries. During the Iran-Iraq War, a variant of this security system seemed possible for a few years. Though generally favorable to Iraq, the GCC countries were not considered as belligerents by Iran. This changed when GCC tankers became targets and when Iran tried to use the Mecca pilgrimage for political purposes.

This kind of security arrangement would be unlikely if the relationship between Iraq and Iran improves, largely as a response to mutual ostracism by the West. A strategy of dual containment on the part of the United States, or an increase in Kurdish self-assertion would accelerate limited rapprochement. A long-term improvement in relations is problematic, since both nations are rivals over time for Western support—the one to annul internationally imposed sanctions and the other to normalize its relations with the West. A long series of unsettled bilateral problems, such as the Iranian interest in having some influence over Iraqi Shiites and Iraqi support for the People's Mujahideen, further complicate the prospects for improvement. These factors explain the relatively limited improvement of the past two years, despite continuous calls for the normalization of relations between the two countries.

Unless a radical change occurs in Iraqi politics, the relationship between Iraq and Iran is likely to be characterized by mutual suspicion and will reduce the likelihood of a security condominium by the two large Persian Gulf powers. GCC countries cannot, however, position themselves equidistant between Tehran and Baghdad. Despite the recent war in Kuwait, Iran has been historically much more threatening: Iran has many channels to the Gulf, which enmeshes it with all the GCC countries, whereas Iraqi pressure is felt directly only in Kuwait and, to a lesser extent, in northern Saudi Arabia. Finally, GCC regimes have linguistic and sectarian affinities with the Arab and Sunni regime in Baghdad that do not exist with Iran. The present level of fear from revanchist Iraq is therefore somehow exceptional. If and when these fears are reduced, Iran's attempts to build a dominant position in the Gulf will once more become the central security preoccupation of most GCC governments.

The Damascus Declaration Model. For some time immediately after the Gulf War in 1991, the idea of introducing troops from Arab and Islamic countries was current. This concept identified two different sources of threat: while the most intense would be dealt with by Western forces stationed "over the horizon," Arab troops (Syrian, Egyptian, and Moroccan) would deal with less intense challenges, by adding their strength to GCC military capabilities. Many precedents existed for such an arrangement. Jordanian troops were stationed temporarily on the Saudi-Yemeni border, Pakistanis were stationed for many years in Saudi Arabia, and Moroccan troops were stationed in the UAE. The central idea was to create a collective rather than a bilateral arrangement and to offer some financial compensation for the contributing countries in return.

While Iraq was the principal object of containment, the strongest opposition to this scheme came from Iran. Iran would not accept the idea of bringing in troops either from hostile Egypt or from friendly Syria: the model of the Damascus Declaration implied that while Iran would be excluded from the arrangement, nonriparian Arab states would be natural participants. A fundamental Iranian strategic principle is that Persian Gulf politics should be dissociated from Arab politics. The shah opposed Nasserist inroads in the Gulf for this reason, as Tehran today opposes the model of the Damascus Declaration.

Iranian opposition was far less effective than the reservations of GCC members in aborting the Damascus Declaration. The Saudi foreign minister allegedly was chastised by his king for having accepted the arrangement, and the Kuwaiti press strongly opposed the plan. It soon appeared that most GCC countries were indeed opposed to an agreement that had been accepted by their foreign ministers in the heat of the crisis. Actions by Kuwaitis to show their impatience with Egyptian troops in their country immediately after the war irritated Cairo. GCC leaders have tried to bury the Damascus agreement without antagonizing Cairo or Damascus. Egypt has never really accepted the Persian Gulf states' rejection of the declaration, while Syria was more realistically content to accept several billion dollars from Gulf countries without pressing for implementation of the formula.

Most were never convinced of the feasibility of the formula. Obvious technical reasons militate against it: neither Syria nor Egypt is in a position to resist successfully an Iranian or Iraqi large-scale challenge to the GCC countries, of the order of magnitude of Iraq's challenge to Kuwait. More important, Egypt and Syria have been perceived as threats to Persian Gulf security at different times. The Yemen war was, after all, an attempt by Nasserist Egypt to coerce Saudi Arabia through its Yemeni surrogate. All Arab countries of the Middle East have, at one time or another, tried to extract concessions from Saudi Arabia or other GCC countries. Iraq's invasion of Kuwait was an intense expression of a general tendency on the part of non-GCC Arab countries to extract resources from GCC countries. Less intense forms of intimidation have been used by almost all Arab countries in the past. Consequently, non-Gulf Arab countries are not seen as reliable allies, thus militating against a long-term deployment of their troops in the GCC.

A final reason for the failure of the Damascus Declaration formula is the reluctance of the GCC governments to become embroiled in the Arab-Israeli conflict. The GCC countries would like to distance themselves as much as possible from this dispute; Iraq would like to be involved but knows that it cannot play an important role; and Iran would like to be very much engaged, through Hezbollah, Islamic militancy, and an alliance with Syria. It is possible that Iran may eventually accept the U.S. view that it should not engage in the Arab-Israeli issue in exchange for recognition of its stakes and status in the Persian Gulf. This is precisely the outcome that the GCC governments fear most—hence Saudi objection to Hezbollah in Lebanon. By being present as a *partie intéressée* on the Palestinian issue, Iran can visibly challenge the passivity of the Gulf monarchies and, at the same time, develop a bargaining chip that can be exchanged for a more visible role in the Gulf.

Once a peace agreement with the Arabs is signed, Israel might also serve as an effective outside factor in the Persian Gulf balance of power. Israel has much more to offer to the GCC governments in military and intelligence capabilities than does Syria or Egypt. Israel's access to the United States is also helpful in facilitating U.S. military sales to the GCC. Israel could also receive considerable benefit from close connections with Gulf governments. This inverted Damascus Declaration seems improbable. The GCC countries (contrary to the Maghrebi, for example) have no interest in antagonizing their own population and the rest of the Arab world by drawing closer to Israel or to speeding up the normalization of their relations. If sustaining the presence of Western troops is problematic, to appear as Israel's partner would be even more so. In any case, such a development could not be expected without a comprehensive peace in which not only the Palestine Liberation Organization (PLO) but also Syria is satisfied.

The Dominant Model: Externally Imposed Security

Dual Containment. Containment has been effective in advancing the peace process between Israel and the Palestinians. One could easily consider that without the sanctions imposed upon them, both Iraq and Libya could have played a much more active role in opposing the agreement between Israel and the PLO, Iran would have been more successful in doing so, and Syria would have been an even more reluctant participant in the peace process.

A major difficulty with the strategy of dual containment is the very superficial equivalence drawn between two very different countries. An ostracized country that can still produce and sell its oil on the international market (such as Libya or Iran) is in a much more comfortable position than one that is prevented from doing so, and though both Iraq and Iran seem to be prepared to improve their relations with the United States, should such an opportunity become available, Iraq would ask for much less than Iran, because it is indeed starting from a much more difficult position.

Another problem with containment is that it may be able to deter clear violations of international law, but it is much less efficient in deterring sabotage, hostile actions, and terrorism where local elements engage in violent action. If a large-scale Iraqi or Iranian military attack is not likely in the near future, smaller-scale and lower-intensity actions are more likely and, indeed, are happening, sometimes with the complicity of GCC citizens.

Effective containment also presupposes the agreement of many other powers not to sell advanced weapons and not to transfer advanced technology. Such an agreement is only feasible in an international system where basic arrangements are already in place. Recent developments in Turkey and Russia indicate that both nations, though for different reasons, cannot and will not sustain a boycott of either Iraq or Iran for a long period. If the Kurdish issue were to flare up again in Turkey and if the Turkish leadership then concludes that only an alliance with Iraq could suppress the Kurds, such an alliance is very likely. Also, Russian and Iranian positions are often similar in Azerbaijan and central Asia.

Containment is effective only as long as the contained country does not feel sufficiently desperate to challenge the sanctions as a better option than the continuation of an unacceptable status quo. Containment also has a temporal dimension. It becomes counterproductive when it ensures the regime's survival in the short term and engenders deep-rooted animosity vis-à-vis the West in the longer term. The sanctions are viewed by the Iraqi people not as a legitimate punishment of their leader but rather as an undeserved punishment of their country.

The other evident risk of dual containment is the promotion of a rapprochement or even an alliance between Iran and Iraq. A rapprochement would be a destabilizing factor in the area; even if the likelihood of the two making a joint attack on any Persian Gulf target is very low, one would be freer to attack if the other were neutralized, and both, together or separately, would be freer to harass Gulf countries.

A mixture of sanctions, warnings, and threats against the two countries is currently U.S. policy. The use of force against Iran (1988) and, more spectacularly, against Iraq (1991) is evidence that deterrence as practiced in the 1980s has been replaced by a willingness to use massive force, which translates into deterrence over a longer period. If any government tries to alter the territorial status quo through force, it will be immediately punished on a very large scale. Nowhere else in the world but in the Persian Gulf has such determination been shown by the West, which leads both Iraq's and Iran's leaders to understand that what Milosevic or Aideed are permitted to do is not applicable to them. The very special position of the Gulf has been very much reaffirmed by the complacency with which other aggressors have been treated.

Active Interventionism. Active intervention raises large questions concerning the kind of ad hoc coalition that is necessary and sufficient, the roles of the U.N. and NATO, the role of regional allies, and the kinds of forces that are needed. In the absence of a general framework, Kuwait has signed a number of individual treaties with the United States, Britain, and France. Russia is in the peculiar situation of having treaties of friendship with both Iraq and Kuwait. The capacity to construct an international coalition depends less on the regional situation than on the evolution of the international system in the next few years. One has, for example, to consider that trade disputes may make a Western alliance less likely in the future. On the other hand, if and when sanctions against Iraq and Iran are lifted, it will naturally give as many Western (notably oil) companies as possible a vested interest in constraining actions by their governments against them. On the other hand, it is likely that Western countries will be more willing to engage in military action in the Persian Gulf when the oil market is soft.

Local regimes with enough freedom to call for and politically "cover" intervention are also indispensable. In 1990, had Iraq remained in Kuwait, Saudi Arabia could have become so "satellized" that the royal family would have been unable to call for Western protection. The cost associated with active interventionism is the thinning out of the authority of local regimes as their reliance on foreign protection becomes more visible day by day. The risk of the "puppetization" of the ruling families in GCC countries is real.

Radical Change in the Political Status Quo

A radical change in the domestic political status quo, such as the collapse of the Iraqi regime or the Saudi monarchy, is possible. Already, the scope of political discourse is being widened. In Saudi Arabia, the famous Nasiha memorandum presented by some hundred clerics to the king in 1992 devoted a full chapter to the discussion of military questions and another memorandum was dedicated to the analysis of foreign affairs. The new chairman of the Majlis, ash-Shoura, specifically stated that military and diplomatic affairs are within the prerogatives of the Majlis. In Kuwait, where new regulations for arms contracts have been put into effect, arms procurement policies are now scrutinized by Parliament and defense policies are openly challenged by parliamentarians. There is growing, though modest, accountability of GCC governments to civil society. Though institutional adjustments are still modest, the trend is clear: politics are being "nationalized," in the sense that the public is much more conscious of what is happening and is demanding greater levels of participation in decision making. National consciousness would normally make these societies more immune to external attempts to destabilize ruling families. Western governments, however, will not be able to continue to deal with these countries in patron-client terms. Royal and princely families are probably going to be much more constrained by their domestic public opinion than they have been in the past.

Radical Change in the Territorial Status Quo

Despite many calls for unity or for secession, the territorial status quo in the Persian Gulf was established after World War II. It would, however, be unwise to accept the permanence of the state. All around the Gulf, the territorial status quo is more vulnerable than is commonly thought. Even though the Iraqi attempt to annex Kuwait failed, annexation of a sovereign state was attempted and failed only because of the deployment of a huge international coalition. Such a coalition is not easily assembled. Iran's control over Abu Musa and the Tunbs islands was achieved by a successful fait accompli. On the fringe of the Arabian Peninsula, the collapse of South Yemen's Soviet patron led to its implosion and to the reunification of Yemen. Iraqi Kurdistan is independent in all but name. A Palestinian entity is in the making, and the future of Jordan is in question.

A change in the territorial status quo is neither an irredentist dream nor a secessionist utopia. In the past few years, separatism and reunification have increased. In the Persian Gulf, these developments are widely known. In practical terms, the reunification of Yemen was viewed as a negative precedent. The territorial status quo in the Arabian Peninsula was altered, and a country that can field many more soldiers than any of its neighbors was created. The possibility of territorial change increases the attachment of the smaller Gulf countries to their legal sovereignty, which could be threatened by friend and foe alike. The extremely nervous reaction in Qatar in the Khafus incident is a case in point. More generally, the refusal of the GCC to standardize armaments is an indirect way of stressing independence from Saudi Arabia. On the other hand, Iran, Iraq, and Yemen, where the social fabric is much more complex than in the GCC, are more seriously threatened by disintegration. The Azeri question and Kurdish separatism remain unsettled in Iran, while Iraqi Kurds now enjoy a large degree of autonomy. Yemeni tribalism is intense, and the risks of civil war are real. An important confidence-building measure could be the recognition of the territorial integrity of states in the Gulf, as would be a pledge to refrain from intervention in the internal affairs of others.

Conclusion

The status quo is permanently threatened in the Gulf because it is organically unbalanced: wealth and power do not overlap, frustrations are high, and external interventions to impose or to maintain the status quo are frequent. Consequently, Western interventionism will be the critical factor in the years to come, at least as long as oil represents a strategic asset for those who produce and those who protect those producers. In the short run, the most sensitive issue is the ability of the pro-Western local regimes to maintain themselves in power and to be politically able to offer a cover for these protective but intrusive Western umbrellas.

Although Iran, Iraq, and Yemen are viewed as possible sources of tension or aggression, they do not have the same objectives and do not command the same strength. Instead of the present strategy of dual containment, the West should treat these three countries on an ad hoc basis: some of their fears can be alleviated, some of their requests are legitimate, and some of their needs can be met. A relaxation of the sanctions on Iraq is long overdue. An open political dialogue with Iran could be useful. A Manichaean policy, where the good "Gulfies" have to be permanently defended against two villains in Baghdad and Tehran, is a good scenario for a Western movie, but not for mid- and long-term security in the Persian Gulf.

Notes

1. See Ghassan Salamé, "The Middle East: Elusive Security, Indefinable Region," *Security Dialogue* 25, no. 1 (1994): 17–35.

2. Rosemarie Said Zahlan, *The Making of the Modern Gulf States* (London: Unwin Hyman, 1989), 12.

3. Ahmad Mustapha Abu-Hakima, *The Modern History of Kuwait 1750–1965*, n.p., n.d., 134.

4. Zahlan, *The Making of the Modern Gulf States*, 7.

5. Ibid., 18.

6. "The essence of the matter was not confined to the fact that the imperial [British] influence and treaties of protection had 'frozen' tribal leadership or rule in the hands of those who had signed the treaties, but it extended to another matter of utmost importance, namely the broadening of the authority of the ruler himself and his successors in the ruling family which under the natural state system was limited." Khaldoun Hassan al-Naquib, *Society and State in the Gulf and Arabian Peninsula* (London: Routledge, 1990), 59.

7. For a study of the relationship between a mission-oriented regional policy and the lack of democracy at home, see Ghassan Salamé, ed., *Democracy without Democrats: The Renewal of Politics in the Muslim World* (New York: St. Martin's Press, 1994).

8. For a detailed discussion of oil in relation to stability, see Ghassan Salamé, "Un pétro-dinar belligène," *Maghreb-Machrek* 133 (summer 1993).

Part II.
REGIONAL ACTORS

4

ALTERNATIVE FUTURES FOR IRAN: IMPLICATIONS FOR REGIONAL SECURITY

Shaul Bakhash

Since the Islamic revolution in 1979, Iran's foreign policy has been characterized by what (for want of a better term) we may describe as a struggle between ideologues and pragmatists, radicals and moderates; by the powerful, contradictory currents generated by the revolution itself; and by the sensitivity of foreign policy to the play of domestic politics and personalities. (The terms "ideologue," "pragmatist," "radical," and "moderate," if lacking in precision, are nevertheless useful for the purposes of this chapter. More exact senses in which the terms are used here emerge in the course of this chapter.)

On the one hand, especially in recent years, Iran has displayed a desire for secure borders, good relations with its neighbors, and the benefits of trade and access to technology and markets that reintegration into the international community should bring. On the other hand, the ideology of the revolution and the convictions of some of its leaders impels Iran to support radical Islamic movements outside its own borders and to seek to challenge and transform an international order that it believes is dominated by a hostile United States and its Western allies.

Iran's dealings with other states and with the international community in general have thus alternated between accommodation and confrontation. Sometimes, both policies have been pursued at once. Repeatedly, initiatives to normalize relations with one or a group of countries have come to grief against powerful currents generated by the revolution itself or by the resistance or actions of influential clerics or of political leaders and political groups. In February 1989, for example, in a turnabout typical of the conduct of foreign policy since the revolution,

Ayatollah Khomeini wrecked several months of a careful fence-mending effort by Ali-Akbar Hashemi-Rafsanjani with European states (an effort which Khomeini himself had sanctioned) by pronouncing a death sentence against the writer Salman Rushdie.

Within the ruling groups, divisions between ideologues and pragmatists have not always been clear-cut. For example, Iran's first president, Abol-Hassan Bani-Sadr, believed the conservative Arab states of the Persian Gulf deserved to be swept away by popular revolutions; he was also the architect of the sweeping nationalizations of the early revolutionary period. Nevertheless, he opposed the taking of American hostages and sought their early release, and he lost his presidency in 1981 in part because of his efforts to curb the revolutionary courts, Revolutionary Guards, and revolutionary *komitehs* (committees).

The current *faqih* (supreme leader), Ayatollah Ali Khamenei, is now identified with the foreign-policy radicals, yet in 1987, he was taken to task by Ayatollah Khomeini for a sermon in which he argued for the primacy of the rule of law and the constitution. The current president of Iran, Ali-Akbar Hashemi-Rafsanjani, is most closely identified with the pragmatists, but following the Palestine Liberation Organization's recognition of Israel's right to exist in May 1989, Rafsanjani called on Palestinians "to execute five Americans, or English, or French" for every martyred Palestinian.[1] He was instrumental in helping secure the release of American hostages in Lebanon after the 1990–91 Gulf War, yet numerous Iranian opposition figures in Europe have been assassinated during his presidency. The Iranian government has been implicated in a number of these assassinations, and it is highly unlikely they could have taken place without the approval, the knowledge, or at least the acquiescence of Iran's highest officials, including the president.[2]

Nevertheless, broadly speaking, it has been possible to discern differences between the radicals and the pragmatists on a number of foreign and domestic policy issues. In foreign policy, the radicals generally have favored a confrontational attitude toward the West, exporting the revolution and providing propaganda and material support for Islamic and other opposition movements in the region and farther afield. The most radical among them have also favored using strong-arm methods, terrorism, and assassination to serve these ends, irrespective of the consequences for Iran's diplomatic relations. For example, when an Iranian consular official was arrested in Manchester, England, in May 1987 on a shoplifting charge, the second-ranking British diplomat in Tehran was abducted by armed men and severely beaten. A month later, when French authorities issued a warrant for the arrest of a member of the Iranian embassy staff in Paris in connection with a series of bombings in the French capital, a French diplomat was charged with smuggling and illegal foreign-exchange transactions, and a "spontaneous" crowd appeared before the French embassy in Tehran to harass French diplomats and their families. The Iranian refusal to surrender the embassy staff member wanted by the French authorities eventually led to a break in diplomatic relations. Iranian officials, including the interior minister, were implicated when a hijacked Kuwaiti airliner was given permission to land in Mashhad, in northern Iran, in August 1987 and were implicated also in the sabotage of Kuwaiti oil installations earlier that year.

At home, the radicals have remained committed to state control of the economy, including foreign trade and domestic distribution of essential items and basic consumer goods, to extensive land distribution, and to continuation of subsidies for basic necessities. They have displayed hostility toward foreign and domestic private entrepreneurial capital. They also have stressed an end to economic "dependence"—that is, reliance on foreign goods, services and financing—and often have interpreted economic "independence" and "self-sufficiency" as a form of economic autarchy.

The pragmatists, in contrast, have sought to repair relations with Western European countries and the Arab states of the Middle East, to reintegrate Iran into the international community, to reduce (but certainly not to eliminate) the state's role in the economy, and to encourage a greater role for the private sector. More technocratic in orientation, the pragmatists have tended to prefer economic development to revolutionary purity.

Ascendancy of the Pragmatists

Rafsanjani emerged as the architect of the pragmatist's agenda. He is credited with finally persuading Khomeini to accept a cease-fire in the Iran-Iraq War. Immediately following the end of the Iran-Iraq War in 1988, when Khomeini was still alive, and following Khomeini's death in 1989, Rafsanjani, first as Speaker of the Majlis (Parliament) and then as president, began to pursue the pragmatist agenda with increasing confidence and consistency and to exercise greater control over both domestic policy and foreign policy.

In the foreign-policy field, even before the 1990–91 Kuwait crisis and Gulf War, he began to normalize Iran's relations with the United Kingdom and France. He used the cover of the Gulf War to resume diplomatic relations with Saudi Arabia, Egypt, and Jordan. All these were highly controversial and politically risky measures. During the Gulf War, Iran, for all intents and purposes, aligned itself with the aims of the United States-led alliance. Clearly, it was in Iran's national interest to do so. Nevertheless, Rafsanjani did not succumb to the blandishments of the radical faction in the Majlis, who were opposed to the U.S. military presence in the Persian Gulf and one of whom urged Iran to ally itself with Iraq against the United States. Iran was steadfast in rejecting the annexation of Kuwait by Iraq—more steadfast, it should be pointed out, than a number of Arab governments. It made no move to break the United Nations-imposed trade embargo against Iraq or to help Baghdad in any other way, despite Saddam Hussein's offer of a treaty formally ending the Iran-Iraq War on terms favorable to Iran.

Iran did provide support to the Shiite uprising that erupted in southern Iraq at the end of the Gulf War, but, given the powerful emotions aroused in Iran by the killing of Shiites and the attack of Saddam's troops on Shiite shrines, what is striking is how little rather than how much Iran did. Again, Tehran acted with restraint. In the aftermath of the Gulf War, Iran finally brought its leverage to bear in securing the release of American and other Western hostages in Beirut, and Roger Cooper, an Englishman who had been held for five years in Iran on spying charges, was released. Iran worked assiduously in the postwar period to improve relations with Saudi Arabia and the Persian Gulf states.

At home, Rafsanjani displayed a similar ability to overcome the resistance of a radical faction within the ruling group to a whole range of his policies. The five-year development plan (1989–94) approved by the Majlis provided for foreign borrowing of up to $27 billion. Foreign borrowing had been a taboo concept in the revolutionary lexicon. Rafsanjani gathered around him a team of economists and technocrats committed to the ideas of privatization, rationalization of foreign exchange rates, a substantial role in the economy for the domestic and foreign private sectors, a gradual withdrawal of subsidies for all but the most essential items, and reduced import controls.

In 1990, by a kind of clever constitutional gerrymandering, Rafsanjani and his allies managed to exclude from the Assembly of Experts—the body that elects the faqih—prominent figures of the radical faction. In parliamentary elections in 1992, he again displayed his dominance over the political process. Virtually all of the prominent clerics and figures identified with the radical faction were excluded from the new Majlis. Rafsanjani also pushed through a reorganization of the security forces, with the primary purpose of bringing two revolutionary organizations, the Revolutionary Guards and the revolutionary committees, under greater central control. The revolutionary committees were merged with the national police and the gendarmerie into a single internal security organization. The Revolutionary Guards and the regular army, at least in principle, were brought under a joint command.

Many observers read these developments as indications of a gradual but steady triumph of moderates over radicals, of pragmatists over ideologues—and rightly so. The evidence of more reasonable councils prevailing in Tehran was incontrovertible. Yet by 1992, the move toward more pragmatic policies at home and abroad appeared to be under considerable attack, and there was ample evidence of a reversion to the more radical, ideologically based policies of the past.

Foreign Policy Incoherence and Its Causes

Since 1992, a degree of incoherence has characterized Iranian foreign (and domestic) policy, in the sense that Iran appears to be pursuing conflicting and incompatible ends. For example, Iran continues to seek foreign credits and investments and the participation of foreign firms in major industrial projects; it continues to work for better relations with the Persian Gulf states and even to court opinion makers in the United States.[3] To the World Bank and the International Monetary Fund, Iran's Central Bank and its key economic officials have sought to project the image of a government firmly committed to privatization and to responsible fiscal policies. But calls to Iranian businessmen to return notwithstanding, property seizures continue to take place in Iran on the flimsiest of grounds. At the same time, the government has engaged in rhetoric and a pattern of behavior that has caused concern in Europe and the United States and among Arab states of the Middle East, exacerbating relations with individual states and undermining long-term economic objectives.

Iran's assertion of rights in Abu Musa in 1993 was clumsy and counterproductive. There is a revival of anti-American rhetoric that, even in the troubled history of Iran-United States relations, is striking for its persistence, pervasiveness, and vehemence. The commitment to radical Islamic causes, which seemed on the wane, once again shapes, and sometimes dominates, foreign policy. Thus, Iran has supported the largely isolated and radical Islamic regime in Sudan, despite the damage this has done to Iran's relations with Egypt and its image elsewhere. The government has vehemently opposed the Arab-Israeli peace process. On the eve of the opening of the Madrid Conference in the Arab-Israeli peace process in October 1991, Iran invited to a conference in Tehran 400 representatives from forty-five countries, including representatives of radical, rejectionist Palestinian groups and terrorist organizations, such as Ahmad Jabril, leader of the Popular Front for the Liberation of Palestine, and Fathi al-Shaqaqi, secretary-general of Islamic Jihad.[4] It has denounced in uncompromising terms the agreement signed in September 1993 by PLO chairman Yasir Arafat and Israeli foreign minister Shimon Peres.

The mindless assassination of Iranian dissidents abroad has continued. The former Iranian prime minister, Shapour Bakhtiar, who posed no threat to the regime, was assassinated in Paris in August 1991, on the eve of a long-planned (and, for Iran, vitally important) visit to Tehran by French president François Mitterand, causing Mitterand to cancel his visit. On both domestic policy and foreign policy, the leadership is once again speaking in many—and often conflicting—voices. Particularly on "Islamic" issues, the Iranian posture has been increasingly activist and confrontational.

This development is rooted in the Iranian domestic environment as well as the regional and international environment, and it reflects the influence of conflicting aims and considerations. Regarding the Persian Gulf states and in other states bordering Iran, the Islamic republic's foreign policy is dictated by traditional Iranian interests. Iran's desire to play a large role in the Persian Gulf and ensure the security of its borders is nothing new. Iran's foreign policy is also shaped by its perception of regional and international threats to Iran or, at least, to regional stability. In Europe and Japan, Iran gives priority to enlisting their participation in its economic development plans. In the newly independent states in Soviet Central Asia and the Caucasus, Iran seeks influence and markets, but appears motivated primarily by a desire to prevent disorder and ensure stability along Iran's northern frontier.

Iran's foreign policy is also shaped by attitudes generated by the culture of the revolution itself and Iran's claim to leadership of the Islamic world against a hostile, exploitative West; by the ideologies of various domestic constituencies, who are not always in agreement with one another; by the fragmented nature of clerical leadership and bureaucratic authority; and by the narrow popular base of the regime. Pragmatism thus competes with revolutionary ideology; the desire for better relations with Persian Gulf neighbors, Middle East states, and Europe competes with a search for influence abroad (in the Middle East, in Africa), which articulates itself in the language of revolutionary Islam. In shaping foreign policy, the government has to contend with influential clerics in and out of the government who do not hesitate to articulate views which may oppose, or complicate, official policy. From 1990 to 1992, Rafsanjani seemed largely successful in shielding foreign policy from the influence of these various forces, but they seem once again on the ascendant.

Iran's armaments program has caused much adverse comment abroad,[5] but Iran's estimate of its own security interests and its perception of regional developments offer partial explanations for arms acquisition. Instability is endemic along Iran's borders with the former Soviet republics and with Central Asia, as well as along its eastern frontier with Afghanistan. The posture of Iraq, with which there is still no peace treaty, remains menacing, and from the Iranian perspective there is no certainty that Iraq's offensive missile capability or its program for the production of weapons of mass destruction have been adequately neutralized. Even today, Iraq's weaponry is superior to Iran's. Again from the Iranian perspective, given Washington's inscrutable ways and the history of cooperation between Saddam Hussein and the West, the rehabilitation of Saddam is always a possibility.

Iran feels beleaguered and vulnerable in other ways. The U.S. posture appears particularly threatening. Washington has branded Iran a "terrorist" and an "outlaw" state. It has accused Iran of seeking to obtain weapons of mass destruction and to destabilize other regional countries. It has attempted to deny Iran access to international arms markets. It has also sought to persuade China, its European allies, and Japan to deny Iran "dual purpose" technology, investments, and credits. It has opposed recent World Bank loans to Iran. In May 1993, the director for the Middle East and South Asia on the National Security Council, Martin Indyk, described Iran as a state hostile to U.S. interests and engaged in subverting governments friendly to the United States. He declared it the aim of the Clinton administration to press for wider adherence by the international community to trade and weapons transfer sanctions against Iran and, lumping Iran and Iraq together, articulated a policy of "dual containment" toward the two countries.[6] In an article in *Foreign Affairs* in March 1994, the U.S. national security adviser, Anthony Lake, further elaborated and refined the policy of dual containment. He described Iran and Iraq as among a number of "backlash" states that the United States must contain and neutralize and repeated many of the criticisms of Iran articulated by Indyk and other U.S. officials. Lake also stressed that under dual containment, the United States did not regard Iran and Iraq in the same light. While the United States sought a change in the regime in Iraq, in Iran it sought modification in government policies and behavior—including Iran's program to acquire weapons of mass destruction, its support for radical Islamic regimes bent on subverting the regional order and regional states, its opposition to the Arab-Israeli peace process, its use of terrorism abroad against its own citizens, and its abuse of human rights at home. Lake said that the United States was prepared for an "authoritative dialogue" with Iran.[7] However, this distinction was lost on Iran's leaders, who remain apprehensive regarding U.S. intentions and the large U.S. military presence in the Persian Gulf. Iran's harsh anti-United States rhetoric and its strenuous opposition to U.S. policies in the region stem at least in part from a perception in Tehran that the United States seeks to isolate and damage Iran.

In addition, from the Iranian perspective, nothing came of the promise to Iran in President Bush's 1989 inaugural address that "good will breeds good will." Iran feels that the United States did not reciprocate after Iran helped secure the release of American hostages in Lebanon.

Iran has traditionally claimed for itself a large voice and a leading role in Persian Gulf affairs, whether under the shah or the Islamic republic, by virtue of its size, population, and long coastline on the Gulf. Its most important resource, oil, lies in onshore fields adjacent to the Gulf or offshore, in the Gulf itself. The Iran-Iraq War and the U.S. re-flagging of Kuwaiti ships underlined the vulnerability of Iranian oil exports and Iranian shipping to interdiction. Thus, Iran is extremely sensitive to exclusion, or any perception of an attempt at exclusion, from arrangements regarding Persian Gulf security.

Nothing came of suggestions following the Gulf War for collective security arrangements among the regional states. The Bush administration, which halfheartedly promoted such ideas, did not put much effort into developing them, and there was little enthusiasm for collective security arrangements among the Arab states of the Persian Gulf. Nevertheless, Iran believed that there was a deliberate attempt, orchestrated by the United States, to exclude it from these discussions. For obvious reasons, Iran also opposed the so-called Damascus Accords (from which it was excluded and which also proved abortive) that would have given Egypt and Syria a role in guaranteeing Persian Gulf security. Iranian officials are no doubt aware that Iran benefits substantially from the military and trade sanctions imposed on Iraq by the United States and its allies, but they cannot admit this publicly. They fear that the United States and its allies are conspiring to break up Iraq, or at least to compromise severely Iraq's sovereignty, and that this is but a prelude or precedent for similar action against Iran. Iran's insistence that the United States should remove its forces from the Persian Gulf and that Gulf security be left to the regional states is thus dictated partly by its desire to play to public opinion, partly by the belief that the U.S. presence diminishes Iran's weight and limits its leverage with the Arab states in the Gulf, and partly by its suspicion of ultimate U.S. intentions.

The Claim to Islamic Leadership

The idea that Iran constitutes the vanguard—the model and pacesetter—in a worldwide Islamic awakening is bound up with the culture of the revolution. Iran's leaders and propagandists claimed leadership for Khomeini, not only of Iran's Shiites but of Shiites everywhere, and not only of the world's Shiites but of all Muslims. "Hope of the world's disinherited" was one of the many titles by which his followers referred to him. However, the inclination to act on the claim of leadership of the Islamic world seemed on the wane in the period of pragmatic ascendancy from 1990 to 1992. Now, it is once again central to foreign policy considerations in a number of areas.

In brief, Iran's leaders believe that the Islamic revolution was the first genuine and effective blow by Muslims against Western imperialism, hegemony, economic exploitation, and cultural domination. They see the Iranian revolution as an example to Muslims everywhere. In the Iranian view, the West, led by the United States, fears Iran and is determined to ensure that the Islamic revolution does not succeed precisely because it threatens Western domination of the Islamic world. It is thus incumbent on Iran to stand firm and to speak for, encourage, and support Islamic movements abroad.

At the same time, Iran's leaders view themselves as competing for the hearts and minds of Muslims against various rival claimants: the "corrupting" attractions of Western culture; secularists of all stripes; leaders of Middle East states who, whatever their pretensions, lack true dedication to Islam; and states, such as Saudi Arabia, that boast Islamic credentials and compete with Iran by funding Islamic movements in many states in the region and outside it.

These ideas echo the views of both senior clerics and religious figures lower down in the clerical hierarchy; of elements in the revolutionary organizations, such as the Revolutionary Guards, the revolutionary committees, and the paramilitary *basij* forces; and of an important faction in the Majlis. The regime thus views its support for a variety of Islamic movements as contributing to its legitimacy among important constituencies both at home and abroad. Moreover, at a time when the regime feels isolated and beleaguered, it feels that support for radical Islamic movements has a nuisance value and can provide Iran with bargaining chips in dealing with the outside world. Past Iranian support for the Hezbollah factions holding American and European hostages in Lebanon, for example, not only enhanced Iran's standing with Hezbollah, but also gave Iran leverage with the countries whose nationals were held hostage—or so the Iranians assumed. Iran's "weight," its claim to be heard, is enhanced, its leaders calculate, precisely to the degree that it can deploy Hezbollah in military excursions into the Israeli security zone in Lebanon, disrupt the Arab-Israeli peace process, or, directly or by extension, cause the United States and its friends difficulties in, say, Sudan or the West Bank.

But there is more. The alacrity with which Iran embraced the new government in Sudan suggests that Iran continues to feel impelled to support regimes that label themselves Islamic, continues to look for opportunities to spread its influence far afield (in this case, in Africa), and continues to see Islam as the main vehicle through which it can accomplish this aim.

In Lebanon, Iran also backs the more radical forces. But in Lebanon, the Iranian position is more substantial. Historically, there have been scholarly and family links between Shiite clerical families in Iran and Lebanon. In addition to the presence in Lebanon of Iranian Revolutionary Guards and the support and training that Iran provides to armed Hezbollah factions, Iran has helped fund a substantial infrastructure of schools, clinics, day-care centers, and religious seminaries in Lebanon. It has protégés among important Shiite clerics and preachers, who regularly visit Tehran. The Iranian investment in Lebanon has thus been considerable, and Iran has secured a position there that it is unlikely to give up easily. Iran may be willing to pressure Hezbollah to release American and European hostages in Lebanon or even (as occurred in July 1993) to curb Hezbollah military activity in the Israeli security zone in southern Lebanon, but it will always be reluctant to push Hezbollah so far as to risk its influence with the organization. It will seek to protect the position it has built up for itself in Lebanon, and it will continue to try and use Hezbollah and Lebanon as a base from which to attack and undermine the state of Israel.

The Iranian presence in Lebanon was initially facilitated by Syria (Iranian official visitors, the rotation of Iranian Revolutionary Guards serving with Hezbollah, and Iranian arms and material assistance to Shiite communities have had to pass through Damascus to get to Lebanon) and is still dependent to a degree on Syrian acquiescence, but it has now assumed a life of its own. Syrian president Hafiz al-Assad has helped facilitate the Iranian presence in Lebanon and Iranian support for Hezbollah, even in armed confrontation with Israel, because this serves Syria's purpose. Hezbollah helps make the Israeli position in southern Lebanon more difficult, and President Assad need not take responsibility for its actions or cross-border raids.[8]

Nevertheless, the Iranian and Syrian positions, particularly on peace talks with Israel and the Gaza-Jericho agreement between Israel and the PLO, have begun to diverge, and they will diverge further still if there is a Syrian-Israeli (and a Lebanese-Israeli) peace agreement. If and when that day comes, Hezbollah will have to be curbed, either by the Syrians or by the Lebanese army, with Syria's blessing. Strain in the Iranian-Syrian relationship will then be inevitable, and Hezbollah's position (and therefore Iran's) in Lebanon will be threatened. If comprehensive peace agreements are signed, furthermore, Iran, as one of the few naysayers to the peace process, may find itself further isolated internationally.

However, Iran's leaders have defined Israel as a core issue on which compromise is not possible. They have linked opposition to Israel's existence with the regime's Islamic legitimacy. Moreover, Iran's leaders calculate that the peace process may still break down, which would vindicate Iran in its position that the Palestinians have been offered little or nothing. Iran's leaders may also believe that even if peace agreements are signed, their protégés on the West Bank and in Lebanon—Hamas and Hezbollah—can continue to be part of the political process and contest elections for Parliament, local councils, and professional bodies and yet capitalize on inevitable popular discontent by posing as critics and rejectionists of the peace accords.

Iran has thus adopted a position of uncompromising hostility toward the Arab-Israeli peace talks and the Israeli-PLO Agreement of September 1993.[9] Following the Israeli-PLO Agreement, Iran's faqih, Ali Khamenei, described Yasir Arafat as "that puny, ill-reputed, blackguard," the agreement itself as "illegitimate," and the acquiescence in the agreement by Arab leaders as "treachery" and "surrender." He declared the issue of Palestine "an Islamic matter," on which presumably all Muslims must have a say, and he asserted that the home of the Palestinian people, "usurped" years ago, "must be returned to the Palestinian nation in toto and unconditionally."[10] Similarly harsh condemnations of the peace accords were made by President Rafsanjani, the speaker of the Majlis, and other senior officials and clerics.

In all this, Iran is motivated by a variety of considerations. Iran's leaders have long made support of the Palestinian cause, the return of Palestine to the Palestinians and of Jerusalem to Muslim control, and the eradication of the state of Israel a cornerstone of Iran's claim to speak for the entire Islamic world. They cannot appear to be ready to compromise on this crucial issue. The Iranian position may also reflect personal commitments among some of Iran's leaders.[11] Like the Hezbollah in Lebanon, Hamas represents what appears to be an effective asset in challenging the West and Israel and undermining Western interests. Iran also sees opportunities to become the leading speaker for a new rejectionist front, to win new supporters among Islamic constituencies, and to enhance its revolutionary Islamic image.[12]

At the same time, not being directly involved in the Arab-Israeli issue and being geographically far from the Arab-Israeli confrontation, Iran (not unlike some Arab states at various times in the long history of the Arab-Israeli conflict) can afford to be totally uncompromising on the question of peace talks or recognition of Israel. Iran may also be concerned that peace between the Arabs and the Israelis may be detrimental to its own diplomatic, economic, and military ambitions in the Persian Gulf and further afield in the Middle East. For example, an Israel free to trade and maintain diplomatic relations with the Persian Gulf states would compete with Iran's ambitions in this area, and Arab-Israeli peace, as already noted, is fraught with problems for Iran's position in Lebanon and its relations with Syria.[13]

The Khamenei Factor

Iran's commitment to radical Islamic causes outside Iran's borders has been reinforced, after a hiatus following the death of Ayatollah Khomeini in 1989, by the positions adopted by his successor as faqih, Ayatollah Ali Khamenei. Even before assuming supreme leadership, Ayatollah Khamenei held strong opinions on the United States, Israel, and the corrupting effects of Western culture. He also expressed a strong commitment to Islamic movements abroad. Since his election as faqih, he has articulated these positions with greater force and frequency.

He sees himself as the heir to Khomeini's mantle, and he has claimed for himself—and his supporters have claimed for him—the same right to absolute obedience as was asserted on Khomeini's behalf. His religious rulings, his supporters have asserted, must, like Khomeini's decrees, take precedence over the rulings of all other clerics. Like Khomeini, Ayatollah Khamenei feels that it is incumbent on him to speak out on questions of import to Muslims.

This inclination is reinforced by the difficulty he has had—and as any successor would have faced—in filling Khomeini's shoes or exercising the immense authority Khomeini enjoyed. At the time of his election, moreover, Khamenei did not fill all the requirements for the office of faqih, in terms of scholarly eminence and legal learning, specified under the constitution. The constitution had to be amended to make his succession possible. His authority has been more vulnerable to challenge than was Khomeini's.[14] Ayatollah Khamenei has thus often taken the lead in articulating the Iranian position against Israel, the United States, and Western cultural influence and in support of Islamic movements, whether in Bosnia or the West Bank, as a means of bolstering his position with domestic constituencies.

Khamenei's hard-line position may also stem from his conviction that Iran should negotiate with the United States only from a position of strength. Whatever the reasons, Ayatollah Khamenei's hand in the shaping of foreign policy appears considerable, and the position he has articulated makes difficult the kind of deliberate fence-mending policy that the government pursued at the time of the Gulf War. In 1990, Khamenei did not stand in the way of Rafsanjani's decision to resume diplomatic relations with Egypt, Saudi Arabia, or Jordan or his policy of implicit cooperation with the U.S.-led alliance against Iraq. He has since been inclined to take a more active role and to set the tone for foreign policy. The resulting change is striking.

Domestic Discontent and Foreign Policy

Domestic politics and economic problems reinforce this more confrontational foreign policy line. In the 1992 parliamentary elections, as noted, President Rafsanjani succeeded in excluding from the new Majlis most of the prominent clerics and other figures associated with the radical faction. But he ended up with a Majlis in which social conservatives dominate. These deputies have generally taken a conservative, Islamic position on such issues as women's dress and permissiveness in film, theater, art, television, and the press. While their primary concern is not foreign policy, their discomfort with Western cultural influence in Iran and their suspicion of easy traffic with Europe, let alone the United States, complicates a policy of rapprochement with the West.

As noted above, even before his election as president, Rafsanjani became the chief spokesman for an economic policy that emphasized economic over ideological goals, a larger share in the economy for both the domestic and the foreign private sectors, and a deliberate effort to attract foreign capital and technology. He secured the endorsement of Ayatollah Khomeini for this policy and it underlay the projections of the first and second five-year development plans (1989–94 and 1994–99). The attempt at normalizing Iran's relations with the international community that Rafsanjani initiated in 1988–89 and resumed in 1990 was fueled in large part by economic considerations.

Huge funds were required for reconstruction of the extensive damage to oil installations, ports, electric power plants, roads, and other infrastructure and to several cities as a result of the eight-year Iran-Iraq War. The industries and enterprises seized by the state from private owners after the revolution (almost all large- and medium-scale industry was taken over) were run inefficiently. Productivity was well below prerevolution levels. By the government's own admission, per capita income in 1989–90 was around 51 per cent of its prerevolution, 1977–78 level at fixed prices, and due to falling oil revenues, a growing population, and the fall in the purchasing power of the dollar, per capita foreign exchange earnings from oil exports were about one-quarter their prerevolution levels. A rate of population growth of 3.2 per cent was adding 1.8 million persons to the population each year. To feed, house, educate, and eventually provide gainful employment for this population would require extensive capital investment, and this, the government concluded, required both foreign and domestic private-sector involvement.

The new economic program initially met with some success. According to the Central Bank, by August 1992, Iran secured $15 billion in medium- to long-term loan commitments, although foreign sources put the amount at no more than $12 billion.[15] Government investment in petrochemical, steel, metals, electric power generation, and infrastructure accelerated. Some rationalization of foreign exchange rates took place. Import restrictions were considerably eased, and government involvement in retail distribution was restricted. Gross domestic product grew by 4.2 per cent in 1990 and 8.6 per cent in 1991.

But foreign and private-sector investment lagged well below plan targets, and many plan targets were not met. Privatization did not proceed very far, in part because the Foundation for the Disinherited and other parastatal organizations in control of hundreds of nationalized and expropriated industries and enterprises resisted the divestment program. Mismanagement and excessive imports in 1991 and 1992 led to a large foreign debt, estimated at around $13.6 billion in December 1991 and as much as $30 billion in short- and medium-term debts by 1993.[16] Retrenchment, import restrictions, a credit squeeze, raw-materials and spare-parts shortages, and idle factory capacity followed. Inflation remained high. The gap in incomes between rich and poor—between a privileged elite of importers, contractors and industrialists with government connections, some high government officials and clerics, those in the professions, and a somewhat larger group of shopkeepers, and skilled or self-employed workers (such as plumbers and electricians), on the one hand, and white-collar workers, civil servants, and the mass of the working population, on the other—remained substantial. Corruption was endemic and widespread.

Public discontent with economic and general conditions led to serious riots in Mashhad and other cities in the summer of 1992 and again in Qazvin in mid-1994. Urban unrest could erupt again. A politically correct, hard-line foreign policy is in some ways compensation for the inability of the state to make good on its promises at home. To suppress the riots in the summer of 1992, the government was forced to rely on the basij paramilitary forces. This experience may have led the regime to conclude that its ultimate survival rests on the forces born out of the revolution itself and that the loyalty of these security forces requires a hard-line foreign policy, rhetorically hostile to the United States and the West and supportive of revolutionary Islamic causes.

The more pragmatic, more moderate foreign policy that Rafsanjani tried to fashion following Khomeini's death has also been hampered by the fragmented nature of clerical and government leadership. Within the revolutionary organizations, such as the Revolutionary Guards and the revolutionary komitehs and the basij forces, in the Majlis, among members of the clerical community (some of high standing, some among the rank-and-file provincial clergy), there is resistance to normalization of relations with the West, to measures that are seen as abandonment of revolutionary principles. Among present and former members of the

Majlis and the clergy and in newspapers, such as *Salaam* and *Kayhan*, there are voices all too ready to charge the government with violating Khomeini's legacy.

Rafsanjani had to face harsh criticism when he resumed diplomatic relations with Saudi Arabia and Egypt. His attempts to explain Khomeini's "death sentence" decree against Salman Rushdie in a way that would minimize friction with European states were quickly attacked.[17] Since 1990, Rafsanjani advisers and officials close to him have on numerous occasions urged a dialogue with the United States. Presumably they were speaking with the president's knowledge, but their views were invariably drowned out in a wave of press protest.

However, it is also the case that the government is to a large degree the prisoner of its own rhetoric. The demonizing of the United States (and of the West in general) is largely the government's own doing. The government is sensitive to the opinion of its various constituencies within the revolutionary organizations—opinion which, admittedly, can be easily mobilized by clerics and leaders within the ruling group—but these constituencies are narrow. A very small percentage of the population is actually involved in the political process. Nevertheless, when the United States remains the country of first choice for Iranians who wish to study abroad and is the country of residence of several hundred thousand Iranians, many with relatives in Iran, and when Western goods and lifestyles are so much part of the way of life of the very substantial Iranian middle class (in the broadest sense), it is difficult to believe that the population as a whole shares the anti-American, or anti-Western, rhetoric of the state. Again, given housing shortages, urban crowding, and similar problems, it is difficult to believe that the bulk of politically aware Iranians prefer their government to expend resources, and attention, on foreign involvements—say, in the Sudan or even the West Bank—rather than on domestic issues or that they support policies that seem to imply that Iran must be forever in confrontation with the rest of the world.

These questions, in any case, are not openly debated. In the absence of such debate, one could argue that the foreign-policy priorities of the regime reflect the priorities of the narrow ruling group and its various, fairly limited constituencies and that the more moderate, more pragmatic foreign policy that President Rafsanjani appeared to be pursuing depends for its success not only on the resolution of conflicting agendas within the ruling group but also on the broadening, rather than the narrowing, of the regime's political base.

"Selective" Radicalism

Iran's foreign-policy posture—even on the questions of Islam and Palestine—is not consistent. The revival of an activist, interventionist, confrontational style in foreign policy is selective, and it applies to some areas or countries and to some issues, and not to others. A striking example of this is Iranian policy toward the newly independent states in the Caucasus and Central Asia. Iranian policy toward these regions has been marked by restraint. There is no evidence that Iran has tried to stir up radical Islamic sentiments in the area. It has been careful not to allow their already strained relations with Turkey to be exacerbated in a competition for influence in the newly independent republics. Rather than stirring up Islamic sentiments, it has sought to mediate differences between Armenia and Azerbaijan, and, for a while, it was more supportive of the Armenians than the Azeris, who should presumably be seen as Islamic Iran's "natural" constituency. In contrast to Iran's strident protests over the treatment of Muslims in Bosnia and Somalia, the government has been relatively silent over the treatment by Russian troops of Persian speakers on the Afghanistan-Tajikistan border. Iran also has generally acquiesced in the setbacks suffered in Tajikistan by the Persian-speaking Tajiks (who culturally identify with Iran) at the hands of Uzbeks and their allies. The Iranian government has sought to exploit opportunities for expanded trade, but, like the shah's regime, it has accorded priority to order and stability along its borders.

This is not altogether surprising. Throughout the Iran-Iraq War, Iran maintained good relations with the United Arab Emirates and (except for brief periods) with Kuwait, although these states were openly assisting the Iraqi war effort. Its harsh condemnation of the Arab-Israeli peace proposal notwithstanding, Iran has continued to repair its relations with Saudi Arabia and the Persian Gulf states that, after all, support this "treasonous" policy. Although in the mid-1980s relations with both France and Great Britain were badly disrupted, Iran more recently has not allowed its conflicts with the United States and its general fulminations against the West to affect its trade relations with Western Europe.

There are some ready explanations of these apparent anomalies. Iran today attaches importance to stability and order along its borders with Pakistan, Afghanistan, Turkey, the Persian Gulf states, and the new republics of the Caucasus and Central Asia. It saves its Islamic radicalism for countries and places distant from Iran—Lebanon, the West Bank, Sudan. In Europe (and now also in the Persian Gulf), pragmatism and economic interests prevail over ideology. In Central Asia and the Caucasus, good relations with Russia are also a concern. Key individuals care more intensely about certain regions of the world or certain issues than they do about others. For example, Khamenei is greatly concerned about the fate of Palestinian Muslims, but far less so about the fate of Muslims in Tajikistan.

To state the obvious, Iran's foreign policy, whether in its ideological or in its pragmatic variety, is not of one piece. The success of the pragmatists lies precisely in their ability to immunize certain areas of foreign policy against the ideological or radical impulse. The ability to pursue radical and pragmatic foreign policies simultaneously has been a source of both strength and weakness for the regime.

Conclusion

What direction might Iran's foreign policy take in the near future? Three alternatives seem possible.

First, the more pragmatic policies of 1989 to 1992 may once again dominate and truly shape foreign policy. At the moment, this does not appear likely. The reasons are implicit in the preceding analysis.

The perception of Iran as leader of a worldwide, revolutionary Islamic movement, and as well as the belief that maintaining this role should assume a high foreign-policy priority, has once again become dominant within the ruling group, or, to put it another way, those in the leadership committed to such a role for Iran have come to play a much greater role in shaping foreign policy. At the same time, the faqih, Khamenei, has concluded that his legitimacy derives largely from a successful assertion of his claim to leadership of the Islamic world and that this requires him to champion the cause of Islamic movements that, generally, take a hostile attitude toward the West or are attempting to replace national governments or challenge the international order. Moreover, the abandonment of maximalist Palestinian demands implicit in the current negotiation between the Israelis and the Arabs and Palestinians has been defined by Iran as a core issue on which no compromise is possible.

With the United States particularly, the prospects for accommodation appear dim, and the grounds for further acrimony appear extensive. The United States demands a modification of Iranian behavior regarding what, to Iran, are core issues (such as Palestine or Iran's support for Islamic movements) or regarding issues of national interest, such as weapons acquisition and rearmament. The Iranian regime fears that it is being isolated by the United States and targeted for some dire retribution. Its sense of being beleaguered only reinforces its inclination to adopt a confrontational posture. Domestically (largely due to conditions of the regime's own making), any attempt at an accommodation with the United States would be attacked as a sellout of revolutionary principles.

The popular base of the regime is narrow. It rests (or so the regime appears to have concluded), on socially conservative forces and those elements that the regime rightly or wrongly assumes to be committed to Islamic issues, to anti-Americanism, and to a confrontational posture in foreign policy. At the same time, the regime (again, rightly or wrongly) imagines that these policies appeal to the inchoate, unorganized mass in society. Rafsanjani might attempt to develop a base of support within the broad middle class, but such an attempt involves considerable political risk. Rafsanjani is unlikely to secure the support of other key members of the leadership in this attempt, which would require concessions to the middle class—on civil rights and freedoms, traffic with the West, privileged access to civil-service jobs and universities now reserved for those with "revolutionary" credentials, a curb on official corruption— that the government is unprepared to make.

A second possibility is that the government will revert to an all-round "revolutionary" stance in foreign policy and accept the cost of such a policy in terms of further isolation and exacerbated relations with the West, the Persian Gulf states, and Arab countries. This, too, seems unlikely. Iran's economic development and industrialization programs, access to suppliers of basic necessities (food and pharmaceuticals and some spare parts and raw materials) and technology require good working relations with the West and Japan. The government, it is true, is not overly sensitive to or constrained by public opinion. Nevertheless, the government has itself made economic performance a yardstick by which it must be measured, and it must always take care that economic discontent does not articulate itself in the form of political unrest.

The Islamic government has generally continued the monarchy's policy of seeking to maintain working relations with Iran's immediate neighbors (Iraq, the Persian Gulf states, Turkey, Afghanistan and Pakistan, and the Soviet Union, and now its successor states). Iraq aside, with all these states (and especially with Saudi Arabia and Kuwait and, to a lesser extent, with Turkey) there have been periods of tension. But Iran has consistently sought to avoid a serious deterioration in relations and to maintain stability on its borders.

The technocracy does not make policy, but it is in a position to shape it. Also, insofar as the government's technocrats draw up plans and focus attention on economic development, refineries, steel mills, construction, and borrowing and securing credit from international financial institutions, they keep Iran engaged and entangled with the international community. In brief, there are numerous factors that make it unlikely that

Iran will revert to a posture where radical ideology will dominate foreign policy to the exclusion of more pragmatic considerations.

The third, and most likely possibility is that Iranian foreign policy will continue to be characterized by conflicting aims and purposes—by both ideology and pragmatism, both moderation and radicalism, both accommodation to and confrontation with the outside world.

It may appear that I have merely (and artificially) posited two extreme scenarios in order conveniently to opt for the "centrist" resolution, but there are scholars and analysts of Iran who define the Islamic republic precisely in terms of these two extremes. Some analysts argue that the commitment to radical ideology in foreign policy is an expression of the nature of the regime, that the Islamic republic cannot abandon this policy and retain its essential character, and that, short of a major internal upheaval, there are few prospects for the emergence of a moderate, pragmatic Iran. There are also analysts who argue that the radical streak in Iranian foreign policy is a remnant of early revolutionary zeal and that the regime is evolving, with some backsliding, into a state like other, "normal" states in the international community. But there are compelling reasons why the regime's foreign-policy behavior is likely to continue to reflect both of these characteristics, and for some time to come.

First, a foreign policy of competing and conflicting purposes reflects accurately divisions within the leadership itself and among the politically significant constituencies from which the leadership draws its support.

Second, such a foreign policy would be consistent with the patterns of the past. Since the revolution in 1979, periods of pragmatism and moderation in foreign policy have alternated with more radical, ideologically driven periods. Repeatedly, a domestic or international incident has caused significant turnabouts in the rhetoric and substance of foreign policy, or the regime has appeared moderate and reasonable on some issues, or in relation to certain regions or countries of the world, and radical and ideologically driven on others.

Third, the regime (or its foreign-affairs practitioners) has shown an ability to maintain and manipulate a foreign policy of conflicting purposes without sustaining (in the regime's calculations) unacceptable levels of damage to the national interest. Iran has learned that the international community will tolerate inconsistency and contradiction in Iran's international behavior.

Iran has maintained tolerable relations with the United States' Western European allies and Japan even as relations with the United States remained strained or deteriorated, and Washington has succeeded only to a very limited extent in persuading Japan and governments in Europe to curtail their trade, technical, and financial exchanges with Iran.

American intercession notwithstanding, China has not stopped arms sales to the Iranians. The assassination of Iranian dissidents on French, Austrian, German, and Swiss soil did not materially affect the relations of these countries with Iran. In 1994, Japan and leading European states rescheduled Iran's debts. Members of the European Union urged Iran to moderate its vociferous opposition to the Arab-Israeli peace process, but they acquiesced without strenuous objection when Iran continued as before.

Finally, while it is obvious that foreign-policy radicalism is costly to the regime, oil revenues are still sufficient (although increasingly less so) to meet the government's basic requirements. The economic and diplomatic costs of foreign policy radicalism are not sufficiently high to cause the regime to reconsider and adopt a consistently and determinedly different course—at least, not yet.

Notes

1. Foreign Broadcast Information Service, Near East and South Asia (FBIS/NESA), 8 May 1989, p. 60. Rafsanjani later claimed he had been misunderstood. See FBIS/NESA, 11 May 1989, pp. 45–46.

2. In a report to be issued in 1995, Human Rights Watch records forty assassinations of Iranian dissidents abroad between 1980 and 1994. By far the largest number of these assassinations occurred after Khomeini's death in 1989; the most recent, at the time of the report, in August 1994. Human Rights Watch concludes that these assassinations reveal a clear pattern of state-sponsored terrorism in which the Iranian government is implicated.

3. One example of Iranian courting of U.S. opinion makers was the establishment in 1992 of the Foundation for Iranian-American Relations, which was committed to improving relations between the two countries. Its publication, *U.S.-Iran Review*, provided useful information on the Iranian economy; gave the Iranian perspective on U.S. policies affecting Iran; tried to depict Iranian armament, human rights, and foreign policy in a favorable light; and depicted Iran as offering attractive opportunities for foreign trade and investment. (*U.S.-Iran Review* ceased publication in early 1995.) A second publication along similar lines was *Iran Business Monitor*, published in New York City by the Center for Iranian Trade and Development.

4. FBIS/NESA, 21 October 1991, p. 55.

5. See, for example, Patrick Clawson, *Iran's Challenge to the West: How, When and Why?* (Washington, D.C.: Washington Institute for Near East Policy, 1993). Clawson depicts Iran as a state bent on regional hegemony, involved in a major arms buildup that includes a nuclear weapons capacity, and dangerous to its Persian Gulf neighbors and to Western interests.

6. See Indyk's 18 May 1993 remarks at the Washington Institute for Near East Policy, reprinted in part in the institute's bulletin, *Policywatch*, of 21 May 1993.

7. Anthony Lake, "Confronting Backlash States," *Foreign Affairs* 73, no. 2 (March/April 1994).

8. An interesting instance of this policy and its ramifications occurred in July 1993, when Hezbollah used antitank rockets and other heavy weapons against the Israelis, inviting massive Israeli retaliation, in the worst outbreak of violence between the two adversaries in southern Lebanon in a decade. U.S. Congressman Tom Lantos subsequently disclosed that just days before the Hezbollah incursions, an Iran Air 747, guarded by Syrian troops, unloaded antitank rockets and other weapons at Damascus Airport. The weapons were trucked off to Lebanon under military escort. See "Iranian Arms Sent by Syria, US Says," *New York Times*, 29 July 1993. The Hezbollah raids ended, and Israeli troops withdrew, after a visit to Damascus by the Iranian foreign minister, and President Clinton subsequently praised Syrian "restraint" during the hostilities. The incident suggests the following conclusions: that Iran is willing to go so far as to supply heavy weapons to Hezbollah for its anti-Israeli campaign, knowing full well that detection is possible; that President Assad, using the thin cover of deniability, was willing to permit this at a time when Syrian-Israeli talks over Israeli withdrawal seemed stalled (the size and intensity of Israel's retaliation against Hezbollah are probably to be explained by this evidence of large Iranian arms transfers and Syrian complicity); and that Syria and Iran are capable of preventing serious Hezbollah armed activity if they are persuaded that the price to be paid is too high. On this occasion, it appears that Assad, having made his point, was able to enlist the Iranians in getting Hezbollah to put a stop to its operations.

9. The chairman of the Parliament Foreign Relations Committee, Hassan Ruhani, told the Austrian press agency on 22 September 1993 that while Iran opposes the Israeli-PLO Agreement, it will not take any action against the PLO or attempt to obstruct the peace process. His statement, attacked in the Iranian press, was subsequently "corrected" by the official Iranian news agency but not fully withdrawn. It appears to have been intended for European consumption and can hardly be construed as representing the official Iranian position, given the statements by Khamenei, Rafsanjani, and other leading Iranian officials. Iran has since repeatedly affirmed its opposition to peace and reiterated the view that Israel is an illegitimate state that must be dismantled, with a Palestinian state created on all of mandate Palestine.

10. FBIS\NESA, 17 September 1993, pp. 49–50.

11. Khamenei, for example, has over many years given prominence in public statements to the need to "liberate" Palestine, and he has been a consistently harsh critic of Israel. Rafsanjani has a reputation for readiness to make a deal on most issues, but he may also harbor strong feelings on the matter of Palestine and Israel. See, for example, his 1989 sermon, reported in FBIS/NESA, 8 May 1989, pp. 58–63.

12. For example, Iran's ambassador to Germany explained in an interview that Iran's position on Palestine would strengthen Iran's standing in the Islamic world because this was the position of one billion Muslims.

13. Iranian newspapers have referred to the access to lucrative Arab markets that Israel hopes to secure through a peace agreement. See, for example, the columns by H. Fathi and F. Assef in the Tehran daily *Abrar*, cited in *Mideast Mirror*, 6

September 1993, p. 13, and by M. J. Larijani in *Ettelaat*, cited in *Mideast Mirror*, 17 September 1993, p. 6.

14. For a discussion of Khamenei's attempt to assume Khomeini's mantle and the challenges posed to his claims to supreme leadership, see Shaul Bakhash, "Iran: The Crisis of Legitimacy," in *Middle Eastern Lectures*, ed. Martin Kramer (Tel Aviv: University of Tel-Aviv Press, 1994), pp. 105–112.

15. Jahangir Amuzegar, *Iran's Economy under the Islamic Republic* (London and New York: I. B. Tauris, 1994), p. 136.

16. Amuzegar, *Iran's Economy*, p. 161.

17. Rafsanjani attempted in 1990 to suggest that Khomeini's *fatwa* (religious opinion) pronouncing a death sentence against Rushdie was the judgment of a single jurist and (by implication) that other jurists might have other, contrary opinions. See FBIS/NESA, 16 February 1990, p. 49, and Rafsanjani's attempt to respond to criticism by somewhat modifying this view in FBIS/NESA, 20 February 1990, p. 67. For numerous statements that rejected the Rafsanjani view, see the views expressed by Ayatollah Mahdavi-Kani, who called Khomeini's decree "irrevocable" and said Rushdie should be killed (FBIS/NESA, 27 February 1990, pp. 39–40) and by Chief Justice Mohammad Yazdi, who stated that all Muslims have a duty to carry out Khomeini's decree (FBIS/NESA, 28 February 1990, p. 58).

5

IRAN'S NATIONAL SECURITY: THREATS AND INTERESTS

Shahram Chubin

Iran's position as a revolutionary Islamic state does not mesh with the current international order. The international system today is not a congenial place for revolutionary powers. Given that the Iranian regime emphasizes its Islamic and revolutionary tendencies more than its Iranian components, tension and confrontation between Iran and the outside world are a foregone conclusion.

The end of the Cold War has created further difficulties for Iran by reducing the leverage of states lacking intrinsic power. The increasing importance of economic forms of power places Iran and other states lacking this capability at a distinct disadvantage. As states accustomed to exploiting the bipolar system have less room to maneuver, the unity of the nonaligned states has become more differentiated and fragmented.

Though unsettled and unclear, the international political system of the 1990s demonstrates a marked tendency to accept the United States as the premier power. The United States is able to create coalitions and assemble votes in support of its interests with apparent ease and impunity, making the threat of a unipolar world more real when viewed from Tehran rather than Washington or London. Countries hostile to the United States no longer have an automatic protector and must manage on their own. The United States, no longer counter-balanced by the Soviet Union, appears free to dominate and manipulate international institutions for American interests.

U.S. superiority has been demonstrated time and again since the end of the Cold War and is seen as a major threat by the Iranian regime. Washington is able to intervene selectively; it chose to do so in Haiti while preferring to stay out of Bosnia thus far. The United States can be energetic militarily on some issues, such as Iraqi weapons of mass destruction, while ignoring proliferation problems, such as Israel's nuclear weapons. From the Iranian viewpoint, the pattern is clear. U.S. policy embodies a double standard in which Islamic interests are ignored in the Israeli-occupied territories, Bosnia, and Algeria, while Islamic states such as Iraq and Libya are treated punitively. Meanwhile U.S. allies—notably Israel and its accumulation of nuclear weapons—are not bothered.

Iran feels particularly threatened by the U.S. ability to control the United Nations and promote new concepts that challenge Iranian security. The new tendency to talk about "failed states," to deny the absolute nature of sovereignty, and to seriously consider the "right of and duty to intervene" are notable examples of Iran's concerns. Tehran believes that these ideas threaten to encourage and legitimize the breakup of existing states with the enclaves in northern and southern Iraq serving as a vivid example. If such a precedent were established, Iran fears that interventions in defense of minorities would be sanctioned and secessionist movements on the basis of self-determination might be encouraged. Maps could be redrawn in Iraq, in Iran's northern provinces (Azerbaijan) and potentially among Iran's Turcomans, Tajiks, and Baluch populations. With the rise of ethnic consciousness in Afghanistan, the breakup of existing states could become a reality, and Iran as a polyglot empire—where some 50 percent of the population is either not ethnically Persian or is non-Persian speaking—cannot welcome this possibility.

Iran is located in the middle of several actual or potential conflict zones. Two recent wars and numerous crises in the Persian Gulf that resulted in two massive foreign deployments in the past decade, demonstrate the difficulties of maintaining peace in the region by solely regional means. The United States has strengthened its military presence in the region near Iran's vulnerable oil installations.

In addition to the "traditional" problems of balance in the Persian Gulf, Iran has become more intimately connected to the Arab-Israeli zone. Both the politics of the two regions and the range of weapons systems have reinforced these linkages, as was vividly demonstrated by Iraq's missiles, which fell on Israel and Saudi Arabia simultaneously. The risks of Iran's direct involvement in the Arab-Israeli conflict appear to have grown appreciably as a result of Iran's declaratory policies, support for opposition groups, and pattern of arms acquisitions. Rhetoric and the dynamics of arms purchases rather than a deliberate policy to confront Israel could see the two countries militarily entangled in the future.

The breakup of the Soviet Union removed a proximate threat to Iran but left a frontier of instability and turmoil in the Transcaucasus and Central Asia. None of the states in these regions constitutes a military threat to Iran in the short term, but their wars and disputes threaten to spill over into Iran and to entangle Iran with Central Asia, Turkey, and Russia. There is also uncertainty about the future role of Russia, which has shown a willingness to reassert its power in its "near abroad," forcefully and directly in Tajikistan and Chechnya and no less emphatically—albeit indirectly—in Azerbaijan and Georgia.

While it would be an exaggeration in light of the turmoil and volatility taking place on practically all of Iran's borders to say that Iran faces no security problems, Iran has no urgent, overwhelming, or concrete security problem. Instead, threats appear diffuse and generalized, potential rather than actual, contributing to a sense of insecurity without providing a focus for that feeling. In short, Iran's insecurity is more a product of its view of the current international system than a reflection of the regional environment. Iran is markedly revisionist about the international hierarchy, which it considers unjustly dominated by, and configured for, the interests of the arrogant Western powers. This same system marginalizes the Muslims and the meek oppressed. Part of Iran's revolutionary identity is grounded in resisting this unjust system. Islamic Iran must be seen to be striving and to have a presence internationally on all issues that concern Muslims and propagate the revolution's values as widely as possible. This revolutionary Muslim activism is considered part of the regime's mandate, an important source of its political legitimacy.

Whether or not Iranian activism is actually a response to a cruel, U.S.-dominated international system is unclear, but the perception tends to make it an important political issue at least among the dominant factions jockeying for power. Clearly the importance of revolutionary activity abroad for the regime's legitimacy is not absolute. It depends on several factors, including the domestic political circumstances, the balance of internal forces, the availability of alternative domestic sources of legitimation (e.g., economic success), the availability of resources, and the prevailing interpretation of Iran's proper role (which can be militantly ideological or pragmatically tempered).

Nevertheless, revolutionary activism in foreign policy is important for a regime that has failed to build support through other channels. Tehran has failed to routinize charisma or institutionalize the revolution; the regime still needs to appeal to, and stir, that section of the population that remains mobilized and supportive. This is where regional instability near Iran and further afield in the Middle East fuels Iran's revolutionary image. In Afghanistan, Kashmir, Tajikistan, Turkey, Iraq, Bosnia, Tunisia, Algeria, Sudan, Israel, southern Lebanon, Egypt, and Zambia, Iran is accused of supporting revolutionary or terrorist forces. The United States also accuses it of having a worldwide terrorist infrastructure and there are reports of terrorist activity in Thailand and the Philippines. Putting aside the degree to which Iran is a complicating factor rather than prime cause in these very different areas, Iran is able to plug into changes going on and at times claim an important role. Revolutionary change that benefits Iran's brand of Islam, or revolutionary Iran's interests, can be condoned. Domestically Iran can claim that regional change validates its revolutionary Islamic model and can point to U.S. hostility as proof that it is still taken seriously as a threat and as an alternative model or source of values.

Iran's specific type of revolutionary impulse has been formed by history and national psychology. It is impelled by a sense of grievance and militancy stemming from the frustrations and anger at past manipulation by outside powers. The problem is compounded by a sense of impotence at the backwardness of the country in the face of the bulldozer of Westernization, which has plowed into developing countries in the guise of modernization. Iran, a Shiite state (though overall the Shiites only account for some 15 percent of Islamic adherents), is a peculiarity in Islam, and this gives Iran's actions a special flavor. Iran's claims to represent Islam are not so readily entertained by other Sunni Muslim states. Indeed some, like the Wahhabi Saudis, consider Shiism at best as a heterodox sect. The result is that when it comes to universal Islamic issues such as Palestine, Iran has to try harder. The Shiite factor may also account for Iran's cultivation of a sense of victimization, or martyr complex. Its leaders have found it congenial to point to Iran's isolation, claiming that it is meritorious and desirable:

> Iran is alone in the world today. The power of the people of Iran today is at its zenith; the same applies to the Iranian Government. The government is very powerful,very dear; those in positions of power in the world pay attention to the Government of Iran. The people and the government are strong and capable; they know what they are doing. At the same time, they are lonely and oppressed. We are alone in the world today. No power in the world supports us today.[1]

Precisely because of the absence of imminent and direct threats to its national security, Islamic Iran is able to indulge itself in concerns about threats to the revolution and its values.

From the outset, Iran has correctly identified the major threat as coming from the West. Hence its insistence, contrary to logic and history, in 1979, that the United States constituted a greater threat to the Islamic Republic of Iran than the Soviet Union. It meant the United States was a threat to the IRI *as a revolution* not to Iran as a nation-state. The end of the Cold War, the breakup of the Soviet Union, the end of the war with Iraq, and Iraq's defeat in 1991 removed two prominent threats to Iran's national security. Iran however continues to focus on the other cultural threat and refers to cultural bullets discharged by the Western media in the form of ideas and values that threaten to undermine the Islamic republic. Against these threats it can only resist, compete with other values or isolate itself. Iran appears to be trying a little of each by banning or limiting satellite television receivers and competing in the production of videos and the promotion of Islam abroad.

Iran's opposition to the current international order and its values, hierarchy, and distribution of power has taken the form of support for revolutionary change. In the early years of the revolution, it was evident in Iran's rejection of the nation-state and secular nationalism and an insistence on the "community of believers" as the appropriate unit of account. Iran now promotes state-to-state relations and denies any intention of intervening in the affairs of other states—except by setting an example. Practical considerations have brought about a change in policy; good relations with neighbors are essential for Iran's interests. At the same time, however, Iran, as a revolution, retains the people-to-people level of relations, which has it involved or implicated in some way in subversive, terrorist, and revolutionary activity across a broad swath of states in the developing world. This dualism incorporates both relations with states and ties with their opposition movements, normalization, and subversion. Iran wants both the benefits of conventional diplomacy and the fruits of intrigue; such a policy reflects in equal parts duplicity and incoherence. The duplicity is simple: as long as things are unclear or unproven, the game can be played with relatively little risk. The incoherence stems from domestic divisions with differently motivated factions at work, often at cross-purposes, with no one able to impose order. Thus the revolutionary consensus consists of going along on several tracks to see what turns up.

Related to this is a curious psychology in which the Islamic republic sees little relationship between its own acts and the hostility of the United States or its neighbors. It is quick to detect conspiracies where others are concerned but slow to see how its own acts may stimulate responses. In both its Islamic and its general revolutionary activity, it creates enemies and security threats that complicate its own existence.

Iran's military buildup is a case in point. Its dimensions and pace are not extravagant given Iran's loss of material through natural attrition and war over the past fifteen years, or by reference to the buildup of its neighbors.[2] Criticism appearing in the West on the buildup and on accusations regarding nuclear weapons stem, however, from the nature of the regime in Iran.[3] Given Tehran's hostility, there is an understandable tendency in the West to assume the worst, to extrapolate current spending into the future, to suspect an incipient nuclear program not unlike that of Iraq, and to focus on it in its early stages before it is too late. Even though one could make a plausible case for not exaggerating

Iran's prospective military capability,[4] the fact is that Iran is seen through the lens of states that witness its ambiguous and not-so-ambiguous regional policies and are concerned by its threats. As a result of Iran's own actions and rhetoric, Iran's legitimate security interests are thus given short shrift by the most powerful states of the international community. This, of course, reinforces Iran's view that there is a conspiracy afoot and sharpens its sense of grievance, never admitting that the catalyst may be found in its own actions.

Where does this leave Iran? The short answer is that it will remain a captive of its domestic politics. If incoherence persists in the absence of a strong center that imposes one line, rhetorical and possibly real confrontations with the West will remain a distinct possibility. Domestic volatility is another variable. Yet another factor is regional instability that may provide opportunities that Iran may find difficult to resist or to disclaim as its own.

Iran, although a nuisance in the area of subversion, will not be a military threat in the region, though there are some threatening scenarios. It has no reliable sources of military supply. It will take some time to rebuild its military, and the opportunity costs will be high. Finally, there is little disposition in Iran for military adventurism. Yet the risk of an inadvertent crisis with the United States or Israel cannot be discounted. Nor can the possibility that Iran might gain access to sufficient fissile material from the republics of the former Soviet Union and circumvent one of the critical bottlenecks on the way toward nuclear weapons. There is also the possibility that Iran will strengthen defense cooperation and enhance its capabilities with other "rogue" or discontented states. This could include North Korea, Pakistan, and Syria, and, depending on their evolution, Russia, China, or India.

These possibilities aside, Iran faces formidable constraints. It is without a dependable ally inside or outside the region. None of the states mentioned above values its relations with Iran more than its relations with the United States; all are correspondingly susceptible to U.S. pressure or inducement, should it be applied or offered. Iran has structural obstacles to the advancement of its power; both the Persian-Arab divide and the Shiite-Sunni split make the extension of Iranian influence problematic, casting doubt on the so-called Islamic axis on which Iran has pinned its hopes.

Furthermore, although revisionist in terms of *status,* Iran is not a *territorial* revisionist. It has an undoubted interest in regional stability. It does not seek a change on any of its borders. As a state without any overland pipelines, it remains more dependent than other major oil producers on the Persian Gulf for its oil exports, the principal source of its revenues, as well as the principal waterway for its commerce. With its large population and reconstruction requirements, Iran remains very sensitive to the price of oil and to its own export quota. This gives it strong incentives to cooperate with Saudi Arabia. Iran's economic needs, including access to credit and technology, also militate in favor of pragmatic relations with the industrial world and the West. Iran's oil and economic infrastructure remains very vulnerable to punitive attacks by extraregional states. Iran's various programs also remain sensitive to the costs of embargoes and denial regimes. As the price for revolutionary agitation rises for the IRI, its leaders will have to consider whether the political benefits of a revolutionary posture at home outweigh its costs to Iran's economic well-being, a key and probably increasingly critical yardstick in the legitimacy of the regime at home.

The United States

In Iranian eyes, the new world order is dominated by the United States. This is a threat to Iranian interests and potentially to its security, as defined in terms of either regime or revolution. In Tehran's view, the emergence of a new era in which the United States is no longer effectively balanced and is free to act as arrogantly as it wants does not bode well for states insistent on maintaining their own independence and values. The fruits of American dominance are already evident in the peace process imposed on the Arab states, which is a barely disguised surrender of Arab-Palestinian rights.[5] U.S. policy toward Iraq also fits this pattern. It is intended to weaken Iraq and make it incapable of resisting the so-called peace process. Hence, U.S. policy toward Saddam Hussein has nothing to do with Kuwait or human rights; rather it is related to the balance of power in the Middle East. The threat to Iraq's territorial integrity can be seen as consistent with the same script: enclaves, safe areas, and no-flight zones are an implicit threat to dismantle Iraq to make it a more compliant party in the Middle East negotiations.

Iran views the encouragement of the claims of the Kurds and others, talk of self-determination, and the right of secession as thinly disguised threats against Iran as well. The new challenge to absolute sovereignty in the name of human rights is thus seen as a direct threat to Iran, a warning about what to expect in the future. Iran takes such threats seriously because of signs of the government's inability to meet economic expectations and needs and of the increased restiveness of various groups in the country. Over time, the threat of restiveness especially in areas bordering unstable states (Azerbaijan, Afghanistan, Baluchistan) might become more serious. In short, Iran worries about the consequences of seeking to maintain its autonomy and follow independent policies, often in opposition to the United States or its allies.

Iran sees its interest in terms of a continuum starting with regime security, advancing to national integrity, and finally ending with the advancement of the revolution. It will not pursue goals that will destabilize the regime, however congenial to the revolution. However, it will also balance revolutionary goals and those more narrowly seen in terms of national interest. The process is not a scientific one, dependent as it is on domestic politics and factionalism. Therefore, there is always a chance that the claims of the revolution will be given precedence over, and conflict with, those of nationalism.

Iran's differences with the United States stem from both global and regional causes. Global differences relate to attitudes toward the international status quo; the regional differences relate to specific differences over such issues as U.S. support for Israel and the selective American approach to arms control and technology transfers or the U.S. military presence in the Persian Gulf. Iran's arms programs, especially to the extent that they involve weapons of mass destruction (and especially nuclear weapons), can be seen primarily as an attempt, dictated by global objectives, to achieve equality in status. Iran also seeks to acquire a shield against U.S. bullying. The conventional arms buildup in the Persian Gulf (antiship missiles and Kilo-class submarines) also should be seen as intended to inhibit or deter U.S. intervention.

This is far from suggesting any intention on the part of Iran to confront the United States. In light of recent events, Iran has no reason to have illusions about its military capability to resist the determined U.S. military machine. Iran does feel frustrated and threatened by the U.S. military presence in the Persian Gulf, which increasingly looks like it may become permanent. Tehran resents the May 1993 United States policy of "dual containment" that puts Iran and Iraq into the same category of states and seeks to exclude them from any regional role.[6] It has officially protested U.S. naval exercises in the Persian Gulf as causing "unreasonable restrictions" and "nuisance"[7] and sees the United States as manufacturing crises and overreacting to them in order to increase its military foothold in the region. In the most recent crisis in October 1994, Iran's leadership observed:

It is obvious that global arrogance is thinking of consolidating its stronghold in this region by whatever means possible.... What is your business in the Persian Gulf? The security of the Persian Gulf is none of your business. Why should you come from another corner of the world to interfere in this region? What is the justification for coming here, to a region that does not belong to you in any way, just under the excuse that Iraq intended to move troops?[8]

Iranian leaders believe that the United States is exaggerating Iran's arms purchases and depicting its intentions as hostile in order to sell arms to the GCC states and to increase their sense of reliance on them:

> They (Britain and the U.S.) have injected them (the GCC) with the idea that Iran is a threat to them. . . . The Americans wish to pick their pockets. They want to buy oil cheaply and not give them anything. And the little they give them they take back in return for weapons that are no use to them. . . . The security of the Persian Gulf states is very important to us. We would never dream of destabilizing them.[9]

Iran sees U.S. policy as confrontational, and its arms policies seem intended to anticipate a sharp engagement. Since the United States would certainly prevail, it is doubtful that Iran would seek such a confrontation. A collision will depend on the degree to which Iran seeks to extend the third of its interests, the goals of the revolution, for there is otherwise no direct source of dispute.

There are, however, areas in which a showdown between the two states are possible, even likely, depending on Iran's policies and on the degree to which the United States decides to be internationally active. Primary among these is the issue of international terrorism and the degree to which Iran is involved and implicated in serious cases. Miscalculation or underestimation of U.S. concern could lead to a crisis, confrontation, and even hostilities. This is more likely to be the case if Iran were seeking to use this instrument to sabotage a Middle East peace agreement, for example, rather than more ambiguously trying to intimidate one of the Persian Gulf states.

Weapons of mass destruction are another area of potential confrontation and hostilities. If Iran were seen to be cheating on obligations assumed under the Nuclear Nonproliferation Treaty or the Chemical Weapons Convention, or even if it sought to leave the NPT, with the implication of seeking freedom to develop nuclear weapons, there would be a strong likelihood, in light of the case of Iraq, of internationally sanctioned coercive disarmament. Iran sees the entire question of weapons of mass destruction as evidence of Western hypocrisy. The West continues to rely on these weapons and is selective about proliferation concerns in cases like Iraq and Israel. Iran sees attempts at controlling them to be an excuse to deny some targeted states technology necessary for their development. In short, Iran sees this issue as symptomatic of the general inequity of the current international system, based on power and arrogance. If Iran were to become involved in hostilities with the Arab states of the Persian Gulf, which appears a remote possibility in light of the renewed and more explicit security commitment by the United States, there would be a strong presumption of the latter's involvement. This could range from an increase in the size of the U.S. presence for deterrent purposes, to the provision of manpower and weapons for defense, through to full-scale involvement, including punitive or disarming strikes on Iranian forces or infrastructure.

These scenarios are not imminent or inevitable, but they are the most likely areas where Iran and the United States might clash directly. They are not top priorities of the Iranian leadership, but they could occur from miscalculation or from illusions about Iran's ability to keep some program or action secret. In general, though, Iran feels the cultural threat that the United States represents. While insisting on the spiritual void at the heart of materialism and the lack of social justice in capitalism, Iran sees the pervasive appeal of modern culture among the young, which it is difficult to block given the permeability of borders and the intrusions of new technologies. In this sense, Iranians are fighting a rear-guard action against the inevitable.

Iran and Israel

Iran sees the question of Palestine-Israel as a Muslim, rather than an Arab, issue. It is an issue that Iran has sought to exploit as a card in Middle East politics. By taking a radically rejectionist position against the peace process or the recognition of the state of Israel and by supporting opposition elements, Iran has sought to use the issue as a card for entry into the region's politics. Its extreme position is intended to polish its Muslim credentials, which, as noted, are not accepted by all Muslim states. For Iran, the Palestinian cause is an issue on which it can take an extreme position, embarrass the Arab states, pose as a protector of Muslim rights and dignity, and do so from a distance with little risk and investment.

Israel is high in Iran's demonology but not equally high in its list of national security priorities. Tehran's support for the Palestinian cause is evident in its opposition to the peace process, support for the Lebanese Hezbollah in their struggle to evict Israel from South Lebanon, and militant rhetoric refusing to recognize the Jewish state's existence. Iran has also funded and supported the militant Hamas and Islamic Jihad movements based in the Gaza Strip, which compete with the mainstream Palestinian secular organizations for supporters. Iran's support for a new rejectionist front has alienated the Palestine Liberation Organization (PLO), Egypt, and the Gulf states, although Syria finds it convenient as a reminder to Israel of what may be in store if an agreement is not reached on the Golan Heights.

The issue of Israel is a foreign policy rather than a security question, an interest rather than a vital interest. It is not intended to become a major Iranian preoccupation to the point of military engagement. Although

Iran's attitude toward Israel has visibly hardened since 1991, it is not at all clear that this is a product of a strategic decision. There is domestic political credit to be gained in depicting the regime as uniquely principled and indomitable where Muslim questions are concerned. Whether Iran has considered its policy in light of an eventual Israel-Syria agreement, which would sever the land link between Iran and Israel through Lebanon, is altogether another matter. Iranian revolutionary leaders do not acknowledge that taking extreme positions on an issue that is some distance from Iran's frontiers may have serious consequences. Yet while Iran may not intend any military commitment against Israel, that country cannot afford, after the case of Iraq, to doubt the plain meaning of words. Israel has thus been conscious since 1991 of the need to counter Iran's military programs, especially its long-range missiles[10] and a suspected nuclear weapons program. Therefore, Israel has sought long-range F-15E aircraft for possible strikes against Iran. It has warned Iran against developing weapons of mass destruction and supporting terrorism aimed against Israel.

Iran, obsessed by its own grievances and agenda, has not fully considered the effects that its harsh rhetoric might have on Israel's defense planning and Israeli concern about Iran's military build-up especially in the area of unconventional weapons. Iran's rejectionist posture has propelled it to the forefront of states opposing Israel; it is seen as a potential threat and as a consequence has risen in the ranks of Israel's potential adversaries. Iran, on the other hand, considers Israel a distant foe but has not considered confrontation with it militarily or based its military planning on scenarios involving Israel.[11] As suggested earlier, Iran is already preoccupied with more proximate and direct security threats around its borders. Nevertheless given the sensitivity of Israel to the subject of unconventional weapons and the thoroughness of its defense planning and, on the other side, Iran's tendency to substitute rhetoric for thought, there is a risk that confrontation between these two states could occur. The risks are enhanced by the fact that Iran's weapons acquisition program could pose a direct threat to Israel and hence create and constitute a dynamic independent of any intentions.

Russia and the Commonwealth of Independent States

If the IRI formally adopted a policy of "neither East nor West" in 1979, in practice the emphasis has been on seeing the United States as the greater Satan. Iran began to enlist the Soviet Union as a diplomatic partner seriously toward the end of the 1980s. It sought to cultivate its northern neighbor but was handicapped by the continuing Soviet involvement in

Afghanistan. In June 1989, newly elected President Rafsanjani, on his first foreign visit, showed Iran's willingness to deal with the Soviet Union by curbing any inclination to exacerbate Islamic agitation in that country. To seal this pragmatic *modus vivendi*, Islamic Iran and the Soviet Union signed their first arms agreements. Accordingly in January 1990, Iran's reaction to the disturbances in Azerbaijan was conservative, more concerned about the border area and relations with Moscow than in encouraging resistance or promoting independence among the Azeris. The last thing Tehran expected and arguably wanted was the collapse of the Soviet Union (as opposed to Communism, which Khomeini anticipated when he sent a letter of Gorbachev in early 1989), and it was extremely slow to accept it, doing so with little enthusiasm in late 1991.

For Iran the north is unknown territory—an area with which there has been little direct interaction and on which there is little expertise. During the Cold War the north appeared predictable; Iranian diplomacy could be energetic and imaginative elsewhere. The Soviet Union effectively stabilized a border that has not been in dispute. Attempts to exploit Iran's ethnic divisions in Kurdistan (in the Kurdish republic of Mahabad) and Azerbaijan after World War II has made Iran wary of calling into question the basis on which the frontier has been established. In some senses, the *glacis* established by Soviet power in the south was also a buffer zone for Iran, settling what could otherwise have been a source of instability.

The collapse of the Soviet Union has also seen the end of exclusive or uncontested Russian influence in the southern republics, opening them up to external influences from Iran, Turkey, China, Pakistan, or the Arab states. The weakening of the border zone has seen a more porous frontier region in which the possibility of Iranian influence northwards at least coexists with that of forces and ideas from the north infiltrating toward the south, where Iran's often sizable minorities straddle the frontier region (Azeri Turks, Turcomans, and Tajiks). If Iran has ambitions in the north to increase its influence and to create a constituency of Islamic states to offset that of the Arab world, that interest is not in territorial expansion. The prospect of more responsibilities in today's setting of limited resources is unwelcome. Furthermore Iran's primary interest is in keeping good relations with Russia. Russia is becoming an important potential source for Iranian technology, including arms. In addition, after the Cold War, Russia may become a more important actor in Persian Gulf politics than it ever was as a superpower with a bloc and an empire. Both considerations dictate restraint on the part of Iran and an attempt to keep on the right side of its northern neighbor.

Iran has shown a willingness to defer to Russian sensitivities in its "near abroad." Iran has not contested the Russian dispatch of some 15,000 troops to Tajikistan's bloody and now lengthy civil war or criticized its active intervention in other disputes. Similarly, the regular refrain from the Russian right and military of the threat from the south ("Muslims on the Volga") and of the Islamic threat as justifications for maintaining large forces, developing antitheater ballistic missiles, not reducing arms stocks, or honoring arms control agreements has not elicited an Iranian response (although Turkey has protested to its NATO allies). Iran has not responded either to Russia's extraordinary historical statement that Iran and Turkey are interloper states in Central Asia and the Transcaucasus. Russia's policies after empire are more uncertain and her domestic politics are, to put it mildly, volatile. Russia is looking for a new role to play; it is developing rapid-reaction forces to protect its borders and possibly its dispersed nationals. Its soldiers talk about the threat of Islamic fundamentalism. They point to Tajikistan as a case of forward defense, where the Commonwealth of Independent States (CIS) borders have been at risk from outside.

Iran is occasionally named as a potential threat. In its attempt to convince the CIS members of the need for military cooperation and thus Russian help, Russia might be tempted to exaggerate the external threat. With no clear security threat to the West and none in the immediate future in the East, emphasis on the southern periphery is natural. Protecting Russian nationals, defending the CIS borders, and stopping Islam may be enough of a program to carry the Central Asian states and Armenia, but Azerbaijan and Georgia have proven more resistant and hence the target of strong-arm tactics. It is possible, even probable, that Russia could relapse into extreme nationalism and in seeking a belt of good neighborly states revert to bullying or imperialism. In this fluid zone where newly independent states are being established and are working out their domestic structures as well as their regional relationships, orientations, and alignments, instability is inevitable and the potential for conflict is ever present. What are the scenarios of conflict with Russia?

Direct Hostilities   This outcome is not likely except as a result of competitive intervention by the two states on opposite sides in a civil war (such as Tajikistan) or an interstate war such as that between Azerbaijan and Armenia. Thus far, Iran has been cautious in both of these cases. It has not taken sides in the latter conflict. In the case of Tajikistan, despite a preference for the Islamic opposition, Iran has been unwilling to commit itself very far. Perhaps it was constrained by the lack of a contiguous border or by resource limitations. But its behavior was significant, because it does not appear that Iran will have as favorable an opportunity or terrain in another republic.

In general, the risk of Iran and Russia being sucked into opposite sides in a regional war appears remote. But the principal uncertainty in this would be the state of politics in Moscow (and Tehran) rather than in the republics.

Generalized Instability   A breakdown of governments in the Caucasus could lead to intervention by Iran, Turkey, and Russia. The fear of *spillovers* from these sources of instability would be the principal concern.

Unravelling of Either Iran or Russia In such a context, the response of either government to what it might perceive as the others' intervention or encouragement of hostile forces could become more belligerent, leading to hostilities.

In general, conflict between Russia and Iran does not appear to rank high on the list of conflict scenarios for Iran. This may be due, in part, to the difficulty of predicting specific scenarios. What can be said, however, is that the principal uncertainty, besides inevitable change and instability in the Transcaucasus and Central Asia, is in Russia's future course. A need to find foreign enemies and threats and a fixation on Islam could lead to a deterioration of relations with Iran and even conflict. On the other hand, there is little reason to suppose that Iran is so anxious to promote change in its north that by intervention it would risk a deterioration of relations, let alone confrontation, with Russia. Iran sees its major future problems to be with the United States. Iran has every incentive to seek to maintain good ties with Moscow[12]; it has switched its air force to Soviet aircraft and will need Russia as a reliable source of supply in the future if it is to develop an air force worthy of the name.

Turkey

Iran has no territorial differences with Turkey and relations have been reasonably good if not particularly warm for most of the past century. The Cold War gave the two states a common interest vis-à-vis the Soviet Union and a common ally. The revolutionary government in Iran, however, came to look on Turkey as a potential U.S. stalking horse in the region and resented its move to secularism as a form of apostasy; in its extreme manifestations, this resentment took the form of propaganda attacks on Turkey and support for Islamic elements in that country. Turkey's neutrality in the first Gulf War and the passing of Iran's extreme ideological phase has seen the development of pragmatic relations between the two states. Since the second Gulf War the two countries have increased their consultations without dropping their mutual mistrust.

Iran has a healthy respect for Turkey's martial traditions and prowess and would not consider the country a likely pushover. Further Turkey has much improved its military equipment over the past decade and deployed a large section of its army to the provinces of the southeast to combat a Kurdish insurgency movement. In addition to its security relationship with the United States and the West, Turkey itself is a formidable force by local standards, surely a cautionary factor where Iran is concerned. Iran and Turkey came to an agreement in mid-1994 not to support or give shelter to each others' opponents. In effect this means that Iran will drop support for the militant and Marxist Kurdish Workers' Party (PKK), while Turkey will restrict the activities of the Mujahideen. Iran and Turkey do not have any direct dispute, which makes a confrontation between these two states unlikely. They have a common interest with Syria in seeing a settlement of the Kurdish question in Iraq in a way that does not exacerbate their own problems with Kurdish populations or increase pressure for an independent Kurdish state. Second, on a different level, Iran is under no illusions that it has any influence with Turkey's 'Alavi Muslims who, though akin to the Shiites, are not comparable to their Iranian counterparts.

How might this relatively stable relationship change and cause conflict between Iran and Turkey? The most direct threat to each state appears to have been regulated by the accord on the PKK and Mojahedin.

But another category of potential conflict arises from Iranian-Turkish competition for influence in the Transcaucasus, especially in Azerbaijan. There Turkish support for Azeri unification and independence (united and free) would constitute de facto support for secession from Iran and thus constitute a threat to Iran's territorial integrity. Iran has links with the Azeris, and both are Shiite. The Azeris, however, are closer to the Turks ethnically (they share a common language), but share cultural ties with both neighbors. If this delicate balance were upset by either side, conflict could result. Iranian-Turkish competition elsewhere in the north is also possible, animated by the search for allies and influence and leverage over the other. Here as with Russia, there is a risk of competitive interventions on opposite sides of local quarrels, of spillovers, and of being drawn into opposite sides of wars. These risks would be increased if Turkey becomes more aggressively pan-Turkic, perhaps as a result of setbacks in relations with the West or due to domestic pressures.[13]

There are other scenarios for Turkish-Iranian conflicts. If either Turkey or Iran were to improve relations with Russia to the other's disadvantage, suspicions would increase, making for more strenuous competition and an increased probability of conflict. Greater tensions between Iran and the United States, with Turkey clearly on the latter's side, especially if it were included in military activity (as in Desert Storm), might see clashes between Iran and Turkey. In general though, despite the different "models" the two countries are said to represent, the most likely area of conflict is in the north, where rules have not yet been worked out and where indigenous instability and the risk of miscalculation could be said to be greatest.

Iraq

Contrary to contemporary conventional wisdom, Iraq is not Iran's traditional nemesis. It has, however, been a problem for Iran since Iraq chose an exaggerated form of Arab Nationalism that at once subjugates its own Shiite citizens and propels it into attempts at regional leadership. Since the second Gulf War, Iraq appears as a threat more for its weakness than for its potential strength, though this may prove transitory. Iraq may still emerge phoenix-like from the ashes for a third attempt at regional military hegemony.

Iran has no territorial claims on Iraq and little sympathy for its rulers. Iranian leaders have expressed a preference for a popular government in that country but have indicated a willingness to accept the existing regime if it survives. While Iran would like to increase its influence in Iraq, the only Arab country where a majority of the population is Shiite and also where important Shiite shrines are located, the first Gulf War laid to rest the idea that sectarian affiliations were stronger than those of culture and ethnicity. With the evaporation of any idea of unity, Iran would gladly settle for a friendly Iraq. Since the spring of 1991 and thereafter, Iran's efforts in Iraq can only be called desultory. However, Iraq's future is uncertain, and the range of possible sources of conflict between two neighbors, which have fought a long and bitter war and continue to interact intimately on a number of levels, is correspondingly large.

We can note three political scenarios for Iraq and examine their likely effects on conflict: a weakened, if not chastened, Baathist Iraq equals more of the same; a disintegrating Iraq, a free-for-all; an Iraq under new management, revanchist or reformed?

A Continuation of Iraq This is not totally unwelcome to Iran. True, as long as Saddam Hussein is around there are bound to be crises, and some may get out of control as with the near miss in October 1994. Furthermore Saddam's political survival and the resultant uncertainty provides the United States with an excuse for remaining in the vicinity of the Persian Gulf. But against this there are benefits: Iraq, isolated and economically weak, is unable to rearm; its absence from Persian Gulf politics has increased Iran's weight in the region; and as long as Iraq is unable to export oil it leaves other exporters like Iran with a larger and much-needed export quota, which will have to be reduced when Iraq re-enters the oil market.[14]

On the negative side, the continuation of Iraq's present uncertainty tends to increase political jockeying for power in the region. Iran is concerned lest the U.N.-sponsored enclaves or safe-zones in the north and south become the kernels of new states. Iran is especially worried by the possibility that this would set a precedent for U.S.-led interventions and the dismemberment of states. The possibility of a Kurdish state emerging from the current turmoil in Iraq is also worrisome. To avoid conflict and to harmonize their approaches, Iran, Turkey, and Syria have stepped up their consultations. At the same time the various Iraqi opposition forces have coordinated their activities so that Kurdish, Shiite, and secular forces are at least in broad agreement.

A Disintegrating Iraq If Iraqi disintegration were to be a slow-motion affair, it would heighten the risks of competitive intervention by Iran and Turkey and hence increase the risk of war between these two states. Saudi concerns might also cause pressure for U.S. intervention. In this scenario, the central government's failure might lead to the effective autonomy of parts of the country in the north and southeast in particular. Today's coordination and consultations would appear to be intended to reduce the risks of this happening. In general, Iran is unlikely to be keen on annexing parts of Iraq or seeing others do so. Given the risks of such an act, in terms of international reaction and relations with the Arab states, as well as the practical difficulties of absorption, it does not appear likely. However, if the Kurds were to uncharacteristically unite and press for self-determination or even statehood, the impact on Iran's Kurds, especially the dissident group fighting Tehran and stationed in Iraq, would be serious.

Revived Iraq on the Rampage A nationalist successor to Saddam Hussein might not only bring Iraq out of its isolation but also set about rectifying past wrongs, real and imagined. Foremost among these, after the reassertion of the central government's authority, might be an attempt to improve its access to the Persian Gulf and an attempt to settle old scores with its neighbors, starting with the smallest. Such a regime might seek to revive Iraq's weapons programs, assuming that the skilled manpower was still available. An alternative and more subtle approach for Saddam's successors might be to ingratiate themselves with the other Arab states by offering Iraq as a counterweight to Iran. It could ask in chastened terms to join the GCC and acknowledge Saudi Arabia in particular as a regional power. Such a regime might be more focused on avenging itself on Iran than on its immediate Arab neighbors. Depending on its composition, it might continue the repression of Shiites internally while confronting Iran regionally.

Another possibility is an Iraqi regime that works with Iran against the West and its regional allies. This alliance might look to and find Yemen a ready partner and in combination they could easily dominate the Persian Gulf-Arabian peninsula. I have emphasized Iraqi initiatives, because I do not believe that Iran is bent on revenge for the Iraqi attack in 1980. Indeed, Iran since mid-1994 has called for the lifting of the sanctions on Iraq and its reintegration into the region.[15] There are admittedly several unresolved issues, such as the prisoner of war (POW) question, and from the Iranian view, the question of reparations is still outstanding. Border clashes could become possible in areas where claims overlap or have not been definitively demarcated. The status of the Shatt al Arab still awaits definitive and formal legal regulation. The situation in the Shatt al Arab remains ambiguous, and the status of Umm Qasr tentative, for in the absence of significant trade a *modus vivendi* on the waterway between Iraq and Iran is not really tested. None of these issues is the stuff of wars unless the relations between the two regimes are otherwise conflictual. In light of Iraq's weakness for the immediate future and Iran's military build-up, the possibility of war between these two states is not very high in the short to medium term (15 years). After that, if the current Iraqi regime lasts and retains some of its capabilities in the area of weapons of mass destruction, it may seek seeks vengeance against Kuwait or Iran; this possibility must be considered by both states.

Iran and the Persian Gulf States

Iran faces no threat from the Persian Gulf states and has no significant active claims against those states. Plausible scenarios that might give rise to tensions are plentiful, but given the nature of external powers' interests and recently affirmed commitments, the likelihood of conflict is harder to visualize. However, precisely because this region has seen considerable turmoil in the space of little more than a decade, witnessing a major revolution, two wars, and foreign interventions, there is no reason to suspect that it will be insulated from further instability in the coming decade. It is most unlikely that, absent Iraq, the Arab states of the Persian Gulf will pose a threat to, or attack, Iran. But they may well act in a manner considered provocative by Iran and cause it to seek a reversal or to do them harm.

We can categorize the provocative types of behavior thus:

- Seeking a qualitative edge on the grounds that they need access to superior arms to offset Iran's manpower superiority (and by systematically exaggerating Iran's threat to keep the Western powers involved).

- Intensifying their arms and security relationship with the United States, which impinges on Iran's security when this results in a conspicuous and inhibiting U.S. military presence in the region.
- Seeking to conclude an Arab-U.S. defense arrangement ostensibly intended to contribute to regional security but in actuality to exclude Iran and block a regional arrangement. This type of deliberate polarization will exacerbate Iran's sense of encirclement.
- The deliberate playing of the Arab nationalist card regionally, perhaps by seeking to regain territory claimed to belong to the Arabs. Arab regimes, like Iraq, have shown themselves quite capable of playing foreign policy for domestic purposes. Saudi Arabia, too, has used or manipulated this area to strengthen its claims to leadership of the Arabian peninsula. Periodic cries about Arab islands and Arab land play well domestically and may become "real," that is, imagined rather than fictional irredenta. There is scope for miscalculation here. So too is there room for misjudgment of foreign support. As Russia becomes more involved in Persian Gulf politics and with U.S. backing assured, the Arab states may take this reassurance as license.

What of the Iranian threat to the Persian Gulf? Iran's current arms buildup cannot be sustained for very long, and it reflects little more than the goal to restore at least on paper its military power eroded over the past decade and a half. It does not necessarily reflect a decision to use this power coercively. The Iran-Iraq War showed the limited value of the use of coercive force, and the second Gulf War demonstrated the high costs awaiting an aggressor. Iran has always taken a proprietary attitude toward the Persian Gulf; this is an outgrowth of geopolitics as much as ideology. But it is also a reminder that Tehran is sensitive about the U.S. presence, the Arab military build-up, and loose and provocative talk about the security of the region being exclusively an Arab affair.

Scenarios involving the use of force could include:

- **A resource grab.** This would involve essentially a rerun of Iraq-Kuwait, with a desperate and poor Iran seeking to compensate for domestic economic failure by diverting energy abroad to pick up new resources. A variant might be to use intimidation against one state, like Qatar, to obtain access to its gas resources. This scenario is not impossible but is not likely either.
- Miscalculation and escalation from thwarted ambitions and frustration. The Abu Musa affair of 1992[16] is still shrouded in sea mist, but at the least it was a probe by Iran to broaden its *de facto* authority on an island whose sovereignty is still contested with Sharjah. Was Iran

seeking to test the limits of the Arabs' solidarity? Was it seeking to encroach on Sharjah's claim to sovereignty incrementally without giving it enough cause to react? Was it Tehran's attempt to use the diversion of Iraq to remind the Gulf states quietly that it was a factor in Persian Gulf politics? Probably all of the above. The episode demonstrated Tehran's capacity for miscalculation of the Arab response. The furor created by the Arabs in the GCC and the Arab League also showed the degree to which such probes could be used tactically by the Arabs to cement their relationship with the West. It also demonstrated Arab sensitivity not to repeat their failure in the Kuwait crisis to raise the alarm early, before a major crisis erupted.[17]

Miscalculation all around suggests that in crises actions are not very predictable. On the other hand, the divide between Arab and Persian in the Persian Gulf has been clearly delineated over the past decade and is hardly ambiguous. This makes the next two types of scenarios less likely than they were in the 1970s and early 1980s.

- **Iranian support for one side in an intra-Arab dispute.** Iran might back, say, Qatar against Saudi Arabia in a territorial dispute. Such backing is, however, unlikely to take a military form.

- **Iranian support for Shi'i or people of Iranian ancestry.** The mistreatment of such populations in one of the Arab states would be a key criteria. Such discrimination and harsh treatment is commonplace in Kuwait and Saudi Arabia, but in the latter perhaps rather less so than before. This scenario would not likely lead to a military conflict, but more probably one in which, at most, Iran would act as a protector and use its diplomatic influence.

- **Support for subversive forces.** This could be an issue on the Arabian peninsula, perhaps with a coup in Saudi Arabia. The *advantages* of undertaking low-level threats against the Arab states may be obvious: they are reminders of Iran's presence; they are deniable; and they might have major strategic results leading to regimes that are more revolutionary or at least anti-Western. The *disadvantages* are: such support might be revealed with costly consequences, such as a Western military reaction; the results might rebound in unexpected ways; adverse repercussions for future relations with Saudi Arabia could impair cooperation in OPEC.

This last scenario, Iran using its power to intimidate its neighbors, if only to ensure that its interests are taken into account, cannot be discounted. From the perspective of the Islamic republic, the threat posed to it by the United States through the local states is not something that can be ignored. At the least, the U.S. military presence is a potential threat. On a daily basis, it acts to inhibit Iran's diplomacy in the region, which is what it is designed to do. It certainly makes the Arab Persian Gulf states more resistant to Iran's overtures. This type of containment adds to Tehran's frustration. It may be an additional reason for looking at nuclear weapons.[18] In the meantime Iran's interests would be best served by good relations with the Arab states.

Conclusion

Iran is not presently threatened militarily on any of its borders by any particular state. The risk of interstate war occurring as a result of a deliberate decision by one of its neighbors, as in September 1980 or August 1990, or by a decision by Iranian authorities appears remote. However, its northern, western, and eastern border regions are scenes of turmoil and local war that could affect Iran. With change repressed so long in the Caucasus, the energy spilling out now promises a prolonged era of crises. To the West, Iraq is similarly unstable, and its territorial integrity and political future uncertain. Turkey appears a reasonably well-known quantity by comparison. So, too, does the Persian Gulf, which has the advantage of having had a shakeout in the crises of recent years; these crises should have reduced the scope for miscalculation. But in a region where domestic politics are notoriously ethnocentric and volatile, and where they dictate foreign policy with few buffers or correctives to make them more realistic and less obtuse, this is no consolation. Wars may occur less from design or rational decision than from organizational or cognitive failures. This is not to argue that the area is noticeably steeped in rationality, but to suggest that the overwhelming lesson of recent years is the risk run by states seeking to extend themselves by military force. Decisions to run the risk, like Saddam Hussein's various actions, cannot be discounted. In general, though, the Iranian regime is more risk-averse and more indirect. War is more likely to occur for reasons stemming from mistakes deriving from the general turmoil than from deliberate calculation.

In light of the considerable concern regarding Iran's military programs shown by many regional states including the Gulf states, Israel, and the United States, it is important to situate Iran in its strategic environment and context. This provides a proper perspective on the subject. Iran is located at a point where the Soviet empire has disintegrated, where states are unravelling and where conflict among overlapping ethnic groups (Azeris, Tajiks, Baluchis, Kurds) could spillover to several states. Assessments of Iran's policies that do not take into account these pressures will tend to overestimate both its capacity in terms of resources and energy and its interest in revisionism and upsetting the status quo.

Notes

1. Address of Ayatollah Ali Khamenei, leader of the Islamic revolution to the Islamic Guards Corps, Tehran, Voice of the IRI, 16 January in FBIS-NES 94-011, 18 January 1994, p.79.

2. See Shahram Chubin, *Iran's National Security Policy: Interests, Capabilities and Impact* (Washington, D.C.: Carnegie Endowment, 1994).

3. See Seth Carus, "Proliferation and Security in Southwest Asia," *Washington Quarterly* 17, no. 2 (spring 1994): 135.

4. The buildup will be limited by problems of supply, assimilation and force structure, vague doctrine, financial limitations, and political constraints.

5. This view is not uniquely that of the IRI; it is shared by Hamas and some of the Arab masses to a far greater extent than is admitted in Washington. See Robert Fisk, "Arabs Search for Honour in the Peace," *The Independent on Sunday*, 23 October 1994, p. 11.

6. See Geoffrey Kemp, *Forever Enemies: American Policy and the Islamic Republic of Iran* (Washington, D.C.: Carnegie Endowment, 1994).

7. See Islamic Republic News Agency (IRNA) reported by Tehran radio 1 October in ME/2117 MED/5, 5 October 1994.

8. Ayatollah Ali Khamene'i, Voice of the IRI, Tehran, 12 October in ME/2126 MED/15, 14 October 1994.

9. President Hashemi Rafsanjani, Friday Sermon, Voice of IRI, 7 October in ME/2122 MED/2127 MED/17, 10 October 1994.

10. For instance, the 1,000-kilometer-range No-Dong from North Korea is due to be delivered to Tehran soon.

11. It is possible that Iran seeks the long-range No-Dong missile that reaches Israel to deter an Israeli strike against its industries or nuclear installations.

12. Iran is concerned, for example, that the United States's pressure on Russia does not lead to a diminution in the transfer of arms or prevent cooperation in the development of nuclear technology. The United States made clear that it was putting pressure on Russia during President Yeltsin's visit to Washington in September 1994 See "Not all is Changed," *The Economist*, 1 October 1994, 64.

13. See Graham Fuller and Ian Lesser, *Turkey's New Geopolitics: From the Balkans to Western China* (Boulder, Colo.: Westview, 1993).

14. This last issue will, of course, vary with the state of demand prevailing at the time; if demand increases the reabsorption of Iraq may be less problematic at least for Iran, for it is Saudi Arabia that has benefitted most from the Iraqi absence.

15. This was first expressed by the Foreign Minister Ali Akbar Velayati on a visit to Oman. See "Iran Urges End to Iraq Embargo," (A.P.) *International Herald Tribune*, 9 September 1994, p. 1. (For the Iraqi dynamics, see the chapter by Charles Tripp in this volume.)

16. See the accompanying chapter in this volume by Shaul Bakhash, "Alternative Futures for Iran: Implications for Regional Security."

17. See Shahram Chubin, "Regional Politics and the Conflict," in Alex Danchev and Dan Keohane, eds., *International Perspectives on the Gulf Conflict* (London: Macmillan, 1994), 1–22 (in association with St. Antony's College).

18. See Shahram Chubin, "Does Iran Want Nuclear Weapons?" *Survival* 37, no. 1 (spring 1995): 86–104.

6

THE FUTURE OF IRAQ AND OF REGIONAL SECURITY

Charles Tripp

Speculation about the future government of Iraq has tended to revolve around two axes, depending upon particular interpretations of Iraq's past. On the one hand, it is clear that neither the Baathist regime nor Saddam Hussein's ascendancy within it nor indeed the impulses to war and to rebellion that Iraq has witnessed in recent decades came out of nowhere. Each was to some extent the product of forces that had already been at work in Iraqi society, and consequently some account must be taken of the power of these same forces to continue to shape Iraqi regimes and their policies, possibly compounded by the events of the past few years. On the other hand, there are those who would argue that the impact of these very events and of the kind of regime that was responsible for them have caused Iraqis radically to rethink their future. In this view, a more pluralist, open Iraqi society could yet be created on the basis of the widespread disillusionment associated with a succession of authoritarian, nationalist regimes.

In some respects, these visions are strategic visions, connected as much with the promotion of a particular kind of future for Iraq as with disinterested speculation about that future. Saddam Hussein is trying to convince the Iraqis themselves—and perhaps certain outside powers—that, whatever their opinion of him and his clan, the uncertainties and the social disruption that would attend his overthrow would be far worse. For the opposition parties, the task is, of course, to persuade both the Iraqis and outside powers of the opposite. Domestically, the promise is that the overthrow of Saddam Hussein will open up the opportunity for a dramatic liberation of the Iraqi people from the various forms of oppression under that they have been suffering. As far as the outside powers are concerned, the Iraqi opposition is keen to persuade them that political change in Iraq is possible with a minimum of violence or social disruption and that the regime established on the ruins of Saddam Hussein's dictatorship will be a peaceful one, intent more on creating the conditions for internal freedoms than on foreign adventures.

There is, of course, no way of saying with certainty what Iraq will look like two, five, or ten years from now. However, it is worth thinking about the degree to which these two contrasting visions—each symptomatic of forces currently at work in Iraqi society—will have a decisive impact in the future. On the one hand, an effort should be made to understand the degree to which the vision of a strong, centralized, authoritarian state, based on a mixture of patrimonialism and coercion, presently articulated by Saddam Hussein and his supporters, may have a grip on the imaginations of those who are in a position to shape the future in Iraq. On the other hand, the social weight of the alternatives to such a vision should be assessed in order to understand whether a very different principle of power can in fact be instituted in Iraq and can be expected to last in the teeth of the opposition that any radical departure is likely to provoke in various sectors of society and state.

In the specific context of regional security, the questions to be asked concern the degree to which such changes as have taken place or might yet take place in Iraqi political society may be associated with changing perceptions of Iraq's neighbors. The danger here is that, precisely because of the dire record of the present regime in Iraq, the belief will grow that any future government will conduct itself in a way that is diametrically opposed to the adventurist and violent policies of Saddam Hussein. To temper this tendency, some effort should be made to understand the degree to which similar impulses—if not necessarily identical reactions—will run through any government of Iraq that wishes to retain sufficient domestic authority to govern the country.

To examine these questions, it is necessary first to look at the foundations and the potential of the forms of power in Iraq. Such an examination aims to determine the most likely general form of the future government of Iraq, which must use the social and the cognitive "material" of Iraqi political society to remain in power, allied to the resources of the state itself. Second, it is necessary to assess the implications of these possible outcomes as far as the neighbors of Iraq are concerned. In particular, an examination of the link between Iraq's geostrategic "givens" and the condition of its political society is necessary to understand the very specific forms of mutual interaction between domestic and regional politics that may characterize Iraq's relations with it neighbors.

Foundations and Possibilities of the Forms of Power in Iraq

Perhaps the best way to start thinking about the nature of power in Iraq and the relevant divisions of its political society is with the idea of the "community of trust"—that is, the group of people who have sufficient trust in one another to act collectively as a political unit. Often linked to or associated with a dominant leader, the community of trust is a structure closely intertwined with the processes of patrimonialism, whereby both patron and clients sustain each other in some—if not in equal—measure. It does not imply that this trust will be unquestioning or absolute; there have been too many cases in Iraqi history of close associates falling out and coming into severe conflict with one another. Nor does it mean that the individuals concerned may not have potentially conflicting ambitions. Rather, it should be seen as delineating those who are more likely than not to cooperate on some of the fundamental questions of Iraqi politics and public life. In addition, the term refers to the unquantifiable ties that often bind the followers or clients to the patrimonial leader, supplementing the more material rewards that they derive from association with a powerful individual.

In Iraq, these groups have almost overwhelmingly been based on kinship ties, either in the form of imagined common tribal ancestry or in the more immediately identifiable form of membership in the extended family. Given the pattern of Iraqi social development, this form has also been reinforced by common origins in the sense of geographical locality and, to some extent, socioeconomic position, often supplemented in both cases by common ethnic or sectarian identities.[1] It has been common knowledge that the present regime of Saddam Hussein has been heavily weighted in favor of his immediate and distant relatives in the inner circles of power. Just as the key elements of the coercive apparatus at his command—the Special Forces, the Presidential Guard, and the two key divisions of the Republican Guard—are largely recruited from his tribal-regional homeland. This does not mean that all the people favored by Saddam Hussein come from this background; rather, it means that those who are placed in positions that give them a degree of unsupervised power have been largely from this "community." It is a community defined by the leader and maintained by him, but its origins lie in the roots of Iraqi society. Equally, as the crises besetting Iraq have built up, this community consists of people so closely identified with Saddam Hussein that he can have some confidence that their fear that they may share his fate gives them a strong incentive to work to preserve his rule.

Even a cursory glance at Iraqi political history will make it clear that such an organization of power has been visible, in one form or another, since the foundation of the state. For much of the time, indeed, it could be said to have been the prevalent mode of organizing power, regardless of the fact that a growing number of Iraqis regarded such forms with increasing distaste. During the last decades of the monarchy, there were those who hoped that a genuinely new beginning might be possible, based on the ideologies and the new forms of association that had emerged under the rather tolerant authoritarianism of the Hashemite dynasty. Disillusionment followed the overthrow of the monarchy in 1958. With the revolution of that year and the series of fierce and bloody conflicts between the various members of the antimonarchical alliance in the years that followed, it became abundantly clear that the universalist forms of identity associated with various political parties had little grip on Iraqi society. Although each could boast its fierce adherents, neither communism nor Iraqi nationalism nor Arab nationalism nor Baathism was able to forge a community of trust based on ideas of common political identity and purpose sufficient to dominate Iraqi society and to create the institutions of a public state. Instead, the tried and tested forms of conspiracy among those who trusted one another implicitly, largely because of common background, led to the overthrow of regimes, the splitting of political parties, and the bypassing, or simple suspension, of state institutions.[2]

Under the Aref brothers, and then under the leadership of the men from the Takrit district, or more accurately from the Al Bu Nasir, the governance of Iraq passed into the hands of patrimonial leaders who, nevertheless, saw some utility in maintaining a facade of ideological conviction. Some Iraqis took the ideals of Baathism seriously. The vast majority, however, saw it simply as a new language that had to be learned in order to get ahead. By and large, the latter have proved to be the survivors, the ideologues having been picked off in successive purges. The outcome of this process for the present organization and the potential organization of forms of power in Iraq has been manifold.

First, it is evident that the apparent public institutions of power are only as solid as their underlying social bonds of trust and patronage. Thus, it is not the formal institution that matters in the organization of power, but rather the informal networks underlying it. This is the way in which the power of the regime is organized, and it is also likely to shape, if not dictate, the patterns of opposition. In other words, successful, rather than merely principled, opposition will perforce have to adopt some of the characteristics of the regime if it is not to be dispersed at its first appearance. In some circumstances, this may mean the successful recruitment of members of Saddam Hussein's inner circle, or at least of those with access to that circle and to the person of Saddam Hussein himself.

Second, the logic of patrimonialism means, of course, that Saddam Hussein is the target. To break the networks of reward and punishment which sustain his regime, his elimination is required. This has a number of consequences that clearly affect the opposition, but may also affect the kind of regime that is likely to come to power in Iraq. The most obvious effect is to encourage the belief that with the removal of Saddam Hussein, the most important obstacle will have been removed from the path to the creation of whatever image of a future Iraqi political order various opposition parties hold. However, his centrality to the kind of the political order that his regime represents should not be exaggerated. There are many in socially, as well as politically, powerful positions in Iraq who may have no illusions about Saddam Hussein's competence or qualities, but who nevertheless would probably agree with him that his form of patrimonial, authoritarian rule is the kind the country in some way "needs."

This is particularly important in view of the role that violence must play in the installation of any new government in Iraq. The present regime has organized things in such a way that its removal can only be contemplated by those who are psychologically prepared and actually equipped to use considerable force. As the rebellions of March 1991 demonstrated, such force would have to be both better organized within the Iraqi military and less ethnically or communally specific than the Kurdish and Shiite uprisings. In other words, a substantial or a key part of the Iraqi officer corps and armed forces would have to be prepared not simply to remove Saddam Hussein, but also to take on in armed combat the forces that he has organized specifically to protect the regime. Thus, any opposition move to establish a new government in Iraq would only be able to come to power owing a considerable debt to the members of the officer corps whose assistance will be fundamental to the undertaking.

It is clearly impossible to say what the precise motivations, or indeed the political views, of these officers would be. Nevertheless, it is in the nature of the Iraqi officer corps, and indeed of Iraqi political society, that any successful coup would have to be organized by a community of trust or communities of trust, as outlined above. That is, conspiracy on this scale could only succeed where two conditions are met. First, the conspirators must be linked to each other in some way that encourages the implicit belief that they would not be betrayed. Second, they must believe that the future political order for which they would be clearing the way would not place in jeopardy the interests of that community of trust, its identity, or its social allies. This does not mean necessarily that the conspirators would share any particular identity, although the part that would be played by Sunni Arab officers in any such coup would undoubtedly be decisive. Rather, it means that, given the present structure and attitudes of the officer corps, two particular features would almost certainly be visible: clannishness and self-righteousness.

The decisive structural feature would be the clannish nature of the heart of any conspiracy, quite possibly bringing together both Sunni and Shiite officers from significant military clans. Given the alternative focus of the Kurdish zone and the difficulties faced by Kurdish officers in the Iraqi armed forces, these conspirators are more likely to be Arab than Kurdish. It is probable that such officers would share a sense of Iraqi nationalism, as defined by the dominant Arab sector of the population. It is equally probable that they would share, in some measure, a feeling of the appropriateness of the way in which they had operated, reinforcing the patrimonial and particularistic logic of the community of trust. The concept of *al-Intisab*, with all its many overtones in an Iraqi context, would be something that such officers could share and that would, in large measure, shape their view about the proper handling of power.[3] It is against this background that one should realistically expect any future government of Iraq to be formed. The problem of the prominence of the officer corps in determining the success of any group or coalition that wishes to constitute itself as the future government of Iraq is likely to show itself in a number of ways.

First, the Iraqi officer corps has been deeply implicated in the adventurism and the repression associated with this regime. Clearly, many of its members have also become disillusioned with the competence and wisdom of Saddam Hussein and some have defected to the opposition or have sought to kill him. The fact remains, however, that the bulk of the officer corps has remained loyal, even at the most critical moment of the regime's existence, following the defeat in Kuwait, regardless of ethnic, regional, or sectarian background.

Second, there is the question of status, in the sense of the status of the officer corps in the future of Iraq and also in the sense of the status of the various informal groupings that link members of the officer corps to larger social formations, providing the recruiting ground and the political culture on which generations of Iraqi officers have drawn. In this respect, the problem for future Iraqi governments may lie in any determined attempt they might make to reinstate a clear political distinction between the civil and the military. Regardless of whether they will in fact do so, the opposition forces at present perceive themselves as determinedly civilian. Indeed, the great majority of them have made this commitment part of their public identity, which will evidently present something of a problem in the future.

Third, it seems almost certain that each opposition grouping will already have its own particular connections and objects of cultivation within the officer corps. The special relationships thus forged in opposition will be expected to bear fruit once a coup d'état has succeeded and a new government is formed. The question that will arise, once the fragile unanimity of opposition has broken down, will be whether the groups concerned can avoid the temptation of seeking to settle any argument by force, or by the threat of force, perhaps calling upon their officer allies once again. Given the past record of Iraqi governments and of countries where people have sought to make a similar transition, there is a very evident danger here of the reemergence of someone, or some group, able to command effective force and to use it in pursuit of a political vision.

Lastly, some account must be taken of the irregular forces at the disposal of various Iraqi opposition groups. These forces—most notably the Sadr Brigade of the Supreme Council for the Islamic Revolution in Iraq (SCIRI) and the substantial forces under the command of the Kurdish parties—are objects of suspicion, and will remain so, for the bulk of the Iraqi officer corps. Quite apart from their ideological or party-political affiliations, they represent a principle that conflicts with the status of the Iraqi armed forces as the monopolizers of the means of coercion in Iraq. Again, unless these forces are dispersed and lose their association with any particular political grouping, the suspicion will remain that they will be used as a form of militia to boost the political fortunes of their patrons. Not only would this alienate much of the Iraqi officer corps, as military men, but it also would tempt other political actors who have no such militias at their disposal to look for allies within the armed forces who might be able to neutralize such groups. This holds up the ominous prospect of a return to the early years of Iraqi independence, or of the unsettled period following the revolution of 1958.

This is the background of the potential, but also of the limitations, of the forms of power in Iraq. It is on these foundations and under these particular conditions that any future government must be constructed, and the dynamics at work are those that will, in general, shape both its future course and its survival. Given these conditions, it seems realistic to think of three possible forms of future government in Iraq. The first would be the result of a move from within the present structure of clannish military power to dispose of Saddam Hussein and to replace him with another member of the clan, one who is better able to convince the international community of the "normalization" of Iraq and to oversee its readmittance into the community of nations. The second would be the mobilization of other clans within the military apparatus that would work in combination to overthrow the rule of Saddam Hussein and the Al Bu Nasir clans, but keep the principle of patrimonial order and the existing hierarchies of privilege more or less intact. The third would be the result of an alliance between a combination of external opposition forces, such as the Iraqi National Congress (INC), and well-placed military commanders within Iraq, specifically intended to bring about a radically different kind of political order in Iraq, founded on the publicly declared principles of the opposition coalition.

There is also, of course, a fourth possibility: a period of bloody military civil war, as one aspiring group of conspirators takes on others who might be seeking to defend the present regime or to look after their own interests. Given the military infrastructure, this cannot be ruled out. However, it seems unlikely that such a period would last long, let alone that it would lead to the dismemberment of the state, as some have suggested. It is more probable that it would lead to some kind of temporary truce, as the various army factions come together to try to work out what would be in their best collective interest, even minimally defined.[4]

Precisely because it seems inevitable that any change of regime in Iraq must be brought about by conspiracy and by violent military action through the participation of a substantial part of the officer corps, there is little purpose in speculating further upon the exact personnel or identities of the officers concerned. Evidence of the kind that would make such speculation moderately plausible is simply unavailable. Instead, the three scenarios postulated above should, in general terms, frame the discussion of the nature of the future government of Iraq. It is in the light of these possibilities—and of the limitations of the kinds of political regime which might emerge—that some effort can be made to think of the implications of such developments both for the future of Iraq and for the kinds of relationships that can be expected to develop between Iraq and its neighbors.

Domestic Insecurities and Regional Relations

We remind [Iraq's enemies] that Iraq . . . will not be a laboratory for their evil experiments. It will not be another Lebanon.

—Republic of Iraq Radio, 22 March 1991

A common theme has emerged throughout Iraqi history, understandably, perhaps, in the light of the ways in that Iraq has been governed since its establishment, but disturbingly for Iraq's relations with neighboring states. This has been the sensed vulnerability of Iraqi political society to the machinations of Iraq's regional neighbors, working through groups in Iraqi society that are taken to be disaffected with the existing dispensation of power. The opportunism of their imagined relentless hostility to the existing political order is presumed to combine with the malign intentions of international forces, facing Iraqi governments in each decade with coalitions of internal and external enemies. Regardless of whether this has actually been the case, it has been the chief way in which domestic political opposition has been portrayed by the government of the day, either as part of a conscious strategy to discredit domestic opposition forces or because this is really the way in which the Iraqi government and those who rely upon it tend to regard the rest of Iraqi society and the world beyond the borders of Iraq.

In thinking about the security of Iraq, the rulers of the state have long had to face two central questions concerning the very existence of Iraq. These tend to emerge sharply in public debate or in the public discourse of the regime, whenever a crisis looms in domestic, as in regional, politics. The two questions are part of Iraq's historical-political legacy, as well as of its geopolitical situation. In the first place, there is the realization that Iraq is a new entity, created by the British Empire primarily to satisfy the needs of the empire. With the disappearance of that empire and thus the logic of its Middle Eastern policies, the permanence of its legacies in the region must clearly be called into question. The second question is a result of longer, but no less unsettling, historical forces and concerns Iraq's status as a "frontier state." As in all such frontier zones, identities have become blurred and do not conform to the neat lines of the frontiers of territorial states depicted on maps of the region. Thus, although Iraqi governments have sought to portray the state as guarding the frontier of the Arab world from the non-Arab peoples to the east, the situation of Iraqi society is more complex than that portrayal would suggest. It is true that Iraq's population is primarily Arabic speaking, but the Arabic speakers are divided, in sectarian terms, between Sunni and Shiite. The latter not only constitute the majority of the Arab population, but also share a nominal sectarian identity with the Persians to the east. Furthermore, in this frontier zone, 22 percent or so of the population of the state are Kurdish.

The results of these legacies have been visible throughout the twentieth-century existence of Iraq. In the first place, successive governments have sought to overcome this feeling of impermanence and uncertain identity through a strident brand of Iraqi nationalism, insisting on the glorious history of a five-thousand-year-old Iraqi nation. This course has been pursued with no less vigor by Iraqi governments, such as the present one, which have sought to portray themselves as the standard-bearers of Arab nationalism.[5] Equally, the lurking fear of social and political disintegration may well have contributed to the notorious violence of Iraqi political conflict. The present regime may have developed this aspect to a new degree of intensity, but Iraqi political history has always been dogged by violence born of insecurity, the roots of which lie in the belief that the future of the state may be at stake in any given political dispute.

Thus, crucial psychosocial insecurities feed into what might be called the situational or objective insecurities that derive from more conventional concerns regarding the vulnerability of the state's resources to regional disruption or exploitation. In the light of the three possible future regimes in Iraq, it is worth thinking about the ways in which these distinctive insecurities will affect them in turn. If Saddam Hussein's successor proves to be someone from his own clan, it would clearly be politic for the new government to proclaim amnesties, congresses of national reconciliation, dialogue with all Iraqis, and so forth. Not only would it give the government a certain breathing space before disillusionment sets in, but it would also be a signal to the international community that things have changed in Iraq and that sanctions, the debt, and the punitive reparations bills should no longer be imposed on the "reformed" government in Baghdad. Given Iraq's present plight and the motivation underlying any possible "insider" coup, the rehabilitation of Iraq in the international community would be a driving imperative.

However, an insider coup that keeps power firmly in the hands of the Al Bu Nasir or, at a stretch, in those of the clans of the Takrit region would obviously produce a regime that would have no desire to see the political order of Iraq changed in any substantial way. The people who might carry out such a coup and form the heart of the new government would, after all, have to act preemptively: they would have to take the risk of removing Saddam Hussein in the belief that the longer he stays at the helm, the greater the danger to the political order and privileges from which they have so substantially benefited. It would scarcely be their intention, therefore, to pave the way for a radical reconstruction of the political order of Iraq or of the socioeconomic order that has both sustained and been promoted by that dispensation of power. This does not necessarily rule out tactical concessions to various groups, if they were thought prudent for reasons of domestic or international acceptance. However, as with similar concessions made in the 1970s, the regime would be on the lookout for an opportunity to claw them back, and it would be fierce in refusing to yield anything that might permanently alter the balance of forces within Iraq.

Nor would the situation be very different if other military clans seize power on their own initiative. Although these clans are outside the immediate kinship structure that has sustained Saddam Hussein, they are nevertheless very much pillars of the social structure that has enabled him to rule Iraq. While it is true that at various times during the past twenty years, clans from the districts of al-Rawa, Sammarra, Mosul, and al-Dur have occasionally come under suspicion and have therefore fallen into disfavor, leading to the arrest and execution of some of the officers connected with them, the clannish structure as a whole has proved a major beneficiary of Saddam Hussein's rule. By all accounts, this has extended as well to members of the nominally Shiite clans of the middle and lower Euphrates and from the rural districts east of Baghdad. Consequently, it seems highly improbable that such men would make so dangerous a move as to conspire to overthrow Saddam Hussein unless they feel fairly confident that the kind of order they are aiming at would be sufficiently similar to that of the past twenty or so years as not to alarm—and to cause to resist—all the other military clans on which they might have to rely. In other words, the motivation for such men to destroy the present regime would have more to do with securing their own position of privilege than with opening up the country to radical new possibilities in its political and socioeconomic structures.

However, these other military clans too would probably consider it necessary and desirable to enter into dialogue with all the other factions of Iraqi society in the early months of the new regime. The purpose of such a dialogue, after all, would be not simply to impress upon the world community the reformed nature of power in Iraq, but also to gauge the strength and the intentions of these groups. The decisive moment would come when they would be called upon to yield power, or when one group or another would make significant reform of the political structure of the state a condition for continuing such a dialogue. It would be then that one would begin to see the true colors of the regime, in the kinds of alliances it would seek to make and the groups it would seek to patronize in order to outflank those whose demands it finds incompatible with its own vision of power. It is impossible to predict these developments in any detail. However, it seems fairly certain that—given the initial, and perhaps the ultimate, location of power in Iraq in the hands of the armed forces and security services—there will be an underlying concern to preserve the patrimonial system. This is the system with which they are familiar: they know how to operate it and, furthermore, it forms part of their moral universe. In general, the patrimonial system accords with their self-image and with their ideas about how people should conduct themselves and about the proper and honorable way of handling public affairs. When new principles are introduced, as were between 1958 and 1963, the armed forces and the security services can become dangerously insecure, and their reaction is likely to be violent. This will be one of the major obstacles that the third possible form of government would have to overcome.

Any government that comes in under the flag of some form of civilian coalition, such as the INC, would have had to rely upon connections and conspiracies within the officer corps.[6] Only such an organization of military force would be able to carry out the coup that would allow the return of the largely exiled public opposition figures to Baghdad. On their return, the difficulties they would face would be similar to those faced by other exile groups, able to take up office only with the assistance of the real power brokers. In other words, they would be uncertain of their own bases of support, and, given the legacy of the various regimes which have ruled Iraq, the methods of mobilizing and capitalizing upon such support as they might enjoy would not necessarily be clear or straightforward.

A coalition grouping, such as the INC, which nominally brings together parties, factions, and individuals of very diverse views and which is, in any case, unable to impose any kind of discipline on its members, would undoubtedly fall apart into its constituent elements once the task of overthrowing Saddam Hussein was achieved. As an expression of the plurality of views in Iraqi society, this disintegration would not necessarily be a bad thing in itself. In fact, it would be a necessary process of self-definition and political argument if Iraq is ever to achieve a more open political society. The danger would come from the context in which this process might be occurring. Some of the views cherished in exile (and no doubt within Iraq as well)—for a better Iraq, for a country that can escape from the legacies that have made the dictatorship of Saddam Hussein possible—will have radical implications for the reordering not simply of the formal political, institutional structure of the country, but also of the social and economic relationships that have, in the last analysis, determined where political power should lie in Iraq. These implications, whether secular or Islamic in inspiration, may alarm the power brokers in the army and among the sectors in society that have benefited from and wish to see a continuation of the largely patrimonial system of reward and privilege. Equally, some of these visions and plans for the future of Iraq may be mutually exclusive. The fear of exclusion may lead one faction or another to seek an alliance with those in the armed forces or security services who are troubled by the prospect of their own exclusion from the reward system of the Iraqi state. If the country is not to lapse into the factionalism and the violence of the years following the revolution of 1958, both the army officer corps and the leaders of the various political parties and factions will have to demonstrate a good deal more self-discipline and self-restraint than they did at that time.

The most obvious fear under the present regime has been the degree to which Iran might seek to exploit sectarian disaffection among the Shiite population of Iraq. During the past fifteen years, communal resentments have been voiced in the numerous Islamic protest groups that have found fertile ground among the Shiites, playing as much on their social and political grievances as on their sectarian complaints. In fact, there has never been a single Shiite "community" in Iraq in a political sense; rather, there have been different groups and categories and communities among the Shiites.[7] This is scarcely surprising, given the different histories and socioeconomic experiences of the large numbers of Shiites who constitute 50 percent or so of Iraq's inhabitants.

A regime that comes out of the present dispensation and that shares many of the prejudices and personnel of the present regime would clearly find it difficult to give any ground to organizations such as SCIRI or Al-Da'wa. In response to international sensitivity, the active military campaign against alleged "agents" of these organizations in the southern marshes would be discontinued. But there are other, more discreet and probably more effective, ways of both guarding against the possibility of an insurrection instigated by Al-Da'wa and ensuring the security of the frontier with Iran.

A broadly similar logic would apply to the second possibility: a successor government formed by rival military clans to those of the present dispensation. Whether exclusively Sunni Arab or as a coalition of Sunni and Shiite Arab officers, such a government might initially declare an amnesty and might grant certain basic freedoms. However, this would depend upon the degree to which SCIRI, Al-Da'wa, and other organizations seek seriously to implement their programs of transforming the Iraqi state into an Islamic republic of some kind—or upon the degree to which it is feared in many sections of the population that this is what they are trying to do. In these circumstances, the old mistrust of these organizations' loyalty to the Iraqi state and the suspicion that Iran is working through them to weaken Iraq would almost certainly resurface.

In some respects, this is the specter that hangs over the future of these organizations, even in the third possible scenario, of a government initially formed by a coalition of forces, such as those that presently constitute the INC. The main Shiite-based organizations, SCIRI and Al-Da'wa, are both nominally members of the INC. In this capacity, it is clear that there has been a conscious effort in both organizations—but with more conviction in Al-Da'wa than in SCIRI—to reassure their Iraqi allies that they are not agents of the Iranian government.

Should some form of varied, INC-style coalition government come to power, there will be a limit to the extent to which SCIRI or Al-Da'wa would be able to submerge their own programs and priorities in the coalition. If nothing else, SCIRI's and Al-Da'wa's own constituencies—should they be able to mobilize them openly—will begin to demand a distinctive Islamicist thrust to the policies of organizations that have staked their claim to a distinct identity on that basis. In this respect, there is also a danger that this fragmentation and the fragmentation of the former INC will be reflected in the pattern of military politics in Iraq.

Precisely because of the fears of radical restructuring, this would contribute to the reassertion of the control of the military clans and their various allies, all of whom might be terrified by the prospect of Islamic government and of the leverage this would be expected to give Iran over Iraq.

The same anxieties can be seen to apply in relation to the Kurdish populations of the north. The notorious *anfal* of 1988 to 1989 was an example of how the Iraqi government believed that the Kurdish threat could be neutralized: communities were uprooted and destroyed in an effort to isolate Kurdish areas from contact with Iran, and a systematic purge was carried out within Kurdistan to destroy the Kurdish nationalist forces.

It is difficult to envisage any Iraqi regime that has formed itself out of the remnants of the present ruling elite agreeing to measures that would place the oil wealth and the coercive control of Iraqi Kurdistan exclusively in the hands of an autonomous Kurdish leadership. It is clear from the record of the 1970s that a regime such as this might be able to grant a measure of symbolic autonomy to the Kurds, but it would rather go to war than allow the Kurds genuine political or economic autonomy. This seems to be a feature common to any regime dominated by the Arab tribes and networks of military-patrimonial rule. They might not have any ideological objection to expressions of Kurdish cultural identity, but they are highly intolerant of any attempt by the Kurdish nationalist parties to establish their independence.

The public aspiration of the Kurdish Front is that the future government of Iraq should take the form of the third option outlined above. That is, the hope exists that some coalition, such as the INC (of which the Kurdish Front is a member and for which the Kurdish leadership has provided a base in the Kurdish zone of Iraq), will come to power in Baghdad, pledged to oversee the transformation of Iraq into a democratic, federal state. In such a framework, it is believed, the demands of the Kurds would be easily accommodated and the aspirations for real autonomy could be realized.[8] This might well be the case. However, as has been indicated above, the problem lies not in articulating such a possible future for Iraq but in making it come about.

The problem lies in the fact that the very nature of the federal, democratic regime demanded by the Kurdish Front represents precisely the kind of radical transformation of both the formal and the informal structures of Iraqi political society that will provoke formidable opposition. While one can imagine that opposition to Kurdish autonomy will have one focus in the (overwhelmingly non-Kurdish) officer corps of the Iraqi armed forces, there may be many others who might be truly alarmed by the notion. This brings with it the danger of a lapse back into the cycles of military intervention and clannish, conspiratorial politics.

As far as the leaders of the Kurdish Front are concerned, they are faced by a series of unenviable choices. They can press home their demands for full autonomy with such single-mindedness that they provoke substantial opposition in Baghdad. Alternatively, they can back-pedal on those demands, in the hope that this will not panic the new and possibly fragile coalition in Baghdad. However, this will cause them considerable difficulties in their own constituencies. Should they prove unable to influence the shape of government in Baghdad (which is highly likely), they can only take defensive measures similar to those that have served them in the past: they can negotiate tactical deals with the Baghdad government in the hope of buying time and in the hope that a new and more amenable governing coalition might come to power through conspiracy; they can play a part in such conspiracies, precisely to keep the government of Baghdad off balance, in the hope of preventing the emergence of a second Saddam Hussein; and there are the twin possibilities of appealing to outside protection and mobilizing military forces to establish de facto autonomy.

While attention has focused on the plight of the Shiites and the Kurds and their suspected disloyalty to the central government of Iraq, it should also be noted that both under this government and under previous governments, the regional loyalties of much of the Sunni Arab section of the population has also come under suspicion. The dominant fear in this regard appears to have been—and still to be—that those who espouse an Arab nationalist creed might start looking for their inspiration beyond the borders of Iraq itself and thus become agents of the enemies of the Iraqi government in the Arab world. Throughout the 1960s, the suspicion fell on those who looked to Nasser and to Egypt for leadership, rather than to the government in Baghdad. Under the present, nominally Baathist regime, the fear has been that the Syrian Baath might find among disaffected members of the Iraqi Baath party willing accomplices for President Assad's regional ambitions. This has led to occasional, often ferocious purges of the Iraqi Baath and has contributed to the enduring hostility between the Baathist regimes of Baghdad and Damascus. In the light of the events of 1990 to 1991, the influence of Saudi Arabia may also play a part—real or imagined—in shaping the loyalties of members of the Iraqi officer corps.

For any Iraqi government, including the present one, that rules dictatorially, domestic insecurities will be reflected in and will contribute to regional insecurities. In some sections of the population, such as the Shiites and the Kurds, whose members are excluded in large measure from the most powerful positions in the state, the suspicion is that a collective ideal (sectarian, Islamicist, or Kurdish nationalist) may begin to work among them, transforming them into a fifth column at the service of Iraq's regional enemies. However, even where such a collective hostility cannot be assumed to exist—as among the clans of the Sunni Arab population, for example—the fear is that disaffection may lead to conspiracy with Iraq's regional enemies, not necessarily for idealistic reasons, but purely out of opportunism. Thus, disillusioned Baathists are assumed to be working hand in hand with the Syrian government, and disgruntled military officers and others are seen to be sponsored by Saudi Arabia. In regimes such as the present one, which are composed of a self-selected elite, often linked by kinship ties, all other Iraqis are in some senses "outsiders" and all are, therefore, potential collaborators with the regime's many regional enemies, imagined or real.

Geostrategic Situation and Regional Vulnerabilities

At the same time, in addition to these "subjective" security fears, there are a number of what might be called "situational" or "objective" security concerns, stemming from Iraq's geographical situation. Regardless of the regime in power in Iraq, one glance at the map will make it clear that Iraq is heavily dependent upon the goodwill of its neighbors for its economic and strategic security. It is a virtually landlocked state, and its only access to the sea, at the head of the Persian Gulf, depends upon the cooperation of Iran on one side and of Kuwait on the other. In addition, the Tigris and the Euphrates, the two great rivers that run through Iraq and that lie at the heart of the successive civilizations of Mesopotamia, have their origins outside the borders of Iraq, in Turkey and Iran, respectively. Furthermore, Iraq's enormous natural wealth of oil is only realizable if it can be exported from the country. For Iraq to do so in substantial quantities, the oil must pass either through the sole Iraqi sea outlet, at al-Faw, or through pipelines across Turkey, Syria, or Saudi Arabia.

Just as in any territorial state, regardless of the form of its government or the particular array of regional allies or enemies at any particular time, there are certain fears in Iraq concerning the state's situational vulnerability in the region. These fears appear to revolve around four main themes: the defensibility of frontiers, access to the sea, vulnerability of oil resources, and water shortages. All of these fears may be connected with the vulnerabilities outlined in the preceding section, and they are exacerbated by the legacy of Iraq as an imperial creation, where boundaries were drawn that may be regarded now as somehow unfair or unacceptable. Consequently, although the handling of the issues that might arise from these fears may be associated with the style and insecurities of a particular government of Iraq, the concerns from which they arise would be of central importance to any government of the Iraqi state.

Concern about the defensibility of the frontiers of Iraq has taken two particular forms. The first, mentioned in the foregoing section, has to do with the permeability of those frontiers to regional forces seeking to encourage disaffection and rebellion within Iraq. Thus, the mountains of Kurdistan and the marshes of the south have been seen by successive Iraqi governments as areas that are difficult for the central authorities to control and that are also permeable to infiltration from Iran and from Turkey. The anfal in Kurdistan of 1988 to 1989 was in part aimed at bringing the area back under the control of the central government. Equally, the present operations aimed at draining the marshes and destroying them as potential refuges for opponents of the government are intended to "seal" that particular border.[9]

The second concern about the defensibility of borders has more to do with conventional military operations. In this regard, the vulnerability of the narrowing south of Iraq, in which Basra is situated, is considerably greater than that of Baghdad. Nevertheless, as became apparent during the war with Iran, the awareness of the country's relative lack of strategic depth and the fear of the demographic and military weight of Iran were powerful incentives to devise other means of the defense. It seems almost certain that it was with this context in mind that the Iraqi government began to develop its programs for the production of weapons of mass destruction. The development of missile technology and the development of chemical, biological, and nuclear weapons were not perhaps primarily expressions of a single Iraqi leader's ambition; rather, they may have grown out of the insecurity of the Iraqi leadership as a whole when contemplating its "frontier" location. There is good reason to suppose that this is a factor that will shape successive Iraqi governments' security concerns well into the future, regardless of the form of the regime.

Related to these concerns about the vulnerability of Iraq's frontiers is the concern about its lines of communication and trade with the outside world. In this respect, there is a commonly voiced complaint in Iraq that its frontiers were deliberately drawn by the British to ensure the weakness and vulnerability of Iraq, particularly in regard to access to the sea. The strength of feeling behind this and the insecurities to which it has given rise have been all too evident both in the conflict with Iran over the Shatt al-Arab and with Kuwait over access to the port of Umm Qasr. In the latter case, of course, it became conflated with the claim to Kuwait itself as a "natural" part of Iraq, "unnaturally" split off from the motherland by the stratagems of the British imperialists.[10] Again, these are complaints and claims that have been associated with Iraqi governments since the establishment of the state itself (needless to say, not much has been heard from the same sources about the possible revision of the border demarcation that included Kirkuk in Iraqi territory), and they are likely to continue to be of relevance to Iraq's regional relationships.[11]

In part, the fear of the Iraqi government (now realized and enforced by the U.N. embargo) is that Iraq will be prevented from exporting oil, because its relatively limited access to the sea will make it dependent upon those countries through which Iraqi oil must transit by way of pipelines. The vulnerability of oil pipelines to hostile regional states has been amply demonstrated, and, despite diversification of routes for the export of oil, the concern will remain. However, there is another concern that clearly animated the Iraqi government before August 1990 and that is likely to do so again, once Iraqi oil comes onto the market. This involves not the physical security of the oil itself, but the security or stability of the price that Iraq can expect to gain for its oil. In the context of the needs of the Iraqi economy, as defined by its government, the inability of Iraq to prevent other countries from overproducing, and from thereby diminishing income accruing to Iraq, made it powerless to protect its national interests.

Even allowing for the usual hyperbole associated with such pronouncements, the bitter denunciations by Saddam Hussein of the Persian Gulf's oil-producing states prior to the invasion of Kuwait suggested a sense of insecurity and crisis shared by many in Iraq—a sense of insecurity, furthermore, that the other oil producers were ill-advised to ignore.[12] In principle, therefore, Iraqi concerns about the security of its oil production and pricing may be a complicating factor in its relations with most of its regional neighbors: the pipelines across Turkey, Syria, and Saudi Arabia sharpen the sense of physical vulnerability, while the pricing and production policies of Saudi Arabia, Kuwait, the United Arab Emirates, and Iran excite fears for the security of Iraq's national income.

Of equal potential concern are Iraq's fears about the security of its water supplies. As a country that depends very largely upon the two river systems of the Tigris and the Euphrates, Iraq is uniquely sensitive to upstream developments on either of these two rivers. These are the perennial fears of the downstream state in any such system, but where political enmity is added to water fears, an explosive atmosphere of insecurity and resentment is created. Thus, Iranian irrigation works on the tributaries of the Tigris have added to the suspicion that already exists in Iraq that this will be yet one more weapon that the Iranian state will use to establish its regional hegemony. Of even greater concern, given their scale, are the implications for the future flow of the Euphrates in Iraq of the works being conducted in Turkey on the GAP project and in Syria on the Assad Dam. These concerns were sharp enough before Iraq's present state of isolation, but now there is a belief that Iraq's voice will no longer be heard or given equal weight in discussions on how to manage these international water systems, or indeed that water will deliberately be used as an instrument of state power to further weaken Iraq.

These fears are unlikely to dissipate with the passing of the present government of Iraq. Equally, even if the future political dispensation in Iraq should be radically different from that which has hitherto existed, there is every reason to believe that the underlying concerns outlined above will work powerfully on Iraqi perceptions of the region. Although these fears may be managed differently, they will form the underlying basis on which Iraqi governments will judge the security of the country's interests—as well as the standard against which opposition forces will be able to judge how well any particular government is protecting those interests. How explosive they will be will largely depend upon the vulnerabilities and insecurities of the regime in power at the time. The past record indicates that it will be difficult to disentangle these situational concerns from those concerns arising from the determination of Iraqi governments to maintain intact a particular, clannish dispensation of power within the country, and thus it will be difficult to disentangle them from all the subjective or socially derived insecurities outlined above.

As long as Iraq is governed by authoritarian regimes, relying on a mixture of force and bribery as well as on networks of the *Ahl al-Thiqa* (people implicitly trusted by the rulers, usually, but not exclusively on account of their common origins), then the insecurities outlined above— that is, the fears of the potential disintegration of the state due to social disaffection—will be amplified among the rulers at any given moment. This is all the more likely as long as the dominant ruling network continues to come almost exclusively from clans of the Sunni Arab minority. Fear of unknown networks and impulses and ambitions among other sectors of the population will clearly exaggerate or lend a certain sharpness to the suspicion that they may form a conduit for regional hostility.

Political insecurity is preeminently the fear that others will use whatever means are at hand to advance their interests at the expense of one's own. The structure and history of Iraq's political society, as well as the strategies of this regime and most of its predecessors, have ensured that there is no national political community in Iraq, but rather that there are numerous communities, more or less attached at any one time to the central government in Baghdad. In part resulting from and in part reinforcing this sociopolitical atomization, there is no consensus in Iraq on the rules by which interest should be pursued or power should be used. In such conditions, it is not surprising that there is little room for compromise and that politics becomes a ruthless struggle in which all means are deployed to avoid the annihilation defeat would bring. Not only does this intensify the violent potential of Iraqi politics, but it also inevitably draws in Iraq's regional neighbors, either as active supporters of one faction or another or else as targets of the Iraqi government's suspicion. As long as this condition exists, it will be difficult to disengage the sensed vulnerabilities of Iraq's geostrategic situation from the genuine political insecurities of its government.

Recent Experiences and Sharpened Fears

There can be little doubt that, whatever they feel about their government, the events of the past ten years have tended to sharpen Iraqis' fears about the regional threats to their security. First, there was the war with Iran of 1980 to 1988, which also witnessed an anti-Iraq alliance between Iran and Syria. Second, there was the rising tension with the Persian Gulf oil producers and Iraq's major creditors, Kuwait and Saudi Arabia, which resulted in Iraq's invasion of Kuwait in 1990. This, in turn, produced the international and regional alliance that unleashed Operation Desert Storm and drove Iraq from Kuwait. Third, these events sparked the Kurdish and the Shiite rebellions, resulting eventually in Baghdad's loss of control over much of the north of the country. Meanwhile, since 1990, Iraq has been under a strict U.N. sanctions regime, as well as being subjected to an enforced disarmament program. Lastly, there were the air and missile attacks of January and June 1993, carried out by the United States, with assistance from some of its allies. The civilian casualties that resulted from both of these raids can only have heightened the general sense of vulnerability of many Iraqis and may have assisted the Iraqi government in some measure.

Indeed, it has been noticeable that all of these events have been used by the present government to promote its view of the perils, both internal and regional, that face the Iraqis—and to justify the government's own domination of the state, as well as to exculpate itself from the charge that its own miscalculations have brought these disasters upon Iraq.[13] Even with the passing of this government, the experiences of these years, whatever blame may be assigned to Saddam Hussein by his successors, will leave a legacy, both in the objective situation of Iraq and in the attitudes of many Iraqis towards the region. In part the effect may be sharpened by the discovery, made by Saddam Hussein to his cost during the Kuwait crisis, that the ending of the Cold War had removed the possibility of playing one great power off against another. Hitherto, even though Iraq's regional enemies might have looked to a superpower patron to enhance their strength relative to that of Iraq, it had at least been open to Iraq to seek to check such a move by looking for a superpower patron of its own. This had formed an essential part of Iraq's regional strategy and had constituted a form of security guarantee, even if that guarantee was not always as solid as it was imagined to be.[14] With the collapse of the USSR, such a move was no longer possible and Iraq had to experience, unmediated, both regional and international enmity that it did not have the resources to resist. The effect of this has been to sharpen the sense of isolation in Iraq and, if anything, to heighten the insecurities experienced as a result of the events of the previous decade or so.

As far as the objective situation is concerned, borders have been redrawn in favor of Iraq's regional enemies. In the case of Iran, the Iraqi government conceded in August 1990 that it would recognize once again the border settlements of the 1975 Algiers Agreement. This involves minor Iraqi territorial concessions along its land frontier and, more importantly, recognition of Iran's claims to sovereignty over half of the Shatt al Arab. The original Algiers Agreement had been denounced and, indeed, abrogated by Saddam Hussein in 1980 on the pretext that it had been signed under coercive pressure from Iran. Furthermore, the move in 1990 was transparently an attempt to extricate Iraq from the international isolation that followed its invasion of Kuwait and to enlist Iranian support (which failed to materialize). Consequently, the attitude of the Iraqi government to the Algiers Agreement as an unjust settlement forced upon a vulnerable Iraq is unlikely to have changed. In addition, the territorial concessions had been portrayed by Saddam Hussein, when he thought he was in a position to reverse them, as a shameful infringement of Iraqi sovereignty and had thus made themselves known to an Iraqi public that had probably hitherto been relatively oblivious to them. To have been obliged, under the duress of the "Atlanticist-Zionist conspiracy," as the Gulf War alliance is called by the Iraqi media, to cede territory once again to Iran is not a stable foundation for future relations. The probability is that this will simply have reinforced the tendency in Iraq to link regional and international enmity with designs on Iraq's geostrategic security.

Much of the same must apply with regard to the U.N. decision on the demarcation of the Iraqi border with Kuwait. It was inevitable that this border should have received particular attention in the aftermath of the Gulf War. Iraq's general claims to sovereignty over the whole of Kuwait, as well as the specific claims to ill-defined areas along the border and the gradual encroachment of Iraq on Kuwaiti territory in the vicinity of Umm Qasr during the preceding decade made it imperative for the Kuwaiti government to gain international recognition for the exact frontier between the two states. It was hoped that this not only would reinforce the territorial identity of Kuwait as a separate sovereign state, but also would deter future Iraqi coercive pressure in the areas of disputed sovereignty.

The result of the U.N. commission's finding was to redraw Iraq's de facto southern frontier wholly in Kuwait's favor. For roughly the two hundred kilometers of the Iraqi-Kuwait border, the frontier line was shifted northward by six hundred meters in Kuwait's favor. This meant not simply that Iraq lost six of the oil wells in the disputed Rumaila oil field, but, more seriously for Iraq, that it had to give up a substantial portion of the naval base it had constructed during the previous decade at Umm Qasr. At a stroke, therefore, the U.N. had inflamed two sensitive nerves in Iraq's sensed insecurity. Quite apart from the general humiliation of the settlement, Iraq had been weakened in an economic sense by losing oil fields and in a strategic sense by having its access to the waters of the Persian Gulf further restricted. The sensitivity of the issue was visible not simply in the furious Iraqi government reaction to the U.N. findings, which was to be expected, but also in the initial protest of the Iraqi opposition at the terms of this settlement.[15] Once again, the question of the effect of this on general Iraqi perceptions of the security of the state and its place in the region—quite apart from the specific problem that this may create in the future for Iraqi-Kuwaiti relations under whatever government comes to power in Iraq—must arise.

An additional legacy of the recent war has been the measure of independence allowed to the Kurdish communities of the north through international protection. The removal of Baghdad's control of the northern zone, the emergence of a lively and diverse (if sometimes violent) Kurdish political life, the holding of largely free general elections in 1992, and the formation of what is essentially a Kurdish government of the area have been looked upon with apprehension, and not simply by the present government in Baghdad. The Kurdish parties have sought to allay some of these fears, at least amongst fellow Iraqi opponents of Saddam Hussein, by encouraging them to base themselves in Kurdistan as part of Iraq.

However, it may be difficult for the Kurds to allay the suspicion of many that their ultimate objective is separation from the Iraqi state. While it is true that the main Kurdish parties deny any such ambition at present and continue to proclaim their goal as being the establishment of a federal Iraqi state, the longer the present situation in the north persists, the more enduring will be the legacy of the Kurds' experience of self-government and relative autonomy. Under such circumstances, it is hard to foresee their willing incorporation into an Iraqi state of the kind that has hitherto existed. Indeed, they have made it plain that their adherence to a unitary Iraqi state in the future must depend upon its radical reconstruction as a federal, democratic state. For precisely the reasons outlined above, this would entail a dramatic revolution in Iraqi political society and, despite the vicissitudes of the recent past and the present, the prospect of such a revolution may fill many Iraqis with dread.

Another consequence of recent developments that clearly places most Iraqis in the same situation is Iraq's economic situation. Iraqis in general have to cope with the consequences both of the international trade embargo, which remains in force and in the longer term, and the massive Iraqi debt accumulated during the years of war with Iran and augmented by the reparations bill associated with that war and with the invasion of Kuwait. Although it seems clear that Saddam Hussein has managed to retain control of sufficient foreign currency reserves to ensure that those whom he favors and whose support he needs do not suffer unduly as a result of the sanctions against Iraq, no such safety net exists for the remainder of the population. They will undoubtedly see their plight as part of general enmity against Iraq, particularly as the circumstances of the institution of the sanctions begin to recede into the past. The present government, of course, has every interest in encouraging Iraqis to believe themselves to be the subject of international conspiracy, since that shifts the responsibility from Saddam Hussein for creating the situation in which international hostility was initially aroused. The more he stresses the thesis that this hostility is part of the unjust and malign structure of world power, the more will Iraqis in general look upon the world as predatory in its relations with Iraq. In the economic sphere, this will be brought home to Iraqis in their everyday lives, depending upon the mitigating arrangements for the debt and reparations that may be negotiated with an Iraqi successor to Saddam Hussein.[16]

It is not difficult to believe that the shared adversity of most of the inhabitants of Iraq will have left its mark on the collective imagination of Iraqis. The memory of war with Iran, in which perhaps 120,000 Iraqis lost their lives and the memory of the widespread destruction and hardship caused by the military operations of Operation Desert Storm, in which most of Iraq's regional neighbors participated directly or indirectly, are not going to fade quickly. They will tend to color the images of the destructive power that lurks in the region, reinforcing the sense of peril and insecurity on which authoritarian Iraqi governments have relied so successfully to achieve their own leadership ambitions. This is, in sum, the troubling legacy of the past fifteen years, overlaid on an already heightened sense of insecurity. It is not that Saddam Hussein has created a new set of security fears, but rather that the very violence and disruption of Iraq under his leadership has provoked the hostility of precisely the forces that were wary of Iraq in the first place. In reacting, however, these forces may well have left the impression that they were hostile to Iraq all along and had simply been looking for an excuse to mount an attack on Iraq's national interests. Again, this is the version of events currently propagated by the present regime, and there is reason to suppose that it is regarded as plausible within Iraq.[17]

Conclusion: Responses and Future Concerns

In response to this legacy, with which any future government of Iraq will have to deal, a number of strategies are conceivable, although certain forms of government might find it easier to pursue some than to pursue others. Specifically, in this context, it is worth thinking about the possibility that the kinds of fears outlined above, combined with particular reasons for dispute with a neighbor, might lead to armed conflict. This consideration involves, first, seeking to gain an impression of the utility of force in the eyes of the imaginable governments of Iraq. Second, insofar as the management of disputes is concerned, it is worth thinking about the degree to which any Iraqi government might be expected to be willing—or to be permitted—to join some form of collective or regional organization for the settlement of disputes.

In connection with the first question, it has always been noticeable that until the attack on Iran in 1980, successive Iraqi governments had been extremely cautious and sparing in their use of the armed forces of the state beyond its borders. Instead, the history of the Iraqi armed forces has largely been one of suppressing internal rebellion and maintaining domestic order. The change came about in large measure because of the changed circumstances both of Iraq itself and of its neighbor Iran. These presented the government of Iraq with the means to build up the armed forces of the state on the basis of Iraq's vast oil revenues, as well as the perceived opportunity—perhaps even the need—to curb the power of the new Iranian regime. The invasion and occupation of Kuwait in 1990 was itself an indirect product of the eight-year war with Iran—a move that reflected both the desperation of those years and the military might that Iraq had accumulated. Of course, the decision to use war as the instrument of opportunity was taken by the particular regime of Saddam Hussein, on the basis of specific (if sometimes obscure) calculations of threat and advantage.

For any future government of Iraq, even one that comes out of the circles of clansmen and kinsmen who constitute the present regime, the disastrous results of those decisions will be all too clear. Indeed, their corrosive effects on the hierarchies of privilege within Iraq will probably be the catalyst that will bring about the decisive coup d'état. Such considerations will almost certainly rule out the regional use of force in the way it has been used by Saddam Hussein. This does not mean, however, that Iraq's military potential will be neglected. On the contrary, in a government that is installed or run by the military clans of the Iraqi officer corps, any decision to downgrade the armed forces would be a difficult one to take. Precisely because of the many other claims there will be on the state's resources in the period of economic recuperation and reconstruction that would be certain to follow the demise of Saddam Hussein, the share to be allocated to the armed forces would be a subject of controversy. It is almost certain that this controversy would be heightened by the fact that for every Iraqi who might think that it was the exaggerated belief in the capacity of the armed forces that was responsible for the present predicament of the country, there would be several who would believe that the crises of the past fifteen years had reemphasized Iraq's need for a powerful military establishment.

The impulse to continue enhancing the capacity of the armed forces of Iraq would therefore be a strong one, regardless of which government comes to power. However, it is probably safe to say that all of the three possible future regimes suggested in this chapter would avoid committing those armed forces in any foreign adventure if they could possibly help it. The old caution, born of the knowledge of the potential vulnerability of the state, seems likely to reassert itself. Caution does not necessarily imply conciliation, however. There may be any number of means of pursuing one's regional enemies. The preceding pages have discussed a number of difficult issues that are going to characterize Iraq's relations with most of its neighbors for some time to come. Some of these issues can be negotiated or "frozen." Where it is not possible for an Iraqi government to take such a low-key stance, military posturing, political subversion, and cross-border infiltration may be tactics used to respond to what the Iraqi government may regard as a threat in kind.[18]

As far as the second question—that of conflict management—is concerned, it seems highly unlikely that any Iraqi government would be willing to allow others to dictate its security policy and requirements. In this, of course, the Iraqi government has much in common with most of its neighbors, undermining the idea of collective regional security organizations with or without Iraq, whatever outward forms are adopted. However, more specifically, too much has passed between Iraq and its neighbors during the past twenty or so years for any trust to exist that in a collective security arrangement, the other parties would have the security of Iraq or of the Iraqi regime at heart. Even without such a wounding string of experiences and the mistrust they have helped to foster, the nature of Iraq's security concerns are such (as outlined above) that it would be extraordinarily difficult for an Iraqi government to surrender any power of decision or arbitration to an organization that it does not itself dominate in some form. This remains true of any of the foreseeable governments of a post-Saddam Hussein Iraq.

For all of these possible governments, conflict avoidance would seem to be the key strategy, but in such a way regionally—as in domestic politics—that nothing is given away that would permanently alter the balance of power. The ability to avoid conflict will depend in part upon the condition of the regime in Iraq. In this connection, it is perhaps worrisome that there were probably many in the upper echelons of the Iraqi political and military establishments who shared most of Saddam Hussein's illusions in 1980 and in 1990, before they were so rudely shattered. However, these illusions were also in part fostered by the behavior of the governments of Iran and Kuwait, respectively, and by the condition of the region. These factors will also be influential in persuading a future Iraqi government from pursuing its aims by overt military force or in dissuading it from doing so. Only by examining the possible futures, therefore, of Iraq's neighbors will one be able to make an estimate of the balance of threat and opportunity that they might represent for the Iraqi government of the day—possibly persuading yet another leader in Iraq to decide, as in 1980 and 1990, that the potential advantages of initiating conflict far outweigh the risks of doing so.

Notes

1. H. Batatu, *The Old Social Classes and the Revolutionary Movements of Iraq* (Princeton, N.J.: Princeton University Press, 1978), 44–50.

2. Alaa Tahir, *Irak: aux origines du régime militaire* (Paris: Editions l'Harmattan, 1989), 177–242.

3. *al-Intisab* means "belonging," "membership," or "related to" in the context of families, clans and groups, but it also has overtones of "fitting" or "proper." In other words, there is a normative order suggested by the fact of association or relationship.

4. The analogy would be with the Syrian officers' conference at Homs in 1962, when the many factions of the Syrian officer corps came together to try to hammer out a way of settling their differences short of civil war, having each seized control in different parts of the country.

5. See Saddam Hussein's speech in commemoration of Michel Aflaq, founder of the Baath party, on 29 July 1989 (*Al-Mu'allafat al-Kamila*, Baghdad: Dar al-Shu'un al-Thaqafiyya al-'Amma, 1989, pt. 18, 365–71); also A. Baram, "Culture in the Service of Wataniyya," *Asian and African Studies* 17 (1983): 266.

6. For details of the INC and its component elements, see Rend Rahim Francke "The Opposition," in *Iraq since the Gulf War*, ed. F. Hazelton (London: Zed Books, 1994), 153–77.

7. See J. N. Wiley, *The Islamic Movement of Iraqi Shi'as* (Boulder: Lynne Rienner, 1992), 31–71.

8. Falaq al-Din Kakai, "The Kurdish Parliament," in *Iraq since the Gulf War*, ed. F. Hazelton (London: Zed Books, 1994), 129–33.

9. J. Hiltman, "Diverting Water, Displacing Iraq's Marsh People," *Middle East Report* 181/23, no. 2 (March/April 1993): 36.

10. See, for instance, Saddam Hussein's speech to the Iraqi National Assembly on 7 August 1990: "Kuwait is joining the motherland, just as are Jahra and Ahmadi [towns in Kuwait] and all the villages, all the good people and all the good land that was detached from Iraq some time ago." Republic of Iraq Radio, 8 August 1990, quoted in BBC SWB ME/0839 A/4, 10 August 1990.

11. The most obvious previous example is Abd al-Karim Qassim's revival of the claim to Kuwait in 1961. See U. Dann, *Iraq under Qassem—A Political History 1958–1963* (New York: Praeger, 1969), 349–53.

12. See the text of Tariq Aziz's letter to the secretary general of the Arab League, elaborating on Saddam Hussein's speech commemorating the revolution of 1968. Both exhibit a nice mixture of Iraqi national interest and pan-Arab outrage vis-à-vis Kuwait. Quoted in BBC SWB ME/0820 A/4–7, 19 July 1990.

13. See the Political Statement of the Twelfth Pan-Arab Congress of the Arab Socialist Baath Party, "The Mother of Battles Congress," held in December 1992. Iraqi News Agency report, 10 January 1993, quoted in BBC SWB ME/1585 A/6–8, 13 January 1993.

14. See, for instance, Iraqi indignation at the USSR for failing to supply Iraq with sufficient armaments in the early stages of the Iran-Iraq War. Republic of Iraq Radio, 15 March 1981, quoted in Foreign Broadcast Information Service MEA (E1), 17 March 1981.

15. *The Guardian*, 30 April 1992; see also Tariq Aziz's statement reported on Radio Monte Carlo, 27 April 1992, quoted in BBC SWB ME/1367 A/7, 29 April 1992.

16. For some indications of the impact that the sanctions were having in 1991, see J. Dreze and H. Gazder, *Hunger and Poverty in Iraq 1991,* DEP Paper no. 32, (London: London School of Economics and Political Science, September 1991).

17. For the way in which these events are presented, see *Al-Qadisiyya,* 9 October 1994, quoted in BBC SWB ME/2123 MED/7, 11 October 1994 and the Iraqi National Assembly message to Saddam Hussein, Republic of Iraq Radio, 17 October 1994, quoted in BBC SWB ME/2130 MED/14, 19 October 1994.

18. A good example of such tactics, as practiced by the regime of Saddam Hussein, could be seen in the so-called crisis of October 1994. See M. Jansen, "Saddam's Phoney Crisis," *Middle East International,* 21 October 1994, 4–5.

7

OF NOT BEING A LONE WOLF: GEOGRAPHY, DOMESTIC PLAYS, AND TURKISH FOREIGN POLICY IN THE MIDDLE EAST

Soli Özel

> *Turkey is a lone wolf without instinctive friends or allies*
> —Bülent Nuri Eren

Domestically and internationally, the Turkish Republic is at a turning point. To an unprecedented degree, Turkey's domestic political dynamics and international setting influence each other and define each other's limits and possibilities. Current policy choices will have a bearing on the future domestic regime of the country as well as on its alliance relations. In the post-Cold War environment, Turkey's relations with Europe, the United States, and the Middle Eastern countries as well as its contribution to a stable security regime in the Persian Gulf region await a restructuring.

This chapter traces the foundations and the antecedents for "internationalist" and "nationalist" foreign policy visions that are currently competing to establish the direction of Turkish foreign policy in the emerging new world order (or disorder). It offers a perspective on their viability in the new regional and international configurations Turkey faces. It also identifies the problems, both domestic and international, that will have a bearing on the evolution of Turkey's foreign policy in its adjacent regions and toward its erstwhile allies.

Today, Turkish society is engaged in the most open debate about its political future and the nature of its international relations and commitments since the founding of the republic. This impassioned debate unfolding inside the country heralds both the democratization of foreign policy and the ominous possibility of a policy taken hostage by emotions or frozen conceptions of political realities. Whether Turkey belongs to the first division of advanced democratic countries or the third division of illiberal, corrupt, and impoverished countries will be established by this choice. For now, the country hangs suspended between two alternatives, like the bridges on the Bosporus that unite Europe and Asia without belonging to either.

Turkey, the West, and the Middle East

The end of the Cold War had a profound impact on both the domestic and the international politics of Turkey. The country's relations with both its Western allies and its regional neighbors entered a period of transformation. The outcome of this process is still undetermined, but relations with the Western world in particular are undergoing a serious crisis.

Turkey's four-decade-long alliance with the West was as much a response to its own well-founded security anxieties vis-à-vis the Soviet Union as it was the natural culmination of domestic choices, going back to the establishment of the Turkish Republic. The founders of the republic originally decided to pursue, in a substantially more radical fashion, the westernization programs they inherited from the Ottoman Empire. In one sweep, they rejected the Ottoman heritage, secularized the polity, cut the country off from its history by changing the alphabet, and embarked on a program of development that equated modernization with westernization, all in an overwhelmingly Muslim and conservative country. They aimed at creating new, westernized Turkish citizens out of a people whose self-identification was strictly communitarian.[1] The corresponding international strategy of this early republican period was to secure nonthreatening and even friendly relations with the Soviet Union, disengage from the Middle East, and by the mid-1930s engage in a rapprochement with Britain. In their domestic and international politics, the ruling elite of the republic were not accountable to the Turkish public, and hence they enjoyed a free hand in their endeavors.

Having stayed out of the Second World War by a policy of "active neutrality," Turkey found itself in a position of splendid isolation in the immediate aftermath of the war.[2] The Turkish government was basically on its own when it had to cope with the crisis of 1945 that originated with the Soviet decision not to renew the Turco-Soviet Treaty of Neutrality and Nonaggression of 1925. This challenge was followed by Molotov's oral communication to the Turkish ambassador in Moscow concerning Soviet claims over two Turkish provinces in the northeast and bases on the Straits.[3] The resolution of this crisis by Turkey's incorporation into the Western alliance terminated any chance of returning to the prewar policy of neutrality and good relations with the Soviets. On the other hand, the new alliance brought to Turkey, chronically short of capital and unable to attract much direct foreign investment, "strategic rents" allowing it "to exchange concessions in the accommodating market of Cold War politics for more foreign aid."[4] As discussed below, the corollary of this approach in dealing with the Middle East was a total insensitivity to nationalist aspirations and the assumption of an aggressive "Western" posture in regional politics.

In retrospect, the degree to which Turkey has identified its Cold War interests with those of the West, and particularly the United States, looks either audacious or delusory.[5] What makes this even more astonishing is that this unabashed identification with Western perspectives and policies in the international arena was the handiwork of a government whose historical mission had been to tame Turkey's radically secular westernization and to let the country's Muslim identity resurface.[6]

While political radicalism and pan-Arab nationalism swept the Arab world during the 1950s, Turkey zealously pursued a policy of projecting Western interests even when this offended the Arab states. In an attempt to tighten the Western security chain around the Soviet Union, Turkey actively participated in the creation of the Baghdad Pact and proposed that ex-British colonies join the pact with their former colonial master. As Andrew Mango notes, the Baghdad Pact, which included Iraq, Pakistan, the United Kingdom, and Iran, "was flawed from the start: the US which had urged it did not enter it as a full member" for fear of alienating irreversibly Nasser's Egypt.[7]

A series of other blunders did almost irreparable damage to Turkey's relations with and reputation in the Arab Middle East. Massing troops on the Syrian border to stop a radicalization of Syria's government in 1957, allowing U.S. marines to use the Incirlik air base to intervene in the Lebanese crisis of 1958, and voting in favor of France at the United Nations during the Algerian war of independence are some of the most spectacular of these policies that alienated Middle Eastern countries. This attitude vis-à-vis the Arab Middle East only began to change after the first Cyprus crisis of 1964.[8]

The new foreign policy sought to repair relations with Arab countries in order to generate support for the Turkish Cypriot community and for Turkish positions on the Cyprus issue. Before the Six-Day War "Turkey displayed understanding of the Egyptian position and refused to join with the group of 'maritime powers' demanding the reopening of the Gulf of Aqaba to Israeli shipping."[9] During the 1973 Arab-Israeli War, the Turks sided with the Arabs by denying the United States the use of U.S.

bases to help supply the Israelis, just as they allowed Soviet planes to use their airspace to rush aid to the Syrians. In 1969, Turkey made its first major break with Ataturkist principles in international relations by participating in the Organization of the Islamic Conference in Rabat, Morocco.[10]

As Turkey undergoes the most profound economic, social, and political crises of the republican period, Ankara also finds itself involved in the affairs of the Middle East with unprecedented intensity.[11] In a sense, this involvement can be considered the redressing of a balance that was long overdue. Turkey, from the inception of the republic, aspired to be of the West both in its domestic institutions and in its international associations. Consequently, the Middle East was treated first with benign neglect (1925–49), then with Cold War assertiveness (1950–64), and then with cautious rapprochement and gradual warming of relations as expediency demanded (1965–90).[12] As a perceptive historian of the Ottoman Empire, Paul Wittek, has argued, the rulers of Anatolia have always had to be Janus-faced and look both East and West.[13] While this balance is being fully restored, one question still lingers: Will the West disown a country that made a conscious choice to be part of Western civilization from the days of its foundation and has been a formal ally since the advent of the Cold War, and then disengages as its usefulness seems to have expired? The answer to this question has important implications for Turkey's domestic order and its relations with the Middle East.

The Third Incarnation

For the third time in a century, the map of Europe is changing. Also for the third time in this century, the map of the Middle East is being redrawn. In the first two instances, the relation between the transformations in Europe and the Middle East was unambiguously causal. After World War I, the imperialist powers carved out of the defunct Ottoman empire a subsystem of dependent states and mandates. Following World War II, as those states in the Middle East gained their independence, the victorious allies sanctioned the creation of Israel and changed the map again. In the aftermath of the Cold War, the relation between the two dynamics of change is not as visibly causal. The end of the Cold War and Operation Desert Storm expedited the creation of a Palestinian political entity or state. The aborted toppling of the regime in Baghdad by the rebellions in the south and the north of Iraq created greater instability, which, in turn, has created the possibility of a partitioning of Iraq among its constituent communities.

With or without a Kurdish or Shiite state, eastern Mesopotamia and the Persian Gulf will continue to be unstable and vulnerable to either regime or boundary changes. Whereas the Middle Eastern subsystem comprising Syria, Lebanon, Israel, Jordan, Palestine, and Egypt is proceeding toward maturity, the remaining areas, and the Persian Gulf in particular, constitute an immature subsystem with an inherent inability to achieve a balance of power that might lead to a stable environment. The stability of this subsystem currently depends on the active involvement of the United States and is perpetually undermined by the asymmetry of military power among the three main actors—Iran, Iraq, and Saudi Arabia—and the fragility of the domestic orders in most of the constituent countries.

The immaturity of the state subsystem that makes the Persian Gulf region prone to violence and chronic instability also obtains in the other two regions that constitute what Duygu Bazoḡlu Sezer calls "the expanded Middle East"—namely, the Balkans and the Caucasus, where the map has also changed recently.[14] Situated at the center of these geopolitical fault lines, Turkey faces the challenge of redefining both its security interests and its strategic vision and the challenge of rearranging its domestic order. Failure to meet these challenges might result in the further destabilization of Turkey's polity, in its exit from the club of liberal-democratic countries of the West, or even in the weakening of its secular orientation.

It can be confidently postulated that the strategic value of Turkey's geography remains high, and, concomitantly, so does the importance of its domestic stability. Therefore, in view of the continuing fragmentation of the Turkish political system, which popularizes and empowers marginal movements, the current adversarial nature of Turkey's relations with its Western allies is all the more worrisome for regional security.

Did Saddam Resurrect Turkey?

Iraq's invasion of Kuwait is arguably a turning point in the modern history of the Middle East. In this way, it is akin to the partition of Palestine, the subsequent defeat of the Arab armies by the Israelis, and to the shattering of populist Arab nationalism due to the catastrophe of the June 1967 war for the Arab states. Many observers believe it was also a turning point in Turkey's relations with the Middle East and for the definition of its new strategic value. Henri Barkey argues that "the Gulf War provided the first opportunity for Turkey to salvage some of its lost geopolitical importance."[15] Philip Robins suggests that Turkey's policy in this crisis broke two of the cardinal rules of its foreign policy toward the Middle East that had been carefully nurtured since the Cyprus crisis of 1964, in an effort to remove the bitter legacy of the Baghdad Pact days.[16] These two principles were noninterference in the domestic affairs of the

Middle East, and the separation of the Middle East from Turkey's role within the Western alliance.[17] Robins cautions, however, that "it is too early to establish whether the Turkish stance towards the region more generally has been affected by its policy reevaluation in the immediate crisis. Much depends on the consequences of the crisis and, most importantly, the postwar security arrangements."[18]

In a sense, both Barkey's and Robin's observations were correct. In view of current Turkish foreign-policy making, Robins's caution is well warranted. The conventional view that judged strategic importance only in the context of the Cold War was prone to discount Turkey in the new strategic calculations because of the cataclysmic changes in world politics since the advent of Gorbachev in the Soviet Union.[19] Writing as the Cold War was waning, one of the most astute observers of Turkish politics, Dankwart Rustow, called Turkey "the Forgotten Ally."[20] Had it not been for the folly of Saddam Hussein's invasion of Kuwait, which triggered the Gulf War, and the subsequent disintegration of the Soviet Union, a second edition of the book in the 1990s might very well have called Turkey "the Dumped Ally."

The "revolutions of 1989" transformed strategic calculations in a world accustomed to bipolarity and led to a downgrading of Turkey's strategic value. Such reassessments were not unprecedented. A close observer of Turkish foreign policy, Bruce Kuniholm, notes that "when Western relations with the Soviet Union were troubled (e.g., in 1946–48, 1950–53, 1979, or 1980–84), relations with Turkey were generally good. During periods of détente, relations between Turkey and the West became more troubled as one or another party raised questions about the relationship and challenged the other's notion of reciprocity."[21]

The Gulf War and the transformation of the Islamic-Turkic hinterland of the former Soviet Union into independent republics changed the picture and underscored the shortsightedness of this latest devaluation. In fact, following the events of 1990 and 1991, Turkey aspires to be one of the shapers of the future international order. Many outside commentators joined the chorus hailing the dawn of a new era for Turkey in international relations.[22]

Nevertheless, there was also a significant but considerably underexplored change that took place in the formulation of Turkey's foreign policy prior to the "Leninist extinction" and to Operation Desert Storm.[23] This change, which potentially had critical long-term consequences, undergirded the late president Turgut Özal's new strategic vision as well. The main tenets of what constituted Turkey's "national interest"—or, more correctly, the ordering of these tenets—underwent a quiet shift in the 1980s. Of the three tenets—territorial integrity, peace, and continued economic and social development—territorial integrity always took precedence in Turkey's history,[24] and the other two could always be sacrificed if the territorial integrity of the republic was perceived to be threatened. Özal's innovation during the Iran-Iraq War was to change this ordering and base the maintenance of both territorial integrity and peace on successful economic development.[25]

Such an evolution was not totally unexpected, since the shift in priorities coincided with the restructuring of the Turkish economy that began in early 1980, continued under the brutal military rule of 1980 to 1983, and gained further momentum during Özal's early prime minister-ship, between 1983 and 1987. During that period, the developmental model based on import substitution that Turkey had pursued in the previous two or three decades was replaced by one of export promotion. The reorientation of the economy toward export promotion was facilitated by the opening of markets in the Middle East, particularly in Iran and Iraq, which had been closed by a bitter and bloody war that lasted nearly eight years.[26] Taking advantage of the rift between the United States and the European countries as to the proper course to follow toward revolutionary Iran and the appropriate response to the Iran-Iraq war, Turkey found interstices for self-interested action.[27]

Özal's redefinition of what constituted strategic importance in the post-Cold War environment made the loss of Turkey's strategic impor-tance appear less immediate and absolute. Prime Minister Özal, like a good nineteenth-century English liberal, had faith that extensive economic relations between nations would generate nonbelligerence. He also observed that a nation's power would be measured increasingly by its economic strength. In that sense, Turkey's emphasis in the 1980s on domestic economic development as the central tenet of national security presumed a world order where strategic importance would be increas-ingly measured by economic viability and prowess. Özal was weary of the overdependence of Turkey on the United States for its defense and the overdetermination of this relation by defense and security concerns.[28] Throughout his rule, he insisted on improved economic relations with the United States and chose to ask for more trade rather than debt relief or more aid after the Gulf War.

Özal also believed in improving Turkey's economic relations with all the surrounding regions. Enjoying the advantage of a ten-year lead time in economic modernization and market reform, Turkey could be an example to the countries that needed to transform their economies along the same lines. An anecdote that opens the new book written by the former general manager of Turkish Airlines suggests that already in 1988, Özal saw the Central Asian Republics of the Soviet Union as Turkey's new economic frontier and its stepping-stones to the growing economies of the Asian Pacific.[29] Sharing some of Özal's assumptions and in search of a new paradigm for Turkish foreign policy, Ankara's former ambassador in Washington, Şükrü Elekdağ, published an article in a Turkish journal at the beginning of 1992. He argued that in the post-Cold War era Turkey needed to develop an "ecostrategy."[30] Postulating that in the future Turkey's importance would be a function more of its economic health and relations with its neighboring regions and the Western world than its militarily advantageous location, Elekdağ supported the development of regional cooperation organizations, such as the Black Sea Economic Cooperation Organization. Özal himself took the lead in the formation of this organization.

The 1991 war against Iraq enabled Turkey to perform a new strategic mission. The geostrategic alliance fashioned against the Soviet threat could now be redefined. Turkey could be the bulwark of a new arrangement designed to secure free access to oil threatened by the inherent instability of the region.

This sea change started during the second cold war of the 1980s and gradually but perceptibly began to define Turkey's foreign policy under Özal. What, in retrospect, was the swan song of the Cold War intensified in the aftermath of the Iranian revolution and the invasion of Afghanistan by the Soviet Union. Both of these historical events helped resurrect Turkey's military and strategic importance. The renewed strategic value of Turkey brought it some much needed military aid—and later even the capability to produce its own F-16s.

Unlike the early periods of the Cold War, though, when Turkey continuously pursued policies that alienated it from the Arab world, the 1980s witnessed unprecedented closeness in relations with a wide range of Arab countries (with the exception of Syria). As noted, this more nuanced and sensitive relationship with Middle Eastern countries was built upon fifteen years of rapprochement with the Arab world that began in the immediate aftermath of the infamous "Johnson letter."[31] During the Iran-Iraq War, Turkey repeatedly gave assurances to Arab countries that it would not allow the U.S. Rapid Deployment Force to operate from Turkish bases, despite the Defense and Economic Cooperation Agreement Turkey had signed with the United States. By so acting, Turkey was, of course, adhering to the principle of keeping its alliance obligations and the politics of the region separate.

Here, a short detour might be in order. For the Arab countries, the only fixed principle until the crisis of 1990 was to not permit foreign troops to be stationed on their territory. In the Persian Gulf crisis, a threat from within the region demolished this principle and challenged both the existing regimes and the international system. By crossing the fabled "line in the sand," Saddam "was questioning the legitimacy of *all* Iraq's borders"[32] (emphasis added). More than that, "the invasion had deeper roots in the post-Ottoman syndrome. In a sense, Saddam's aggression represented the logical extension of Arab efforts to throw off Western domination, to undo the post-Ottoman divisions."[33] In a region where the legitimacy of borders is at best questionable, the Iraqi challenge triggered a scramble by all of the neighboring regimes to defend their claims. It drew Turkey into Middle Eastern affairs, despite misgivings in Ankara. In the process, Turkey broke its principle of not taking sides in inter-Arab conflicts, and the global dimension of the conflict forced Ankara to alter its strategic stance. Özal's policy during the Gulf crisis reflected an unequivocal choice to put all of Turkey's weight on the side of the Western alliance, underscoring its Western orientation. Özal, the most "Islamic" of all mainstream Turkish political leaders, reaffirmed Turkey's ties to the Western alliance at a time when the end of the Cold War seemed to diminish Turkey's strategic importance and to reduce its influence to purely Middle Eastern affairs.

Özal's Vision

While the rapid collapse of the Leninist world, the Gulf War, and the disintegration of the Soviet Union dismayed and confused many politicians, through all these events Özal remained confident that Turkey could pursue a more activist foreign policy. He saw that the end of the bipolar world order and the flux in international relations would create an opportunity for Turkey to reposition itself and to project its interests in the three regions of which it was part.[34] Disclaiming any territorial ambitions, Özal thought Turkey could act as a role model for the newly emerging republics of the Caucasus and central Asia, helping them make the transition to becoming secular, democratic countries with market-oriented economies. Turkey's historical ties to these countries could be reinforced by financial and technical assistance. The economic integration of these regions into the world economy could be facilitated through their ties to Turkey. Turkey would become a conduit for Western investments in the region, thus facilitating its own economic development.

Özal thought Turkey's vocation was to become a critical link in the flow of goods and services between Europe and Asia. To be able to play this role properly, Turkey needed both a close relationship with Azerbaijan, which was its gateway to central Asia, and open access through the Balkans to Europe. Özal viewed the Balkans as Turkey's door to Europe, particularly as the European Community grew increasingly fortresslike and less receptive to Turkish petitions for admission.

Özal's proposals for twin pipelines that would carry the waters of the Seyhan and Ceyhan Rivers in southern Turkey to all countries in the region that are chronically short of water should be seen as part of this general framework. In his "peace pipeline" scheme, six million cubic meters a day would flow to the Arab world through the "Western" and "gulf" pipelines.[35] If this project succeeded in reducing the suspicion and mistrust that divided Turkey and the Arab countries to its south, it could form the cornerstone for wider regional economic integration.

Özal's bold vision certainly challenged the traditional maxim that "Turkey is a small power, which by definition implies that in general she is in the position of responding to what happens in the external environment rather than shaping that environment."[36] Özal intended to reshape Turkey's environment.

A more active and engaged foreign policy would enable Turkey to create its own sphere of autonomous activity, freeing Ankara from the confinement of serving purely Western interests. It is, indeed, this new space that accounts for "the inversely proportional increase in Turkey's strategic value and geopolitical role as its strategic significance in NATO diminishes."[37] The Persian Gulf crisis was undoubtedly the most significant development insofar as it raised questions about the basic principles of Turkish foreign policy and highlighted the confining conditions created by its domestic political and ideological structures.

Substantively and stylistically, Özal's conduct of Turkey's foreign policy during the Persian Gulf crisis and the Gulf War was pathbreaking. A country accustomed to keeping a low profile in international relations and comfortable with doing nothing more than what is absolutely necessary chose instead to take an initiating, high-profile role. The decision to actively join the U.S.-led U.N. coalition against Iraqi aggression reflected Turkey's new perspective on security that was developed just prior to the crisis.

In December 1989, the then Turkish foreign minister, Mesut Yılmaz, convened a meeting in Vienna, Austria, of Turkey's ambassadors in Europe. The participants concluded that in the future, the primary security threats to Turkey would come from its southern and possibly its western borders. In fact, only three months before the Iraqis, strapped for cash, took their "tanks to the bank,"[38] Saddam Hussein openly threatened the visiting Turkish prime minister, Yildirim Akbulut.[39] In this context, it was rather disinguous for some Turkish observers to claim that Özal's role in the Persian Gulf crisis had been dictated by the West and that he subordinated Turkish diplomacy completely to the whims and desires of the United States. Rather, Özal used the opportunity that the U.N. coalition presented to take on an adversary that Turkey would have had to confront sooner or later. The war neutralized one of Ankara's most serious potential security problems and consequently broadened its room for maneuver in pursuit of a new regional and international strategy.[40]

Yet most of Turkey's political establishment opposed both the substance and the style of Özal's policies—as if opposing the U.N. campaign was a real option. In the course of the crisis, a foreign minister, a defense minister, and the chief of staff of the military resigned their posts in disagreement with Özal. The disparate forces that opposed Özal's Gulf War policies coalesced and prevented Özal from dominating the conduct of foreign policy after the general elections of 1991. Süleyman Demirel, whose political vision remained highly insular and who was philosophically averse to any type of boldness, formed the new government at that time and thwarted most of his former top aides' bolder (more eccentric?) initiatives.

Following Özal's death, most of his initiatives were blunted, but not overturned. Nevertheless, "Özalist" policies did not quite survive their architect. The obsession with Turkey's territorial integrity, fortified by a belief in a never-ending conspiracy to dismember it through Kurdish separatism, partially accounts for this reversal.

The Habitual Strikes Back

The Özalist project was ambitious, the international environment was accommodating, and Özal himself was resourceful and imaginative. However, Turkey's history, the inadequacy of its domestic order, and the sclerosis of its political and state elites (perhaps compounded by Özal's own vanity and shortcomings) proved to be formidable, if not insurmountable, obstacles to the realization of his objectives. The old strategic consensus was broken irreparably during the Gulf War, despite the elite's stiff resistance to Özal's policies, but the success Özal enjoyed in breaking with the old consensus was not repeated in the formation of a new one that would put Turkey irreversibly on a different path in foreign policy. Equally, Özal failed to convince the general public that the new foreign policy, necessitated by Turkey's aspiration to "regional power" status, required a reordering of domestic politics.

To become a significant actor in international relations, Turkey had to reform its economic system further, integrating it more fully into the world economy and liberating its resources by downsizing the public sector. Only a more robust economy could sustain Özal's ambitious foreign policy. The domestic political coalition of vested interests that opposed any restructuring of the economy proved to be formidable, though. Some businesspersons, bureaucrats, politicians, and public-sector workers vehemently opposed attempts to integrate Turkish economy into the world, fearing losses in income, profits, patronage, and employment. After Prime Minister Çiller's economic stabilization package, there was even less enthusiasm for a program of modernization and privatization that would arguably generate further hardship for large segments of the population.

In domestic politics, the most controversial and, in the long run, the most consequential of Özal's actions was his redefinition of the Kurdish issue and his effort to open the entire matter to national debate. The smear campaign to which he was subjected because of his position on the Kurdish question (and his intimate relations with the Iraqi Kurdish leadership) underscored the difficulty of attempting radical departures from Turkey's "official ideology" and national security taboos.

The obstructionism and vilification that Özal faced as he searched for a new "strategic partnership" with the United States was another case in point. This controversial aspect of Özal's thinking, predicated upon the transitory nature of a unipolar world where there existed an "uncertain balance," was seen as old-fashioned subservience to a much-vilified United States rather than an attempt to fashion a new relationship between the two countries.[41] By working closely with the United States, Özal paradoxically created the conditions for new international political openings; this fact escaped the attention or the comprehension of a majority of his detractors and commentators.

Today, two years after Özal's death, his strategic outlook and plans are under serious conceptual and ideological attack. In a trend that accelerated during the tenure of Mümtaz Soysal as minister of foreign affairs (August to December 1994), Turkish foreign policy showed signs of responding to Third Worldist and nationalist views with undertones of anti-Westernism emanating from the public. Turkey's entire post–World War II orientation in strategic matters and its "civilizational" choice to become part of the West faced a new "populist"-cum-democratic challenge.[42]

A partial explanation for this shift and its popularity with the general public can be found in the general disenchantment with the West and the belief that Turkey's interests and concerns were being given short shrift by its allies. Western policies on Bosnia-Herzegovina looked suspiciously like "appeasement" of the Serbs at best, and complicity with war criminals from a sense of Christian solidarity at worst.[43] Turkey's concerns went unheeded by its allies, who also excluded Ankara from the major councils where a solution to the Bosnia problem was discussed. These developments exacerbated the feeling of distrust toward the West among the general public.[44]

There was also the brutal awakening from the euphoria generated by the collapse of the Soviet Union and the entry into the international system of the Turks' long-lost "cousins" in Azerbaijan and the central Asian republics of the Commonwealth of Independent States. The conflict in the Caucasus also intensified suspicions of a Western conspiracy to deprive Turkey of influence in its expanded post-Cold War zone of national interest. The Conference on Security and Cooperation in Europe (now the Organization for Security and Cooperation in Europe) failed to adjudicate the conflict between Armenia and Azerbaijan over the autonomous region of Nagorno-Karabakh. As a result, Armenia occupied almost a fifth of the lands of Azerbaijan proper, with indirect Russian assistance. Russia grew increasingly assertive throughout its "near abroad," and the West appeared to acquiesce. The enthusiastic reception of Samuel Huntington's controversial essay "The Clash of Civilizations?" in Turkey highlighted the fact that, for many Turks, a vision of the world that pitted the rest against the West—and, in particular, the world of Islam against the world of Christianity—was essentially valid. Such a conceptualization of the nature of international relations in the new era (and the fact that Huntington himself categorized Turkey as a "torn country") further fueled the ongoing national debate about identity and the appropriate direction of international relations for the country.[45]

Nowhere has the Western orientation of Turkey's foreign policy come under such intense scrutiny and created such disenchantment with the general public as in the Middle East. A real or imagined sense of betrayal and undercompensation for Turkey's stance during the Gulf War combined with the very real and severe economic costs of continuing the embargo against Iraq are putting a heavy strain on relations among Turkey, the United States, and Europe.[46] Continuing criticism of Turkey's human-rights record (especially by Western Europeans, but increasingly by the U.S. Congress) in its handling of the Kurdish problem and the growing pressures on Ankara to devise a "political solution" to this issue are also fueling the so-called Sèvres phobia of Turkey's traditional elite.[47] As a result, by the time Özal died, both the elite and the popular constituencies for a more "nationalist" (read "parochial") policy were in place. This brought a qualitative change to the conduct of Turkey's foreign policy.

In Search of Moments Past

The moment for Turkey to become a regional power, so full of promise between 1990 and 1993, has probably passed. As noted, the redefinition of Turkey's strategic interests necessitated a more engaged relationship with the surrounding regions that collectively make up the expanded Middle East.

Turkey's security policies toward the Middle East or the Persian Gulf should, then, be evaluated in relationship to this broader area. Turkey has tried to maintain friendly contact with all of the countries in the region, allowing Ankara to offer its services as a mediator between conflicting parties at appropriate times. This role was to build upon the historical legacy of the Ottoman Empire. For example, the Turkish prime minister made a well-publicized visit to Israel in November 1994, and the two countries are increasing their cooperation in security as well as trade and tourism. Israeli expertise in agricultural technology is being put to use in Turkey's giant Southeast Anatolian Project, and Israeli tourists constituted one of the larger groups visiting Turkey in 1994. President Demirel's trip to Jordan in August 1994 was similarly well publicized, and the two countries' approaches to regional problems seem to be converging.

Since the expanded Middle East, in which Turkey has political, economic, and security interests, overlaps in the north with part of the Russian near abroad, some rivalry between the two countries was inevitable. The Russians expressed their anxiety about growing Turkish influence in the former Soviet states in a letter that President Yeltsin sent to Demirel in September 1993. By sending this letter "Yeltsin sent shock waves through Turkey. . . . He reportedly declared that force ceilings established by the CFE treaty for the North Caucasus districts were falling short of responding to Russia's needs, adding that they faced the risk of non-implementation."[48]

Particularly in the Caucasus, despite efforts by both Özal and Demirel to be reassuring, Russia's foreign policy and security establishments remained suspicious of Turkey's motives. Resurrecting the politics of "the Caucasian Triangle" (that is, the historical rivalry in the Caucasus among Iran, Russia, and Turkey),[49] "Russia has responded by trying to limit Istanbul's [sic] role in the Nagorno-Karabakh peace process and prevent Turkey from becoming a primary transhipment point for oil from Azerbaijan."[50] In September 1994, Azerbaijan signed "a $7 billion agreement with Western oil companies and a Turkish partner to develop Caspian Sea oil fields."[51] Ankara would like this oil, and the oil from Kazakhstan, to reach world markets via a pipeline that would go through Turkey. Russia opposes the shipment of either country's oil through Turkey and would prefer that its Black Sea port of Novorossiysk be the outlet from which the oil could be sent to world markets via Bulgaria and Greece. Already uneasy about the volume of naval traffic on the Bosporus, Turkey opposes any measures that would use waterways under its control to increase this traffic. This clash of interests led Turkey and Russia to play a fencing game in the Caucasus in 1993 and 1994 that still continues.

Turkey's equivocation about and subsequent acquiescence to the Azeri coup d'état engineered by militia leader Suret Huseyinov,[52] which ultimately deposed President Elchibey in June 1993, initially eroded its prestige and influence in Baku.[53] Gaidar Aliyev, who was installed as president after the coup and was widely seen as "Moscow's man," was almost overthrown by the same Huseyinov after Aliyev signed an oil agreement with the Western consortium, which now included the Russian Lukoil. Ironically, the imperatives of geopolitics and the desire to maintain some autonomy from Moscow brought Aliyev to the point of signing the same oil agreement that he had suspended when he replaced Elchibey as president.

Turkey would need the support of the Western allies if it hoped to regain lost ground in Azerbaijan and to secure the passage of the pipelines that would transport Kazakh and Caucasian oil to the port of Ceyhan in southern Turkey. If built, this pipeline is expected to turn Ceyhan into a new Rotterdam. The policy of the United States on this matter would be particularly critical. But Washington's tendency to treat Moscow with deference and to yield to Russian aspirations in the near abroad, compounded by the increasingly problematic nature of the relations between Turkey and the United States over policy toward Iraq and the Kurds, meant that this support never fully developed.[54]

The "return" of the Russians to their near abroad had a positive impact on the relations between Turkey and the third element of the Caucasian Triangle, Iran. Much has been made of the Turkish-Iranian rivalry over the Muslim republics of the former Soviet Union when they gained their independence. Whether the central Asian republics would choose as their model secular, democratic, and free-market-oriented Turkey or the Islamic Republic of Iran was debated endlessly. Ultimately both countries' power to affect developments in the new republics proved limited. Rivalry flared in earnest only in the Caucasus, over the Nagorno-Karabakh conflict. The Iranians feared the passionate nationalism of the Popular Front in Azerbaijan and its leader, Elchibey, who saw northern Iran as southern Azerbaijan. This led Tehran to support the Armenians against Baku. Considerably less worried about Iran than about Turkey, the Russians signed two agreements with Iran, "one envisaging regular political consultations, the other cooperation in economic military and nuclear matters."[55] The Russians also sold arms to the Iranians.

While Russian domestic politics were in turmoil at the end of 1993, those veterans of the Afghan War who were responsible for devising Moscow's new security policies managed to reestablish Russian dominance in almost all the territories of the former Soviet Union. By the end of 1993, both Azerbaijan and Georgia grudgingly but helplessly joined the CIS. The rise of the radical right in Russian politics and the ascent of ultranationalist Vladimir Zhirinovsky, however, had the effect of bringing Turkey and Iran closer together.[56] The two countries were already coordinating their policies on the Kurdish issue to prevent, at any cost, the emergence of an independent Kurdish state in the "safe haven" established in northern Iraq at the end of the Gulf War.[57] They were also cooperating in the Economic Cooperation Organization, which brought together Pakistan, Iran, Turkey, and the central Asian republics in a regional economic development scheme. Demirel's high-visibility visit to Iran in July underscored the improvement in relations, although Ankara still blamed Iran for supporting the Kurdish Workers Party (PKK), for sponsoring terrorist activities inside Turkey against secular intellectuals, and for supporting Islamic movements. According to Barkey, "Iran perceives Turkey as a US-sponsored competitor seeking to limit its influence among the newly independent republics of Central Asia. Thus, Iranian support for the PKK is a means of checking what it sees as Turkey's growing ambitions throughout the region."[58] Yet both Özal and Demirel maintained an open and cordial dialogue with President Rafsanjani. Turkey is even willing to play the role of the intermediary in helping Iran establish better political relations with the world community.

Continuities and Changes

The Özalist vision and the reprioritizing of the principles of Turkey's national security led to an outward-looking policy. Overcoming the rigidity of physical and political borders, Turkey tried to extend its influence, primarily economically, to all surrounding areas, to act as a broker between the West and the expanded Middle East, and to benefit economically and politically from Turkey's increasing importance as a gateway.[59] Another corollary of this approach was to use the United States as leverage on many regional issues and to secure U.S. backing to resolve contentious issues on Turkey's own terms. To attain such a level of autonomy from and cooperation with the United States, Özal also acknowledged that Turkey's domestic political order had to be liberalized and democratized.

The evolving antithesis to this approach to Turkey's international relations is predicated on the primacy of Turkey's territorial integrity, and it had as its corollary inward-looking policies. The restoration and perpetuation of the traditional order takes precedence over international engagements and obligations. This nationalist alternative strategy reflects a deep concern about a possible Western conspiracy to weaken Turkey, perhaps by sponsoring the creation of a "puppet" Kurdish state. The nationalist perspective also counts on Turkey's geographic location to create political leverage. This approach began to seriously jeopardize Turkey's relations with Europe and increasingly with the United States.

Unless the practitioners of such a perspective were simply determined to disengage Turkey from the West, only two explanations explain the pursuit of such policies:

1. In the terminology that Professor Soysal, minister of foreign affairs between July and December of 1994, introduced into the Turkish political lexicon, Turkey had to follow an "honorable" foreign policy and maintain its distance and independence from the United States while pursuing its own interests. Particularly with respect to Iraq, such a vision singularly ignores the limits of unilateral action in the existing international environment and disregards the sensitive equilibriums of linkages that exist for Turkey's diverse interests in the surrounding regions.

2. Anticipating that Turkey's strategic value would rise to something like its Cold War level as Western discomfort with an increasingly assertive and perhaps aggressive Russia increased, some policymakers believe that the pressures on Turkey over human rights and democratization would subside, as they always have in the past.

Since the end of the Gulf War and the establishment of the Kurdish safe haven, relations between the United States and Turkey have oscillated between very warm and problematic. The presence and purpose of Operation Provide Comfort progressively became a contentious issue in Turkey because of growing and more effective PKK activities in the region. American pressure on Turkey about its human-rights record and a variety of other issues helped to undermine what once appeared to be a solid partnership.

The issues of contention between Turkey and the United States fall into two categories: (1) direct bilateral problems and (2) different and sometimes contrary approaches to a number of international developments that constitute indirect problems. The second category includes the problems of Bosnia, the Caucasus, and attitudes toward Russia's near-abroad policy. In the first category, five topics increasingly sour bilateral relations:

1. Human rights: In past relations with Turkey, the United States (unlike the European Community) rarely emphasized human-rights violations. However, if the nebulous policy of "enlargement" becomes operational, the issue of human rights may surge to the fore as a new and determinant factor in the relations between the two countries.[60]

2. Aid: The U.S. Congress made 10 percent of U.S. aid to Turkey conditional on improvements in human rights and the

withdrawal of Turkish troops from Cyprus. The Turkish government rejected that portion of the aid package in September 1994.

3. Cyprus: The unresolved problem of Cyprus continues to cast its shadow on bilateral relations as Turkey resists pressures to abandon its unilateral intervention on behalf of the Turkish Cypriot community and to accept a diplomatic solution.

4. Policy toward Iraq.

5. The Kurdish problem, which is intimately related to the human rights question.

The last two issues are, by far, the most troublesome between the two countries. They call for a more thorough treatment.

Turkish-American Debate over Policy toward Iraq

Until Saddam Hussein moved his troops near the Kuwaiti border in October 1994, "making the mother of all blunders,"[61] Turkish policy toward Iraq was on a fast track towards conciliation. Occurring on the eve of a critical U.N. Security Council vote that might have given him some respite, the almost incomprehensible move by the Iraqi leader killed all Turkish initiatives, along with hopes that Turkey could be instrumental in easing Iraq's way back into the international system.

The root causes of Turkey's tilt toward a policy that is more "understanding" of Iraq can be traced back to the unfinished task at the end of the Gulf War. There is no doubt that Özal's policy expected Saddam Hussein, if not the Baath regime, to be removed from power. The inconclusive end to the war, the flood of Kurdish refugees on Turkey's borders that ensued from the bloody repression of the Kurdish insurgency tolerated by President Bush, and the fact that Turkey ended up suffering the economic consequences of the sanctions regime instead of getting a share of the "spoils" at the "victors' table" all contributed to the weakening of public support for pro-U.S. policies.[62] Any residual support for Özal's policies was further eroded by the deepening of Turkey's economic crisis in 1994, which brought about a substantial decline in gross national product, increased unemployment, and produced an inflation rate of over 100 percent. Consequently, "under economic and political pressure, the Turkish government is seeking to normalize ties with Iraq without breaking the U.N.-imposed sanctions."[63]

The new approach that prevailed toward Iraq in the post-Özal era also reflected the growing importance of a social dynamic with three dimensions:

1. The general public increasingly blamed both its economic vicis-
    situdes and the spread of PKK violence to the embargo and the
    presence of "Poised Hammer" (Operation Provide Comfort).
2. Nationalist elites (including a wide spectrum of political posi-
    tions, from protofascists to Kemalists to social democrats) be-
    came wary of the vacuum in northern Iraq, because they feared
    that it might serve as the midwife for that most undesirable child,
    an independent Kurdistan.
3. Finally, important constituencies saw the economic oppor-
    tunities that lifting the sanctions against Iraq might create and,
    for that reason, supported the Russian and French initiatives for
    lifting the embargo, without realizing that both of these countries
    (particularly the latter) would not directly challenge the United
    States.

The common denominator among these three groups is their inability
to view Turkey's strategic interests from a broader perspective. That
perspective would require an appreciation of Turkey's objective conditions and the region's delicate political equilibriums that place Turkish-
Iraqi relations in the context of a larger strategic equation. The
proponents of this approach hoped to resurrect the Saadabad Pact of
1937, which allied Turkey, Iran, Iraq, and Afghanistan. In the spirit of that
pact, there was "an understanding that Iran, Iraq and Turkey would
co-operate in suppressing any Kurdish nationalist movement intent on
altering the political status quo in the region."[64] The political status quo
had already been changed, though, by the consequences of Saddam
Hussein's actions in 1991, and the Kurdish issue is more prominently on
the world's agenda now than it has ever been before. Even if the regional
balances of the northern tier, the Arabian Peninsula, or the world system
at large are not conducive to the emergence of a Kurdish state, the
resolution of Turkey's Kurdish problem will still require more imaginative approaches than that provided by a pact signed in 1937.

Turkey also continued its efforts to put together an agreement
whereby it would be allowed to flush oil two and a half times through
the pipelines that it closed in August 1990 as part of the economic
embargo against Iraq. This move was also defended on technical
grounds, because it would help to avoid corrosion of the pipelines.
Having suffered the devastating material consequences of halted
economic activity, declining revenue, skyrocketing unemployment, and
a surge in violence, Turkey was within its rights to ask for relief. Ankara
should have received more help sooner in this quest, but the United States
is distant from the region and does not have to bear directly the price of
its own passive policy toward Iraq. Yet what had started as a Turkish
search to find a multifaceted solution to the Iraqi pipeline problem by

engaging the other Persian Gulf states, such as Saudi Arabia, gradually evolved into a policy of appeasing Baghdad.

After a long and arduous process, the Turkish foreign ministry drafted a resolution to be approved by the U.N. Security Council for flushing the oil inside the pipeline and dispensing the revenues accruing to Iraq from its sale. This draft was prepared with the full knowledge and consent of all of the parties to its provisions. At the last moment, however, the Iraqi regime objected to the distribution by the Turkish Red Cross of the essential goods procured with this money. Those who had a better understanding of Saddam's regime and saw it as a source of instability for the entire region felt a bitter vindication when, at the last moment, he reneged on this agreement. This act of bad faith and Saddam's subsequent military maneuvers along his borders with Kuwait ended any possibility of flushing the oil so long as he remained in power.

The alternative approach to relations with Iraq, articulated by Özal, projected unremitting hostility towards Saddam and the Baathist regime. This approach was more sanguine about the Kurdish safe haven and the efforts by the Kurds to create institutions of self-governance. Özal argued that

> it would be a lot more useful for us to have influence over these groups (the KDP, the Kurdistan Democratic Party, and the PUK, the Patriotic Union of Kurdistan) in Northern Iraq rather than letting them be influenced by external forces that have dubious intentions. We should try to keep them under our spell as much as possible and even try to assume the role of their guarantors. We know that the Saddam regime supports the PKK and helps it any way it can. If Saddam succeeds along with the PKK, in weakening the Kurds and the Turcomans of northern Iraq, then the terrorist organization will be better situated to maneuver in those territories. It also goes without saying that it does not serve our interests to make enemies of Talabani and Barzani in addition to the PKK.[65]

Özal was confident that a Kurdish state could not be formed against Turkey's will. Hence, he thought the proper course to take would be to exercise some kind of economic and political overlordship in northern Iraq, maintain good relations with the Kurdish groups, and make sure that Turkey would be party to all developments concerning the Kurdish region. In fact, one of the consequences of the reversal of these policies vis-à-vis northern Iraq after Özal's death has been the alienation from Ankara of the Kurdish leaders Jelal Talabani and Masud Barzani, respectively the leaders of PUK and KDP, whom the Turks had encouraged to negotiate with Saddam. As a result, Turkey was excluded from the developments that led to the reconciliation talks between the two leaders whose forces had battled against each other earlier. This last position revealed once more the contradictions in Turkey's approach to the security problems in northern Iraq. Earlier, the two Kurdish leaders were given the responsibility to contain the PKK in the region after Turkey's military operation there in 1992. Turkey's ambiguity vis-à-vis the protected Kurdish zone in northern Iraq and the recurring battles between the two dominant Kurdish groups, KDP and PUK, weakened this arrangement and created a vacuum that the PKK took advantage of to set up bases from which to attack targets inside Turkey. This, in turn, led to the massive military operation in northern Iraq that the Turkish army undertook with 35,000 troops in March 1995, at great political and financial cost to the country. Upon withdrawal of the troops, the only internationally acceptable solution to the security problem in northern Iraq turned out to be the resurrection of the 1992 agreement, whereby the KDP and the PUK would be made responsible for containing and controlling the PKK and the Turkish government would extend financial and other assistance to the Kurdish zone.

Turkish-American Debate over the Kurdish Problem

The Kurdish issue is part of the larger problem of human rights. The United States, which has declared the PKK a terrorist organization, has joined other Western countries in putting pressure on Turkey for a "political solution" to this problem. Turkey's domestic Kurdish problem is also the key to the pattern of domestic alliances that favors one foreign policy option or the other vis-à-vis Iraq and the Middle East. Those who favor a more liberal and integrationist (as opposed to assimilationist) approach to the resolution of the Kurdish problem tend to favor a less rigid policy towards northern Iraq.

The Sèvres-phobic nationalist approach, which continues to insist upon the primacy of territorial integrity, brings together a coterie of Kemalists, ultranationalists, Islamists, and nationalist social democrats who view the world through lenses heavily tinted by conspiracy theories. They tend to view U.S. foreign policy toward Iraq prior to the invasion of Kuwait as deliberate entrapment of Saddam Hussein, which led to the dominance of the region by the United States. Even today, this camp tends to view Western support for the protected Kurdish zone in northern Iraq and Western concern about Turkey's handling of the Kurdish problem as reflections of a Western desire to break Turkey (and Iraq) into smaller, more manageable states.

The founding principles of the Turkish Republic barred the political expression of four ideologies: Islamism, Kurdish nationalism, liberalism, and communism. The social and economic development of the country and the transformation of the ideological map of the world have already rendered three of these bans meaningless. Communism became a relic, Islamism prospered as the population of Turkey mobilized and moved into the cities, and economic (but not political) liberalism found grudging acceptance. Such was not the fate of Kurdish nationalism. In an unpublished paper in which he reviews Turkey's taboos, historian Heath Lowry argues that "central to the creation of Turkish nationalism, i.e., to the ideological foundation of the state, was the well-entrenched taboo against any kind of emphasis of one's ethnicity."[66] Hence, all references to the Kurds, who fought in the war of independence alongside the Turks, and to the Kurdistan, which sent representatives to the first National Assembly of 1920 to 1923, suddenly disappeared from political discourse after 1924. Because of its close association with the question of territorial integrity, any discussion of Kurdish nationalism continues to be anathema to the state elite in Turkey.

The current Kurdish problem has political and military-terrorist facets. The Turkish state is well equipped to react to the challenge of military-terrorist violence and fight the PKK.[67] It concentrates on military means to eradicate the organization and rejoices at every sign of perceived weakness on the part of the PKK and its leadership. At the same time, it continues to ignore the wider, nonmilitary dimensions of the problem. As Philip Robins observed in his analysis of reactions to the PKK's unilateral declaration of a ceasefire in March 1993, "the PKK was regarded as being desperate to stave off hostilities in order to rebuild its communications and its morale. Underlying this view was a widely held assumption that the Kurdish problem for Turkey was in essence that of an estranged minority operating beyond the frontier under the patronage of Turkey's hostile Middle Eastern neighbors."[68]

Nationalist ideology notwithstanding, Turkey is a multiethnic, multicultural society. The revolutionary elite who founded the republic willed it to be homogeneous and denied the existence of ethnic identities. To a large extent, they succeeded in assimilating different ethnic groups by subsuming diverse identities in a unifying Turkish citizenship. Ethnic identity never became a barrier to social mobility, yet there was a cost. Lowry notes that for the Kurds as well as other ethnic groups, "the cost of fully entering life in the new republic was the denial of one's ethnicity. To anyone willing to do so all doors were opened."[69] More than seventy years after the founding of the republic, the fear of fragmentation that led to the formulation of such a policy is no longer valid. The problem today is how to accommodate the desires of Turkey's citizens to express their particularities. This new development reflects on the richness of the country's heritage and its culture. In a new era, when ethnic identity and indeed ethnic nationalism are fixed parts of the global, social, and political landscape, a new understanding of these issues is required.

The Turkish military has enjoyed success in the civil war this past year, managing to quell PKK violence and break the organizational structure of the party in Turkey proper.[70] It is a pyrrhic victory, though, since the price of this success has been devastating. In 1994 between TL 250 trillion and TL 500 trillion (approximately $15 billion) was spent to prosecute the war and for related expenses.[71] Close to fifteen thousand deaths, both military and civilian, have occurred, along with countless casualties, since 1984, when the PKK attacks began. According to some cabinet members, close to two thousand villages and hamlets have been destroyed.[72] More than one million people were forced to migrate to big cities in Turkey (some also fled to northern Iraq), becoming refugees in their own country and thereby increasing the risk of urban violence. Other costs include the growing enmity of citizens against the state, declining revenues from tourism, the burden on an already crippled economy, paralysis in political relations with Western Europe, and strains in relations with the United States. Turkish security and diplomatic power have been severely undermined because of the disproportionate allocation of human, material, and monetary resources in the southeast of the country. The credibility of Turkey's deterrent capability is reduced by this vast investment of resources in one region alone.[73]

One would assume that these costs are being incurred to preserve "the indivisible unity of the country with its state and its nation," as the Constitution stipulates. But even if this end justified the means, it could still not conceal the imbalance between the costs (economic, social, and political) and the limited value of the objectives achieved. The coffins of the young soldiers killed in action that find their way to western Turkey foster resentment and hatred against Turkish citizens of Kurdish origin who have been living in the region for years, if not for generations.[74] The social peace between Kurds and Turks, based on a shared religion and easygoing interactions, is increasingly fragile. Such a development threatens to tear the social fabric of the country apart by accentuating communal differences and boundaries. As Lowry notes, "Turkish-Kurdish ethnic violence continues to spread away from southeast Anatolia . . . (and) partially and fully assimilated Kurds living far from their traditional homeland are having their ethnicity forced upon them by the actions of a Turkish majority growing increasingly apprehensive about the unrest spreading from the southeast."[75]

Perhaps if there were a parallel program of political and cultural reforms, one could more readily accept the necessity of these measures. Turkey's allies have, after all, been encouraging the Turkish leadership to undertake these reforms. Not only are reforms an appropriate approach to help resolve the Kurdish problem, but they are also part of Turkey's obligations stemming from treaties and charters to which it was a signatory. Turkey's friends and allies tried to convince Ankara that a war on the Kurds, which would divide the country and aggravate an already unstable region, was not in their interests. Alas, the Turkish political class tended to equate reform proposals with "capitulation to terrorists." This mind-set, viscerally intolerant of any diversion from the accepted code, led to the lifting of the immunities of Democratic Labor Party (a Kurdish nationalist party) deputies and, scandalously, to their incarceration.[76] The outcome of their trial, everyone agrees, will depend on the balance of political forces within the country, and not on recognized principles of justice. Such action forecloses the possibility of a political resolution of this increasingly dangerous problem by leaving the PKK as the only viable Kurdish organization. While the Turkish elite denies the very existence of a Kurdish problem and sees ethnic nationalism as nothing more than a symptom of imperialist meddling that weakens the state, it is difficult to think of a political solution. A country where between a quarter and a third of the deputies in the National Assembly are of Kurdish origin requires a more sensible approach to the resolution of its most intractable problem. In an age when negotiations between Israel and Hamas over a code of behavior are in the realm of the possible, Turkey cannot continue to deny the scope of the Kurdish problem. Some political space must be created for nonviolent Kurdish groups to come forward and assume the responsibility of mediators. The irony is that obstructing the moderates can only serve the purposes of the PKK. Its leader, Abdullah Ocalan, having recently declared in an interview with the British Broadcasting Corporation that the Kurds do not seek independence, is waiting in the wings for his political opportunity.[77]

"Irony Can Write the Preface to Tragedy"[78]

It is quite evident that the Kurdish problem is the focal point of a network of domestic and international policy issues. These issues will determine the degree of continuity, stability, and dependability of the Turkish political order, which, in turn, will affect whether the Turkish contribution to the regional subsystems will be stabilizing or destabilizing. Domestically, the current approach to the Kurdish problem is the last line of defense and the refuge of an unimaginative political elite, adamant that it will prevent any change in the existing political arrangements. Internationally, it weakens and could even possibly sever Turkey's affinity, if not its political relationships, with the West and relegate it to the company of pariah states such as Iran, Iraq, and Syria. Turkey should, by all means, enjoy good relations with Iran and Syria and a post-Saddam Iraq. It should also pursue policies of accommodation with Iran that might not fit well with the confrontational policies of the United States. Allies can and do differ in particular policies so long as the foundations of their collaboration remain intact. Turkey shares many interests with Iran, a country with which it has had no border problems for over three hundred years. Turkey also needs Iranian cooperation to pursue some of Ankara's more ambitious projects, such as the gas pipeline from Turkmenistan.

With Syria as well, bridges ought to be built to dispel some of the bitterness and mistrust generated by colonial meddling and a long and selectively remembered history of Ottoman rule. Syrian (or Iranian and Iraqi) support for the PKK is just mischief. It will fade away once the more important bilateral issues are dealt with in the context of peace in the Mashreq. Turkey and Syria will then have the choice of squandering their resources in belligerency or of cooperating for economic development. Most analysts suggest that once the Syrian-Israeli peace is signed, there will be increasing tensions between Syria and Turkey—particularly, disputes over sharing water resources. A state of belligerency is expected. If this were to happen, then Turkish diplomacy would need the deterrent power of a well-equipped and well-prepared army that is not locked in a fight against its own citizens.

Turkey's political *qibla* still ought to be the liberal democracies of the West, because alternative political arrangements for its domestic order are totally inadequate to keep together a society as differentiated and developed as Turkey. Furthermore, Turkey's constructive role in the Middle East and the Persian Gulf region can continue only if Ankara maintains its close association with the West. Continuing the affinity with the West when the latter's own forces of modernity seem to have run out of steam and when a degree of justifiable anti-Westernism is rampant in non-Western societies is a more difficult position to defend for Turkey's modernized elites. There is indeed something irritating, no matter how justified, about European lectures on human rights, when in Bosnia the Europeans themselves have managed nothing better than diplomatic double-talk as a country was being raped and a nation's right to independence was being violated. The Europe of the Enlightenment demonstrated that it could not accommodate Islam in its midst no matter how "European" that Islam might have been.[79] For Turks, it is disconcerting to hear sermons about "minority rights" based on preconceived models constructed with inadequate knowledge of history and mistaken analogies, when the challenge is to secure the equality of all citizens in a new political contract.

Yet Turkey ought to continue to model its political standards on Western ideals, both for the sake of its citizens and for its destiny as a nation. Turkey can no more detach itself from the West and become solely a Middle Eastern country than it could have become an exclusively Western country under Ataturk. Even Turkey's Islamists will find that efforts to impress upon the country a monolithic worldview are unlikely to succeed permanently. They will make their contribution to the evolution of Turkish democracy only if they can understand and assimilate this reality.

In an almost prophetic article written in 1989, Duygu Bazoğlu Sezer argued that "Turkish historical experience gives strikingly consistent evidence of being rather receptive, even if very gradually and somewhat grudgingly, to the persuasive powers of external stimuli as opposed to the internal."[80] In the post-Cold War environment, the absence of more rigidly defined rules for international conduct makes this observation only slightly less salient. Turkey faces an environment that has yet to deal with all the tremors that followed the Gulf War and the Leninist extinction. For the international system, Turkey's stability and its ability to constructively reshape the region will be far more valuable than the West might think today. At one level, international stimuli may exacerbate the xenophobic tendencies that seem to overwhelm rational perspective and discourse in Turkey's domestic politics today. However, for the first time in its political history, Turkey also has a mature, well-entrenched, and relatively sizable liberal middle class that could be the agent of a domestic dynamic that would integrate Turkey with the liberal and globalist currents in the world. Yet, given the erosion in the legitimacy of the westernization project in Turkey, the external stimuli in favor of liberalization and democratization coming from the West need to be subtle.

The case was made above that Özal's globalist policies ran afoul of an unreconstructed domestic political order. I also argued that the dynamics of Turkey's surrounding regions and its alliances would not allow a complete restoration of a domestic status quo ante, no matter how threatening Russian power might become. Hence, the onus is on the rulers and citizens of Turkey to understand their geography and regional politics in the context of a fast-changing world where there will be no second chance, for some time to come, to join the advanced world. The degree of freedom enjoyed by the state elite in the conduct of foreign policy since the 1920s is no longer possible. It may not even be desirable. However, Turkey cannot afford to let its foreign policy become hostage to domestic political considerations, particularly when the domestic political scene is so fragmented.

Ultimately, the destiny of the country will be in the hands of its citizens. The Turks would do well to remember the wise words of their best-known Sufi poet, Celaleddin-i Rumi, who wrote that "gone with yesterday, my love, is all that was yesterday's, now's the time to say new things." Heeding this advice will help establish a proper balance between what domestic resources can bear and what the international environment can allow, tolerate, or encourage. As George Liska suggests, "just as the dialectic between freedom and necessity draws the boundaries of choice, and the resistance of actuality to aspiration delimits the area of change, so to expose contemporary events to principles and patterns evidenced historically is to narrow the range of present options and future developments."[81] Time and politics will tell whether Turkey will be able to find its proper course and play the constructive role that its geography and history bestow upon it in the expanded Middle East.

I would like to thank Bill Quandt, AAAS, and the editors, Geoffrey Kemp and Janice Gross Stein, for giving me the opportunity to write this piece. I accumulated even further personal and intellectual debts to Yahya Sadowski, who obviously has nothing to do with all the shortcomings of this paper.

Notes

1. Serif Mardin, "Religion and Secularism in Modern Turkey," in *Atatürk: Founder of a Modern State*, eds. Ali Kazancıgil and Ergun Ozbudun (London: C. Hurst, 1981), especially pp. 112–116.

2. Selim Deringil, *Turkish Foreign Policy during the Second World War* (Cambridge: Cambridge University Press, 1989), chap. 9.

3. For this crisis and the story of Turkey's inclusion in the Truman Doctrine, see Stephen G. Xydis, "New Light on the Big Three Crisis over Turkey in 1945," *Middle East Journal* 14 (fall 1960): 416–432, and the classic book by Bruce R. Kuniholm, *The Origins of the Cold War in the Near East* (Princeton, N.J.: Princeton University Press, 1994), chaps. 4–6. For a different interpretation of this period's developments, see Melvyn Leffler, "Strategy, Diplomacy and the Cold War: US, Turkey and NATO: 1945–1952," *Journal of American History* 71 (March 1985): 807–25.

4. Çağlar Keyder, *State and Class in Turkey* (London: Verso, 1987), 136.

5. For two examples of such uncompromising identification of Turkish national identity and interests with those of the West, see Bulent Nuri Eren, "The Middle East and Turkey in World Affairs," in *Annals of the American Association of Political and Social Sciences*, July 1951, 72–80; and Fatin Rüstü Zorlu, "A Turkish View of World Affairs: A Bridge Between East and West" (speech delivered at Colgate University, Hamilton, NY, 1 July 1959), *Vital Speeches of the Day*, 1 September 1959.

6. Reşat Kasaba, "Populism and Democracy in Turkey: 1946–1961," in *Rules and Rights in the Middle East*, eds. Ellis Goldberg, Reşat Kasaba, and Joel Migdal (Seattle: University of Washington Press, 1993), 43–68.

7. Andrew Mango, "Turkish Policy in the Middle East," in *Turkish Foreign Policy: New Prospects*, ed. Clement H. Dodd (Cambridgeshire: Eothen Press, 1992), 62.

8. Süha Bölükbaşı, *Turkish-American Relations and Cyprus* (Lanham, Md.: University Press of America, 1988), 60–81.

9. Philip Robins, *Turkey and the Middle East* (New York: Council on Foreign Relations Press, 1991), 78.

10. Turkey did not become a full member of the conference until 1976, and even then the agreement was not ratified by Parliament.

11. These relations certainly intensified in the last decade, particularly in the aftermath of Operation Desert Storm. For a detailed survey of the evolution of Turkey's relations with the Arab and Muslim worlds, see Mahmut Bali Aykan, *Turkey's Role in the Organization of the Islamic Conference: 1960–1992* (New York: Vantage Press, 1994).

12. In their article "Turkish Foreign Policy toward the Arab-Israeli Conflict: Duality and the Development (1950–1991)" (*Arab Studies Quarterly* 14, no. 4 [fall 1992]), M. Hakan Yavuz and Mujeeb R. Khan suggest "four well-defined phases: (1) the Cold War and Western dominated foreign policy (1947–1964); (2) the Cypriot angle (1964–1973); (3) the petro-dollar oriented policy (1974–1989); and (4) the Gulf Crisis and 'strategic ties' with the USA" (73).

13. Paul Wittek, *The Rise of the Ottoman Empire*, Royal Asiatic Society Monographs 23 (1938; reprint; London: Royal Asiatic Society, 1965).

14. Duygu Bazoğlu Sezer, *Turkey's Political and Security Interests and Policies in the New Geostrategic Environment of the Expanded Middle East* (Washington, D.C.: The Henry L. Stimson Center, 1994).

15. Henri J. Barkey, "Turkish-Arab Relations," The Beirut Review 7 (spring 1994): 10.

16. For the genesis of the Baghdad Pact and Turkey's reasons for pursuing it with such passion, see Mango, "Turkish Policy in the Middle East," 61–63. Richard Robinson also observes that "curiously, the Baghdad Pact represented a Turkish departure from traditional policy of not committing itself irrevocably to any particular position in the Middle East" (*The First Turkish Republic* [Cambridge: Harvard University Press, 1963], 186).

17. Robins, *Turkey and the Middle East*, 65–67.

18. Ibid., 72–73.

19. Sezer has observed that "security in the post-INF period posed a basic dilemma for Turkey's alliance diplomacy. While she advocated a closing of ranks within the alliance in those times of fluidity, centrifugal forces and tendencies on both sides of the Atlantic were pulling the Alliance apart. . . . First, the American skepticism about the continued merits of her security commitment for Europe increased. Second, the Western European publics grew reluctant to support defense expenditures particularly within the Alliance framework. And third, several West European countries increasingly tended to improve the coordination and cooperation of their security policies in institutions and channels outside the Alliance," such as the Western European Union. Duygu Bazoğlu Sezer, "Turkey and the Western Alliance," in *The Political and Socioeconomic Transformation of Turkey*, eds. Atila Eralp, Muharrem Tunay, and Birol Yesilada (Westport, Conn.: Praeger, 1993), 226.

20. Dankwart Rustow, *Turkey: America's Forgotten Ally* (New York: Council on Foreign Relations, 1987).

21. Bruce R. Kuniholm, "After the Gulf War: Turkey and the East," in *The Persian Gulf War: Views from the Social and Behavioral Sciences*, eds. Herbert H. Blumberg and Christopher C. French (Lanham, Md.: University Press of America, 1994), 454.

22. Many authors in Turkey and elsewhere made this argument, which proved to be exaggerated. For a forceful presentation of this argument, see Graham E. Fuller's chapters in Graham E. Fuller et al., *Turkey's New Geopolitics: From the Balkans to Western China* (Boulder, Colo.: Westview Press, 1993).

23. The term is from Ken Jowitt, *New World Disorder: The Leninist Extinction* (Berkeley, Cal.: UC Press, 1992).

24. Robinson, *The First Turkish Republic*, 71. I am indebted to a senior Foreign Ministry official for drawing my attention to the shift in the ordering of these tenets under Özal.

25. "A strong domestic economy, for Özal, was the first condition for a viable national security. . . . International political economy was the essence of Özal's policy". Yavuz and Khan, "Turkish Foreign Policy toward the Arab-Israeli Conflict," 83.

26. For a detailed and tightly argued analysis of Turkey's gains from the Iran-Iraq War, see Henri J. Barkey, "The Silent Victor: Turkey's Role in the Gulf War," in *The Iran-Iraq War: Impact and Implications*, ed. Efraim Karsh (London: MacMillan, 1989). Barkey's conclusion is that "the war opened up many more opportunities than Turkey took advantage of. This is true with respect to both its relations with Western as well as Middle Eastern countries. . . . One would have expected Turkish diplomacy to maximize its country's importance. This was not done" (149).

27. Turkish foreign policy vis-à-vis the Persian Gulf region during "the second cold war" is analyzed in Mahmut Bali Aykan, "Türkiye'nin Basra Körfezi Güvenliği PolitikasI: 1979–1988" (Turkey's Policy toward Gulf Security: 1979–1988), *ODTU Gelisme Dergisi* 21, no. 1 (1994): 23–59.

28. Aykan, "Türkiye'nin Basra Körfezi Güvenliği PolitikasI," 51.

29. Cem Kozlu, *Bir Turkiye Mucizesi Icin: Vizyon Arayislari ve Asya Modelleri* (For a Turkish miracle: Search for a Vision and the Asian Models) (Istanbul: Iş Bankasi Yayinlari, 1994), xi–xv.

30. Şükrü Elekdağ, "Jeo-Stratejiden Eko-Stratejiye" (From Geostrategy to Ecostrategy), *Görüş*, January 1992, 36–44.

31. President Johnson sent a letter to Prime Minister Inönü in June 1964 warning him against the use of U.S. weapons in Cyprus and informing him that the United States and NATO would not feel obligated to defend Turkey if the Soviets chose to attack. Once leaked to the press, the letter poisoned Turkish-U.S. relations for a long time to come. For an analysis of the events that led to the drafting of the letter that is very critical of Inönü's tactics to bring the United States into the diplomatic game on Cyprus, see Süha BölükbaşI, "The Johnson Letter Revisited," *Middle Eastern Studies* 29, no. 3 (July 1993): 505–25.

32. Avi Shlaim, War and Peace in the Middle East (New York: Viking-Penguin, 1994), 96.

33. Ibid., 127.

34. Henri Barkey assesses Turkey's options at the time more pessimistically: "Özal's strategic goals could not be realized. The end of the Cold War undermined Turkey's geopolitical position. In addition, the economic recession, combined with expectations of a peace dividend, limited Western enthusiasm for providing Turkey with substantial amounts of economic and military aid. . . . In short, the role Turkey played during the Gulf crisis has not restored it to a prominent place in Western strategic calculations. In fact, the Kurdish problem demonstrated that Turkey would not become a full strategic partner of the US and NATO in the Middle East; such a partnership would impose too many limitations on Turkish interests and behaviour." Henri Barkey, "Turkey's Kurdish Dilemma," *Survival* (winter 1993–94): 61.

35. See chapter on "The Politics of Water," in Robins, *Turkey and the Middle East,* 87–99. The scheme was supposed to cost $21 billion and the pipelines were expected to have a lifetime of fifty years. These plans also suggested that Turkey wanted to use the most precious natural resource of the future in the region for purposes of economic integration and political cooperation. Yet the Turks had and continue to have a hard time convincing the Arab countries of the "purity" of their intentions.

36. Sezer, "Turkey and the Western Alliance," 216.

37. Cengiz Çandar, "21. Yuzyila Doğru Türkiye: Tarih ve Jeopolitiğin Intikamı" (Turkey toward the Twenty-First Century: The Revenge of History and Geopolitics), in *Türkiye Günlüğü* 19 (summer 1992): 33.

38. This phrase was coined by Amatzia Baram in a talk given at the Johns Hopkins School for Advanced International Studies in Washington, D.C., in February 1994.

39. Prime Minister Akbulut related the following conversation: "In our bilateral talks he [Saddam] told me in very self-assured manner that 'NATO is disintegrating. Your friend, the United States is losing her power. Only those countries that can control their allies are powerful. Nobody listens to the US anymore. She cannot help you.' I was braced for something to follow this tirade. Finally he came forth: 'What are you going to do now?' he asked. . . . He was actually trying to remind me of a nonexisting 'water' problem, and using this was assuming a rather unfriendly attitude towards our country. His words were threatening," from Hulki Cevizoğlu, *Özal'in Korfez Politikasi* (Istanbul, 1991) cited in Soli Özel, "Zirveye Cikis" (The climb to the top) *NOKTA* (Turkish weekly) "Special Supplement on Turgut Özal," 17 April 1993, 23. A slightly different version is found in "Yildirim Akbulut's Memoirs: When I Was Prime Minister," serialized in *Hurriyet,* 10 August 1994, 10.

40. "Ozal seized the opportunity to fully ally himself with the anti-Iraq coalition. His bold early moves . . . also reflected Turkey's concerns about Iraqi nuclear and ballistic warhead ambitions. . . . Prior to the Kuwaiti invasion, Iraq had accelerated its support to the Kurdish Workers Party (PKK) and did not allow Turkey to implement a November 1989 agreement which permitted it to pursue Kurdish fighters into Iraq. Moreover, relations were further strained over the Ataturk dam project and Iraq's refusal to pay its outstanding debt of $1.7 billion to Ankara. . . . Turkish officials were further alarmed when components of Iraq's

planned 'super-gun' were seized in Edirne in the spring." Yavuz and Khan, "Turkish Foreign Policy toward the Arab-Israeli Conflict," 84.

41. A Turkish journalist, Cengiz Çandar, who was very close to Özal, explains this concept in an unpublished paper, "Turkey's Place in the World or the New Turkey in the New World," drafted for the New Democracy Movement.

42. The importance of the relation between Turkey's attempt to westernize and its foreign policy cannot be overstated. As Duygu Sezer argues, "A discussion of Turkey's chosen philosophical-ideological world view as a factor in its security thinking is critical . . . because of the close interdependence between the sustainability of the socio-political order it has inspired and the nature of the external environment." Sezer, *Turkey's Political and Security Interests and Policies in the New Geostrategic Environment of the Expanded Middle East*, 4.

43. See Tanıl Bora, *Bosna-Hersek* (Istanbul: Iletisim yayinlari, 1994), chap. 5, for a survey of the Turkish public's reaction to the unfolding tragedy in Bosnia-Herzegovina.

44. It is important to note, for instance, that France initially opposed the inclusion of a Turkish squadron stationed in Italy in the allied air force flying reconnaissance flights over Bosnia.

45. Samuel P. Huntington, "The Clash of Civilizations?" *Foreign Affairs* 72, no. 3 (summer 1993): 42.

46. In addition to annual loss in revenues of about $300 million from the closed oil pipelines, Turkey's loss for 1990 and 1991 is estimated to be about $7 billion.

47. The Treaty of Sèvres divided up the Anatolian possessions of the Ottoman Empire among several national entities, Kurds and Armenians included. The Turkish war of independence was fought to nullify this agreement and maintain the territorial integrity of Asia Minor—hence the sensitivity over Western criticism on the Kurdish issue that leads many to accuse the Western countries of imperialist designs over Turkey and of wishing to divide its territory by supporting Kurdish separatism. Philip Robins makes the same point: "Some 70 years later, however, the Sèvres experience remains fresh in the minds of Turks. The diplomatic lesson drawn by many is that the creation of a Kurdish state will inevitably weaken the Turkish state." "The Overlord State: Turkey and the Kurds," *International Affairs* 69, no. 4 (1993): 659.

48. Sezer, *Turkey's Political and Security Interests and Policies in the New Geostrategic Environment of the Expanded Middle East*, 8.

49. For the politics of the Caucasian Triangle (Iran-Turkey-Russia) in history and today, see A. Fuat Borovalı, "The Caucasian Triangle: Old Scripts, New Versions" (paper presented to the International Studies Association Conference, Washington, D.C., 28 March–1 April 1994).

50. John W. R. Lepingwell, "The Russian Military and Security Policy in the 'Near Abroad,'" *Survival* (autumn 1994): 75.

51. Sami Kohen, "Turkey, Russia Carve Out Power with Oil Routes," *Christian Science Monitor*, 23 November 1994, 14.

52. This was a typical Demirel policy. Afraid of offending the Russians, Demirel recognized the coup against Elchibey as a fait accompli and violated Turkey's

commitment to democratically elected governments. Elchibey's only fault seems to have been his unconditional affection and support for Turkey.

53. Elchibey was due to go to London, England, a day after the coup took place to sign the agreement on the exploration, production, and distribution of Caspian Sea oil with an international consortium that included BOTAŞ, the Turkish state enterprise in charge of the transportation of oil by pipelines in Turkey. Other participants in the consortium were Amoco, Pennzoil, McDermott, Unocal, Ramco, Norwegian Petroleum Company, British Petroleum, and Turkish Petroleum.

54. *Die Zeit* of 11 November 1994 noted that "the CIS state of Azerbaijan has recently made a spectacular deal with a Western oil consortium over three offshore oil fields in the Caspian sea. The fifth largest American firm, Amoco, is a partner. . . . In order for the oil to be exported for gigantic profits, a decision about a pipeline is needed. Washington supports Ankara in its desire to have the line run through Turkey. For geopolitical and economic reasons, Moscow, on the other hand, wants the line to run through Russia." In a more conspiratorial tone, the newspaper also linked the recent disclosures of environmental catastrophes from leaky pipelines in Russia to the U.S. desire to get the oil to go through Turkey. Cited by Alexander Cockburn in *The Nation*, 19 December 1994, 753.

In January 1995, the U.S. ambassador to Turkey presented a letter to the Turkish government that indicated that the United States preferred the pipeline to pass through Turkey and it trajectory from the Caucasus to be determined later. They were unconditionally opposed to its passing through Iran.

55. Sezer, *Turkey's Political and Security Interests and Policies in the New Geostrategic Environment of the Expanded Middle East*, 16.

56. Ibid., 16–17.

57. The tripartite biannual meetings between Iran, Syria, and Turkey were established in November 1992. All three countries were against the formation of an independent Kurdish state, each for its own reasons. Ironically, Turkey also had grievances against both of the others for their support of the PKK.

58. Barkey, "Turkey's Kurdish Dilemma," 63.

59. Özal articulated this vision in a remarkable interview with the editor in chief of *Türkiye Günlüğü* (summer 1992, 15–23).

60. Articulated by U.S. national security adviser Anthony Lake, enlargement involves the United States encouraging the development and consolidation of market economies and democratic polities around the world.

61. *The Economist*, 15 October 1994, 15.

62. Reports of Özal's reasoning for taking such an active role during the crisis, especially his alleged declaration that Turkey would "bet one and get three" out of the war, greatly raised the population's expectations.

63. Sami Kohen, "Turkey Opens Back Door to Relations with Iraq," *Christian Science Monitor*, 8 September 1994, 3.

64. J. M. Abdulghani, *Iraq and Iran: The Years of Crisis* (London: Croom Helm, 1984), 131, cited in Ali Fuat Borovalı, "Kurdish Insurgencies, the Gulf War and Turkey's Changing Role," *Conflict Quarterly* (fall 1987): 31.

65. From a letter Özal sent to Demirel at the end of February 1993. Published as "Özal's Will" in *Hurriyet*, 12 November 1993.

66. Heath W. Lowry, "Challenges to Turkish Democracy in the Decade of the Nineties," 16.

67. For the origins and genesis of the PKK, see Ismet Imset, *The PKK: 20 Years of Separatist Violence* (Ankara: Turkish Daily News Publications, 1993).

68. Robins, "The Overlord State," 669.

69. Lowry, "Challenges to Turkish Democracy in the Decade of the Nineties," 18.

70. Mehmet Ali Birand, "10th Anniversary Review of the PKK's Record," *Sabah*, 22 August 1994. See also Hasan Cemal, "Guneydoğu Notlarî" (Notes from the Southeast), *Sabah*, 9–13 November 1994.

71. Figure given by the 20 October 1994 "Economy" page editor of *Sabah*, Necati Doğru. The lower figure reflects the estimates for 1994 given by many observers in 1993; it is equal to 40 percent of Turkey's export earnings in 1993. If the higher figure is correct, then even a larger share of Turkey's export earnings will have been spent in fighting the PKK in 1994.

72. There have been several notorious instances (Sirnak, Silopi, Lice) of brutal retaliation against "guilty" villages or towns by the Turkish military in the past. One of these incidents, the destruction of a village in the provence of Tunceli (once governed by a special law in mid-1930s) had extensive press coverage in the fall of 1994. On the meaning of this latest incident in an increasingly violent and militarized environment, see the commentary of Sedat Ergin, "Demokrasimizin Tunceli Sinavi" (Turkish democracy's test in Tunceli), *Hurriyet*, 23 October 1994.

73. Turkish war-fighting capability was not high to begin with. The military was overstaffed and underequipped and technologically inadequate to fight a modern war. The military desperately needed to proceed with its modernization program in order to face the challenges to Turkey's security, mostly from the expanded Middle East, in the post-Cold War environment. Based on observations of the military's conduct during the Gulf War, Ian O. Lesser notes that "the military leadership apparently had serious doubts about Turkey's ability to deploy and sustain forces beyond their own territory, or even to conduct large-scale mobile operations on the border with Iraq. In short, close observation of the campaign in the Gulf confirmed the unpreparedness of the Turkish armed forces to wage modern conventional warfare. It has even cast doubt on the value of the relatively modern equipment to be acquired from the allies as a result of the CFE agreement" (Ian O. Lesser, "Bridge or Barrier? Turkey and the West After the Cold War," in *Turkey's New Geopolitics: From the Balkins to Western China*, Graham Fuller et al. eds. [Boulder, Colo.: Westview Press—A RAND Study, 1993], 120). It is quite evident that under the circumstances, the interests of the country would necessitate a speedy resolution of the Kurdish problem so as to free resources and to undertake a comprehensive modernization. Incidentally, such a restructuring of the Turkish military and the need to improve its professional quality might also lead to an altered relation between the military and the civilian authorities.

74. It is estimated that approximately 50 to 60 percent of Turkish citizens of Kurdish origin live in the western provinces of the country.

75. Lowry, "Challenges to Turkish Democracy in the Decade of the Nineties," 22.

76. In fairness, it must be added that some of the Democratic Labor Party's deputies preferred to use their position to fuel the process of polarization rather than to look for opportunities for mediation, as some of them have later acknowledged.

77. "We are not trying to establish an independent Kurdish state. . . . We just want to live freely and on equal terms with Turks. If the Turkish authorities will agree to political negotiations, then we can discuss our proposals in greater detail" (comments made to the British Broadcasting Corporation reported in the *Executive News Digest*, 29 September 1994). Ocalan, whose organization boasts of killing babies and unarmed teachers, is a singularly unsavory character and were it not for the stubborn policies of "repression and repression alone" preferred by successive governments and the military, he could not have become as important a figure as he is today among the Kurds.

78. George Liska, "Coda: The System. Patterns of Persistence and Revolutions within Evolutions," *Russia and the World Order* (Baltimore, Md.: Johns Hopkins University Press, 1980), 187.

79. "The terrible work of Franjo Tudjman in Croatia and Slobodan Milosevic in Serbia has been made easier by the Islamic bogeyman stalking Europe, but there is a great pathos in the nervous Izetbegovic clinging to the pluralist myth of Europe to ward off the dangers all around. For the pluralism of Europe is a myth. . . . It is much more likely that the genuine sons of Europe, the perfect embodiments of its cruel history and dark nationalism and populist frenzy, are Milosevic and Tudjman—and not Izetbegovic. Europe has not been kind to the outsider. It cast out and destroyed its Jews. There is no evidence that it will gladly make a place for Muslims." Fouad Ajami, *The New Republic,* 21 November 1994, 35.

80. Duygu Bazoğlu Sezer, "Turkish Foreign Policy in the Year 2000," in *Turkey in the Year 2000* (Ankara: Turkish Political Science Association, 1989), 115.

81. George Liska, *Ways of Power* (Baltimore, Md.: Johns Hopkins University Press, 1993), 7.

8

CONFLICT IN THE GULF: VIEWS FROM THE GULF COOPERATION COUNCIL

Abdel Monem Said Aly and Hassan Saleh

The nine countries of the Persian Gulf and the Arabian Peninsula (the Gulf Cooperation Council [GCC] states, Iran, Iraq, and Yemen) share many of the pains and ills found in the Third World. All are basically dependent on outside powers for military supplies. All are oil and gas producers, controlling about 60 percent of world oil reserves and 30 percent of gas reserves, with economies that are highly dependent on that one source of income. Yet the states of the region differ in most other areas, including size, population, wealth, levels of economic development and modernization, and military power. The uneven distribution of material resources creates imbalances that enhance ambitions and hegemonic tendencies as well as increase the levels of apprehension, suspicion, and fear. Old and new nations are conscious of their historical legacies, from the ancient times of the Persian Empire to the more recent Persian Gulf wars. Islam, the dominant religion in the region, divides peoples along Sunni-Shiite lines.

Though imbalances of power, historical legacies, and religious divisions have set the stage for confrontation, they are not by themselves enough to generate conflict. Other forces help explain key security threats. In the Persian Gulf and the Arabian Peninsula there are four significant elements.

First, there is an uneven relationship between the wealth of the GCC states and regional population levels. The GCC countries have a total population of 17.6 million (Table 8.1), compared with 54 million for Iran, 17 million for Iraq, and 13.5 million for Yemen (Table 8.2). While the GCC states maintain a fiscal surplus, Iran has a $30 billion foreign debt, Iraq

Table 8.1. Gulf Cooperation Council states' populations, 1992 estimates.

Country	Population			
	Nationals	Nonnationals	(%)	Total
Bahrain	330,000	134,000	(29)	464,000
Kuwait	387,000	803,000	(67)	1,190,000
Oman	1,062,000	380,000	(26)	1,442,000
Qatar	141,000	272,000	(66)	413,000
Saudii Arabia	8,066,400	4,192,600	(34)	12,259,000
United Arab Emirates	531,000	1,294,000	(70)	1,825,000
Total	10,500,000	7,100,000	(40)	17,600,000

Source: Roger Hardy, *Arabia after the Storm: International Stability of the Gulf Arab States* (London: The Royal Institute of International Affairs, 1992), 25.

owes $84 billion (plus reparation payments for the second Gulf War), and Yemen has $8.5 billion in debts.

Second, population asymmetries create areas of tension in most Persian Gulf states. The citizens of Kuwait, Qatar, and the United Arab Emirates (UAE) are minorities in their own countries. Furthermore, the ethnic and religious compositions of the populations on both sides of the Persian Gulf are quite diverse. While Iran, dominated by Persian Shiites, has considerable Arab Shiite and Sunni minorities, the other eight Arab countries have Shiite and Iranian minorities, with the exception of Bahrain (Table 8.3).

In the late 1970s and throughout the 1980s, the Shiite minorities in the GCC states were under a cloud of suspicion. This was mainly because of the Islamic revolution in Iran, the first Persian Gulf war (the Iran-Iraq War), and the Shiite subversion in Bahrain, Kuwait, and Saudi Arabia.

Table 8.2. Iran (1991 estimate), Iraq (1991 estimate), and Yemen (1990 Estimate) populations.

Country	Population
Iran	53,190,000
Iraq	17,903,000
Yemen	11,282,000
Total	85,025,000

Source: *The Europa World Year Book*, 1994.

The second Gulf war, of 1990 to 1991, helped to lift this cloud by providing the Shiites with an opportunity to demonstrate their patriotism in opposing Iraq's occupation of Kuwait. This led to a rapprochement between the Gulf states and Iran, causing fear of Iranian-sponsored activities to decline. This, however, did not end the Shiite grievances.

The Shiites' problems have three dimensions. One part of the problem is sectarian, especially in Saudi Arabia, where the Shiites were once seen as heretics worthy of death. Human-rights issues abound, especially in Bahrain and

Saudi Arabia, where any sign of Shiite activism is harshly crushed. Finally, the Shiite communities in all Persian Gulf states suffer various forms of discrimination. For example, they are often barred from high military and civilian positions.

As a result of this divisive situation, the Shiites in the Persian Gulf states remain susceptible to external influences, especially from Iran. The latest dispute between Iran and the UAE over the islands of Abu Musa, Lesser Tunb, and Greater

Table 8.3. Shiites in the Gulf Cooperation Council States, 1984 estimates.

	Shiites	
Country	Population	As % of nationals
Saudi Arabia	440,000	8
Bahrain	168,000	70
Kuwait	137,000	24
United Arab Emirates	45,000	18
Qatar	11,000	16
Oman	28,000	4

Source: Hardy, *Arabia after the Storm,* 23.

Tunb is a good example, especially since mid-1992, when Iran decided to take full control of Abu Musa. Since a 1971 agreement, Abu Musa had been shared by Sharjah and Tehran. Iran's recent behavior has inflamed the problem and has affected the domestic position of the Shiite communities in the Gulf states. The perception of Iranian expansionism, even if based on only one new incident, undermines the standing of Shiites throughout the Persian Gulf region.

Third, like most Third World countries, the states of the region are new states in the modern sense. They face undefined borders, a problem that was inherited from the time of the colonial powers. These undefined borders have played a major role in armed conflicts in the Persian Gulf. The Buraimi conflict of the 1950s was a direct result of a border dispute between Saudi Arabia, on one side, and Great Britain, representing Abu Dhabi and Oman, on the other side. The Iraq-Iran War of the 1980s was also caused, to a large degree, by the disagreement between the two countries over the ownership of the border area of the Shatt al Arab. The border dispute between Iraq and Kuwait, over the Rumaila Oil field and the ownership of the islands of Bubian and Warbah, was one of the main reasons for the Persian Gulf crisis of 1990 to 1991. All the states in the region have also suffered from smaller border disputes with neighbors. Of these disputes, the Bahrain-Qatar conflict over the Hwar islands and the Fasht Al-Dibal resulted in a military confrontation in 1986. Tensions rose again in 1991, when Qatar submitted its claim to the International Court of Justice in the Hague. In September 1992, the Saudi-Qatar border dispute erupted in an armed clash at Al-Khofus, some 130 kilometers south of Doha. Qatar threatened not to attend the 1992 GCC summit in Abu Dhabi, but Egyptian mediation resulted in the signing of an agreement between the two countries in the Saudi city of Medina. A committee was to be established to demarcate formally the Saudi-Qatari borders, so Qatar attended the GCC summit. As of early 1995, the Saudi-Qatari border had yet to be officially demarcated. Other border issues yet to be solved include Omani-UAE and Saudi-Yemeni disagreements. The border disputes in the Persian Gulf region will continue to present a serious challenge to future Gulf security.

Fourth, and probably most important, the region is divided between conservative, status quo powers and radical and revolutionary powers. The GCC states are traditional, conservative states that find their security and well-being linked to the West. Iran, Iraq, and to some extent Yemen are republics that also spout revolutionary visions of themselves and the regional context in which they live. This includes the Islamic revolutionary ideals of Iran, the Arab nationalist ideology of Iraq, and the mixture of both perspectives in Yemen. Iraq and Iran are clear cases. The situation is more ambivalent in Yemen, however, especially after the northern Yemeni leadership succeeded in crushing the rebellion in the former South Yemen in the summer of 1994, against the wishes of the GCC states with the exception of Qatar. The legitimacy of the state system in the area is often challenged. For the less wealthy, more populated, and radical states, such as Iran, Iraq, and Yemen, the GCC states are up for grabs in the name of the Islamic nation, or the Arab nation, or both.

Persian Gulf Security Environment: The Gulf War, Before and After

The four realities discussed above constituted the basic vulnerabilities of the Arab and Persian Gulf states. To face these threats, these states have devised a security policy based on six elements:

1. The Persian Gulf countries, particularly Saudi Arabia, have increased their military capabilities through the acquisition of high-technology weapons.

2. These states have increased their collective security through the establishment of the GCC and a joint military force under the name of Al-Gizira. The force started small (about five thousand soldiers), but the states hope to enlarge it in the future.

3. These states have attempted to balance regional powers by helping Iraq against Iran and Syria against Iraq, and by keeping lines open with other regional powers, particularly Egypt and Turkey.

4. The states have given considerable economic assistance to major regional powers, such as Syria, Egypt, Iraq, and Yemen. Even Iran was given assistance when it was struck by natural disasters.

5. These states have created the most extensive welfare states in the world for citizens and residents alike to satisfy their populations and reduce socioeconomic and political tensions.

6. These states have consolidated their political and economic relations with the West by following a strong anticommunist and antirevolutionary policy.

These six elements of the Arab and Persian Gulf states' security policy have not been enough to ensure the security of the Gulf. Kuwait was threatened by Iran during the Iran-Iraq War and then invaded by Iraq. Saudi Arabia was threatened directly by Iran, Iraq, and Yemen. Iraq threatened Qatar and the UAE during the Gulf crisis. Iran, from time to time, has threatened Bahrain. All these threats put the issue of Gulf security at the top of the post-Gulf War agenda. Several security schemes were introduced for the area during and after the Gulf War. The most notable of these was a U.S. proposal. On 6 March 1991, President Bush, speaking to a joint session of the U.S. Congress, defined four key challenges that would have to be met in the Middle East:

1. Creating shared security arrangements in the region with the help of the United States. This would include U.S. participation in joint exercises involving both air and ground forces and maintaining a U.S. naval presence in the region.

2. Controlling the proliferation of weapons of mass destruction and missile systems.

3. Putting an end to the Arab-Israeli conflict with a comprehensive peace based on the U.N. Security Council resolutions 242 and 338 and principle of the exchange of territory for peace.

4. Fostering economic freedom and prosperity for all the people of the region.

France, Italy, and Spain advocated a European security project for the entire Middle East. The European project was based on the European experience in the Conference on Security and Cooperation in Europe. The idea was to hold a Conference on Security and Cooperation in the Middle East to guarantee existing borders in the area, encourage economic cooperation and regional integration, control the arms race in the area, and promote democracy and respect for human rights.

The third security proposal was made in a speech by Iranian president Hashemi Rafsanjani on 21 September 1990. Rafsanjani called for an Islamic Peace Project based on security arrangements by the GCC countries and Iran. The project called for the replacement of the "foreign" forces in the Persian Gulf with Arab and Iranian forces. It also called for an Islamic court of arbitration to resolve conflicts in the area. Finally, the project called on the Arab and Persian Gulf states to pay for the reconstruction of Iran and Iraq.

Behind the scenes, Egyptian representatives presented a fourth security plan. The Egyptian project called for a new Arab order based on a reinvigorated Arab League, for which the Arab partners in the international coalition to liberate Kuwait would form the cornerstone. The GCC, Egypt, and Syria (the so-called 6+2 formula) could play a moderating role in the Middle East, secure the Persian Gulf through the presence of Egyptian and Syrian forces, and encourage forms of economic and social development in the area.

A fifth idea for regional security came from the GCC itself and included elements of the other proposals. Abdallah Bishara, the GCC secretary general, argued that there should be four components of Persian Gulf security. The first component was the consolidation and further integration of Arab and Persian Gulf states under the banner of the GCC. The experience of political, diplomatic, economic, and military cooperation during the Gulf crisis would be the basis for a new, advanced phase of collective security arrangements. The second component was the consolidation of the strategic relationship among the Arab partners of the international coalition to liberate Kuwait, such as the GCC states, Egypt, and Syria. The third component was the creation of special cooperative relationships with the neighboring Islamic countries, particularly Iran and Turkey. The fourth component was the establishment of security arrangements between the GCC states and Western countries—particularly the United States, the United Kingdom, and France—that would protect the common interests of all parties and especially the flow of oil to the industrial world.

The GCC security approach was an attempt to integrate the best aspects of all the security proposals for the Persian Gulf. However, four years after the Gulf War, there is no sign that the Gulf is more secure than before the war. The survival of Saddam Hussein and his claim on Kuwait has continued the Iraqi threat in a more moderate form. The Iraqi mobilization in southern Iraq in the fall of 1994 and Kuwaiti dependency on the United States to deter this threat provided an example of the continuing problem. In reality, the collective security arrangements among the GCC states have fallen short. The Omani proposal to create a standing Arab-Persian Gulf army of 100,000 soldiers has not developed. In fact, the GCC not only showed few signs of progress toward integration, but also showed signs of disintegration. Border disputes between

Qatar and both Bahrain and Saudi Arabia soon precluded any possibility of collective security arrangements.

Further, the security cooperation between the GCC and Egypt and Syria failed to materialize. On 6 March 1991, immediately after the Gulf War, the two parties signed the Damascus Declaration, which called for security cooperation based on the presence of Egyptian and Syrian forces in Kuwait in exchange for an Arab economic fund to help the development of poorer Arab countries, particularly Egypt and Syria. A few weeks after signing the declaration, Kuwait asked for amendments that reduced the level of security cooperation; Kuwait called for bilateral, not multilateral, relations during times of crisis. By the summer of 1991, Egyptian and Syrian forces had withdrawn from the Persian Gulf. The Arab economic fund was never created. Perhaps the only concrete result was continued meetings between the two sides at the foreign ministerial level.

Cooperation with the neighboring Islamic countries also did not last long. After a short period of reconciliation between the GCC countries and Iran, their relationship was soon filled with apprehension, fear, and acrimony. After resuming diplomatic relations with Saudi Arabia, Iran did not waste much time and politically attacked the GCC, the Damascus Declaration, and the Western military presence in the Persian Gulf states. Iran continued its arms buildup, making other states suspicious of its intentions. It occupied the UAE part of Abu Musa. It took sides with Qatar in the Qatari-Saudi border dispute. The Iranian behavior showed that the Gulf War had created, with the defeat of Iraq, a serious imbalance in the area, and Iran intended to exploit this opening.

The only progress in the security of the Persian Gulf took place in terms of security agreements between the Gulf states and Western countries. Kuwait signed agreements with the United States, the United Kingdom, and France. Western states signed similar agreements with Bahrain and Qatar. The United States had previous agreements with Oman and Saudi Arabia. All these security agreements called for military cooperation to protect the Gulf region.

However, in the absence of an Arab or even an Arab-Persian Gulf dimension for security, the Western-oriented security system cannot guarantee the security of the Gulf alone. More likely than not, it will cause radical forces in the area, particularly Islamic fundamentalists, to accuse the Gulf states of relying on ex-colonialist powers. Iran has already made such accusations. In Saudi Arabia, religious forces have expressed resentment at the presence of foreign forces. With the exception of Kuwait, a long-term reliance on Western countries for security in the Gulf will breed new forms of violence and instability, particularly without a resolution of the Arab-Israeli conflict.

The Military Balance: The New Arms Race

The Gulf War was instrumental in bringing about a new phase in the arms race in the Persian Gulf region and in the entire Middle East. Operation Desert Storm validated and introduced significant doctrinal concepts and combat behavior. Key military lessons of the Gulf War were the importance of the air phase and air assets; the vital role of global reconnaissance and secured communication; twenty-four-hour combat continuity; long-range, accurate firepower; and electronic warfare. During the war, more than 7,400 tons of advanced, precision-guided munitions were used. Laser-guided bombs (GBU-12, GBU-24) were employed by the stealth strike aircraft (F-117) to hit hard targets. High-speed anti-radiation missiles were used to deter surface-to-air-missile radars and control centers. F-15 multirole fighters used low-altitude navigation and targeting infrared for night-system pods to locate and destroy missile sites and missile launchers. Certainly, Operation Desert Storm became a turning point for defense acquisition planning by most of the states in the Gulf. Military planners are now considering a large array of systems that they would have not taken seriously or regarded as important in the past. The Gulf War sparked an arms race. The following is a portrait of the current status of weapon acquisition in the nine countries that affect the military balance in the Gulf.

Iraq

The Iran-Iraq War was instrumental in causing the expansion of the Iraqi army (Table 8.4). In addition to troops and weaponry, by the end of the war Iraq had built up an important armaments industry, whose products included a surface-to-surface missile, based on the Soviet Scud, developed with Egyptian and Argentinean assistance. By 1989 or 1990, Iraq was manufacturing chemical weapons and sophisticated missiles and was not far from acquiring the means to produce nuclear weapons; the essential components of all these systems were being provided by firms in Western Europe and the United States.

During the Gulf War, Iraq suffered considerable

Table 8.4. Expansion of the Iraqi Armed Forces, 1979–88.

Component	No.	
	1979–80	1987–88
Soldiers	190,000	1,000,000
Tanks	1,900	6,310
Combat Aircraft	339	500+
Armored Fighting Vehicles	1,500	4,000

Source: IISS, *The Military Balance 1987–88* (London: International Institute for Strategic Studies, 1987), 100.

military losses. According to the International Institute for Strategic Studies, 41 Iraqi divisions may have been killed off. Destroyed or captured equipment included 3,000 tanks, 1,860 armored vehicles, and 2,140 pieces of artillery; 35 aircraft were shot down, and 115 combat aircraft were flown to Iran. Most of the Iraqi navy was sunk, with the exception of the Italian-made frigates still held in Italy and Egypt. Nonetheless, according to the International Institute for Strategic Studies, Iraq still has a considerable force. It has approximately 382,000 active personnel, 2,200 main battle tanks, 1,980 artillery pieces, about 316 planes, 4,200 armored vehicles, and all of its helicopter force.[1] Although Iraqi military power has been reduced considerably, Iraq remains a military power in the Persian Gulf, with defense and deterrent capabilities. If compared with the GCC states alone, Iraq still could mount sizable offensive operations.

Iran

The current active Western military presence in the Persian Gulf, the policy of permanent prepositioning of defence heavy equipment in the area, and the large-scale arms purchase plans by the Gulf states all create a new security environment for the Iranian regime. Furthermore, Iraq is still considered an important threat to Iran as long as Saddam Hussein remains in power. Iran is making important efforts to reorganize and modernize its armed forces, which suffered severe losses during the long war with Iraq. At the same time, Iran's arms industry has been expanded to support a growing military machine. Between 1984 and 1994, Iran signed arms transfer agreements valued at $19.8 billion in which $16.1 billion worth of arms were delivered. Values of covert U.S. agreements and deliveries in 1985 and 1986 were not included in these estimates, nor were black-market agreements and deliveries. By one estimate, arms deliveries to Iran from 1983 to 1990 were valued at $39.5 billion.

Iran still remains a fundamentalist state that retains its strong desire to expand its Shia Muslim ideas to other countries. Currently, Iran is actively involved in Lebanon and is becoming a growing factor in Sudan. Iran has wide-ranging strategic interests in the Persian Gulf and is conscious of the strong Shiite populations in the area. In an attempt to settle oil and gas disputes with Saudi Arabia and Qatar, Iran could try to impose its wishes by force. Vital oil resources and installations in Saudi Arabia are within 150 kilometers of the Iranian coast, a situation that could permit Tehran to blackmail Riyadh with a tactical missile attack. Such a potential threat produces great risks for disembarkation ports in the Persian Gulf and for intervention forces intending to use these ports. Iran has recently made a very important move in the area by expelling Arab nationals from the island of Abu Musa; this caused considerable concern in the area.

Tehran's most intense political action is currently aimed at the Muslim republics in central Asia, and especially those bordering Iran. Azerbaijan, Turkmenistan, and Tajikistan are all targets for Iranian intervention. There is widespread concern that Iran could acquire nuclear weapons or material from poorly protected stores in the ex-Soviet republics; economic difficulties facing ex-Soviet officers and officials make sales more plausible. Considerable efforts are also under way in Iran to establish research and development and production facilities that could eventually provide nuclear capabilities. Ex-director of the U.S. Central Intelligence Agency Robert M. Gates testified to the U.S. Congress that Iran was seeking the nuclear bomb and could have one by the year 2000. U.S. authorities interfered to block deals between Iran, Argentina, and China to obtain equipment that would have allowed Iran to begin its own nuclear manufacturing. In 1994, Iran signed nuclear cooperation agreements with China and Russia, which presumably will enhance its nuclear capability.

Russia has already agreed to sell Iran a large number of the latest version T-72 main battle tanks, some forty MiG-29s, a few MiG-31s, and two squadrons of Su-24 Fencer strike aircraft. This has allowed the depleted Iranian Air Force to regain its strength in a remarkably short time. A total of 115 Iraqi Air Force combat aircraft escaped to Iranian airports during the Gulf War, and a large percentage of these aircraft are in serviceable condition. At least some of these aircraft could be kept in operation with assistance from Russia or China. Iran also negotiated with Italy the sale of CH-47 Chinook medium-lift helicopters, which could be used for civilian and military purposes.

Recent reports of Iranian arms purchases indicate orders from China, the ex-Soviet states, Brazil, and North Korea. The North Koreans are rapidly becoming one of Iran's best suppliers, with a contract for almost two hundred Scud B and C missiles. Bulgaria delivered over ten thousand rockets and surface-to-air missile launchers from its stocks. Iran is also trying to rebuild its naval capability, a move that could become extremely dangerous to oil shipping routes through the Strait of Hormuz. Iran has recently bought three Kilo-class submarines from Russia that can be used with long-range air patrols and shore-based Silkworm antiship missiles to support Iranian military operations in the Persian Gulf (Table 8.5).

Saudi Arabia

A very ambitious Saudi plan has been announced that calls for the defense forces to be expanded to about 250,000 men over the next five years. This preliminary plan is supposed to bring Saudi forces to the same size and effectiveness level as the coalition forces deployed during the Gulf War. Of course, Operation Desert Storm became a turning point for Saudi defense

Table 8.5. Iran's military power, 1994 estimates.

Weapon	No.	Type and detailed remarks
Main battle tanks	1,245	190 T-54/-55s, 260 Ch T-59s, 150 T-62s, 150 T-72s, 1 *Chieftain* MK 3/5,135 M-47/-48s, 135 M-60 A-1s
Artillery	2,320	Towed, self-propelled, multiple rocket launchers
Surface-to-surface missiles	26	At least 6 Scud B/-Cs, 20 CSS-8s, local-manufacture missile reported to be under development
Air-to-ground weapons	N.A.*	*Dragon, TOW,* AT-3 *Sagger,* AT-4 *Spigot*
Surface-to-air missiles	+240	*Improved Hawk, Rapier, Tigercat,* HQ-2J, SA-7, HN-5, SA-5, FM-80.
Helicopters	452	Under army command, 100 AH-1Js (attack), 40 CH-47Cs (heavy transport), 170 Bell-214 As, 40 AB-205 As, 90 AB-206s, 12 AB-212s, 30 Bell-204s, 5 Hughes 300Cs, 5 RH-53Ds, 10 SH-53Ds, 10 SA-319s, 40 UH-1Hs
Combat aircraft	295	60 F-4D/Es, 60 F-5E/Fs, 30 Su-24s, 60 F-14s, 25 F-7s, 30 MiG-29s
Support aircraft	81	5 P-3Fs, 1 RC-130, 8 RF-4Es, 4 Boeing 707s, 9 Boeing 747 Fs, 11 Boeing 707s, 1 Boeing 727, 19 C-130 E/Hs, 3 *Commander* 690s, 15 F-27s, 5 *Falcons*
Navy Facilities	10	*Kamam* class
Submarines	2	*Kilo* class
Destroyers	2	*Babr* class
Corvettes	2	*Bayandor* class
Inshore patrol craft	33	3 *Kaivans,* 3 *Porvin* PCIs, 1 *Bogomol*-PFI, 3 *Chaho* PFIs, some 10 other PFIs, some 13 hovercraft
Naval helicopters	11	3 SH-3Ds, 6 AB-212 ASWs, 2 RH-53Ds
Manpower	351,000	Reserves add 350,000, and the Revolutionary Guard, 120,000

*N.A., Not available

Source: International Institute for Strategic Studies, *The Military Balance 1994–1995* (London: International Institute for Strategic Studies, 1994), 128–129.

Table 8.6. Saudi Arabia's military power, 1994 estimates.

Weapon	No.	Type and detailed remarks
Main battle tanks	770	30 M-1A2 *Abrams*, 290 AMX-20s, 450 M-60A3s
Artillery	1,060	Guns, howitzers, multiple rocket launchers, mortars
Surface-to-surface missiles	40	10 CCS-2s, 40 misc.
Air-to-ground weapons	N.A.	*TOW*-2, M-47 *Dragon*, *HOT*
Surface-to-air missiles	309	40 *Croales*, 128 MIM-23 B *Improved HAWKs*, 141 *Shahines*
Combat aircraft	292	51 F-5Es, 44 *Tornado* IDSs, 24 *Tornado* ADVs, 78 F-15Cs, 20 F-15Ds
Support aircraft	128	49 transports, 97 trainers
Patrol and coastal combatants	29	9 missile craft (*Al Siddiq* class), 3 torpedo craft (*Dammam* class), 17 patrol craft
Frigates	8	4 *Madina* class, 4 *Badr* class
Manpower	104,000	National Guard adds 57,000

Source: International Institute for Strategic Studies, *The Military Balance 1994–1995*, 137–38.

planning, just as it did for other countries of the Middle East. Saudi planners are now considering a large array of U.S. systems that they would not have taken seriously, or regarded as important, before the Gulf War.

Over the years, Riyadh has pursued a prudent diversification policy, procuring from non-U.S. sources items that the United States could not or would not deliver (for example, the British Tornado strike aircraft and the Chinese DF-SA intermediate-range ballistic missile). The Saudis often grow weary with U.S. caution over the transfer of technology and Washington's fear of upsetting the Middle East regional balance. However, there are now five airborne-warning-and-control-system (AWACS) planes in the Saudi inventory and more than 98 F-15 fighters. For its ground forces, Saudi Arabia will have up to 465 M-1A2 Abrams main battle tanks and some 600 M-2 Bradley mechanized infantry combat vehicles in its inventory before the year 2000, and it already deploys more than 60 multiple-launch artillery rocket systems. In addition, the Saudi forces use Stinger Man-Pads, the Bell 406 Combat Scout, and AH-64 Apache helicopters. They also have 116 TOW launchers with 2,000 an-titank guided missiles. Some recent arms requests include 150-plus Hell-Fire antitank missiles and more than 2,000 Maverick air-to-surface missiles. Among other things, the Al-Yamamah 1 expansion program called for 48 Tornado IDS, 24 Tornado ADV, and 30 Hawk trainers, and deliveries are being completed. Al-Yamamah 2 calls for the further dispatch of 48 Tornados, 60 Hawk, and 40 WS-70A Blackhawk helicopters. Six Patriot batteries with 384 missiles are on order, and a further 14 batteries have been requested.

Finally, Saudi Arabia has succeeded in opening discussions for the purchase of an additional four AWACS, with an estimated cost of $1.5 billion to $2 billion. It was also reported that Saudi Arabia is considering becoming a full-equity member of the European Fighter Aircraft. Table 8.6 shows the current capabilities of Saudi Arabia.

Other Gulf States

The other five states of the GCC have smaller military establishments, yet they face tremendous military challenges from Iran and Iraq. They could hardly face such a threat without outside help from either the United States or other Arab states. Kuwait's armed forces were severely beaten during the early stages of the Iraqi invasion, with most of their equipment destroyed. To rebuild its armed forces with the best equipment, Kuwait is expected to spend over $9 billion on arms purchases in the near future, plus other defense-related expenditures. Among the major weapon systems being procured are 40 F/A-18 Hornet fighters, currently being delivered under a $1.9 billion contract. Furthermore, a $2.5 billion deal covers the purchase of several Patriot and improved Hawk air-defense missile batteries. After negotiations with both the United Kingdom and the United States regarding the selection of a new main battle tank to rebuild the Kuwaiti armed forces, Kuwait has chosen to buy 236 U.S. M-1A2 tanks, to be delivered over a two-year period starting in 1994. It was reported also that Kuwait ordered French naval equipment, including Simonneau Marine fast patrol boats, La Combattante 4 fast missile corvettes, Aerospatiale MM-40 Exocet antiship missiles, Matra Mistral air-defense missiles, and possibly Eridan-class mine hunters.

Bahrain is going to purchase the AH-64 Apache attack helicopter, but cost constraints may lead to the upgraded Cobra as an alternative. Some multiple-launch rocket systems were sold, in addition to one squadron of F-16 fighters and two dozen M-60A3 tanks (within a 54-tank deal). The UAE received 45 Mirage 2000s, and it has expressed a need for a second batch of modern fighters. The competition for this follow-on order is largely between additional Mirages and F/A-18C/Ds. The UAE has signaled its preparedness to diversify its traditional supply sources by signing a deal for 500 Russian BMP-series mechanized infantry combat vehicles. The Sultanate of Oman recently signed a £150 million contract to buy two missile corvettes equipped with advanced combat systems. The Qatari Navy is also planning to build four VITA-type large missile craft for £200 million.

Yemen

On 22 May 1990, the Yemen Arab Republic and the People's Democratic Republic of Yemen joined to form the Republic of Yemen. Since then, the country has been going through the difficult process of unification. Domestic and international political and economic problems are creating instability and sometimes anarchy. The extreme poverty in the country and its rigid tribal system are additional factors leading to civil disorder and possibly war. During the Persian Gulf crisis, Yemen took sides with Iraq, leading to the expulsion of 750,000 Yemenis from Saudi Arabia. This deprived Yemen of a major source of hard currency. Newly discovered oil and gas reserves (200,000 barrels per day) are not expected to change the fortunes of Yemen significantly, at least in the short term.

A major reorganization of the armed forces is under way in the wake of the civil war. The war, however, was instrumental in unifying the command of the two armies, which was too difficult to obtain previously. The combined forces are small in terms of active manpower, which totals 65,000 with perhaps 40,000 in reserve. In terms of equipment, however, Yemen has a force of 1,140 main battle tanks, 670 armored personnel carriers, 547 artillery pieces, and 110 combat aircraft. It is possible that this equipment is under-manned and faced with problems of maintenance and spare parts because of the lack of hard currency and the collapse of the Soviet Union.

Conclusion: Conflict Scenarios

The picture emerging from this review demonstrates the following:

There are considerable power imbalances in the Persian Gulf-Arabian Peninsula region. These imbalances are compounded by religious, ideological, demographic, and geostrategic factors that may lead to different forms of conflict.

The region is engaged in a high-level arms race. The Iran-Iraq War and the Gulf War fueled the search for high quality and highly destructive weapons.

In the post-Gulf War period, most regional arrangements for the security of the Persian Gulf did not materialize. Currently, Gulf security is highly dependent on defense and security arrangements between the GCC states and Western countries, particularly in the United States. These agreements by themselves could contribute to insecurities in the area if they are used by radical and revolutionary states, such as Iraq and Iran, to ignite anti-Western and anti-American feelings.

The current military balance in the area is not stable. As different countries in the area—especially Iraq, Iran, and Yemen—look for more weapons, the balance may change. However, in the short run, Iraq does not present a major threat to its neighbors. The international sanctions and the Western presence in the Persian Gulf constitute considerable deterrence, yet if these two elements wane, Iraq under Saddam Hussein could once again pose a major threat. Iran is still suffering from its long war with Iraq. However, its military capability is increasing. The combination of political upheavals, economic crisis, and ideological militancy could produce an adventurous military posture. For the moment, Iran is incapable of launching large-scale operations similar to the 1990 Iraqi invasion of Kuwait. The combined forces of the GCC states are, in theory, capable of providing a solid defense against such actions. However, Iran has enough power to seize small targets (such as Abu Musa or other small islands in the Gulf) and blackmail Bahrain. The northern gas field of Qatar and the oil fields of Saudi Arabia could be targets for Iranian subversion and missiles.

For the foreseeable future, Yemen will be busy with its domestic problems and may not be able to maintain internal stability. Its military is undermanned and incapable of launching large-scale operations against neighbors. Therefore, Iran is currently the major threat for the region. Its anti-status-quo attitude is influencing attitudes in the ex-Soviet Islamic republics and the entire Middle East. Iran stands against the Arab-Israeli peace process and harbors fundamentalist anti-Western feelings. Iran may soon present a threat similar to that posed by Iraq before the Gulf War.

Finally, the border disputes in the region represent a ticking bomb that could easily ignite the area once again and destroy any hope for a future security arrangement in the Persian Gulf. These disputes produced three major armed conflicts, in the 1950s, the 1980s, and in 1990 to 1991, and they could lead to more confrontations in the future. Iran's latest moves on the island of Abu Musa and the continuation of border disputes among the GCC states and between Saudi Arabia and Yemen will certainly lead to future conflicts in the region. Unless a new formula is found to settle these border disputes, future conflict in the Gulf is likely.

N.B. Opinions expressed in this paper are of those the authors and should not be taken as an expression of official government policy.

Notes

1. International Institute for Strategic Studies, *The Military Balance 1994–1995* (London: International Institute for Strategic Studies, 1994), 129–30.

9

ADDRESSING THE KURDISH ISSUE

David McDowall

The fate of Kurdistan became an international issue for the first time at the end of World War I, when the victorious Allies divided the region among themselves. Britain, which had conquered Mesopotamia and had its troops still physically on the ground, was more concerned with the fate of Kurdistan than any of the other Allies.[1] Britain wanted a buffer area that would protect the northern approaches to Mesopotamia. In practice this meant denial of southeast Anatolia to the Turkish nationalists and the Bolsheviks, both of whom were viewed as a potential danger to British regional interests.

Consequently, Britain encouraged the inhabitants of this area to form a state under formal or informal British tutelage. In a lucid and well-informed memorandum at the time, an officer of the British General Staff in Mesopotamia summed up the Kurdish predicament thus:

> Although they are a nation, however, they are a nation without leaders, widely scattered, and at present incapable of self-government. There is practically no education in the country and their tribal chiefs are for the most part mere rustics with no outlook and little influence beyond the confines of their own tribes. The few who have settled abroad and acquired a foreign polish and a wider outlook have to a great extent forfeited their influence in their own country.

> To leave Kurdistan to run itself in the absence of leaders and community of thought is to leave it split up into a hundred warring tribes with no hope of peace in the future and a menace to all its neighbors. The only hope for the future appears to be some form of foreign rule or guidance, and the problem is to find some system that will ensure a measure of law, order, and progress and that will, at the same time, by being in accordance with the national aspirations, be acceptable to the majority of the people.[2]

The author warned, too, of the dangers of leaving the fate of Kurdistan unresolved, ". . . failure to deal adequately now with the Kurdish question will leave a permanent sore threatening for ever the peace of the middle east."

As in so many other cases, events on the ground overtook policymaking. Britain could find no suitable Kurdish political leaders to coalesce Kurdistan into a coherent political entity; without U.S. involvement, an Armenian state further north failed to materialize; and most important of all, the Ottoman government in Istanbul was progressively displaced by a nationalist movement in eastern Anatolia that had no difficulty recruiting Kurdish tribes to support a Muslim cause against the Greek and Armenian danger to the west and east.

Britain, faced with the inevitable, resolved merely to hang on to what it already had, a fringe of mountains that made the military defense of Mesopotamia feasible. Thereafter the Kurdish issue was considered virtually a private and domestic concern to the states in which the Kurds had the misfortune to find themselves.

The Kurdish Issue: A Regional and International Matter

The dismal forecast of the issue becoming "a running sore threatening for ever the peace of the middle east" has hardly been borne out by events. At best, the Kurdish question has disturbed the waters only intermittently, and usually only internally to individual states of the region. It is difficult to argue a case for Kurdistan's centrality in the question of strategic security in the Middle East.

For obvious reasons no regional or world power has ever taken that view. The Kurds themselves still do not represent a coherent and united force, even if regional governments have occasionally feared that this might happen.[3] Landlocked, the Kurds have no access to the materiel necessary for the conduct of conventional war. They represent a military problem only as a guerrilla force, and therefore remain an issue of internal security.

However much Turkey, Iraq, Syria, and Iran may dislike each other, and even if they yield to the temptation to use the Kurds as a catspaw against a disagreeable neighbor, they have always agreed to deny the Kurds statehood.[4] It is partly because of the danger of expanding its Kurdish component that Turkey has even refrained from seizing the vilayet of Mosul, to which it has historic claims, in spite of considerable temptation to do so.[5]

For the great powers, ever since the confirmation of new international borders following World War I, there has been an overwhelming reluctance to redraw the map. In 1919 Britain was momentarily tempted to waive the interests of the enfeebled Qajars to include Iran's Kurds within its sphere of influence, but decided against it.[6] The Soviet Union momentarily contemplated bringing the Azerbaijani and Mahabad republics under its protection in 1946.[7] It, too, thought better of it. Like the regional contestants, external powers have been happy to use the Kurds to discomfit regional adversaries but not to allow them sufficient independence to create a state.[8]

In 1991 the creation of a safe haven in northern Iraq, followed by a no-fly zone north of Latitude 36 created a precedent that seemed to suggest a change in international attitudes. For the first time the United Nations broke its rule of noninterference in a member's internal affairs and allowed intervention on behalf of Iraq's Kurds, who were mentioned specifically by name in U.N. Security Council Resolution (UNSCR) 688.

UNSCR 688 understandably excited Kurdish hopes that at long last the international community would come to grips with the Kurdish question. This hope has not been realized. On the contrary, the coalition was driven by considerations of domestic popular outrage (inflamed by distressing television coverage of Kurdish suffering) and by the question of regional security, in this case the pragmatic need to get Iraq's Kurds off Turkey's border. As such it was as much (and possibly more) an act of solidarity with Turkey (coalition member and NATO ally) as an act of humanitarian concern.[9] The Kurds thus remain cruelly confined by a unanimity of view among the regional states and the international community that no new borders will be drawn.

It is tempting, therefore, to accept the widely believed view that the Kurdish issue is important only in moments of government weakness, summed up in a proverb used elsewhere as the title of an article on the Kurds during the Iran-Iraq war: "when the cat is away, the mice will play."[10] Certainly this is how the Kurdish question normally manifests itself, but the steady advance of Kurdish identity in Turkey and Iraq, and the West's involvement in Iraq, suggests that the issue cannot be dismissed so easily.

The Kurdish View of the Kurdish Issue

For the Kurds themselves, of course, the Kurdish issue is on a wholly different scale from regional or external government perceptions. It is about their political future, and it is painful to them that their present and future security remains a peripheral issue to the outside world. Their identity is, to a great extent, qualified by the differing treatment they have experienced from their various non-Kurdish rulers since 1918. In all three countries—Iran, Iraq, and Turkey—Kurds have wanted to govern themselves, but in each case this desire has different nuances.

In Turkey Kurdish identity per se was denied by government for three generations, in fact until early 1991. Kurdish risings were put down with measures close to genocide,[11] and there can be little doubt that in the late 1920s Turkey did indeed contemplate measures similar to those taken against the Armenians. In 1927 Turkey's Foreign Minister expressed an unambiguous view of Kurds:

> in their case, their cultural level is so low, their mentality so backward, that they cannot be simply in the general Turkish body politic. . . . They will die out, economically unfitted for the struggle for life in competition with the more advanced and cultured Turks . . . as many as can will emigrate into Persia and Iraq, while the rest will simply undergo the elimination of the unfit.[12]

The Kurds survived because the task of eliminating them was not feasible, but they were banished to the periphery of Turkish national life as "mountain Turks." Kurds who disowned their origins and embraced a Turkish identity wholeheartedly were not discriminated against and could and did achieve high office.

In Turkey, therefore, the Kurdish struggle has been fundamentally one for recognition and for equality of opportunity *as Kurds*. In the face of persistent denial of these basic rights, Kurds have become committed to the idea of independence from a regime under which Turkish Kurds do not believe that basic political rights can be achieved. The extremes of Kurdish nationalism, one might say, have been fostered by the extremes of its denial.

In Iran and Iraq, however, no such denial of identity took place. In Iran Kurdishness has remained closely associated with Sunni identity, in opposition to the Shiism of the state and of its immediate neighbors. This is a long-standing phenomenon, with intermittent conflict between Shiite Azeris and Sunni Kurds in Western Azerbaijan[13] and the deliberate use of Shiites in positions of authority over Kurdish areas by the Pahlavis and the Islamic Republic. Ironically, Kurds consider Azeri Turks (but not Sunni Turks) "ajam" (meaning Iranian in Turkish), using the term incorrectly to denote their religious rather than ethnic identity (Azeris are Shia).[14]

In Iraq, where national feeling evolved more rapidly than in either Iran or Turkey, Kurds were driven by their distaste for Arab rule. At no time did they seriously object en masse to being part of Iraq, but they wanted self-administration (later, full autonomy) and full cultural rights—things accepted by Baghdad in theory but not implemented in practice because successive Arab regimes believed that concessions of this kind would lead eventually to a secessionist movement. While that fear may be understandable, it is questionable whether it is realistic. Iraqi Kurdistan remains economically interdependent with the rest of Iraq, as it has been throughout this century. If they were not already aware of their position of economic weakness as a landlocked entity, the period of relative political independence since April 1991 will have reinforced the message of acute vulnerability to their neighbors' policies.

General Progress of the Kurdish Movement since the Second World War

The progress of the Kurdish nationalist movement since 1945 is partly a response to the repression inherent in the centralizing processes of the states that govern the Kurds. But it is equally about change in social relations and in the economy.

In Turkey, the Kurdish struggle is arguably as much against economic neglect as against military repression by the state, and this has been expressed in attacks on Kurdish landlords who are seen as auxiliaries to the state apparatus that represses the Kurdish people. Those traveling eastward across Turkey will recognize the transition from an industrializing society to a less developed economy. Per capita income in the Kurdish provinces is less than half the national average.[15] It is a world of grinding poverty, making Kurdish nationalism as much an economic as an ethnic issue.[16] It is no accident that Abdallah Ocalan and his cofounders of the PKK (the Kurdistan Workers Party) commenced their careers in Turkish leftist groups committed to class war. Ocalan and his colleagues were denounced by the Turkish left for giving the national question primacy over the class factor. The first party program in 1977 enunciated the minimum objective of the creation of an independent nonaligned Kurdistan state in the region: Turkish Kurds would lead in this process of state building, and the state would be based on Marxist-Leninist principles.[17]

In Iraq, the importance and leadership of certain families in the national movement has transcended class issues. The class dimension was largely resolved when the Hashemites, whose rule had depended on the chiefs, were overthrown in 1958. The Kurdish movement in Iraq rapidly lost its class connotations thereafter, in spite of the fashionable appeal to leftist ideas of class and national liberation. Despite their rhetoric in the 1970s and 1980s, there was never any great likelihood that the Iraqi Kurdish leaders were seriously interested in social revolution, once the power of the tribal chiefs was clearly in decline.[18] They welcomed the social evolution that was now naturally taking place, wanted autonomy and a fair share of national assets, and in their more exuberant moments, hinted at the distant dream of an independent Kurdistan.

In Iran, agrarian land reform of 1962 and the accelerating process of urbanization destroyed the old control of the local magnate class and led to mass sympathy for the Kurdish national movement among a rapidly growing proletariat. This was accelerated by the sense of alienation from the state, personified by the Pahlavi dynasty. Furthermore, in spite of religious differences, but possibly because of their ethnic and linguistic affinity, Iran's Kurds never seriously hankered after full independence after the collapse of the Mahabad Republic in 1946.[19]

The Kurdish movement, particularly in Turkey and Iran, has also been characterized by large-scale migration. In Turkey's case, this has led to possibly 5 out of Turkey's 12 million Kurds living outside Kurdistan. Istanbul, with probably over 2 million of them, is the largest concentration of Kurds anywhere. In Iran large numbers of Kurds now travel out of Kurdistan seasonally in search of work, to Khuzistan in search of employment in the oil industry, or to other industrial centers, most notably Tabriz and Tehran.

In both Turkey and Iran, some migrant Kurds have quietly dropped their Kurdish identity, but for others, Kurdish nationalism has acquired a new political virulence as recent migrants seek to rediscover their own identity in the context of anonymous, oppressive, and alien environments. (Those familiar with the story of Beirut in the late 1960s and early 1970s should not be surprised by this fact.) Since much of the driving force of Kurdish nationalism in both countries derives from repression and alienation, the political leadership of the state can no longer assume that centralization and urbanization leads to a more homogeneous state. Clearly this is not necessarily so.

Labor migration out of Kurdistan, both in Turkey and Iran, represents a potential communal as well as security problem for the state, but it also presents the Kurdish national movement with a dilemma. On the one hand it can mobilize the disaffected in a disruptive campaign of sabotage and urban guerrilla war against the state. On the other, the reality beyond the rhetoric of secession would be economically disastrous for the growing number of Kurds who need to migrate in search of work.

Fault Lines Within the Kurdish Movement

Implicit in any discussion of the Kurdish movement is the existence of a Kurdish nation per se. It might, however, be more accurate to say that while most Kurds pay lip service to the idea of one Kurdish nation, there remains a real problem about the degree of homogeneity necessary for the effective national unification of all Kurds. Let us consider some aspects.

International Borders

The rhetoric of Kurdish national unity crossing international boundaries goes back over sixty years,[20] but it remains questionable how far the ideal has been realized. International borders remain an obvious impediment, and these have become increasingly impermeable. Until 1939 a substantial measure of social intercourse and trade took place informally among the Kurds of Iraq, Iran, and Turkey, but since then it has been in decline. Today, cross-border social liaison is much reduced and in spite of considerable smuggling, the economy of each part of Kurdistan is integrated into the state in which it finds itself. This is true for the marketing and purchase of commodities and, of course, in the search for employment. And increasingly, work is found, as exemplified in labor migration, within the non-Kurdish part of the state. Moreover, Kurds are subject to different dominant cultures—Turkish, Arab, and Persian. Whether they like it or not, the Kurds in each country are inevitably drawn into the prevailing cultural ambiance in which they must function effectively. As citizens of these countries they can and do participate in a wider context beyond the confines of Kurdistan. Such factors tend to give Kurdishness its own distinctive quality in each country, and this distinctiveness is likely to grow, not decrease.[21]

Language Difference

But there are longer-standing phenomena. Kurds have still not resolved the basic impediment of language difference. Whether one describes the difference between northern (Kirmanji) and southern (Sorani) Kurdish as one of dialect or of language, the effect is the same. Educated Kurds can cross the barrier without too much difficulty, but for those with little education, communication is much harder. The dialect divide does not follow international borders. Iraqi Kurds along the northern border area (Bahdinan) are Kirmanji speakers and therefore feel greater linguistic affinity to Turkish Kurds than to other Iraqi Kurds to the south. The latter, as Soran speakers, feel closer linguistically to most Iranian Kurds than they do to Turkish Kurds. Apart from their strongly felt nationalism, it is the fact of living together in a predominantly Arab state that draws Kirmanji—and Sorani—speaking Kurds together in Iraq. In Iran a minority from Urumiya northwards speak Kirmanji. In both Turkey and Iran there are substantial numbers who speak neither main dialect.[22] There is also the problem of script, Latin in Turkey, Persian in Iran and Iraq, (and Cyrillic in the ex-Soviet Union). In Turkey there has been a widespread loss of the Kurdish language, and it is possible that Kurdish language identity may also be slowly disappearing. Most migrant families lose their Kurdish, as do many townsfolk, even in Kurdistan.

Religion

Although all Sunni Kurds belong to the Shafii school of jurisprudence, religion complicates rather than advances Kurdish unity. In Turkey and Iran there are substantial minorities that are not Sunni. In Turkey a large Alevi community exists, possibly fifteen million strong, of whom perhaps three million are Kurds.[23] Observant Sunni Muslims, be they Turkish or Kurd, view Alevis as *kafir*. Although the majority of Alevi Kurds support the national struggle, some Alevis understandably feel more at home with Turkish Alevis than they do with Sunni Kurds. And within Sunni Kurdish society religious feeling remains strong, particularly in rural areas, where education is weak or nonexistent and where the authority of religious shaikhs remains strong. Sunnism here can be stronger than Kurdism, and there is a conflict between secular and religious Kurdish nationalism. It is no accident that some of the strongholds of Turkey's right-wing religious party, Refat, lie in the Kurdish countryside.

In Iran, too, religion is divisive. Mention has already been made of the Sunni-Shiite divide. At least 15 (and possibly 20) percent of Iran's Kurds are Shiites, living in Kirmanshah (Bakhtiran) province. In 1979 they sided with the Islamic Republic against the call of Kurdish nationalism further north with its Sunni connotations. Today, following the disastrous war with Iraq, Shiite Kurds feel much more sympathy for the nationalist call further north. However, the 200,000 or so Ahl al Haqq, another extreme heterodox group, have largely eschewed Kurdish nationalism, in favor of the Islamic Republic, a policy based, as it was under the Pahlavis, on the need to survive in a potentially hostile climate.[24]

In Iraq the Islamic movement still seems minuscule.[25] Yet whereas it garnered only 4 percent of the vote in the Kurdish election of May 1992, a year later it was thought that it could attract double that vote or more.[26] Indeed the major armed clashes between the Islamic Movement of Kurdistan (IMK) and the PUK in December 1993 resulted from a growing contest for the same support, and this conflict was renewed in May 1994 when the IMK seized Halabja and Khurmal. How far the IMK has created a popular following will be revealed if elections are held in May 1995 as currently proposed.

Tribalism and Neotribalism

Today traditional tribalism is firmly in retreat, although clan or tribal leaders continue to play a role, both in Turkey and Iraq.[27] In its place, however, "neotribalism" is manifest in political life, evident in patronage repaid by loyalty to individuals or families, most clearly seen in the Barzani family, but practiced very widely. It was a clear phenomenon among the pro-government *jash* prior to the 1991 uprising organized either under tribal chiefs (thereby reviving tribalism) or under local strongmen who profited from their ability to raise local retainers and to hire these out to government. Such quasimilitary organizations may currently be in abeyance but might well revive under appropriate circumstances.

Political loyalties among ordinary people are largely determined by geographical location, dominant local patrons, local politics, and family consensus. Leaders, and the rewards they can offer (gainful employment for the humble, authority for the ambitious), are infinitely more important than party ideology. Indeed, as in the political process elsewhere in the Middle East, ideology can easily be a facade for public consumption. Behind it operates the real (patriarchy) system. In the election of 1992, it was difficult to discern any defining ideological differences between any of the secular Kurdish parties.[28] These kinds of attachments impede the creation of a more homogeneous society in which ideas about social organization, economics, or political relationships with neighbors can take precedence over personal loyalty.

Outside Interference

Finally there is the question of Kurdish susceptibility to external manipulation, widely recognized among Kurds themselves as damaging to their struggle. They have been coopted easily by their own non-Kurdish governments and by regional or external players in order to unbalance an adversary.[29] Kurdish willingness to cooperate with outsiders has often been determined by disputes within Kurdish ranks. When one tribe enjoyed strong government support, its rival would almost automatically support the opposition. Such behavior continues even since the decline of tribes and the formation of parties and has been profoundly damaging to pan-Kurdish cooperation.[30]

The Current Situation

Iraq

It is, of course the Iraqi context that springs most readily to mind. Iraqi Kurds remain dependent upon international protection against genocide and for support against the economic war being waged by Baghdad. The coalition (and most notably Turkey) is willing to provide only the minimum support consonant with basic physical survival. Members fear that their electorates will hold them accountable if there is a repetition of the televised scenes of human suffering of March–April 1991. They also fear that another mass flight to the border will damage efforts to restore stability to the region. On the other hand, the coalition has no intention of allowing Iraqi Kurdistan real independence; it was on this basis that Turkey allowed its allies use of the Incirlik airbase (Iran also cooperates with this policy).

Consequently, the Kurds are caught in a highly unsatisfactory political and economic condition, knowing how precarious their situation is. They must assume that one day coalition protection will no longer be there. Consequently the total political independence from Baghdad that they currently enjoy is much less attractive than an accepted, but more modest, autonomy agreement. It was in order to achieve such an agreement with Baghdad that the Kurdistan Front negotiated a revised autonomy agreement in the summer of 1991. It broke off that negotiation because it was unable to exact the concessions it wanted regarding disputed areas, the exclusion of Baghdad's secret police network from the region, and the introduction of democracy in Iraq. But it also hoped that the international community might act as guarantor of an agreement and believed that Saddam was unlikely to remain in power for long.

It is on this last, so far unfulfilled, hope that the Kurdistan Front remains in close dialogue with other Iraq opposition groups in the hope that together they might construct a post-Saddam Iraq in a way that suits their political values. The Kurdistan Front now favors a federal structure for Iraq, offering something more than autonomy but less than full independence for the Kurds. A federal solution is grudgingly accepted by other opposition groups, who remain uncomfortable with federalism.[31]

However, while the Kurdish forces represent the strongest component of the opposition forces, they are no match for the Iraqi army. The Kurdish leadership knows it would have to come to a rapid accommodation with Baghdad should coalition air cover be withdrawn or prove an inadequate deterrent. Masud Barzani has reportedly maintained a dialogue with Baghdad as a precaution against just such an eventuality.

Inside Kurdistan the Kurds are discovering the difficulties of creating a credible political structure for themselves. In May 1992 they demonstrated their ability to hold free democratic elections and to abide by the result. This in itself was an achievement. Yet it was a controversial path. Externally it demanded a reaction from an international community reluctant to acknowledge any act that implied the breakup of Iraq. Internally, Kurdish society, like the rest of Iraq, had no previous experience of democratic practice, and there was no guarantee its elected representatives would honor the democratic institutions that the election promised.

The Kurdish parliament and government have been denied international recognition. In order to continue to deal with the outside world, Masud Barzani and Jalal Talabani decided not to take part in the government formed to administer Kurdistan. By refraining from participation, however, it was inevitable that real power remained in the two-party headquarters rather than with the Kurdish Regional Government (KRG). The government is responsible for administration but largely impotent in policy matters. Furthermore, because the election outcome was so evenly balanced between the Kurdistan Democratic Party and the Patriotic Union of Kurdistan, the government is shared on a 50–50 basis. Where a minister belongs to one party, his deputy belongs to the other. In practice, two parallel administrations or patronage systems (as Kurdish skeptics would describe them) exist, reaching all the way to the police on the street, in an uneasy coexistence between two rival neotribes. Even at the top level, rivalry between Barzani and Talabani has created, in the words of another senior Kurdish politician "detente without entente."[32] As a consequence, democracy has had no chance to fulfill its promise. By December 1993 frustration (including the resignation of the KRG's first Prime Minister)[33] had led to the formation of an eight-person "strategic committee" designed to overcome the gap between the party leaders and the KRG. Personal tensions, however, prevented the committee from meeting before the failure of the Kurdish leadership to form a credible political system was cruelly exposed. In May 1994 a land dispute[34] near Qala Diza unleashed pent-up rivalry, and widespread fighting between PUK and KDP peshmergas (Kurdish guerillas) rapidly spread across Kurdistan. The IMK, effectively acting as the KDP's ally, crossed from Iran to seize Halabja and Khurmal. A ceasefire was only established in June through Iraqi National Congress (INC) mediation and after hundreds had been killed and thousands displaced. All parties were accused of summary execution of captives.

The impact of the conflict was severe. Kurdistan was left divided into clear zones of party control. Deep bitterness now existed between partisans of each party. The credibility of the KRG in Arbil was now further drastically reduced. Externally, the fighting raised serious questions for Turkey, which wants a stable, and above all PKK-free, environment on its southern border. It suspected the PUK of assisting the PKK revival in order to create difficulties between itself and the KDP (which controls the territory along Turkey's border). In addition Kurdish internecine conflict must have weakened the political commitment of the coalition to its air cover north of Latitude 36.

It has been provisionally agreed to hold fresh elections in May 1995. It is widely expected that the outcome will be more decisive, almost certainly in favor of the KDP. Judging by the events of 1994, such an outcome might precipitate renewed conflict or the secession of PUK areas, if these constitute a large and coherent whole. In short, the emergence of a clear winner may be the first real test of Kurdistan's determination to build a credible electoral system.

Meanwhile Saddam is waging a damaging economic war against Kurdistan, restricting foodstuffs and fuel on which the population depends. Reporting on the human rights situation in Iraq, the U.N. Special Rapporteur stated in February 1994:

> I have to ask for special attention to the fate of the Kurdish people in the north. While the population in other parts of Iraq receive food rations covering some 50 percent of their basic needs, and that is already far too little, the internal blockade organized by Iraq against the northern Kurdish governorates leads to a situation where only 7–10 percent of the normal rations reach the population that is very much dependent on international aid and assistance. It is only by massive aid from outside that the population can survive.[35]

A war of attrition is going on, with the deliberate deprivation of food and fuel, causing particularly acute hardship in winter. If a Kurdish government in Arbil is unable to function properly, unable to provide basic services, and is manifestly unable to protect the population in the event of a coalition withdrawal, despondency among the people may lead to openly expressed discontent with the leadership.[36] It could even lead to pressure for a negotiated settlement with Baghdad.

Iran

After initial setbacks, Iran defeated its Kurds in the early 1980s. It now holds the area in an iron grip, with frequent roadblocks and military patrols, and air raids on Iranian Kurdish camps inside Iraq. The Kurdistan Democratic Party of Iran (KDPI) and Komala continue their guerrilla war but it is reduced to pinprick attacks. The KDPI openly admits that the only justification for its operations is to keep the idea of Kurdish nationalism alive, and to give Kurds hope. It no longer harbors any serious ambition of bringing Tehran to the negotiating table as a result of its guerrilla operations nor, indeed, to negotiations in the foreseeable future since the last attempt led to the assassination of its leader Abd al Rahman Qasimlu in 1989. Today Iran's Kurds struggle merely to keep their Kurdish identity alive.

Despite its overtly Shiite hue and its mass executions of Kurdish opponents, the Islamic Republic is probably not as hated as was the Pahlavi regime. It does allow modestly more expression of Kurdish identity—for example, it permits Kurdish publications—than did the Pahlavis. However, like the Pahlavis, it governs the Kurds through senior officials who are not Kurds, a major source of discontent. Furthermore,

Tehran has done nothing to compensate for the serious economic neglect of Kurdistan compared with other parts of Iran.[37] Labor migration is another major source of resentment.

Turkey

In contrast to the KDPI, since it began its military campaign in 1984 the PKK has made the Kurdish question the single most important domestic issue in Turkish politics.

The secret of PKK success lies as much in state brutality as in its own strategy. Indeed, the violence of the PKK and Ankara have perfectly complimented each other to polarize the country. Something in excess of one hundred thousand (some say two hundred thousand) troops are now permanently deployed in eastern Turkey. By the end of 1993, a year in which approximately 3,750 perished and 874 villages were destroyed or severely damaged, the death toll (since 1984) exceeded ten thousand.[38] Yet no end is in sight.

Unlike the Iranian and Iraqi contexts, the government refuses recognition of the Kurds as a minority and a liberation movement that, until 1990, claimed that nothing short of full independence would suffice. Even after Ocalan's announcement in April that year that "there is no question of separating from Turkey," independence remains his ultimate objective.[39]

There has been great unwillingness on either side to explore the possibility for compromise. The army continues to believe that any concession whatsoever will logically lead to Kurdish secession.[40] The PKK, for its part, has never evolved a coherent political strategy. Its modus operandi has been guerrilla warfare, to be followed by more conventional military tactics once it had forced the Turkish government onto the defensive. In autumn 1992, a move toward more conventional warfare allowed the Turkish forces a significant victory in cooperation with the Iraqi-Kurdistan Front, which felt compelled to cooperate in order to protect its lifeline through Turkey to the outside world. This defeat for the PKK was a commentary on the bankruptcy of its military strategy: it had not recognized both the potential and limitations of guerrilla war.

The concessions that have been made by Ankara have largely been the product of individuals—most notably the late President Turgut Özal—who have been willing to break with the Ataturk tradition. In any case such concessions have been pitifully small. Spoken Kurdish was allowed in January 1991, written Kurdish in publications a few months later. But these were accompanied by more stringent security conditions in Kurdistan that nullified whatever mollifying effect liberalization may have had. This has been followed by a wave of assassinations of journalists, politicians, and others associated with the Kurdish secular struggle.[41] Government complicity is strongly suspected. There can be little doubt that in 1991 an important opportunity was missed to create a basis of trust.

However, Kurdish political leaders must share some of the responsibility. When twenty-two Kurds were elected to the Grand National Assembly in October 1991, two of them deliberately provoked Turkish MPs with openly nationalist statements, creating a storm of hostility. Both sides cling to declaratory positions rather than search for areas of flexibility.

In March 1993 the PKK proclaimed a ceasefire but the Turkish government—presumably assuming that the concession was a consequence of the defeat the previous autumn—made no significant gesture in return. Its troops continued to search for PKK bases and to kill PKK fighters. In May hardliners in the PKK ambushed and killed off-duty soldiers, and thereby forced Ocalan to abandon the ceasefire and resume the offensive.

Then the PKK staged attacks on Turkish targets in Europe and on tourist sites on Turkey's popular southern coast. The war has resumed, more savage, more expensive (it cost $6 billion in 1993) and more polarizing than ever before.[42] Large numbers of country people have been driven from or fled their villages. Diyarbakr, in 1991 a city of some 500,000 inhabitants exceeded one million by 1994. In July 1993, the state banned the only party with a strong Kurdish identity, the People's Labor Party (HEP), thus denying the Kurds a legitimate Kurdish voice in Parliament. In June 1994 it banned its successor, the Democratic Party (DEP), and its successor, the Peoples Democratic Party (HADEP) probably faces the same fate. In mid-October 1993 the PKK demonstrated the authority it now wielded in Kurdistan. In response to highly selective Turkish reporting of events, it successfully prohibited reporting by both the Turkish and international press from the region, to the anger and embarrassment of Turkey's political and military establishment.

The only advance in Turko-Kurdish relations has grown out of the talks initiated in March 1991 with Iraqi Kurdish leaders. Psychologically, that dialogue made it harder for Turkey to deny its own Kurdish minority, but this is a modest and insubstantial gain.

The Prospects

Iran

One might naturally suppose that Iran had little to fear from the Kurds, but all administrations in this century have regarded Kurdistan nervously.[43] As the Islamic Republic knows, Kurdistan is the natural springboard for all militant opposition groups. However, the greater danger may lie not so much in Kurdistan itself, as with the growing number of Kurds who exist in the slums of Iran's industrial cities. They have both a sense of nationalism and a strong class affinity with the other millions of impoverished people in Iran.

As Iran experiences growing economic difficulty, particularly in the most crucial area, the ability to feed its own rapidly growing population (which doubles every twenty years or so), it is questionable whether the government will be able to control an increasingly discontented urban proletariat living in slum conditions. It is probably only within the process of a popular revolt against the current clerical regime that the Kurds have any hope of achieving local autonomy; consequently, economic rather than ethnic unrest will probably be the driving factor. Under such circumstances an attempt at ethnic autonomy may seem unpromising, but it should be borne in mind that just under half Iran's population is non-Persian, and that there have been moments when previous governments considered decentralization.[44]

In the event of a change in Iran's government resulting from economic conditions and disenchantment with the clerical regime, it is possible that the Kurds and other ethnic minorities might be able to negotiate a degree of self-government. But as Kurds constitute barely 10 percent of Iran's population, this is only likely to be achieved with a central government that is committed to decentralization. No such government is apparent.

Iraq

For Iraq's Kurds the prospects are stark. If Saddam Hussein survives, it is almost inevitable that he will try to reassert his authority over Kurdistan. He may do so through triumphant conquest, but this would trigger mass flight and great human suffering, with the danger of international intervention and of difficulties with Turkey or Iran. It is more likely therefore that he would reconquer Kurdistan by stealth, forcing its acquiescence to Baghdad's authority through economic coercion. His economic blockade of Kurdistan suggests this process is well under way. In spite of past experience it is conceivable that a starving Kurdish population might demand that their leaders seek an accommodation with

Baghdad, particularly if the KRG continues to be perceived as inadequate.

Saddam Hussein may offer the Kurds a fresh round of autonomy
negotiations. If he can, he will use the lifting of sanctions by the international community to contrast the improvement that will take place in the
rest of Iraq with the poverty in Kurdistan. The terms he is likely to offer
will be similar to those offered in 1974, bereft of the substance of
autonomy. Saddam is psychologically incapable of allowing any genuine
democracy or decentralization.

Faced with the dangers of defiance—the mass destruction of Kurdish
life—Kurdish leaders may decide they must concede, deferring the Kurdish struggle until conditions are more propitious. Once in control,
Saddam's security apparatus would resume its purge of Kurdish society.
As long as his security operations do not provoke open conflict or mass
flight, Saddam can assume that the coalition will be reluctant to intervene. However, many Kurds would flee rather than await the possibility
of arrest, and the numbers might be so great as to create a major refugee
problem for Iran and possibly for Turkey.

Is the coalition willing to provide effective protection against these
possibilities? Effective protection is contingent on Turkey's good will and
also makes Kurdistan's temporary political independence from Baghdad
more permanent. One can only speculate that the coalition's commitment
cannot have been strengthened by the conflict in 1994 within the Kurdish
region. Any agreement on autonomy, however unreliable, will probably
persuade the coalition to withdraw its protection. This is the single most
important reason for the Kurds to refuse any agreement with Saddam.

Yet the Kurds must also recognize that economic sanctions against
Iraq are unlikely to endure. Quite apart from the fact that by mid-1994
Iraq had more or less complied with the disarmament requirements of
UNSCR 687, the pressure is building from those states anxious to resume
political and economic relations. France has held talks with Baghdad
since August 1993, Egypt is pressuring for Iraq's rehabilitation, and Iran's
Foreign Minister, Ali Akbar Vilayati, spoke of Iraq's need to reassert
control "up to the border" in the spring of 1994 and sent a delegation to
Baghdad the following June. But for the Kurds it is Turkey's decisions
that will be most dangerous. Because it has lost $2 billion yearly in transit
dues, Turkey has been particularly anxious to reopen the Kirkuk-Mersin
pipeline. In May 1994 Ankara announced the imminent pumping of 8
million barrels in order to clean the pipe. It is possible Turkey may
anticipate the lifting of sanctions by resuming export of Iraq's oil, and
may even allow overland shipment of goods to Iraq. The threat to
suspend the coalition's use of Incirlik airbase could be used as a deterrent
against international coercion to uphold the blockade. It is questionable

whether the coalition, even with the political will, could sustain any credible protection for the Kurds without Turkish assistance.

Moreover, there is no guarantee of sufficient political will, particularly if the coalition faces the prospect of defending warring Iraqi Kurdish fiefdoms. This is the nightmarish possibility Kurdish political leaders must at all costs avoid. Whatever happens externally, the creation of internal unity under the authority of the KRG is essential to the Kurdish region's credibility with the INC and internationally.

Even supposing Saddam is overthrown, the seemingly desperate hope of Iraqi opposition groups, it is probable that he will be succeeded by a member of his own coterie or a senior army officer. The new head of state may come to some autonomy arrangement with the Kurds, but it is questionable whether an agreement with any of the ruling elite in Baghdad will offer the Kurds significantly more than they were offered in 1974. The best hope may be that Saddam's successor would need Kurdish cooperation in order to rebuild Iraq's shattered economy, and that out of this cooperation a more lasting and more trusting arrangement could be achieved. However, Saddam's inner group seems implacably opposed to either democracy or decentralization. Furthermore, there can be no realistic prospect of Baghdad relinquishing its hold on Kirkuk, or on Sanjar and Khaniqin, the former for economic, the latter two for strategic reasons.

There is a remote possibility that the Iraqi National Congress, the main formal opposition group, would be able to participate in a successor government. That is only likely to happen if Saddam's successor feels the need for national reconciliation. There is evidence to suggest that despite clawing his way back from the disaster of 1991, Saddam now presides over a regime in an advanced stage of disintegration, with repeated coup attempts, popular disaffection and large-scale desertions from the armed forces.[45] National reconciliation and the political participation of opposition groups could lead to a fundamental restructuring of Iraq to allow its religious and ethnic components joint participation in government and a measure of autonomy for the Kurds. It remains questionable whether the prospect of an internal collapse of Saddam's regime is likely, and whether any successor regime (even the INC) could happily live with a federal arrangement.

The Kurdish political leadership may feel unable to accept anything short of full autonomy, unless they are prepared for bitter disappointment among their constituencies. But it should be borne in mind that a very substantial portion of the Kurdish population, while wanting autonomy, now has low expectations of the abilities of their political representatives and probably wants above all guarantees from Baghdad that neither forcible resettlement nor arbitrary arrest, torture, and disappearance will happen again. There is also the possibility that the two main parties will disagree over negotiations with Baghdad, and that Baghdad will exploit this division to defeat both or to develop an agreement with one party that will banish the other to the margins of Iraqi political life. Both the PUK and the KDP have been susceptible to such temptations in the past.

With or without a change of regime in Baghdad, if the Kurdistan Front loses coalition protection and is also unable to conclude an agreement with Baghdad, a return to guerrilla warfare, with Iran allowing the guerrillas to operate in the border areas, is a distinct possibility. The furthest Iran might go to cooperate with Iraq would be to "mothball" the Iraqi Kurdish groups, but it will wish to keep them available should the need arise to deal with its old adversary again.

Turkey

The short-term prospects for Turkey's Kurds are also discouraging. Ciller's inability to defy the army and conservative establishment by opening a debate on the Kurdish question, the deepening guerrilla war, and the elimination of any legitimate vehicle for the expression of Kurdish community aspirations all create gloomy short-term prospects. The PKK will have no shortage of recruits, and the security forces will enjoy growing backing from an ill-informed Turkish majority that feels increasingly angry at PKK hostage taking, bomb attacks on civilians and tourists, and outrages against the families of Village Guards. Regardless of the outcome of this war, the failure of Turkey to address the Kurdish issue allows the progressive advance of Kurdish nationalist sentiment in what remains the most economically neglected part of the country. This sentiment leaches out into Turkish Turkey via Kurdistan's migrant labor force. There has been a progressive rise in intercommunal tension between Turks and Kurds, and this drives Kurds to seek secession as the only logical resolution of their predicament.

The most important question, however, concerns the longer term. It remains open to question whether Ciller, or another premier, can recognize and respond to the failure of military repression to suppress Kurdish identity and the radicalization of the Kurdish population in Turkey. The real challenge now for Ankara is to win back the allegiance of the Kurdish electorate, and that requires political and economic, not military, measures.

The growing polarization between the Turkish and Kurdish communities threatens to plunge the country into a level of strife that will at the least discourage foreign investment and might do much deeper damage to the fabric of the republic. If polarization continues to deepen, it may culminate in either ethnic cleansing, as experienced by the Armenians earlier this century, or eventual Kurdish secession after much bloodshed.

Economic development requires liberalization, and it is almost impossible to confine this to the economy but only a minority in the Turkish establishment have recognized that economic investment and expansion depends on confidence, and this confidence depends on a sense of public well-being. It also depends on the community's ability to participate. For the Kurds a striking example of their impaired ability to participate is the South East Anatolia Development Project (GAP). This project proposes, from the 22 dams planned for the Euphrates and Tigris, not only to generate sufficient power to fuel Turkey's industrial expansion program (mainly outside Kurdistan) but also to create widespread, irrigated, capital-intensive agriculture and agro-industries. It is proposed that the local population will benefit from this development project, thereby helping to satisfy the urgent need to improve the local economy. But since the level of education and literacy in the region is so much lower than the national average, it is unlikely that local Kurds will be able to benefit to the extent proportionately.[46] A chief obstacle to educational progress is the insistence on the use of Turkish at primary level, even though large numbers of rural Kurds know no Turkish. Unless Kurds are allowed to learn in their mother tongue, they are unlikely to progress intellectually. Thus economic development is tied to the question of political liberalization.

The government has also repeatedly backed off from the notion of land reform in the area, because the landlord class has been so important in the electoral process of the region.[47] Eight percent of farming families own 51 percent of agricultural land. Eighty percent of rural families either own neither land nor livestock or own under five hectares, an area insufficient for family subsistence let alone capital intensive agriculture. By its plans to create state-run enterprises for small holders, GAP is likely to drive small holders off the land because they will cease to control what little they have.

The proportion of Kurds in the Republic, currently standing at around 20 percent (about 12 of 58 million), will increase as a result of a substantially higher crude birth rate.[48] Therefore the Kurdish problem is likely to deepen, both because of a proportionately higher growth rate among more Kurds and because a growing number will migrate westward. Demographic growth and migration can probably be avoided only by specific efforts to promote the economic and educational development of the Kurdish people in their traditional homeland.

The Kurds, Regional Security, and the International Community

The future of the Kurds may seem important only to countries that have a Kurdish population. But their future has become increasingly important at the international level. The mass flight of Iraqi Kurds creates major regional problems, particularly for Turkey. Having accepted responsibility for protecting the Iraqi Kurds, the U.S., British, and French governments are vulnerable to their own electorates if they appear to abandon the Kurds to a harsh fate. Turkey's stability and economic prospects are likely to be increasingly impaired by its Kurdish problem. Its treatment of the Kurds was one substantive reason why its application to join the European Community in 1987 was indefinitely deferred. PKK bomb attacks along the coast damage Turkey's attractiveness not only to tourism but also to investment.

The failure to deal adequately with the Kurdish question in the post-World War I period has, indeed, left a permanent sore in the region. To that extent our British staff officer of 1919 was correct. One could also point without difficulty to the continuing political divisions within the Kurdish community. However, his proposal "to find some system which will ensure a measure of law, order and progress and which at the same time, by being in accordance with national aspirations, be acceptable to the majority of the people," has clearly failed. Ever since 1921, forcible integration has been the policy adopted by all those attempting to establish their version of stability in the region. Britain gave Iraq a treaty of independence that deliberately omitted any mention of the Kurds. Turkey ignored even the linguistic rights of the Kurds adumbrated in the Treaty of Lausanne. The West has averted its gaze from the Kurdish question, except when either tempted to engage in covert action (the CIA in the 1970s) or forced to intervene (safe havens in 1991).

External powers see regional security defined largely through the balance of power between states and, of course, in terms of their own strategic and economic interests. These concepts of security easily overlook the millions of people who actually inhabit the region. In the Kurdish case, an obvious example was the international response to Halabja, where international law was given no weight in comparison to the regional security consideration of supporting Iraq against Iran. With hindsight, it was arguably a short-sighted policy. Iraq learned that it could violate international law massively with impunity.

The obvious prescription for Western policymakers is that their long-term policy toward all states with a substantial Kurdish minority must encourage political solutions "acceptable to the majority of the people," albeit within the present interstate configuration of the region.

However unwelcome such a policy may be to the governments in the region, there is little alternative since coercive integration is a wholesale failure. The well-being of communities as well as states is an essential component of regional security and economic progress. External powers must take an active interest in assisting the parties involved in the Kurdish issue to reach a modus vivendi that protects the sovereignty of states, but that also brings their Kurdish communities into a more productive relationship with the state. Kurds would no longer be attracted to the use of violence, and regional powers would no longer be able to disturb regional tranquility through the use of the Kurds as proxies.

A core set of principles should now govern the West's policy toward Iraq. Alongside its commitment to Iraq's territorial integrity, the West should indicate that it remains committed to the principles implicit in UNSCR 688 and will use its best efforts to persuade Baghdad that the fundamental rights and freedoms for all Iraq's communities will remain a key factor in its political and economic relations. In a more perfect world where Western powers acted in concert, they might also consider whether some form of international guarantee should be offered to any agreement reached between the Kurds and Baghdad.

Unfortunately, practical considerations make the implementation of such a broad strategy enormously difficult. Neither Baghdad nor Ankara, let alone Tehran, will welcome international involvement, however well-intentioned. Kurds note with some bitterness that the United Nations seems a good deal more concerned with disarming Iraq (UNSCR 687), than it is with the physical safety of Iraq's own population (UNSCR 688). Protection for the Kurds seems essentially a grace-and-favor exercise, contingent on Turkey's cooperation. All three governments—American, French, and British—should consider the potential consequences of ending their commitment and consider whether it is possible to retain a sufficient deterrent should Turkey withdraw its facilities.

The Kurds of Iraq would still like some kind of international guarantee for any agreement they reach with Baghdad. Without international guarantees for a modicum of political and economic rights, long-term stability in Iraqi Kurdistan remains unlikely. Coalition governments should recognize that such guarantees are a necessary component to a long-term solution to the Iraqi crisis and to their own military withdrawal. However, the prospects of an international security guarantee have been reduced by the danger of renewed conflict between the KDP and PUK, and the fragmentation of the Kurdish autonomous region. One practical and immediate measure may be taken regardless of the political difficulties. The West should ensure that Saddam's economic blockade of the Kurds is offset by the provision of adequate foodstuffs and fuel through Turkey to prevent hardship and suffering.

So far Turkey's Kurdish problems have had limited impact on the outside world. But if the outbreak of attacks on Turkish targets internationally is repeated and becomes a feature of the PKK struggle, Turkey's allies will have to consider how to respond. While they will wish to cooperate in counter-insurgency measures, they may conclude that the fundamental need is to persuade Turkey's military leaders that a military solution is not possible and that military action can only usefully be the servant of a political solution. There is no evidence that Turkey is working toward a political solution. Turkey's generals are notoriously unreceptive to liberal messages, and it may be that such messages can only be conveyed credibly by the military men of NATO who have had to struggle with internal guerrilla problems of their own as in Spain and in the United Kingdom. There is likely to be enormous reluctance by Turkey's NATO allies to engage in such meddling. But as with Iraq, those concerned with regional security must recognize the dangers of deteriorating intercommunal relations and passivity.

Notes

1. France was interested, for it intended to acquire Cilicia and had not forgotten that under the now largely redundant Sykes-Picot Agreement it was to acquire northern Mesopotamia and the whole Kurdish fringe area adjacent to these regions. Had it not foundered in 1917, Czarist Russia had hoped to acquire virtually all the eastern edge of Ottoman Kurdistan. The United States was also concerned with Kurdistan, less for its own sake than because President Woodrow Wilson was keenly interested in the idea of creating an Armenian state in eastern Anatolia in which the surviving Armenian community would be assured protection from the "terrible Turk." Having captured Mesopotamia at great cost and having begun to recognize the strategic and economic importance of Northern Mesopotamia, Britain's willingness to allow this region to become a French sphere of influence had rapidly evaporated. In a memorandum a month after the cessation of hostilities, the India Office opined "The future of Kurdistan depends in great measure upon two questions, viz. (i) whether we can induce the French to forego their claims in the Mosul vilayet and (ii) whether, if so, we can unite Mosul with the Mesopotamian State," Great Britain, India Office L/P&S/781 Political Department memorandum on Kurdistan, 14 December 1918.

2. [E.J.R.], *Precis of Affairs in Southern Kurdistan During the Great War* (Baghdad: Government Press, 1919), 18.

3. Turkey, more than its neighbors, has had an almost paranoic fear concerning the coalescence of Kurdish nationalism, ever since the foundation of the republic in 1923.

4. This consensus has been formalized in the Sa'adabad Pact (1937), the Baghdad Pact (1955), the Algiers Agreement (1975), and more recently, the tripartite

agreement of Turkey, Iran, and Syria regarding the territorial integrity of Iraq (1992).

5. This temptation has arisen on at least three occasions: in response to the overthrow of the Hashimites in 1958; when Iran looked as if it might defeat Iraq in the mid-1980s; and finally when Iraq looked as if it would disintegrate following its defeat in the Gulf War in 1991.

6. This was solicited by a number of leading Kurdish tribal chiefs from the eastern slopes of the Zagros at a meeting in Sulaymaniya with the British Acting Civil Commissioner, Arnold Wilson, on 1 December 1918. Later, in 1919, "E.J.R." argued strongly for the inclusion of the West Azerbaijan Kurds in a Kurdish State (though not those further south who appeared "on the whole fairly well satisfied with Persian rule"), [E.J.R.], *Precis of Affairs*, p. 19.

7. Archie Roosevelt, "The Kurdish Republic of Mahabad," in *A People without a Country: The Kurds and Kurdistan*, Gerard Chaliand ed. (New York: Olive Branch Press, 1993), 126.

8. This was true of Russia in Ottoman Anatolia, of Britain in Iran in both world wars, and arguably in Iraq, where collectively, the Kurdish tribes were more powerful than King Faisal's army, not to mention U.S. and Israeli Kurdish policy in Iraq in the 1970s.

9. U.S. forces had a very tight timetable. They used methods close to coercion to encourage Kurds to come down from the mountains. On 9 May 1991, as they were still coming down off the Turkish border, U.S. General Shalikashvili, in charge of the Operation Safe Haven, announced to coalition colleagues on the Safe Haven planning group that there was no intention of U.S. forces remaining on the ground beyond the beginning of June, Confidential information from a member of the Safe Haven planning group. See also David Keene, *The Kurds in Iraq: How Safe Is Their Haven Now?* (London: Save the Children Fund, 1993), 7.

10. Malcolm Yapp, "The Mice Will Play, Kurds, Turks, and the Gulf War," in *The Gulf War, Regional and International Dimensions*, Hanns W. Maull and Otto Pick, eds. (London: Pinter, 1989).

11. See for example, Great Britain, FO 371/12255 Hoare to Chamberlain, Istanbul December 14, 1927; FO 371/14579 Edmonds, "Notes on a tour to Diabekir, Bitlis and Mush," May 1930. Although propagandist documents, Emir Sureya Bedr Khen, *The Case of Kurdistan against Turkey* (Philadelphia: Khoybun, 1929), and Bletch Chirguh, *La Question Kurde* (Cairo: Paul Barbey, 1930) indicate widespread massacres, deportations, and razing of villages involving the probable death of hundreds of thousands of people, 1925–1928.

12. FO 371/12255 Clerk to Chamberlain, Ankara, 4 January 1927. See also FO 371/11557 Clerk to Oliphant, Istanbul, 20 December 1926 reporting the visit of Sir Henry Dobbs to Ankara. This view can hardly have been unrepresentative of cabinet views, since it was in harmony with the kind of government repression actually taking place in Kurdistan at the time.

13. For example, Kurdish massacre of the inhabitants of Miandoab in 1880, confessional conflict during the Simko Rebellion, 1921–1922, and an explosion of tension between Azeris and Kurds in 1942.

14. Margaret Kahn, *Children of the Jinn*, (New York: Seaview, 1980).

15. Turkey, Planning Organization, *The South Eastern Anatolia Project (GAP), Final Master Plan Report* (Ankara: Prime Ministry, 1989), Vol. I.

16. It is my impression that some descendants of Turks who were settled in Turkish Kurdistan after the First World War have quietly assumed Kurdish identity as an expression of anger at state neglect.

17. Ismet Ismet, *The PKK: A Report on Separatist Violence in Turkey 1973–1992* (Ankara: Turkish Daily News, 1992), 15.

18. Talabani and his colleague and mentor, Ibrahim Ahmad, did indeed take a serious leftist view in the 1960s. But by 1980 this was already weakening, despite the rhetoric.

19. It was a moot point whether the nationalists of Mahabad wanted independence (as they were accused) or merely autonomy within Iran (as they claimed).

20. To the foundation of Khoyboun in 1927.

21. Kurds presumably feel no less differently about themselves than, for example, do West and East Germans who find the realities of unity after a separation of less than fifty years distinctly painful.

22. Zaza, spoken by approximately two million Turkish Kurds, and Gurani, spoken by up to 300,000 of Iran's Kurds. Considerable dialect variations exist elsewhere. Dialect differences between one valley and another have declined over the past century; see, for example, Jacques de Morgan, *Mission Scientifique en Perse* (Ernest Leroux, Paris 1895), Vol. II., *passim*.

23. Alevism derives from the extreme heterodox beliefs of the founders of the Safavid dynasty, before they adopted *ithan'ashari* Shiism as the state religion.

24. They even raised battalions to fight alongside Shia units in the Iran-Iraq war.

25. The enormous influence of the shaykhs of the Naqshbandi and Qadiri orders rapidly declined in the middle years of the century, owing to education and also to their displacement as judicial arbiters by local government.

26. Interview with Sami Shurish, specialist on religious movements among Iraqi Kurds, London 1 July 1993.

27. In Turkey tribal chiefs and landlords are still wooed by political parties for the votes they can deliver in elections, and the state and the PKK compete for their loyalty. In Iraq the Harki, Zibari, Baradosti, Khushnaw, and Surchi chiefs distance themselves from the Kurdish national movement largely on account of their longstanding animosity to the Barzani clan, and also because the social dimension of the nationalist program threatens their position.

28. Except for the minuscule party PASOK, whose central plank is full independence, as distinct from the others, which differed largely on what kind of autonomy they sought and the means to obtain it.

29. This is a longstanding phenomenon. In the nineteenth century, Russia and Ottoman Turkey competed for the loyalty of the Kurds of Eastern Anatolia. At the end of the Great War, that competition was essentially between Britain and Turkey. The Ottomans and the Russians sought to undermine Qajar authority by sowing unrest among Iran's Kurds. Britain used the threat of unrest among the

Kurdish tribes to bend the Qajars to their will. More recently the U.S. and Israel, as well as Iran, supported Mulla Mustafa against Baghdad from 1970–75.

30. In 1958–60 Barzani used government backing to deal with old Kurdish enemies. When he himself fell out with Baghdad, such tribes quickly sought Baghdad's sponsorship and became the core out of which the *jash* movement grew. Since 1991 many of the tribal *jash* have kept their distance from the national leadership, forming their own Kurdistan Tribal Society. It remains unclear how they would react if Saddam Hussein reasserted his control of the region. In 1964 Jalal Talabani sided with Baghdad against Barzani after being chased out of the Kurdistan Democratic Party (KDP). Four years later Mulla Mustafa Barzani caught Iranian Kurdish guerrillas fighting for their own autonomy and handed them over to the shah for execution. After the Islamic Revolution, Barzani fighters cooperated with the Islamic Republic in the defeat of the Iranian Kurdish nationalists. More recently, in October 1992, the Iraqi Kurdistan Front cooperated with the Turkish army to defeat Turkey's Kurdish guerrillas just inside Iraq's northern border. In the late 1980s the Turkish government raised a local militia force, called Village Guards. Where some families sympathized with the PKK, their local rivals rallied to the Village Guards. Some villages that refused to cooperate were razed and their inhabitants deported. In other cases the Village Guard apparatus became another system of economic and political power for local landlords.

31. In the case of the Shiites (SCIRI), they were unwilling to talk to "autonomists" at all until they themselves had been hammered by Saddam's forces in south Iraq and needed whatever friends they could obtain.

32. Dr. Mahmud Uthman, pers. comm., 27 July 1993.

33. The PUK leader, Fuad Masum.

34. Space does not permit details, but the land dispute was between a tribal-landlord claimant (KDP) versus nontribal (pro-PUK) alleged squatters, and harked back to dubious land acquisitions made during the period of Mulla Mustafa's ascendancy in 1970.

35. Statement by Max van der Stoel, 28 February, quoted in *Iraq Update*, no. 106, 12 August 1994.

36. In fact, some would argue, the political leadership is part of the economic problem. A huge amount of vitally needed plant has been exported to Iran in order to boost party funds. In March 1993 the people of Panjwin caught a group affiliated to a political party attempting to smuggle the plant for an asphalt factory to Iran. With roads in their current state of disintegration, such behavior does nothing for political authority, *Hawkar*, July/August 1993.

37. On the whole the Pahlavis neglected the peripheries of the state, concentrating on the industrial development of the center and north of the country. But the two main Sunni areas, Kurdistan and Baluchistan, suffered worst of all. See Akbar Aghajanian, "Ethnic Inequality in Iran: An Overview" in *International Journal of Middle East Studies*, no. 15 (1983): 211–24, or Ervand Abrahamian, *Iran Between Two Revolutions* (Princeton, N.J.: Princeton University Press, 1982), 449.

38. See *Hawkar*, no 18–19, June–July 1994; *The Independent*, 23 October 1993.

39. See the statement of Abd allah Ocalan in *Middle East International*, no. 373, 13 April 1990.

40. In April 1990 the regional governor was given sweeping and draconian powers, including forcible population transfer and censorship of the press, Karar-name No. 413, subsequently revised and renumbered 424. Since the accession of Tansu Ciller as Prime Minister in May 1993, the army has strengthened its control of the Kurdish question in Turkey, see *Middle East International*, 22 October 1993.

41. In 1993 alone there were 850 unsolved political murders. This figure includes more than pro-Kurdish journalists, news vendors, members of the Kurdish nationalist People's Labor Party (HEP), and its successor Democratic Party (DEP), teachers, lawyers, writers, and trade unionists, see *Hawkar*, no. 18–19, June–July 1994; *Turkey Briefing* Vol. 7, nos. 2 and 3 (summer, autumn 1993), Vol. 8, no. 2, (summer 1994); *The Independent*, 15 October 1993, *Middle East International*, 22 October 1993.

42. *Hawkar*, no. 18–19, June–July 1994.

43. Quite apart from the Mahabad Republic of 1946, in the early years of the century the tribes of southern Kurdistan dominated the politics of Kirmanshah. A disconsolate Qajar Prince, Salar al Dawla, made repeated attempts to raise these tribes against his brother, the Shah. In the period 1918–1922, the Kurdish chief Simko sought to wrest West Azerbaijan from state control. In the 1920s and 1930s Tehran was repeatedly faced by tribal defiance.

44. In 1951 General Razmara introduced legislation for the decentralization of Iran to meet the ethnic dimension of national life, but he was assassinated before its enactment. In 1979 the Islamic Republic briefly considered the whole question of limited self-government for minorities. Had it felt less threatened it might have moved in that direction.

45. See for example SCIRI, *Iraqi Update*, no. 63, 8 October 1993.

46. Only 70 percent of children enroll in primary education and only 18 percent go on to secondary education in the Southeast area of Turkey. Only 9 percent complete the secondary cycle. Thus, while the national average for literacy is 77 percent, the literacy level in Mardin province, for example, is only 48 percent. Turkey, Prime Ministry State Planning Organization, *The South Eastern Anatolia Project (GAP) Final Master Plan Report*, Vol. II (June 1990) paras. 5.15, 5.16.

47. See Turkey, State Planning Organization, *The South East Anatolia Project (GAP) Final Master Plan Report* (Ankara: Prime Ministry, June 1990) Vol. II., paras. 6.10, 6.11.

48. The crude birth rate for Kurdistan is 3.718 percent compared with a national average of 2.769 percent. In fact the average crude birth rate for the Turkish part of Turkey is 2.586 percent. Turkey, State Institute of Statistics, *1991 Statistical Yearbook of Turkey* (Ankara: Prime Ministry, 1992), 93.

10

SOURCES OF CONFLICT IN THE MIDDLE EAST: THE KURDS

Barham A. Salih

In all, the Kurds comprise a population of some twenty-five to thirty million, a sizable number by any measure. They are the Middle East's fourth largest ethnic-linguistic group, after the Arabs, the Turks, and the Persians. They are a people of unfulfilled national aspirations; they have found their language and culture suppressed, their identity denied, and even their physical existence threatened. Ironically, however, whenever the Kurdish national issue is addressed, the security concerns of their neighbors are invoked. Considering the suffering the Kurds had to endure in past decades, one wonders whose security concerns are more profound and more pertinent.

Today, Kurds fear that the logic of the old regional order will prevail once again when the politics of this region are reshaped. It is a profound concern shared by many Kurds that their rights and aspirations, and their security concerns, will once again be ignored and subordinated to a concept of stability formulated primarily in regional capitals.

Historical Background

The conflicts that have engulfed the Kurdish homeland in recent years find their roots in the post-World War I period: the defeat of the Ottoman empire in 1918 and the allied division of the Ottoman lands afforded the Kurds a fleeting opportunity to gain independence. President Wilson's Fourteen Points, given to the world on January 8, 1918, promised an era of self-determination for all subject peoples. Wilson's twelfth point addressed itself specifically to the nationalities under Ottoman rule. They should be assured of "an absolutely unmolested opportunity of autonomous development." On November 8, three days before the war's end, the British and French governments issued a statement assuring that their aim was ". . . the establishment of national Governments and Administrations drawing their authority from the initiative and free choice of indigenous populations."[1]

The British, who were the major military power in the Middle East when the war came to its close, at first envisaged the creation of an independent Kurdish state or a series of independent or semiindependent Kurdish principalities. The allied powers initially promised a regime of "local autonomy" for the Kurdish inhabited regions, with the option for independence within six months. But these promises were later abandoned and ignored. The plight of the Kurds under the order that emerged in the aftermath of World War I was summarized by the human rights organization, Helsinki Watch, as "a staggering list of human rights abuses; arrests; tortures; murders; assassinations; chemical warfare; mass deportations; expulsions; appalling conditions in refugee camps; denial of ethnic rights to language, literature, and music; and the destruction of villages and towns."

As a result, resistance and conflict have been predominant features of contemporary Kurdish history. Beyond the moral issue of human rights, the Kurdish issue constituted a major destabilizing factor with serious repercussions in the wider regional order. This reality has often been overlooked, as analysts and policymakers considered the issue to be isolated in, and confined to, the mountain strongholds of Kurdistan. Many tended to consider the Kurdish issue as too marginal to have an impact on wider regional stability. But it is instructive to examine a recent episode of Iraqi-Kurdish history to illustrate the inaccuracy of this approach.

The Baath regime, unwilling to concede Kurdish demands for autonomy and self-rule, and unable to crush the Kurdish insurgency militarily, found itself obliged to offer Iran significant territorial concessions at Algiers in 1975 in return for ending Iranian assistance to the Kurdish movement. Saddam Hussein's decision to abrogate the Algiers's Accord was a prelude to the devastating eight-year-war between Iran and Iraq, which was in itself the setting for Iraq's aggression against Kuwait. The recent conflict in the Persian Gulf can be traced, in no small part, to repercussions of the Kurdish national issue in Iraq.

The Kurds have been, and remain, a potent source of regional conflict. They have the further distinction of being the one serious source of conflict in the Middle East that the foreign ministries of the major powers, and many independent analysts as well, have long refused to deal with or even to acknowledge. For decades, diplomats have toiled ceaselessly to resolve the Arab-Israeli conflict. While numerous other regional disputes commanded the attention of policymakers, the Kurds have been ignored or dismissed, looked upon either as a nuisance or a containable conflict, but rarely as a problem requiring attention. Governments have had a Kurdish policy only when they sought to achieve some strategic gain by manipulating the Kurds to serve their own ends. Otherwise, the common reaction has been to wish them away.

Consequently, the Kurdish problem has now reached the point where it can be ignored only at the risk of major upheaval. No stable regional order can be achieved without due consideration to Kurdish aspirations and Kurdish security concerns.

The Kurds in Iraq and the Baath

The advent of the Baath government and its takeover by Saddam Hussein marked a turning point in the relationship between the Kurds and the Arab government in Baghdad. The Baath regime sought to destroy the Kurdish national identity and began escalating a program to transfer Arabs into the Kurdish region. Little by little these transfers became deliberate Iraqi government policy, aimed at expelling Kurds and establishing Arab colonies in the Kurdish heartland. After the defeat of the 1974–75 Kurdish uprising came the first large-scale destruction of Kurdish villages, the first mass exiling of Kurds, and the first mass killings. In the early 1980s, when the war against Iran began to go badly, Saddam Hussein sought to conciliate the Kurds. But once he regained the upper hand, he struck out against them in a frenzy of destruction and killing unlike anything perpetrated by any earlier Iraqi government. Iraqi army poison gas attacks on Kurdish towns and villages during 1987 and 1988 are conservatively estimated to have taken some ten thousand lives. During the infamous "Anfal" campaign of those same years, and in 1989, the Iraqi army erased some four thousand Kurdish villages from the map. Over a half-million Kurds were expelled into so-called new towns that were in reality strategic hamlets that enabled the regime to maintain a tight watch over the population.

It is not surprising, therefore, that the Kurds of Iraq rose in revolt the moment Saddam Hussein's army was defeated in Kuwait in February 1991; that some two million Kurds fled in panic into the mountains, to Turkey, and to Iran, when the Iraqi dictator turned what remained of his forces against them; or that the Kurds have now set up their own regional self-government in the area they control in northern Iraq.

Despite allied intervention in the spring of 1991 and the consequent stabilization of the situation in northern Iraq, the Baath regime continues to harass the Kurds and to try to push them out of their land. Some three hundred thousand Kurds, and also Turkomans, from Kirkuk have been expelled from their homes and now live as refugees in camps inside Kurdish-controlled territory in Iraq. Iraq has sponsored attacks on Kurdish villages, carried out terrorist bombings and murders in Erbil and other Kurdish towns and cities, sought to prevent international humanitarian assistance from reaching the Kurds, clamped an illegal embargo on the Kurdish-administered region, and massed an army of some two hundred thousand along its borders.

Kurdish Security Concerns

The first and most immediate security concern of the Kurds of Iraq is therefore never again to fall under the rule of Saddam Hussein and his regime; and to be protected from them, so long as they remain in power.

Beyond this the Kurds seek from the major powers a change in the patterns of behavior toward them. Traditionally, the major powers have regarded the Kurds as a destabilizing element and have refused to grant legitimacy to their grievances. It is hoped that with the end of the Cold War it will be possible for policymakers to evaluate and view the Kurdish national issue in a more realistic manner, uninhibited by considerations of superpower rivalries.

The regional powers have often collaborated to suppress Kurdish national aspirations, as in the pre-World War II Sa'adabad Pact, the 1975 Algiers accord between Iraq and Iran and the hot pursuit agreement between Turkey and Iraq. Despite the participating powers' assurance to the Kurdish leadership, the periodic tripartite meetings among the Foreign Ministers of Syria, Iran, and Turkey is a cause of great concern and alarm in the Kurdish camp. Despite profound differences in character and outlook, regional powers have managed to collaborate to confront the presumed "Kurdish threat." The principal Kurdish leaderships are adamant in confining the domain of their movements to the boundaries of the states within which they live, but it is feared that this pattern of regional collaboration against the Kurds may ultimately lend support to calls by extremists who advocate a pan-Kurdish strategy transcending present political boundaries.

Historically, two patterns of behavior have prevailed in regard to the Kurdish issue: to attempt to exploit it for perceived short-term national gain, or to ignore the Kurds—in either case with little or no consideration given to the moral, human, or political consequences.

The Iranian-American intervention of the 1970s, in which the Shah of Iran and the Nixon administration provided support to the Kurdish resistance during the 1970s, is a prime example of the first of these two patterns. These Iranian and American actions were aimed not at resolving but at exploiting the Kurdish issue; the Shah wanted satisfaction of his territorial ambitions, and the U.S. wanted to keep the Iraqi army busy at home and away from Israel's borders. In March 1975, after a year's fighting, Saddam Hussein made a deal with the Shah; Iran and the U.S. cut off their aid to the Kurds, and the Kurdish rebellion collapsed. The Kurds suffered terribly, but the Iranians paid an even greater price for the Shah's perfidy a half-decade later when Saddam denounced the 1975 agreement and invaded their country.

The same pattern is found in the behavior of the Baghdad and Tehran governments during the Iran-Iraq War, when each supported Kurdish insurgencies inside the other's borders, solely to weaken the other party.

Some may object that the Kurds have been the too eager recipients of aid, even though the assistance was designed to help the great powers. Today many Kurds would acknowledge that the objection has validity. On the other hand, the oppression suffered by the Kurds under governments intent upon erasing their linguistic, cultural, and ethnic identity left them little alternative; as the saying goes, a drowning man rarely has the luxury of scrutinizing the provenance of the life jacket that is thrown to him.

The second pattern—that of simply ignoring the Kurdish issue and tolerating the abuses perpetuated against the Kurds by the governments under which they live—has been more common but in some instances also more devastating. For decades the world stood by silently while regional governments oppressed and abused their Kurdish citizens. One instance stands out as particularly egregious. In the summer and fall of 1988, when the government of Iraq carried out its systematic program of destroying Kurdish towns and villages and transferring their inhabitants to concentration camp enclosures, the foreign ministries of the major powers, though well-informed about what was happening, either said nothing or protested only very weakly. No steps were taken to penalize Iraq for its action, which was clearly genocidal in nature and in stark violation of international law.

This second pattern is explained by the fact that the Kurds are a minority in the states in which they live. Foreign ministries have never been comfortable dealing with the question of minorities. In traditional diplomacy, the state is sovereign. What a state chooses to do to the population that lives within its borders is its business and no one else's; and even if it is morally repugnant, other governments consider their broader political and economic interests. The principle of realpolitik prevailed.

Governments that oppressed and abused their Kurdish minorities traditionally invoked the principle of sovereignty to shield themselves from being called to account. To cite one example among many: in September 1988, the government of Iraq advanced the excuse of sovereignty to justify its refusal to receive a United Nations team to investigate reports that it had used chemical weapons against its Kurdish population. Iraqi Defense Minister Adnan Khairallah commented that "the Kurds are Iraqis and it is an internal issue." There was, he declared, no justification for the U.N. or any other international party to infringe upon Iraq's sovereignty by independently investigating conditions in the Kurdish area.[2] Although the use of chemical weapons is barred by international law, the world community accepted this Iraqi refusal without protest. Further, no sanctions were levied against Iraq even after it was established beyond question that it had used chemical weapons against its Kurdish population.

If the Kurdish issue is not to become a major source of disruption and conflict in the Middle East in the decades to come, the two patterns must change drastically. Governments must recognize that attempts to exploit Kurdish grievances for short term and expedient political gain can only result in serious long-term complications that will threaten the stability and prosperity of the entire region. Governments must also recognize that times have changed, and that sovereignty is no longer the sole measure of the world order. Since World War II, a vast body of international law has grown up that prohibits states from denying to their ethnic minorities, as to their individual citizens, a broad array of basic rights and freedoms. What a government does to the people who live within its borders is no longer only its business; to the extent that it abuses them, it is everybody's business.

The Kurds and Regional Security: Possible Solutions

The Kurdish issue needs to be put on the world community's agenda, and the Kurds can be no longer treated as the sole concern of the states in which they live. The world community has an obligation to share in the search for a solution that will offer the Kurds the opportunity to shed their unwanted role as a prime source of regional conflict and instability and become responsible citizens contributing to their region's progress and stability.

Generally speaking, there are two possible solutions for the Kurdish problem. One is to unite the Kurds into a single national state. The other is to seek to accommodate them, on terms compatible with their linguistic and cultural heritage and their fundamental human rights, within existing borders. The provisions of the Treaty of Sèvres of 1920 offered a framework for the first of these two solutions. For reasons explained earlier, these provisions were never implemented. The opportunity that existed in the two years following the end of World War I to resolve the Kurdish problem within a nation state was lost.

No more than the first solution—that of the nation-state—the second—that of accommodating the Kurds on terms compatible with their heritage and their fundamental human rights—has not been tried so far. It is urgent now that the effort be made.

The situation of the Kurds of Iraq is unique. The ferocious repression visited upon them by Saddam Hussein's Baath government has few parallels in modern history. The upsurge of Kurdish nationalism in Iraq, and the closing of Kurdish ranks that has developed in recent years, was no doubt, in part, the wholly unintended consequence of Saddam's policies. Initially, the Kurdish leadership made great strides toward the establishment of the institutions of self-government promised to them by the allies after World War I. In May 1992, the first free elections in the history of the Kurdish people—certified free and fair by independent international observers—were held in Iraqi Kurdistan. A parliament and a provisional executive were created under a moderate, secular leadership. Recently, however, the Kurdish entity experienced its first major crisis. On May 1, almost two years after the elections, a seemingly minor land dispute escalated into fighting between the two major Kurdish parties. The fighting quickly spread and engulfed much of the Kurdish-administered region.

The spectacle of the two major Kurdish parties fighting one another was a sad reminder of a tragic history. It should not be taken simply to mean, however, that the Kurdish people have fallen back into older patterns of feuding and divisiveness. The violence demonstrates that the political institutions established following the May 1992 elections are still young. Put to the test, they proved incapable of channeling the rivalry of the two major political parties toward a peaceful solution. While the recklessness and belligerence of some of the players unquestionably fanned the flames of crisis, the causes of violence are as follows.

* The failure of the power-sharing arrangement instituted after the May 1992 elections, which degenerated into deadlock of the political process.

* The reluctance of traditional elements in Kurdish society to relinquish their arms and authority to elected political bodies and the unwillingness of these elements to accept pluralism and democratic methods of peaceful conflict resolution.

* The continuing insidious efforts of Saddam Hussein's government, and neighboring countries, to undermine the Kurdish entity, create instability, and pit Kurds against one another.

* The severe economic deprivation suffered by the people of the Kurdistan region—with urban unemployment running as high as eighty percent and shortages of all essential commodities—as a result of the double embargo imposed by the Baghdad government and by the United Nations.

However, the conflict has been contained. The two major parties to the conflict have held a series of meetings to try to resolve the issues in conflict peacefully. In the latest of these, senior delegations from the two parties met in France between July 16 and 22. The statement issued at the close of the meetings outlined a series of jointly agreed-upon measures. The two sides recognized that the power-sharing arrangement devised after the 1992 elections cannot be sustained and have agreed to revise it fundamentally by widening the base of the Kurdistan regional government and enhancing its authority. They also agreed to implement measures to disarm militias and to create a unified Kurdish Peshmarga force based on the principle of national conscription; and to prepare a new electoral law, compile an accurate electoral register, and hold new parliamentary elections in May 1995, the results of which shall be respected by all sides.

In essence the crisis was symptomatic of problems associated with the transition from a resistance movement to one of the rule of law. Such problems are not unique to the Kurds, but can be seen in almost all cases where the transition toward democracy is challenged by the inertia of obsolete political habits and cultures. It is hoped that out of this crisis a revitalized sense of unity and purpose will consolidate the institutions of civil society and democracy in Iraqi Kurdistan. Arguably, the success of Kurdish democracy can be of profound importance to a wider regional order based on principles of democracy and respect for human rights: in an Iraqi context, the democratic process in Kurdistan could be a prelude for a wider solution to the political crisis in Iraq, and may be the catalyst to democratization of the whole of Iraq.

As a secular and democratic movement, the Kurdish movement in Iraq is strategically placed to make a major contribution to stability in the region. Its democratic character sets an example for the other peoples of Iraq. In pursuit of its vision of a regional order based on democratic values and human rights, the Kurdish leadership has been seeking to play a constructive role in the politics of this region and to show that Kurdish aspirations need not be a threat. To this end the Kurdish leadership has attempted to cultivate relations with its neighbors. But conventional notions of national security of the neighboring countries persist in designating the Kurdish entity in Iraq as a threat. The neighboring countries have yet to come to terms with the Kurdish reality.

The Kurds of Iraq can also contribute to the stability of the Arab world. Long-term security in the Persian Gulf depends on reshaping Iraq's political system in a way that will minimize the possibility for the emergence of another Saddam Hussein in the future. The Kurdish leadership can play a pivotal role in efforts to bring about a pluralistic democratic system of government that will, one hopes, be at peace with itself and with its neighbors.

But to be able to make their contribution to regional stability, the Kurds of Iraq must first survive. The four million who live in the Kurdish self-governing region of northern Iraq are under internal blockade by the Baghdad government. The blockade, established in 1991, prevents the Kurds from acquiring gasoline and fuel for heating from Iraqi refineries as well as medicines and other supplies. Because there is no ready alternate source of refined petroleum products, the Iraqi blockade has caused great suffering, particularly during the winter months. The effects of the blockade have been compounded by sabotage and terrorist actions carried out by Iraqi agents against international relief convoys bringing food, fuel, medicine, and other necessities to Kurdish territory. In December 1993 and January 1994, Saddam Hussein's agents blew up a number of trucks carrying U.S. and U.N. humanitarian assistance to the Kurds. The Baghdad regime has also sent agents inside Kurdish territory to carry out other acts of sabotage and terror.

In addition to the Iraqi blockade, the self-governing territory suffers under the United Nations' embargo against Iraq. This embargo, which was meant to punish Saddam Hussein's regime for its seizure of Kuwait, prevents the Kurds from obtaining badly needed spare parts and equipment to rehabilitate industry and agriculture. It is a serious obstacle to rebuilding the economy of the Kurdish territory, which has been ravaged by war and by the deliberate destruction, by the Baath regime, of over four thousand Kurdish towns and villages.

The biggest threat to the Kurdish territory, however, comes from the very large army that Saddam Hussein has massed along its border. Iraqi forces threatening the Kurdish territory currently number some two hundred thousand; they are equipped with tanks, artillery, and other heavy weaponry and have air support. Were they to attack, the Kurdish forces, equipped with light weapons, might not be able to hold off an Iraqi assault for long. Another mass flight of Kurdish families, in the millions, across the border into Turkey and Iran would ensue and the world community might be faced with a repeat of the crisis in April 1991 that brought about allied intervention.

The deterrent to an Iraqi attack on the Kurdish territory is the allied task force in Turkey, known variously as Operation Provide Comfort or Operation Poised Hammer. So long as he knows that the Western allies are able and determined to oppose a thrust into the Kurdish territory, Saddam Hussein is unlikely to risk renewed aggression. However, uncertainty over the future of the task force—whether the allies will maintain it and whether Ankara will continue to allow its stationing on Turkish soil—risks miscalculation by the Iraqi leader, a trait that has characterized his rule. To reduce the likelihood of a serious miscalculation, the Western allies, and the government of Turkey, should make clear that the allied task force will be maintained so long as Saddam Hussein and his regime in Baghdad remain in power.

The challenge both to the major powers and to regional governments is to cultivate the potential of the Kurdish communities as a pillar of a regional security order. Kurds can play a strategic role in promoting stability, democracy, and respect for human rights. Failure to address Kurdish aspirations will inevitably perpetuate the cycle of violence and instability. The Kurds want to, and can, shed their traditional role as a source of conflict and instability in the Middle East. They want to become a partner with the democracies in the construction of a new, more just, and more secure regional order.

Opinions expressed in this chapter are solely those of the author, and do not necessarily represent views of the Iraqi Kurdish leadership.

Notes

1. Sir Arnold T. Wilson, *Mesopotamia 1917–1920, A Clash of Loyalties*, vol. 2 (London: Oxford University Press, 1931), 102.

2. Middle East Watch, *Human Rights in Iraq* (New Haven, Conn.: Yale University Press, 1990), 80–81.

11

WEAPONS OF MASS DESTRUCTION AND ADVANCED DELIVERY SYSTEMS IN THE MIDDLE EAST

Marvin M. Miller

The proliferation of weapons of mass destruction (WMD) and advanced delivery systems, particularly ballistic and cruise missiles, has been the focus of much international concern since the Gulf War. Major initiatives to restrain both WMD and missiles are in various stages of negotiation and implementation—for example, the extension of the Nuclear Nonproliferation Treaty (NPT), a comprehensive test-ban treaty (CTBT), the Chemical Weapons Convention (CWC), and the Missile Technology Control Regime (MTCR).[1]

The purpose of this chapter is to assess the risks posed by WMD and advanced delivery systems in the Middle East and to suggest what can be done to minimize these risks.[2] Although the proliferation of nuclear weapons is my special interest in this area, this chapter also explores issues related to chemical and biological weapons, as well as delivery systems, especially ballistic missiles.

First, the chapter examines the nature of the WMD and delivery system threats with regard to both their technical requirements and their destructive potential. It also summarizes what is known about the capabilities of states in the region with respect to these technologies. Next, it discusses various ways to reduce the risk of the proliferation of WMD and delivery systems, with special attention to export controls, arms control, and military actions. Finally, the concluding section offers some thoughts about the relationship among several factors that are significant in this context: the risks of further proliferation of WMD and delivery systems in the Middle East, the lessening of political tensions through negotiations (such as those now taking place between Israel and its Arab neighbors), and the possibility that the major powers will provide "leadership by example" in delegitimizing the possession and use of WMD, particularly nuclear weapons.

Nature of the Threat

Technical Requirements for Nuclear, Biological, and Chemical Weapons

The technical requirements for nuclear, biological, and chemical weapons programs are reproduced in Table 11.1. Table 11.2 illustrates that WMD can be delivered by both high-technology and low-technology modes.

Nuclear Weapons

The technology involved in making simple nuclear fission weapons has not changed in more than forty years, but other factors have. For instance, some of the old technology has been declassified, and more will be; new technology simplifies the task; needed dual-use commodities are more available; there are new countries that can supply the technology; there are more people with the relevant scientific knowledge and technological skills; and there are more possibilities to acquire secret design information.

In large measure, the above is also true with regard to more advanced weapons, including those that utilize the process of nuclear fusion as well as fission, that is, boosted and thermonuclear weapons. The consensus in the weapons community is that such advanced weapons require testing at full yield in order to validate design. However, if it is not essential to minimize the weapon's size and weight and to predict its yield precisely, computational power well below the level available in today's personal computers should suffice to develop weapons at all levels of technical sophistication, including fission-fusion bombs, with only a minimal number of such full-scale tests.[3]

However, proliferation of such advanced weapons is not the central concern of the nonproliferation community; rather, it is the development of fission-only warheads that can be delivered by Scud-class ballistic missiles. Unfortunately, the development of such warheads—which might weigh on the order of a thousand kilograms and have yields on the order of a few to tens of kilotons—by most proliferants is credible with *no* full-yield nuclear testing.

Obtaining the required amounts of fissile material for nuclear weapons—either plutonium or highly enriched uranium—remains a greater barrier than weapons design and fabrication. The material of

Table 11.1. Technical hurdles for nuclear, biological, and chemical weapons programs.

	Nuclear	Biological	Chemical
	Nuclear materials or lethal agents production		
Feed materials	Uranium ore, oxide widely available; plutonium and partly enriched uranium dispersed through nuclear power programs, mostly under international safeguards.	Potential biological warfare agents are readily available locally or internationally from natural sources or commercial suppliers.	Many basic chemicals available for commercial purposes; only some nerve gas precursors available for purchase, but ability to manufacture them is spreading.
Scientific and technical personnel	Requires wide variety of expertise and skillful systems integration.	Sophisticated research and development unnecessary to produce commonly known agents. Industrial microbiological personnel widely available.	Organic chemists and chemical engineers widely available.
Design and engineering knowledge	Varies with process, but specific designs for producing either of the two bomb-grade nuclear materials can be difficult to develop: • separation of uranium isotopes to produce highly enriched uranium • reactor production and chemical processing to produce plutonium	Widely published; basic techniques to produce known agents not difficult.	Widely published. Some processes tricky (Iraq had difficulty with tabun cyanation, succeeded at sarin alkylation; however, sarin quality was poor).

Table 11.1. cont.

	Nuclear	Biological	Chemical
Equipment	Varies with different processes, but difficulties can include fabrication, power consumption, large size, and operational complexity: • Electromagnetic separation equipment can be constructed from available, multiple-use parts • Equipment for other processes is more specialized and difficult to buy or build	Widely available for commercial uses. Special containment and waste-treatment equipment may be more difficult to assemble, but are not essential to production.	Most has legitimate industrial applications. Alkylation process is somewhat difficult and is unusual in civilian applications. Special containment and waste treatment equipment may be more difficult to assemble, but are not essential to production.
Plant construction and operation	Costly and challenging. Research reactors or electric power reactors might be converted to plutonium production.	With advent of biotechnology, small-scale facilities now capable of large-scale production.	Dedicated plant not difficult. Conversion of existing commercial chemical plants feasible but not trivial.
Overall cost	Cheapest overt production route for one bomb per year, with no international controls, is about $200 million; larger scale clandestine program could cost 10 to 50 times more, and even then not be assured of success or of remaining hidden.	Enough for large arsenal may cost less than $10 million.	Arsenal for substantial military capability (hundreds of tons of agent) likely to cost tens of millions of dollars.

Table 11.1. cont.

	Nuclear	Biological	Chemical
Weaponization	Black-market purchase of ready-to-use fissile materials or of complete weapons could be many times cheaper.	Principal challenge is maintaining the agent's potency through weapon storage, delivery, and dissemination. Broad-area dissemination not difficult; design of weapons that effectively aerosolize agents for precision delivery challenging (but developed by U.S. by '60s).	Advanced weapons somewhat difficult, but workable munition designs (e.g., bursting smoke device) widely published.
Design and engineering	Heavier, less efficient, lower-yield designs easier, but all pose significant technical challenges.		
Production equipment	Much (e.g., machine tools) dual-use and widely available. Some overlap with conventional munitions production	Must be tightly contained to prevent spread of infection, but the necessary equipment is not hard to build.	Relatively simple, closely related to standard munitions production equipment.

Source: U.S. Congress, Office of Technology Assessment, Proliferation of Weapons of Mass Destruction: Assessing the Risks, OTA-ISC-559 (Washington, D.C.: U.S. Government Printing Office, August 1993), 10–11.

Table 11.2. Weaponizing agents of mass destruction: actual and possible methods of delivery.

Weapon	Nuclear	Biological	Chemical
Aerial bomb	✓	✓	✓
Bomb submunitions		✓	✓
Aerial spray tank		✓	✓
Ballistic missile warhead, nonseparating	✓	✓	✓
Ballistic missile warhead, separating	✓	TP	TP
Reentry vehicle			
Artillery shell	✓	✓	✓
Rocket shell	✓	✓	✓
Mortar shell	✓		✓
Cruise missile warhead	✓	TP	TP
Mine (land)	✓		✓
Mine (sea)	✓		
Antiaircraft missile warhead	✓		
Torpedo	✓		
Transportable clandestine bomb	✓	TP	TP

Key:

✓— Actual Cases

TP — Theoretical possibility

Source: SIPRI, 1975, and OTA. (Table from OTA, *Proliferation of Weapons of Mass Destruction*, 50.)

choice for countries seeking to acquire a nuclear weapons "option" in the 1950s and 1960s, such as Israel and India, was plutonium. This was because the only technology available at that time to enrich uranium to weapons-grade quality—gaseous diffusion—was difficult to master indigenously, expensive, and readily detectable because of its large demands for electric power. Thus, the plutonium route was chosen, even though the material-handling problems involved in producing plutonium and then fabricating it into a weapon are more severe, and the reactor and reprocessing plant needed to produce it are also readily detectable.

The development of the modern gas centrifuge, starting in the 1960s, has changed all of this. Both the power demands and the physical plant required for the gas centrifuge are much smaller than those required for gaseous diffusion for the same level of enrichment capacity. Thus, clandestine construction and operation of such plants may be difficult to detect; moreover, the technology is increasingly available.

Biological Weapons and Chemical Weapons

In contrast to nuclear weapons, where a minimum amount of plutonium or highly enriched uranium—on the order of kilograms to tens of kilograms—is required to make a bomb, there is no such constraint in the case of chemical or biological weapons. Chemical weapons agents, such as the blistering agent (sulfur mustard), the choking agent (phosgene), and the nerve agent (sarin), are man-made, nonliving poisons. Biological weapons agents, such as the bacteria that cause anthrax, tularemia, and plague, are infectious microorganisms that reproduce within the host to cause incapacitation or death. Toxins, such as botulinum and ricin, are poisonous chemicals manufactured by living organisms; as such they share characteristics of both chemical weapons and biological weapons agents.

Besides the fact that there are no minimum material requirements for chemical weapons and biological weapons, the technology base required to manufacture these agents is much less sophisticated, more widely available, and hence, much less costly than in the nuclear case. The much greater lethality of biological weapons as compared with chemical weapons under similar conditions is a direct consequence of the fact that the quantities of material needed to infect are typically several orders of magnitude smaller than those needed to poison. Indeed, against unprotected populations in situations where weather conditions as well as delivery systems are favorable to biological weapons agent dissemination, biological weapons have the potential for inflicting casualties of the same magnitude as a nuclear explosive containing a comparable amount of weapons material.

Thus, biological weapons are truly weapons of mass destruction, while chemical weapons would require massive amounts of material under similar conditions to have comparable lethality. In this sense, chemical weapons are "the poor man's [nuclear] bomb," both in terms of their greater ease of acquisition and the fact that their impact, while potentially devastating against ill-prepared troops and civilian populations, is much smaller than that of nuclear and biological weapons.

For these reasons, there is increasing concern about biological weapons proliferation. For example in testimony before the U.S. Senate Select Committee on Intelligence on 25 January 1994, then director of central intelligence James Woolsey stated, "Nuclear weapons are, of course, a very serious proliferation problem, but they require a good deal more infrastructure, particularly to obtain fissionable material, than biological weapons. . . . Biological weapons can be extraordinarily lethal and rather small, and you have the same kind of problem with distinguishing the dual-use material or technology that you have with chemical weapons."[4]

The above concern is in marked contrast to the attitude that prevailed during the negotiation of the Biological and Toxin Weapons Convention (BTWC), which was signed in 1972 and entered into force in 1975. The BTWC prohibits the development, production, and stockpiling of such weapons, but it provides no mechanism for independent verification of these obligations. At that time, all the Western states and some of the unaligned states were reluctant to accept the minimal safeguards of the convention. In the end, however, they agreed, because they considered it relatively improbable that biological weapons would ever acquire the military popularity of chemical weapons.[5]

The BTWC calls for a review conference every five years. At the reviews in 1986 and 1991, a range of confidence-building measures was agreed upon, including declaration of national biological defense programs, declaration of unusual outbreaks of disease, and encouragement of international contacts and conferences. The 1991 conference also created an Ad Hoc Group of Governmental Experts (VEREX) to evaluate different methods for verifying the convention. The group released its final report in September 1993. It lists twenty-one new measures—including data exchange, exchange visits, remote sensing, and on-site inspections—that "could be useful, to varying degrees, in enhancing confidence" that member states are fulfilling the convention's obligations. At a special conference held in Geneva in September 1994, the state parties—now numbering 134—decided to set up another ad hoc group to consider measures to increase confidence in the BTWC, including the verification measures examined and evaluated in the VEREX Report. It is hoped that the proposals will be ready for the next BTWC Review Conference in 1996.

There is additional concern that new methods in biotechnology, especially genetic engineering, could yield infectious biological warfare agents with higher lethality than known agents.[6] However, according to Meselson, Kaplan, and Makulsky, "it is undoubtedly true that additional agents could be developed by genetic engineering and also by more classical techniques. But no one has even proposed a realistic set of biological, physical, or other properties of a hypothetical novel agent that would endow it with military characteristics fundamentally different from those of known agents."[7]

Delivery Systems

Delivery modes other than combat aircraft, ballistic missiles, and cruise missiles are capable of delivering WMD, for example, trucks, boats, civil aircraft, and artillery. Nevertheless, a focus on the "high-end" systems is warranted, because the simpler systems are not amenable to international control; because there is a high degree of overlap among the countries pursuing WMD and those developing or seeking to acquire high-end systems; and because high-technology delivery systems enable a country to do more damage to a greater number and variety of targets, with greater reliability and potentially at longer range, than do low-technology alternatives.[8]

Ballistic and cruise missiles in particular may have added psychological effects, since they can be harder to defend against, or even to detect, than manned aircraft. By this measure, a ballistic missile is preferable to aircraft or cruise missiles for delivery of a nuclear warhead to a heavily defended and distant target, especially if great accuracy in delivery is not a requirement—for example, such targets as population centers or military bases, rather than missile silos. Moreover, the costs and infrastructure requirements for missile systems are much less than for a modern air force, and, of course, missiles do not "defect." Finally, missile deployment has a strong prestige value.

On the other hand, advanced aircraft are much more readily available on the international marketplace than are missiles, especially since the advent and progressive upgrading of the MTCR. This is important because indigenous development of ballistic missiles with payloads and ranges in excess of about a thousand kilograms and a thousand kilometers, respectively, involve qualitative upgrades of technology compared with currently available Scud-type missiles. A comparison of the ranges and payloads of selected aircraft and ballistic missiles operated by potential proliferant countries shown in Figure 11.1, demonstrates the payload advantage of aircraft. This is important in the case of chemical and large-scale biological attacks, since the damage that can be inflicted depends directly on the amount of agent that can be delivered. Also, aircraft have a strong advantage for attacks against mobile targets or those in unknown positions. Thus, with regard to payload capacity, accuracy, and flexibility in delivery, aircraft have advantages compared with ballistic missiles. However, as noted, missiles are much more difficult to defend against, especially if their chemical or biological payloads are in the form of submunitions.

In contrast to a ballistic missile, a cruise missile sustains flight through aerodynamic lift over most of its flight path. Cruise missiles with ranges on the order of a hundred kilometers or less—such as the French

Figure 11.1. Range and payload of selected aircraft and missiles operated by potential proliferants.

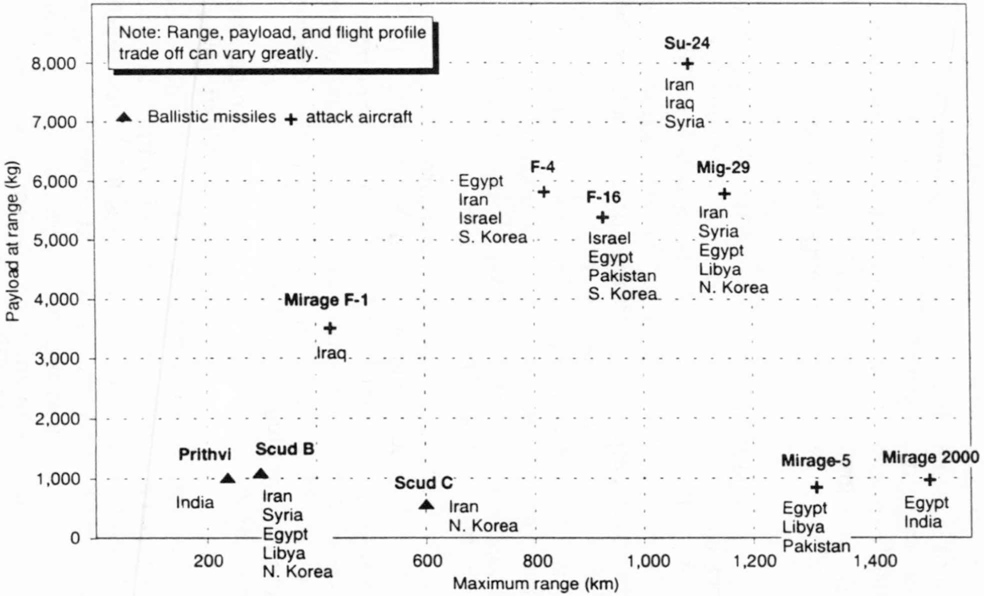

This figure shows nominal ranges and payloads of selected aircraft and missile systems of countries (beyond the 5 nuclear-weapon states) suspected of having or trying to acquire weapons of mass destruction. The graph is not intended to be exhaustive, but only to indicate that each country already possesses aircraft or missile systems of one kind or another that could be adapted to deliver weapons of mass destruction.

Source: OTA, *Proliferation of Weapons of Mass Destruction*, 68.

Exocet, the Chinese Silkworm, and the Soviet Styx—are usually rocket powered, but longer-range ones—such as the U.S. Tomahawk of Gulf War fame—generally use small jet engines.

In the past, indigenous development of guidance and propulsion systems for long-range cruise missiles presented significant barriers for developing countries. However, small jet engines suitable for one time use in a cruise missile are now manufactured in more than twenty countries, and accurate guidance, independent of range and time of flight to the target, can be provided by the Global Positioning System and Glonass satellites of the United States and Russia, respectively.

Although cruise missile payloads are generally less than those of ballistic missiles and much less than those delivered by aircraft—for example, the U.S. Harpoon has a range of 120 to 220 kilometers and a payload of 220 kilograms—the ability of some modern cruise missiles to fly at very low altitudes and low speeds makes them particularly well suited for delivering chemical and biological weapons. While short-range antiship cruise missiles have proliferated even more widely than ballistic missiles, longer-range land-attack systems are not yet available to proliferant countries and may still be amenable to control through the MTCR. Still, cruise missiles may become a significant new threat as a delivery system for WMD in the 1990s.

Destructive Potential of Weapons of Mass Destruction

Illustrative examples of the lethality of WMD and their applications are provided in Figure 11.2 and Tables 11.3 and 11.4. The much higher numbers associated with biological as compared with chemical weapons in Figure 11.2 are a direct result of the former's much greater lethality per unit weight. These estimates are based on the following assumptions: the population is unprotected, the weather conditions are neither the best nor the worst for a chemical or biological weapons attack, and the delivery vehicle is a Scud-type missile with a maximum payload of a thousand kilograms. With ideal (for lethality) population densities and weather, the chemical and biological agents could kill considerably more people than shown in Figure 11.2; under worse conditions, they might kill many fewer, especially if a significant fraction of the population is protected by the provision of filtered air via individual gas masks or in shelters.

As noted in Table 11.4, the consequences of chemical and biological weapons are much less predictable than those of nuclear weapons, because their effects are so dependent on the weather and the degree of chemical protection. In addition, biological weapons—except for some toxins—act more slowly than chemical weapons, taking days or weeks to achieve full effect. Thus, the military utility of chemical and biological

Figure 11.2. Comparing lethal areas of chemical, biological, and nuclear weapons: missile delivery on an overcast day or night, with moderate wind (neither best nor worst case).

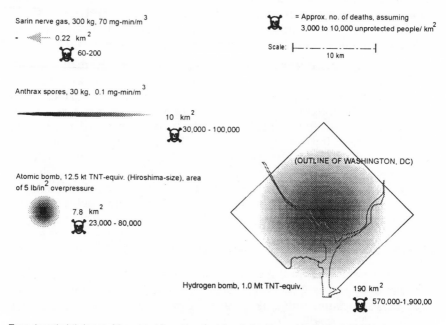

Sarin nerve gas, 300 kg, 70 mg-min/m^3

0.22 km^2

60-200

Anthrax spores, 30 kg, 0.1 mg-min/m^3

10 km^2

30,000 - 100,000

Atomic bomb, 12.5 kt TNT-equiv. (Hiroshima-size), area of 5 lb/in^2 overpressure

7.8 km^2

23,000 - 80,000

= Approx. no. of deaths, assuming 3,000 to 10,000 unprotected people/ km^2

Scale: |—·——·——·——·—| 10 km

(OUTLINE OF WASHINGTON, DC)

Hydrogen bomb, 1.0 Mt TNT-equiv.

190 km^2

570,000-1,900,00

Figure shows the lethal areas of the agents delivered by a Scud-like missile with a maximum payload of 1,000 kg (note that the amount of biological weapon agent assumed would weigh considerably less than this; since the lethality per unit weight is great, the smaller amount considered here would still more than cover a large urban area). The estimates of lethal areas for chemical and biological weapons were prepared using a model that takes account of postulated release height, wind velocity, deposition velocity, height of temperature inversion layer, urban air currents, and residence time in air of the agent. The diagrams show approximate outer contours of areas with sufficient concentrations of agent that 50 percent to 100 percent of the unprotected people would receive fatal doses. Although some people within the defined area would survive, about the same number in the outer, less lethal areas, would die; therefore, the defined areas give approximations of the total number of unprotected people who could be expected to die in each scenario. With ideal (for lethality) population densities and weather, the chemical and biological agents could kill more people than shown here; under worse conditions, they might kill many fewer. The atomic weapons (fission and fusion) are assumed to be air burst for optimum blast and radiation effects, producing little lethal fallout. The lethal area is assumed to be that receiving 5 lb/in^2 of overpressure—enough to level wood or unreinforced brick houses.

SOURCE Office of Technology Assessment, 1993.

(Figure from OTA, *Proliferation of Weapons of Mass Destruction*, 53.)

Table 11.3. Estimated weight requirements for various weapon types.

Weapon type	Illustrative agent	Approximate weight to attack 100 target km² (tons)
Thermonuclear		0.5 (warhead weight)
Biological	*F. tularensis*	5*
Toxin	botulinal toxin	300* (assumes toxin can be stabilized)
Chemical	nerve agent (sarin)	800*

*Based on estimates in *Health Aspects of Chemical and Biological Weapons*, World Health Organization, Geneva, 1970. The estimates depend on a number of uncertain variables and should be regarded as only illustrative. The weight of devices for disseminating the agent payload is assumed to be three times that of the agent for sarin, ten times for botulinal toxin, and twenty-five times for dry *F. tularensis*.

weapons is questionable. However, they can be potent weapons of terror against psychologically unprepared, physically unprotected civilian populations.

Use of Weapons of Mass Destruction

Philip Sabin has carefully examined the historical record with regard to the use of WMD in an attempt to assess efforts to limit or prevent such use.[9] His basic conclusions can be summarized as follows:

- WMD have never been used at the outset of a war; this suggests that a sudden attack with WMD may be less of a risk than hostilities that begin at the conventional level and escalate to WMD use.

- The most important disincentive to the use of WMD has been fear that the enemy would respond in kind. Hopefully, the growing mutual vulnerability of civilian populations in the Middle East may make employment of WMD due to a perceived military superiority in such weapons less likely.

- Had WMD as a whole possessed clear and more tractable military utility in a wider variety of tactical circumstances, their use over the past eighty years would almost certainly have been less restrained. In the Middle East, chemical weapons seem most likely to be used in drawn-out static conflicts, or against unprotected populations like the Kurds. Since so few nuclear weapons will be available (except perhaps to Israel), they are unlikely to be used in tactical operations,

Table 11.4. Applications of weapons of mass destruction compared.

Characteristics	Conventional explosives (for comparison with WMD)	Nuclear	Chemical	Biological
Destructive effects (See Table 1.)	Blast, shrapnel, fire	Blast, fire, thermal radiation, prompt ionizing radiation, radioactive fallout	Poisoning: skin, lungs, nervous system, or blood	Infectious disease or biochemical poisoning
Typical military targets	Military bases and equipment	Similar to targets for conventional munitions (esp. targets hardened against blast)	Infantry concentrations, towed artillery, air bases, ships, ports, staging areas, command centers	Infantry concentrations, air bases, ships, ports, staging areas, command centers
	Command-and-control installation (e.g., command posts, radars); troop concentrations; ships	Enemy nuclear or other WMD facilities		
Typical missions against military targets	Destruction of targets, personnel casualties	Destruction of targets	Unprotected personnel casualties; disruption of operations by requiring protective measures or decontamination	Unprotected personnel casualties; disruption of operations by requiring protective measures or decontamination
		Personnel casualties		
		Intimidation of personnel		
		Disruption of operations by requiring dispersal of units. Disruption of communications by electromagnetic pulse effects.	Demoralization or panic of personnel	Demoralization or panic of personnel

Table 11.4. cont.

Characteristics	Conventional explosives (for comparison with WMD)	Nuclear	Chemical	Biological
Drawbacks as military instrument	Small lethal radius requires either many weapons or great accuracy for most military missions	Potential for great "collateral damage" Risk of retaliation and escalation in kind Radioactive contamination of ground that user may wish to cross or occupy	Relatively large quantities required Protective measures may greatly reduce casualties Leave buildings and equipment reusable by enemy (but persistent agents may require decontamination) With persistent agents, chemical contamination of ground that user may wish to cross or occupy	Protective measures may reduce casualties Most agents degrade quickly; with persistent spores, contamination of ground that user may wish to cross or occupy Leave buildings and equipment reusable by enemy (but persistent spores may require decontamination) Effects depend on weather and time of day; are delayed, unpredictable, or uncontrollable

(Table from OTA, *Proliferation of Weapons of Mass Destruction*, 56.)

but they might be employed for coercive purposes or held in reserve as a counter-city deterrent.

- Throughout history, various weapons have been viewed with opprobrium in particular cultures because they have been perceived as "unfair." Chemical and biological weapons have attracted especially widespread and enduring odium, probably because of their insidious character. Nuclear weapons came to be seen as similarly repulsive, as awareness spread during the 1950s of the effects of fallout and radiation poisoning, with their potential impact upon generations yet unborn. This cultural aversion to the use of WMD extends to military commanders, who have rarely taken the lead in pressing for the use of such weapons and who have often reacted with skepticism or inertia when such use has been suggested to them.

The 1991 Gulf War illustrated the reluctance of Western states to consider the use of WMD, even in retaliation, against ordinary Iraqis thrust into war by Saddam Hussein. How to deter a WMD attack by rogue states, such as Iraq in the face of such perceived distinctions between ruler and ruled, will be a major challenge for Western powers in the future.

- A final restraining influence on the use of WMD has been anticipation of an adverse political reaction on the part of neutral or allied states. Concern about world opinion more generally has had the greatest force when countries have been dependent on outside support and have wished to avoid punitive sanctions. International norms dictating no first use of WMD or no use of WMD under any circumstances, reinforced by declarations to this effect by individual states, can also have a positive impact. As the norm of nonuse of nuclear weapons has become established over time, it has come to exercise a powerful restraint in its own right upon states considering breaking the taboo. Conversely, the taboo on chemical warfare, which developed following the experience with chemical weapons in World War I, has been eroded by the employment of chemical weapons in Vietnam, Yemen, the Persian Gulf, and elsewhere. As a result, it will be easier to breach this threshold again in the future.

In conclusion, Sabin is cautiously optimistic about the future use of WMD in the Middle East: "This pattern of NBC [nuclear/biological/chemical] use [by Iraq] fits squarely with previous historical experience, and suggests that even if NBC capabilities continue to spread within the Middle East, their actual employment in time of conflict is likely to remain severely circumscribed." On the other hand:

> Political instabilities and hatreds in the Middle East are deeper [than between the great powers during the Cold War]; hostile relationships are multipolar rather than bipolar; and an unbridled emphasis on the

building up of deterrent NBC capabilities risks such weapons falling into the hands of terrorists or being assimilated by the various military forces to the point where they are used wherever militarily advantageous.

> In this situation, the ideal outcome remains NBC disarmament as part of the Middle East peace process or through wider global initiatives such as the CWC. Should certain NBC capabilities persist, a major priority is to avoid circumstances in which the use of those capabilities becomes a relatively cost-free option . . . by posing a clearer threat of sanctions against states which initiate such action, whatever the political circumstances.[10]

Regarding the effectiveness of the cultural aversion to WMD as a barrier to possession, and especially use, there are grounds for both optimism and cynicism. Nicholas Sims finds something particularly perverse about chemical and especially biological warfare.[11] He quotes Harris and Paxman to the effect that such warfare is "public health in reverse";[12] it is this characteristic that sets biological and chemical warfare apart even from nuclear weapons. Deep-rooted fear of disease and revulsion at the thought of its being deliberately introduced to spread through potentially vast numbers of people combine to accord biological weapons a very special status of loathsomeness, even compared with chemical weapons.[13]

This notion that both chemical and biological weapons are "beyond the pale" will help the United States and other like-minded countries promote international norms, such as the CWC and the BTWC. However, other states may perceive that U.S. disavowal of such weapons is less a matter of their inhumanity than of a judgment that as long as the United States retains a qualitative edge in advanced conventional weaponry, as well as a powerful nuclear arsenal, global elimination of chemical and biological weapons serves U.S. security interests. In contrast, states lacking both "smart" conventional and nuclear weapons may attempt to acquire nuclear weapons or may view membership in the CWC and the BTWC as a luxury they cannot afford.[14]

It is widely believed that constraints on further proliferation of WMD and missiles in the Middle East, as well as prospects for capping existing arsenals, depend critically on the success of the Arab-Israeli peace process. However, as Sabin has noted, hostile relationships in the region are multipolar, and significant hostile relationships exist outside of the Arab-Israeli context, for example, between Iraq and Iran. Therefore, incentives for WMD in some states in the region will likely remain even if Israel's conflicts with the Palestinians and Syria are resolved on the basis of "land for peace."

State Capabilities and Intentions

Although experts differ on technical issues, such as the military utility of chemical and biological weapons and the effectiveness of ballistic missile defense, the greatest source of uncertainty and controversy in the literature on WMD and advanced delivery systems is public assessments of country capabilities and intentions. This is hardly surprising, since what most concerns a given state (for example, the United States, Russia, or Israel) is proliferation of WMD and advanced delivery systems to countries perceived to be antagonistic to its interests. Proliferation among friendly states may complicate life in various ways—for example, it may serve as an incentive for acquisition of WMD by hostile states—but the primary concern is with the hostile states. Thus, primary concern is not with the weapons themselves, but with who has them. For example, according to Israeli foreign minister Shimon Peres, Israel's greatest danger today is from the combination of nuclear weapons and extremist ideology, such as Islamic fundamentalism: "irrational" states may not be deterred even by a secure second-strike capability.[15]

The differentiation between hostile and friendly proliferation has the obvious problem that regimes may change, leaving capabilities in place. It also has important consequences for the collection and analysis of intelligence information and for how this information is "filtered" in public statements by government officials and supporting documentation. Such filtering—together with unsubstantiated allegations concerning WMD activities in various countries, often created and spread as part of deliberate disinformation campaigns—makes it very difficult to assess the true status of WMD and delivery-system programs without classified access.

Two cases in point are the extent of chemical weapons programs in the Middle East, and Iran's capabilities and intentions with regard to nuclear weapons.

A keen perspective on the former has been given by Julian Perry Robinson.[16] For example, he notes that in March 1991 Admiral Thomas A. Brooks, then director of U.S. Naval intelligence, testified before a congressional committee that no less than twenty-four countries outside NATO and the Warsaw Pact probably possess offensive chemical-warfare capability. These countries included six states in the Middle East: Egypt, Iran, Iraq, Israel, Libya, and Syria.

Robinson concludes that while "chemical-warfare weapons have been in the Middle East for many decades . . . self-interested issue-creation in the West on the theme of chemical proliferation has enhanced the political significance of [such] weapons in the Middle East." This factor, amplified by the spread of advanced-delivery-system technology, may lead to greater importance being attached to such weapons. Robinson is skeptical that this will occur, but even if it does, "the chemical weapons themselves would probably not become especially threatening or destabilizing, for they would certainly induce greater attention to antichemical protection. The real danger would lie rather in the indirect consequences, above all in the boost that would be given to biological warfare armament."[17]

The problems involved in assessing Iranian capabilities and intentions with regard to WMD, particularly nuclear weapons, and missile delivery systems are discussed in a recent paper by Seth Carus.[18] He notes that there are two polar perspectives of the prospects for WMD and missiles in Iran, which he characterizes as the Russian Foreign Intelligence Service and the U.S. Central Intelligence Agency views. In sum, the former stresses the formidable technical and nontechnical constraints on indigenous development of WMD and missiles in Iran, while the latter highlights the hostile nature of the regime and claims clear evidence of active chemical and biological weapons programs as well as an intent to acquire nuclear weapons. Even if the nuclear program is now in an early stage, there is always the risk that external assistance—specifically, from China and the former Soviet Union—could lead to significant progress in a short time.

Carus shares the Foreign Intelligence Service's skepticism regarding Iran's ability to implement its WMD and missile programs successfully: "In fact, Iran may be in a race between its political and military collapse and the development of capabilities needed to make it a major regional power. It is highly possible that Iran may fall apart long before it gets the bomb. *Indeed, political upheaval in Iran could lead to a change in the nature of US concern for Iranian proliferation activities—depending in part on the character of the new regime.*"[19]

However, even if skepticism is warranted, Carus believes that the risk of Iranian nuclearization is great because of the political-military and diplomatic uses to which such weapons can be put. He mentions three: (1) deterrence of U.S. military action; (2) nuclear threats to compel other countries, for example, the Gulf Cooperation Council (GCC), to take Iranian interests into account; and (3) a means of controlling the escalation of any military conflict between the United States and Iran to the latter's advantage.[20] Thus, the Iranian threat is based more on hostile intentions than on current capabilities. If the hostile intentions persist, however, capabilities can be expected to grow, both in WMD and in advanced conventional weapons, such as diesel-powered submarines armed with cruise missiles, which can pose serious problems for the United States and its allies in the region.

Given the above-noted caveats about the tendency to pay "selective attention" to hostile proliferants, Tables 11.5 and 11.6 show data on countries "reportedly" having or trying to acquire WMD.[21] The following is my summary perspective on the WMD and missile programs of selected countries—Israel, Iraq, and Iran—in the Middle East, with an emphasis on nuclear weapons.

Israel. The Israeli nuclear-weapons program has been aptly characterized by the *Economist* magazine as "the world's worst-kept secret."[22] No serious security analyst believes that Israel does not have nuclear weapons, and even Israeli citizens, who tend to be reticent about the subject because of official and self-censorship, find it increasingly cumbersome to use the ambiguous terminology of nuclear "option," "potential," or "capability," instead of "weapons."[23] By now, some matters connected to the nuclear program are well known, such as the origins of the program in the trauma of the Holocaust; the seminal roles played by David Ben-Gurion, Shimon Peres, and Ernst David Bergman; the concerns of U.S. president John Kennedy; and the development during the 1960s of a policy of ambiguity symbolized by the statement that Israel will not be the first state to "introduce" nuclear weapons into the Middle East.[24] These and other aspects of the program should be increasingly documented in the coming years.

However, until 1986 there was little credible information in the public domain about what had been accomplished technically or about the doctrinal and organizational postures that govern the possible use of the arsenal. The detailed information provided by the former Dimona technician Mordechai Vanunu—some of which appeared in the London *Sunday Times* on 5 October 1986—shed important light on the technical accomplishments.[25] Even the most conservative Western estimates now credit Israel with an arsenal of fifty to a hundred warheads, at least some of which incorporate fusion materials in advanced designs. However, these disclosures have only heightened concerns about Israeli nuclear doctrine, about which there is still only speculation. For example, according to Norman Moss, Vanunu's disclosures indicate a nuclear capability far greater than that required for a strategy of defensive last resort. While he credits the possibility that technological and bureaucratic momentum was responsible for the building of more and better weapons, the very existence of such an advanced capability is worrisome: "Future Israeli leaders may have less respect for the nuclear taboo than the superpowers have today and may refuse to see the nuclear bomb as a special kind of weapon to be used only *in extremis*. . . . Nuclear proliferation means proliferating possibilities."[26]

Table 11.5. Countries reportedly trying to acquire nuclear weapons.

Region	Country	Comment
Middle East/ North Africa	Algeria	Possibly interested in nuclear weapons, but currently lacks facilities; has agreed to IAEA inspection of formerly secret, Chinese-supplied nuclear reactor; not a party to the NPT.
	Iran	Reportedly pursuing nuclear weapons, but little public evidence of progress; CIA testimony estimated production unlikely before the end of the decade without foreign assistance.
	Iraq	Massive program uncovered after Persian Gulf War; United Nations has required destruction of most infrastructure, but knowledgeable personnel still in country.
	Israel	Widely believed to have a clandestine nuclear arsenal of approximately 100 weapons.
South Asia	India	Exploded a nuclear device in 1974; probably has sufficient materials for several weapons.
	Pakistan	Undoubtedly has nuclear weapon program, probably successful. U.S. president no longer certifies to U.S. Congress that Pakistan does not possess a nuclear device, suggesting high likelihood that it does.
East Asia	North Korea	Suspicious reactor and reprocessing laboratory; submitted to some IAEA inspections in 1992 and 1993, but refused others; in March 1993, denied IAEA access to suspected reprocessing waste sites and declared its intention to withdraw from NPT (since rescinded).
Latin America	Argentina	In agreement with Brazil, seems to have ceased weapons program. No disclosure of progress towards weapons, but suspected of having developed clandestine enrichment plant, a key step towards weapons.
	Brazil	In agreement with Argentina, has apparently ceased weapons program. In 1987, revealed it had developed the ability to enrich uranium. (Brazil has also had a nuclear power submarine program requiring highly enriched uranium fuel.)
Africa	South Africa	Widely suspected to be very near nuclear-weapon capability, South Africa declared in March 1993 that it had in fact constructed 6 nuclear weapons, but dismantled them in 1990. The South African president promised that South Africa would cooperate fully with the IAEA to assure the world that it was complying with the NPT. Joined NPT in 1991, placed declared weapons-grade uranium under IAEA inspection, and presumably dropped nuclear weapon ambitions.

Source: Leonard S. Spector and Jacqueline R. Smith, *Nuclear Ambitions: The Spread of Nuclear Weapons 1989–1990* (Boulder, Colo.: Westview Press, 1990) and Nuclear Non-Proliferation Project, "Nuclear Proliferation Status Report July 1992" (Washington, DC: Carnegie Endowment for International Peace, 1 July 1992). The latter report also names Libya as "presumed to be seeking N-weapons," but does not cite evidence of indigenous nuclear weapons facilities; and names Syria as identified by a U.S. official as having a "nuclear program with suspicious intentions," but no suspicious facilities have been publicly cited.

(Table and note from OTA, *Proliferation of Weapons,* 64.)

Table 11.6. Countries generally reported as having undeclared offensive chemical and biological warfare capabilities.

Region	CW Capability[a]	BW Program[b]
Middle East	Egypt Iran Iraq* Israel Libya Syria	Iran Iraq* Israel Libya Syria
East Asia	China North Korea Taiwan	China North Korea Taiwan
Southeast Asia	Myanmar (Burma) Vietnam	

*U.N. inspections of Iraq found a considerable chemical arsenal and some evidence of offensive biological weapons research, though no stocks of biological agent. Chemical agents which have been found are being destroyed. Quiescence of Iraqi programs probably depends on continued U.N. monitoring.

a. *Source:* Gordon Burck and Charles C. Flowerree, *International Handbook on Chemical Weapons Proliferation* (New York: Greenwood Press, 1991), 164–71., cite nineteen published reports, from 1985 to 1989, that identify nations suspected by various sources as having chemical weapon programs. In addition, a later publication (Elisa D. Harris, "Towards a Comprehensive Strategy for Halting Chemical and Biological Weapons Proliferation," *Arms Control: Contemporary Security Policy* 12, no. 2 [September 1991], 129), cites statements of U.S. government officials listing suspect countries; also added is *Russian Federation Foreign Intelligence Service Report: A New Challenge After the Cold War: Proliferation of Weapons of Mass Destruction,* JPRS-TND-93-007. OTA has listed here the nations mentioned in two-thirds or more of these sources published since 1989.

b. *Source:* Mentioned in at least four of the following six (i.e., two-thirds): David Fairhall "Eleven Countries Defying Ban on Germ Weapons" (*The Guardian* [London], 5 September 1991, p. 1); Elisa Harris, "Towards a Comprehensive Strategy," (op. cit, 129); Seth Carus, "'The Poor Man's Atomic Bomb?' Biological Weapons in the Middle East" (Washington, DC: The Washington Institute for Near East Policy, Policy Papers No. 23, 1991, 25); and Harvey J. McGeorge, "Chemical Addition," *Defense and Foreign Affairs* (April 1989, p. 17); Russian Federation Foreign Intelligence Service, op. cit., and U.S. Arms Control and Disarmament Agency, "Adherence to and Compliance with Arms Control Agreements and The President's Report to Congress on Soviet Noncompliance with Arms Control" (Washington, DC: ACDA, 14 January 1993).

(Table and notes from OTA, *Proliferation of Weapons of Mass Destruction*, 65.)

These concerns have been echoed and expanded upon by Yezid Sayigh.[27] In particular, he maintains that Israel has incorporated nonconventional capabilities—specifically, nuclear battlefield weapons—in its force structure and operational thinking and that Israel is in a position to wage an offensive nonconventional war, yet remain relatively immune from counterattack.

The statements by Moss and Sayigh raise two basic questions: To what extent are their assertions about a change in Israel's nuclear capability and doctrine credible? and To the extent that they are, is this change incompatible with a policy of defensive last resort?

Not surprisingly, Israel has not responded to these assertions; an essential element of ambiguity is neither to confirm nor to deny. It is plausible, however, that the experiences of the October 1973 war—specifically, the near breakthrough of Syrian forces on the Golan Heights and the threatening attitude of the Soviet Union—convinced Israel to accelerate development of a more flexible nuclear deterrent and the associated delivery systems. No doubt, this was abetted by the technological and bureaucratic momentum referred to by Moss. Indeed, one would expect that the role of these factors in the highly secret, publicly unacknowledged Israeli program was even greater than in the United States. The strategy still seems to be defensive last resort, but there are now more options for executing it than simply launching a nuclear attack against an Arab capital only when Arab troops "reach the gates of Tel Aviv."

Still, the Israeli nuclear program does serve as one (but not the only) rationale for Arab states also to acquire a nuclear capability. To the extent that the Israeli nuclear program remains unconstrained and its rationale remains unacknowledged, it becomes more difficult to maintain a consensus for strong measures to minimize the risk of further proliferation in the Middle East. In response, Bundy, Crow, and Drell believe that the time has come for more Israeli openness about Israel's nuclear program: "The number of those outside Israel who are comforted by the pretense [that Israel does not have nuclear weapons] shrinks, and the number who find it absurd and even offensive grows. The pretense prevents any public defense of the Israeli program by the Israeli government and any effective argument that no state or group need fear an Israeli bomb unless it attempts the destruction of Israel."[28]

While agreeing in principle with Bundy et al., I do not think that an open declaration by Israel of its nuclear status is a good idea. A better way to reassure the international community about the defensive nature of its nuclear posture is by acceptance of verifiable constraints on its program—specifically, a cutoff on further production of weapons-usable materials.[29]

Compared with nuclear weapons, much less is publicly known about Israeli activities with regard to chemical and biological weapons. There has been no equivalent Vanunu, although Marcus Klingberg, a Russian-born scientist from the top-secret Nes Tziona chemical and biological warfare center, was reportedly tried in camera on charges of being a Soviet agent. However, his existence has never been admitted by Israel.[30] With regard to chemical weapons, Cordesman lists a mustard and nerve gas production facility established in 1982 in the Sinai near Dimona, as well as probable stocks of bombs, rockets, and artillery.[31]

Iraq. Provisions of UN Security Council Resolution 687, which established the cease-fire after the Gulf War, also established the UN Special Commission on Iraq (UNSCOM) to carry out the tasks of supervising and executing the elimination of Iraq's biological, chemical, and missile capabilities and monitoring Iraq's compliance. The International Atomic Energy Agency (IAEA) was requested to carry out the corresponding tasks regarding Iraq's nuclear capability with the assistance and cooperation of UNSCOM.

Due to the painstaking and often heroic efforts of the UNSCOM-IAEA inspection teams, most of the massive infrastructure Iraq had created before the Gulf War to develop WMD and missiles has been destroyed. This is no small achievement. Rolf Ekeus, the executive chairman of UNSCOM, noted with regard to nuclear weapons: "Considering that Iraq's initial declaration in May 1991 under Resolution 687 stated that it had no nuclear weapons, no nuclear weapon programme, no weapon grade materials, no knowledge of or activity related to nuclear weapon subsystems, components or manufacture, and no research and development (R&D) facilities related to the production of nuclear weapons, it is quite remarkable that one and a half years after this declaration it is now proven that—with the exception of nuclear weapons—Iraq had all of the above."[32]

Moreover, on 26 November 1993, Iraq finally accepted the plans for future monitoring and verification of Iraq's nonacquisition of proscribed WMD and missiles, as called for in UN Security Council Resolution 715. This monitoring and verification is essential to prevent the reconstitution of Iraqi programs in these areas, once sanctions are lifted and money is again available to acquire key materials and facilities and to pay the knowledgeable scientists and engineers who previously worked on these programs. In the nuclear area, one should expect that Iraq will press for the lifting of UN Security Council Resolution 707, which, inter alia, demands that Iraq halt nuclear activities of any kind, except for medical, agricultural, and industrial purposes, until it is determined that Iraq is in full compliance with Resolution 687 and the terms set forward by the

IAEA. If Resolution 707 is lifted, Iraq will be able to get back into the "peaceful" nuclear business, as a convenient cover for weapons-related activities. This is essentially what is taking place in Iran and North Korea today.

Given the existing experience base in uranium enrichment, Iraq would probably try to reconstitute its gas centrifuge program, perhaps in an underground facility, or hide a chemical enrichment plant in a large chemical-processing complex. Both of these routes are much less detectable than was its major enrichment enterprise before the Gulf War. Of course, that process, electromagnetic isotope separation, was not discovered until after the war! The key issue, however, is What will the response of the international community be after proliferation activities are detected?

Iran. As noted above, there are strong differences of opinion regarding Iran's current capabilities and intentions with regard to WMD and delivery systems. The view of the Clinton administration, as stated by the president's national security adviser, Anthony Lake, is that Iran's WMD are at a relatively early stage of development. In principle, this gives the U.S. government more time to prevent Iran from becoming in five years what Iraq was five years ago. However, Lake acknowledges that the policy of trying to deny Iran the imports needed for its nuclear and chemical programs as well as missiles and missile-related systems does not have the same international support as the draconian measures imposed upon Iraq after the Gulf War.[33]

Despite the success of the United States in persuading Russia, India, and Pakistan, as well as the other Group of Seven countries, to tighten their nuclear-related exports to Iran, Iran continues to try to obtain power and research reactors and recruit scientists under the guise of the need for nuclear power. Although this method of acquiring a nuclear-weapons option has worked in the past, as in India and even to some extent in Iran under the Shah, its effectiveness today is dubious. Nevertheless, Iran will undoubtedly keep trying, and, given the depressed state of the worldwide nuclear industry, it may succeed, despite the best efforts of the United States. Meanwhile Iran will continue its activities, including professing its peaceful intent and inviting in the IAEA, while keeping a keen eye on developments in Iraq and North Korea.

Cordesman raises an alarm about "strong indications that Iran is actively developing biological weapons."[34] As in the nuclear area, it is difficult to separate fact from fancy, given the secrecy that would be expected to surround such efforts as well as deliberate misinformation campaigns by the People's Mujahideen and others. However, it appears likely that Iran, like other states in the Middle East, is keeping a biological weapons option open.

Minimizing the Risks of Proliferation of Weapons of Mass Destruction

The discovery after the Gulf War of large clandestine programs in Iraq to acquire WMD and ballistic missiles has given impetus to efforts by other nations, acting alone or in concert, to increase the scope and effectiveness of the broad array of nonproliferation tools. Although these include traditional means, such as export controls, international safeguards on nuclear materials, and arms-control agreements, much of the recent controversy in the nonproliferation arena has centered on the effectiveness of defensive and offensive military means to "counter" proliferation by destroying a country's WMD (particularly nuclear) assets on the ground, or, if this is impractical, by employing an antiballistic-missile defensive shield against WMD delivered by such systems. A relevant perspective on the overlap between nonproliferation and counterproliferation stratagems is provided in a memo from one of the key players in this domain in the Clinton administration to two of the others:

1. Nonproliferation is the use of the full range of political, economic, and military tools to prevent proliferation, reverse it diplomatically, or protect our interests against an opponent armed with weapons of mass destruction or missiles, should that prove necessary. Nonproliferation tools include: intelligence, global nonproliferation norms and agreements, diplomacy, export controls, security assurances, defenses, and the application of military force.

2. Counterproliferation refers to the activities of the Department of Defense across the full range of U.S. efforts to combat proliferation, including diplomacy, arms control, export controls, and intelligence collection and analysis, with particular responsibility for assuring that U.S. forces and interests can be protected should they confront an adversary armed with weapons of mass destruction or missiles.[35]

Thus, counterproliferation is viewed as a special Department of Defense responsibility, with an emphasis on the need for an enhanced intelligence collection and analysis capability as a necessary condition for possible defensive or offensive actions to counter a threat to U.S. forces and interests.[36] The current stress on counterproliferation originated in the Gulf War, with, for instance, discussions about our failure to detect much of the Iraqi nuclear effort and debates about how the diplomatic and military strategy of the allied coalition would have changed if Iraq had been known to possess nuclear weapons at the time of its invasion of Kuwait. More recently, the heated debate about the benefits and risks of destroying North Korea's nuclear facilities has abated somewhat with the signing of an agreement between the United States and North Korea that requires the latter to dismantle these facilities over time. However, the possible unraveling of this agreement and the inevitable deterioration of the technical barriers to the proliferation of nuclear weapons, particularly the risk of leakage of weapons-usable materials from the former Soviet Union, increase the likelihood that soon counterproliferation will again be a central consideration in deciding how best to respond to the threat of further, especially nuclear, proliferation.

Arms Control

Nuclear Weapons

There are three major initiatives on the current international nuclear arms-control agenda: (1) negotiations related to the NPT extension conference in April 1995, (2) negotiation of a CTBT, and (3) preliminary consideration of a global convention to ban further production of fissile material for nuclear weapons.

To date, the focus of negotiation efforts has been on the NPT and the CTBT. These issues are linked, because many nonnuclear-state parties to the NPT have conditioned their acceptance of its indefinite or long-term extension to the negotiation of a CTBT. Unfortunately, the CTBT negotiation has been delayed by the foot-dragging of the de jure nuclear-weapons states, particularly China and France. Both China and France want to conduct additional tests in order to modernize their arsenals, while China also wants an exemption for "peaceful" nuclear explosions. An initial U.S. proposal (since withdrawn) to allow states to withdraw from the treaty after ten years—without even citing supreme national interest, as is customary in such treaties—has also contributed to skepticism about the degree of U.S. support for a cessation of nuclear testing. In the end, it is almost certain that a CTBT will be negotiated, but it is highly unlikely that agreement will be reached before the start of the NPT extension conference.

All the states in the Middle East that have either a demonstrable interest in acquiring nuclear weapons (Iran, Iraq, and Libya) or have already done so (Israel) have signed and ratified the Partial Test Ban Treaty.[37] There are no indications that any of these states would not also support a CTBT.

The situation with regard to the NPT is different. Israel is the major nonsignatory in the Middle East. While it is on record as in favor of a nuclear-weapons-free Middle East, its preferred means to this end is not the NPT, but rather the negotiation of a nuclear-weapons-free zone in the region.[38] However, it is clear that Israel views a nuclear-weapons-free zone as a long-term goal that can be reached only after an extended period of peaceful relations with its neighbors. Until Israel has greater confidence in their good will *and* has the ability to verify the absence of nuclear-weapons activities on a bilateral basis, it will continue to view its nuclear deterrent as an essential ingredient in guaranteeing its national security and will not relinquish it.

Israel's refusal to sign the NPT anytime soon, if ever, has complicated negotiations for treaty proponents, particularly the United States. For instance, a group of states led by Egypt has linked its support for long-term if not indefinite extension of the treaty to Israeli willingness to also join the treaty. It remains to be seen how far Egypt will go in terms of withholding support for the NPT in the absence of Israeli willingness to join the treaty now or at some future date.

Alternatively, a compromise might be fashioned on the basis of Israeli willingness to consider a cutoff in the production of fissile materials. While a fissile-material cutoff was a primary objective of U.S. arms-control negotiations with the Soviet Union from the Truman through the Johnson administrations, its value as an important nonproliferation, rather than arms control, measure in the Middle East was first advocated by Cohen and Miller, in 1988.[39] The idea met with little enthusiasm initially, but it gained support in the aftermath of the Gulf War, especially after then-president George Bush supported it as part of a menu of U.S. policy objectives to minimize weapons proliferation in the Middle East. However, recent discussions of this issue are based principally on a proposal by President Clinton on 27 September 1993 for a "multilateral convention prohibiting the production of highly enriched uranium or plutonium for nuclear explosive purposes or outside of international safeguards."[40]

Thus, the current initiative is global rather than regional in scope; it seeks to take advantage of the fact that the de jure nuclear-weapons states, particularly the United States and Russia, have no need to produce more weapons material. Its major rationale is to cap the weapons programs of India, Israel, and Pakistan and, in so doing, to bring these countries across some psychological threshold into the nonproliferation regime.[41]

On the other hand, the proposed cutoff convention is silent about stocks of weapons material produced before it takes effect, and thus it tends to legitimate their possession.[42] On this basis, one would anticipate a favorable reaction to the cutoff on the part of Israel, as well as India and

Pakistan. However, some Israelis view the cutoff as a "slippery slope." That is, its negotiation, and more particularly the inspections to verify compliance, which are certain to be an integral part of any agreement, will inevitably underline Israel's nuclear status and may lead to pressure to abandon its nuclear deterrent altogether.

Although the United States would likely offer Israel various non-nuclear inducements (such as access to advanced technology) to agree to a fissile-material cutoff, the heart of the matter for many Israelis is whether Israel could "trade" a cutoff agreement for an increased level of assurance that its neighbors, particularly Iran and Iraq, can be prevented from acquiring nuclear weapons. At this point, the U.S. government has not exerted any public pressure on Israel to join the NPT or to agree to a fissile-material cutoff, perhaps mindful of the difficulties the current Israeli government faces in convincing its citizens that trading "land for peace" in agreements with both the Palestine Liberation Organization and Syria will not endanger Israeli security.

The optimistic view is that once such agreements are in place, substantive discussions on arms control can begin, and hopefully make progress. In particular, the Arab states and Israel may come to view the fissile-material cutoff, credibly verified, as a substantive step towards the goal of a Middle East free of all WMD. However, at this point, negotiations on the cutoff at the Conference on Disarmament in Geneva are moving at a snail's pace, and the United States is concentrating its efforts on promoting it in South Asia, not in the Middle East.

Chemical Weapons

The CWC was opened for signature in January 1993 and will enter into force 180 days after the sixty-fifth state has ratified it. As of March 1995, 159 states had signed the treaty, but only 27 had ratified it. The CWC is, without doubt, a major disarmament and arms control achievement, but also a very complex undertaking, particularly with regard to its extensive and intrusive verification provisions.[43]

A key issue in this regard is the workability of the provisions for challenge inspections. In brief, each state party has the right to request an on-site challenge inspection of any facility or location in the territory of any other state party for the sole purpose of clarifying and resolving any questions concerning possible noncompliance. Frivolous or abusive inspections can be blocked by an Executive Council, but once the inspection is approved, the challenged party must provide quick access to the suspect facility. However, it can protect sensitive installations for security and commercial reasons via restrictions on the perimeters of sites to be inspected and by "managed access" within sites. Managed access may include shrouding sensitive pieces of equipment, restricting sample analysis to the presence or absence of chemicals restricted by the CWC, and using random selective access techniques whereby inspectors gain access only to a given percentage or number of buildings of their choice. The rationale for challenge inspections with managed access is the consensus view that the CWC would not be credible without provisions for detecting prohibited activities at undeclared sites, while at the same time protecting nonprohibited activities from disclosure.

The importance of such provisions goes beyond the CWC. In the nuclear area, a verification regime for the fissile-material cutoff convention must also protect all activities not associated with the production of fissile materials. Indeed, the IAEA is promoting "managed access" as a way of making a state's nuclear activities as transparent to inspectors as possible while protecting nonrelevant sensitive information.[44]

The impact of the CWC on chemical weapons in the Middle East is unclear at present. Important nonsignatories in the region are Egypt, Libya, Iraq, and Syria. Some of these states have linked signing and ratifying the convention to Israeli accession to the NPT. On the other hand, Israel has signed the convention, but it will probably not ratify it unless the above states do likewise.

Biological Weapons

As noted above, the BTWC, which entered into force in 1975, has no provisions for independent verification. However, the perception that such provisions are needed has grown, and it appears that there will be strong support for adding verification teeth to the convention on the basis of the recommendations of the VEREX group.

One important feature of both the BTWC and the CWC is that they are nondiscriminatory—unlike the NPT, which legitimates the possession of nuclear weapons by only five states while all other state parties pledge not to acquire such weapons. Unfortunately, two key Middle Eastern states, Syria and Egypt, have signed, but not ratified, the BTWC, and Israel has not signed.

Arab-Israeli Peace Process

In addition to these international developments, the framework of the Madrid peace conference in October 1991 provides a specific forum—the multilateral working group on regional security and arms control—for discussion of arms control in a regional context, including control of WMD and missiles. At their Cairo meeting, 30 January to 3 February 1994, this group issued the Declaration of Principles and Statements of Intent on Arms Control and Regional Security, which states the following:

In the context of achieving a just, secure, comprehensive, and lasting peace and reconciliation, the participants agree to pursue, inter alia, the following arms control and regional security objectives:

- preventing conflict from occurring through misunderstanding or miscalculation by adopting confidence-and-security building measures that increase transparency and openness and reduce the risk of surprise attack and by developing regional institutional arrangements that enhance security and the process of arms control;
- limiting military spending in the region so that additional resources can be made available to other areas, such as economic and social development;
- reducing stockpiles of conventional arms and preventing a conventional arms race in the region as part of an effort to provide enhanced security at lower levels of armaments and militarization, to reduce the threat of large-scale destruction posed by such weapons, and to move towards force structures that do not exceed legitimate defensive requirements; and
- establishing a zone free of all weapons of mass destruction, including nuclear, chemical, and biological weapons and their delivery systems.

Again, and unfortunately, several of the key regional parties—Iran, Iraq, Libya, and Syria—are not members of this working group.

Export Controls

The realization that controls on the export of technology relevant to the development of WMD and missiles in individual countries would not be effective unless they were coordinated with other suppliers of such technology has led to the creation of several multilateral agreements to control such exports. These agreements and the related export control groups include the following:

- The Nuclear Supplier Group (also known as the London Club) was formed in 1976 to address the export of nuclear technology, including items that have both nuclear and nonnuclear applications (so-called dual- or multiple-use items).
- The Australian Group, formed in 1984, deals with chemical and biological weapons agents and their precursors.
- The MTCR, formed in 1987, addresses missile systems, subsystems, and related technology.[45]

The most important common feature of the export control agreements reached by these groups is that they are not subject to formal coordination, monitoring, or enforcement, although informal consultations among various suppliers are common. No Middle East countries belong to any of these regimes, with the exception of Israel, which agreed in October 1991 to abide by MTCR provisions by the end of 1992 and applied for membership in March 1993.[46]

None of these control regimes is perfect, either with regard to the enforcement of the guidelines via national legislation in the supplier countries or with respect to the inclusion of all significant suppliers within the regime. In the aftermath of the Gulf War, several countries that were criticized for having exported WMD and missile technology to Iraq (for example, Germany) have tightened their export control laws, including providing for stiffer penalties for violations. However, other states, particularly North Korea, continue to export missiles and related technology to countries of proliferation concern in the Middle East, especially Iran.

In this regard, the most newsworthy recent event was the test-firing of four missiles by North Korea into the Sea of Japan in late May 1993. One (or possibly two) of these was the so-called Nodong-1. Estimates based on the missile's size and fuel capacity, as derived from intelligence photos, give the Nodong-1 a range of approximately a thousand kilometers and a payload of some one thousand kilograms. If the range of the Nodong could be extended to about thirteen hundred kilometers, while retaining a thousand-kilogram payload, it would put Japan in range of a nuclear missile attack from North Korea and Israel in range of such an attack from Iran. This assumes, of course, that such missiles can be made operational at such ranges, and, in the case of Israel, that North Korea would be willing—and able—to export such missiles to Iran. This problem underscores the difficulty of pressuring states to adhere to the rules of international regimes and supplier cartels, such as the MTCR, when they feel that their political and economic interests dictate otherwise.

Taking into account the technical requirements for WMD, as discussed above, a rough hierarchy of the efficacy of export controls in preventing proliferation—when enforced!—would be as follows (from best to worst): nuclear (particularly with regard to the technology needed to produce fissile material), chemical, biological. The verification provisions of the CWC, especially the challenge inspections, should also help to detect exports of prohibited chemicals to CWC state parties. Hopefully, similar provisions can be incorporated into the BTWC.

The emphasis given to strengthening WMD and missile export control regimes has thus far not extended to the "human dimension" of the proliferation problem—that is, a coordinated policy to place formal restrictions on the education and training of foreign nationals from countries of proliferation concern at educational institutions in supplier countries. However, such restrictions have been applied in the past in the

United States and other states on an ad hoc basis. In the face of evidence that Iraq both recruited large numbers of scientists and engineers from the Arab world to work on its WMD and missile programs and sent Iraqi students abroad to acquire expertise in weapons-related disciplines, both the U.S. and the United Kingdom governments are considering new measures to deal with this problem. Thus, in the United Kingdom, the universities and the higher-education colleges have recently agreed with the government to accept official guidance about countries and technologies of concern, which they "will take into account when reaching decisions" about accepting overseas researchers "at post-graduate and post-doctoral levels in certain fields of scientific research." This, Parliament was told, is to inhibit access to technologies which could assist in the development of WMD. A previous government proposal that the universities reject all postgraduate applicants from a list of eleven countries and seventeen academic disciplines that in combination were "a prima facie cause for concern" was rejected by the universities.[47]

This is obviously a very sensitive matter: while it is legitimate to exclude "rogues from rogue states," identifying them as such is highly problematic, and such restrictions run counter to established policies of academic freedom and the benefits of raising the educational level of scientists and engineers from developing countries. As noted in a U.S. Office of Technology Assessment report: "Indeed, the dissemination of technologies that have at least some relevance to producing WMD might need not only to be tolerated but encouraged if populations in developing countries are to improve their health, environment, and standard of living."[48]

Military Actions

Since the Gulf War there has been much discussion of two "what if" scenarios, and their implications for future U.S. national security policy: What if Iraq had used chemical weapons against the allied coalition? and what if it had become known that Iraq had nuclear weapons after it invaded Kuwait? Although the Bush administration reiterated the U.S. government's negative security guarantee of no first use of nuclear weapons against a nonnuclear state, first made in 1978, it was silent on the question of its response to an explicit or implicit nuclear threat by Iraq. Fortunately, neither this question nor that of a possible Israeli nuclear response to an Iraqi chemical attack was put to the test. However, Iraq's known nuclear facilities were attacked on the first day of Operation Desert Storm. Moreover, given the risk of future acquisition of nuclear weapons by states hostile to U.S. interests—for example, Iraq, Iran, Libya, and North Korea—the issue of the role of military actions in preventing the acquisition of nuclear weapons by hostile states, or in response to a nuclear attack on U.S. territory or assets in the field, is hardly academic.

Before the Gulf War the best-known example of military action to prevent proliferation was the destruction by Israel of a large French-built research reactor in Iraq in June 1981, just before it was scheduled to start up.[49] The official Israeli rationale for the attack was that the unirradiated highly enriched uranium fuel for the reactor could have been diverted to produce nuclear weapons, or plutonium for the same purpose could be produced during reactor operation. In the aftermath of the attack, most knowledgeable observers, including the Israeli scientist Yuval Ne'eman, concluded that it was unlikely that Iraq could have successfully concealed either a diversion of bomb quantities of highly enriched uranium or the production and separation of bomb quantities of plutonium from the IAEA inspectors or the French technicians who were to remain on-site. Rather, according to Ne'eman, Israel's concern was that Iraq—with the collusion of Western suppliers—was (mis)using its NPT status to gain access to bomb-related nuclear technology and, at the appropriate time, would leave the treaty by invoking Article X.[50]

According to this line of reasoning, attacking the reactor before it went critical was both responsible and effective. It was responsible in an ethical sense, because it avoided the potential for radioactive contamination. It was effective, because it eliminated the key element of a nascent nuclear weapons program before the program grew too large to destroy in a single, surgical strike, using conventional arms. There was widespread sympathy for this view, especially in the United States, where Israel was widely viewed as a valued ally; Iraq, as a rogue state; and France, as an unconscionable nuclear supplier. However, there was also concern that sanctioning attacks on "suspect" nuclear facilities would set a dangerous precedent, including the possibility of "tit for tat" escalation. Thus, would Pakistan retaliate for an attack on its enrichment plant at Kahuta by attacking research or power reactors in India? Similarly, would North Korea target nuclear reactors in South Korea in response to the destruction of its nuclear facilities by the United States? Even if retaliatory means are not available at the time of the attack, rulers like Saddam Hussein have long memories and may in the future have the technical means to threaten U.S. and Israeli nuclear facilities. Indeed, Iraq fired several Scud missiles at the Dimona site in Israel during the Gulf War.

The question of retaliation aside, it seems clear that the Israeli attack only increased the determination of Iraq to acquire nuclear weapons, and Iraq proceeded toward this goal across a broad technical front while cleverly disguising the extent of its efforts. While there is some difference of opinion among the relevant experts on how long it would have taken

Iraq to cross the nuclear threshold if it had not invaded Kuwait in 1990, the United States and its allies may well have confronted a hostile state possessing a nuclear arsenal numbering tens of weapons deliverable by Scud-type missiles by the mid-1990s. What then? In particular, could the United States or Israel rely solely on conventional weapons either to eliminate such a state's nuclear facilities and weapons before they could be used or to respond to a nuclear attack on its territory, military bases, or troops in the field?

This question has been considered in the context of potential U.S. responses by several analysts.[52] Their collective judgment is that conventional weapons can and should suffice: there is no nuclear attack, even in retaliation, that would be both militarily effective and morally acceptable, and hence credible. This conclusion is premised on the following convictions: a nuclear response would put civilians at risk, and this would be extremely unjust; military assets, including nuclear weapons, can be attacked just as effectively by nonnuclear means; the U.S. homeland is unlikely to be threatened; and the symbolism of U.S. nuclear restraint is important.

Note that a policy of no nuclear use, even in retaliation, goes well beyond the U.S. negative security assurance first articulated by Secretary of State Cyrus Vance to the United Nations on 12 June 1978, which reads: "The US will not use nuclear weapons against any non-nuclear state party to the NPT or any comparable internationally binding commitment not to acquire nuclear explosive devices, except in the case of an attack on the US, its territories or armed forces by such a state allied to a nuclear-weapons state or associated with a nuclear-weapons state in carrying out or sustaining the attack."[52]

Although some nonnuclear parties to the NPT have demanded that the United States and the other nuclear-weapons states strengthen and clarify this commitment to no first use of nuclear weapons against avowed nonnuclear states, there is a reluctance to do so on the part of officials in the U.S. defense establishment and their counterparts in the other nuclear-weapons states. They believe that such a commitment could, in theory, weaken deterrence against the use of chemical and biological weapons by nonnuclear states, a threat that is taken more seriously today than it was in 1978. A possible remedy, suggested by the Federation of American Scientists, is to modify the 1978 no-first-use declaration as follows: "The United States will not use nuclear weapons against any state which has provided the US with credible assurances that it is a non-nuclear weapon state, except in response to the use by such states of other weapons of mass destruction."[53]

Even if this formulation were adopted, it does not address the nature of a response to a nuclear attack. While I am sympathetic to the case made by May and Speed, Cropsy, and Arnett that the response should be nonnuclear,[54] it is unrealistic to expect that any nuclear-weapons state would adopt this as declaratory policy.

The acquisition of nuclear weapons and ballistic missiles comparable to the North Korean Nodong in range and payload capability by such states as Iran, Iraq, and Libya would be more threatening for Israel than for the United States. Such missiles could reach Israel, but not the United States, from these states.

This situation would also increase the temptation for Israel to preempt. Since it would be much more difficult for Israel to destroy a large-scale dispersed nuclear program than for the United States to do so, there would be a greater risk that some nuclear weapons and their associated delivery systems would remain after a preemptive attack and could be used to retaliate against Israel. Moreover, adopting a pledge of no first use of nuclear weapons along the lines of that suggested by the Federation of American Scientists might also be more problematic for Israel than for the United States. The historical rationale for the Israeli nuclear program has been to provide a deterrent against any attempt to destroy Israel by overwhelming *conventional* means.

Conclusions

WMD and missile delivery systems already exist in some countries in the Middle East. The primary motivation for the acquisition of such weapons and missiles was the perception that they are essential for the security of the state against rivals that already had them or had superiority in conventional forces and delivery means. An additional motivation was the political power and technical prestige that are still associated with the acquisition of WMD, particularly nuclear weapons and missiles, especially if this is achieved via indigenous programs. However, such acquisition also provides a strong incentive for further proliferation of WMD and missiles in the region, especially with the persistence of disputes over land and resources, suspicions about the desire for peaceful relations professed by most government leaders, and ambitions for regional hegemony.

Since the Gulf War, this prospect for further proliferation, especially to so-called rogue states such as Iran and Iraq, has become a major foreign-policy concern (and dealing with it has become a growth industry) in the West, especially the United States. Much time and energy have been expended by a diverse community of proponents of different ways of minimizing the proliferation risk. A nonexhaustive list of such approaches would include the following:

- Improving intelligence collection and analysis capabilities with regard to clandestine WMD and missile programs;
- Planning for the contingency of disabling or destroying such programs by military force;
- Upgrading the capability of the IAEA to deal with the problem of undeclared nuclear facilities by enlarging its mandate and providing it with relevant intelligence information;
- Negotiating and implementing new arms-control agreements, such as the fissile-material cutoff convention, the CTBT, and the CWC, as well as improving and extending agreements already in effect, such as the BWTC, the MTCR, and the NPT;
- Moving more vigorously to implement the goal of universal nuclear disarmament as embodied by Article VI of the NPT.

Reducing the threat of "hostile" proliferation enjoys wide support among both the public and opinion leaders in the United States, and, with the notable exception of universal nuclear disarmament, all of the above measures are supported by the current U.S. administration. However, other states do not necessarily share the U.S. views about which states are hostile, the efficacy of various nonproliferation strategies, and the dangers of further proliferation. Given the growing availability of WMD and missile technology, this implies that it may not be possible to prevent further proliferation in the Middle East and elsewhere solely by reliance on punitive measures, such as export controls, economic sanctions, and military action.

But is proliferation, including nuclear proliferation, necessarily bad? There has always been a minority view that it is not. In large measure, this view is based on the judgment that the absence of a war, even a conventional one, between the United States and the former Soviet Union since World War II was due to the fear of escalation to mutual nuclear destruction. If nuclear deterrence worked for the superpowers, it is argued, why shouldn't it work elsewhere, for example, in the Middle East?

The counterargument, to which I subscribe, is that reliance on nuclear deterrence was a risky business in the U.S.-Soviet context and would be riskier still in such regions as the Middle East and South Asia. The reasons are political, geographic, and technical. Many of the conflicts in the Middle East—for example, between Israel and some of its Islamic neighbors and between Iraq and Iran—as well as the relations between India and Pakistan are characterized by deeply rooted, almost visceral animosity. Some of these states share common, and disputed, borders, and there are legitimate concerns about the safety and reliability of the command and control systems of newly acquired and often untested WMD, especially in the "fog of war."

What then can be done to lessen the proliferation danger? Fundamentally, the solution lies in reducing proliferation incentives by lessening political tensions between states and promoting democratic norms within them and by reducing the military threat, political power, and prestige associated with existing nuclear weapons—and eventually eliminating them altogether.

Outside powers, international organizations such as the United Nations, and even individuals can often play a useful role in lessening political tensions and promoting democratic norms. However, direct negotiations between the parties themselves are essential, and these must include consideration of arms-control initiatives, whether unilateral, bilateral, or regional, covering both WMD and conventional forces. Such initiatives can build trust between the parties by dealing with concerns that cannot be easily addressed by global agreements, such as the NPT and the CWC, and thus can contribute significantly to the prospects for success in the political negotiations.

As noted above, a forum for discussions of arms control and regional security in the Middle East has been established. However, several regional states of proliferation concern are not members of this forum: Iraq remains an international pariah as long as Saddam Hussein is in power, while Syria and Iran have declined to participate; a peace agreement between Israel and Syria as well as regime changes in Iraq and Iran will probably be required to bring these three states to the table. Meanwhile, both discussions in this forum and those whose aim is to strengthen international norms against the acquisition of WMD should be vigorously pursued. The former provide a valuable mechanism for delegates from Israel and the Arab states to learn more about arms control and to discuss their nations' threat perceptions and concepts of regional security; the latter provide an opportunity for the great powers to provide leadership by example, particularly with regard to nuclear weapons.

The tension between the retention of nuclear weapons by some states on the grounds that they are necessary for national security and their opposition to other states' acquisition of nuclear capability is underscored by the universality of the ban on chemical and biological weapons codified in the CWC and the BTWC. At bottom, the argument for selective retention of nuclear weapons is a slippery slope. Even during the Cold War, when many states chose or were forced to seek shelter under the nuclear umbrellas of the superpowers, France, China, Israel, India, and Pakistan were not persuaded that nuclear abstinence was in their national interests. The breakup of the Soviet Union and its loss of leverage over former clients and allies have increased both the incentives for proliferation and the availability of bomb material and expertise, if not actual weapons, to satisfy such desires.

At the moment, there is guarded optimism that the packages of carrots and sticks that have been crafted to persuade Ukraine and North Korea not to go nuclear in response to real and imagined threats to their security will suffice. However, the response of the international community to the acquisition of nuclear weapons by these states sends a clear message that such weapons are still valuable—politically and economically, if not militarily. It is unlikely that the threat of economic sanctions or military action by a nuclear-armed state, such as the United States, Russia, or Israel, will be enough to halt further proliferation in the future. This would raise the risk that the taboo against nuclear use that has existed since 1945 could be broken in an action-and-reaction cycle, with potentially disastrous consequences in terms of loss of life and global stability.

For a small but growing number of analysts, the only viable solution to the danger posed by the proliferation of WMD is their universal abolition.[55] The recent negotiation of the CWC as well as initiatives to strengthen the BTWC are seen as important steps in this direction. However, the nuclear-weapons states remain convinced that retaining a minimum nuclear deterrent and preventing further nuclear proliferation are essential for their own security, as well as for the stability of the international system. For in a post-Cold War environment characterized by conflict between states and substate actors with large disparities in conventional arms, aspirations to obtain nuclear weapons remain. Given that technical verification means are not foolproof, sooner or later, some rogue state will "break out" of a nuclear-weapons-free world and hold the rest of the world hostage. Thus, it is argued that a nuclear-weapons-free world is neither politically desirable nor technically feasible.

Obviously, nuclear disarmament cannot be realized in an atmosphere characterized by conflict and mistrust among states and disparities in their possession of chemical weapons, biological weapons, and conventional arms. As previously noted, this synergy between control of both conventional arms and weapons of mass destruction, as well as between arms control in general and improvements in the political climate, is widely appreciated in the Middle Eastern context. Thus, if the political climate improves, states will be more relaxed about their neighbor's intentions. Conversely, credible verification modalities can help to build trust. Although verification of a nuclear-weapons-free world could be very demanding, for example, it might require very intrusive inspection or even international control of all ostensibly peaceful nuclear activities, even more problematic is the mind-set that says that it cannot be accomplished. In the wake of the successful effort by Iraq to hide many aspects of its WMD programs and in support of the verification provisions of the CWC, technical means to detect clandestine WMD activities are being significantly upgraded. Moreover, the need for more transparency in ostensibly peaceful nuclear, chemical, and biological activities, ranging from research to the production of, for example, electrical power, chemical feedstocks, and pharmaceuticals to ensure that they are not being misused for weapons purposes is now widely recognized. And instead of building bombs, scientists can play a major role in the realization of a world free of all WMD by refusing to participate in or even "blowing the whistle" on WMD programs that their countries have publicly forsworn. Certainly, much remains to be done to make the above more credible; what is lacking at the moment is a commitment on the part of the nuclear-weapons states to move with serious intent towards the goal of a nuclear-weapons-free-world, and thus to reinvigorate the international nuclear nonproliferation norm.

Eliminating existing WMD capabilities from the Middle East and eliminating incentives for their further acquisition are daunting tasks. However, incremental steps to reduce both WMD stocks and incentives are feasible, and here there are synergisms, both positive and negative, between progress toward defusing regional tensions and the success of initiatives to delegitimize and eventually eliminate WMD on a global basis. The impact of the former on the latter has often been remarked upon, but the reverse connection is also significant. For example, while arms control must address specific regional concerns, including the conventional balance of forces, the potential, for example, for smuggling of nuclear weapons materials from the former Soviet Union and for the sale of long-range missiles by North Korea can have a direct impact on the prospects for WMD acquisition and use in the Middle East. Thus, regional actors are affected by, and can also have a significant influence on, international arms-control negotiations. While their participation in such forums may sometimes be mischievous, it also puts pressure on them to be more accountable for their actions. On balance, such participation should be strongly encouraged.

Notes

1. Of course, conventional weapons delivered by conventional means, such as aerial bombs, can also kill large numbers of people in a relatively short period of time (for example, the destruction of Dresden, Germany, during World War II). Moreover, conventional weapons, including small arms, mines, and artillery, have been responsible for almost all of the more than twenty million deaths in the wars since then, and, in contrast to WMD, very little is being done to halt their proliferation. Indeed, their sale to "responsible" states that can pay for them is promoted by some of the same countries, such as the United States, that oppose,

though selectively, the proliferation of WMD and missiles. This conventional proliferation is dangerous both because the new generation of conventional arms available on the market is increasingly deadly and also because the acquisition of these arms by one state creates incentives for their regional rivals to do the same, or even up the ante by seeking to acquire WMD.

2. Much has been written on this subject, particularly since the Gulf War, but I make frequent reference to three publications in particular: (1) the recently issued report by the U.S. Office of Technology Assessment, *Proliferation of Weapons of Mass Destruction: Assessing the Risks* (cited as *ATR*), OTA-ISC-559 (Washington, D.C.: Office of Technology Assessment, August 1993); (2) a companion background paper, *Technologies Underlying Weapons of Mass Destruction* (cited as *TWMD*), OTA-BP-ISC-115 (Washington, D.C.: Office of Technology Assessment, December 1993); and (3) E. Karsh, M. Navias, and P. Sabin, eds. *Non-Conventional Weapons Proliferation in the Middle East* (Oxford: Clarendon Press, 1993).

3. Richard K. Wallace, "Nuclear Weapons Computational Design Capabilities" (Applied Theoretical Physics Division, Los Alamos National Laboratory, September 1990). Although high-performance computing is not a key "enabling" technology for the design and development of even sophisticated nuclear weapons, numerically controlled precision machine tools that use computers are useful for the fabrication of warhead components as well as components for certain uranium enrichment methods, such as gas centrifuges. However, the key element of such machinery is in most cases not the computer itself, but the control system, software, and feedback loop, which translate computer calculations into, for example, the precise movement of a lathe. For a discussion of this and related issues, see Cameron Brinkley and John R. Harvey, "Export Controls on Dual-Use, High Technology: Implications for National/Economic Security" (summary of a workshop hosted by the Stanford University Center for International Security and Arms Control, 18–19 October 1993).

4. Frank Morring, Jr., "Germ Warfare," *Aerospace Daily*, 31 January 1994, 146.

5. Nicholas A. Sims, *The Diplomacy of Biological Disarmament: Vicissitudes of a Treaty in Force, 1975–85* (London: Macmillan Press, 1988), 62.

6. See, for example, Tomas Bartfal, S. J. Lundin, and Bo Rybeck, "Benefits and Threats of Developments in Biotechnology and Genetic Engineering," in *SIPRI Yearbook 1993: World Armaments and Disarmament* (Oxford: Oxford University Press, 1993), 302–304.

7. Matthew Meselson, Martin M. Kaplan, and Mark A. Makulsky, "Verification of Biological and Toxin Weapons Disarmament," in *Verification: Monitoring Disarmament*, eds. Francesco Calogero, Marvin L. Goldberger, and Sergei P. Kapetza (Boulder Colo.: Westview Press, 1991), 150.

8. For an excellent survey of proliferation systems for the delivery of WMD, see *TWMD*, chap. 5.

9. Philip Sabin, "Restraints on Chemical, Biological and Nuclear Use: Some Lessons from History," in Karsh et al., *Non-Conventional Weapons Proliferation in the Middle East*, 9–30.

10. Ibid., 29.

11. Sims, *The Diplomacy of Biological Disarmament*, 5–6.

12. Robert Harus and Jeremy Paxman, *A Higher Form of Killing: The Secret Story of Gas and Germ Warfare*, (London: Chatto & Windus, 1982), xi–xii.

13. Sims, *The Diplomacy of Biological Disarmament*, 42.

14. Les Aspin, *From Deterrence to Denukeng: Dealing with Proliferation in the 1990s* (Washington, D.C.: U.S. Congress, House Committee on the Armed Services, 1992).

15. Shimon Peres, *The New Middle East* (New York: Henry Holt, 1993), 82–83.

16. Julian Perry Robinson, "Chemical-Weapons Proliferation in the Middle East," in Karsh et al., *Non-Conventional Weapons Proliferation in the Middle East*, 93–94.

17. Ibid., 97–98.

18. Seth Carus, "Proliferation and Security in Southwest Asia," *The Washington Quarterly* (spring 1994): 129–139.

19. Ibid., 135 (Emphasis added).

20. Ibid., 136.

21. More information about WMD and missile programs in the Middle East can be found in the writings of Anthony Cordesman (see, for example, *After the Storm* (Boulder, Colo.: Westview Press, 1993), and *Iran and Iraq: The Military Dimensions of Possible Regional Conflict* (Washington, D.C.: Woodrow Wilson Center, October 1993).

22. "The World's Worst kept Secret," *Economist*, 26 October 1991, 111.

23. An amusing example of this, given its source, is the index to the recently published book by Peres, *The New Middle East*. Under the index heading "nuclear weapons," one finds "Israel's program of, 4–5."

24. For the Holocaust trauma and the roles of Ben-Gurion, Peres, and Bergman, see, for example, Tom Segev, *The Seventh Million* (New York: Hill & Wang, 1993), 367–370.

25. "Revealed: the Secrets of Israel's Nuclear Arsenal," *Sunday Times*, 5 October 1986, 1–3.

26. Norman Moss, "Vanunu, Israel's Bomb, and US Aid," *Bulletin of the Atomic Scientists*, May 1988, 7–8.

27. Yezid Sayigh, "Reversing the Middle East Nuclear Race," *Middle East Report*, July–August 1992, 16–17.

28. McGeorge Bundy, William J. Crow Jr., and Sidney D. Drell, *Reducing the Nuclear Danger* (New York: Council on Foreign Relations, 1993), 69.

29. Avner Cohen and Marvin Miller, "Facing the Unavoidable: Israel's Nuclear Monopoly Revisited" (Defense and Arms Control Studies Program, Massachusetts Institute of Technology, June 1988), and Cohen and Miller, "How to Think about—and Implement—Nuclear Arms Control in the Middle East," *The Washington Quarterly*, spring 1993, 101–113. See also Geoffrey Kemp, "Arms Control and the Arab-Israeli Peace Process," in Karsh et al., *Non-Conventional Weapons Proliferation in the Middle East*, 245–247.

30. Ian Black and Benny Morris, *Israel's Secret Wars: A History of Israel's Intelligence Services* (New York: Grove Weidenfeld, 1991), 442. The book also contains a summary of the Vanunu case, including a convincing rebuttal to the contention

that Vanunu was a deliberate plant. Both with regard to this discussion and with regard to that concerning the Klingberg affair, it is interesting that the book, as published, passed Israeli military censorship.

31. Cordesman, *After the Storm*, 55.

32. Rolf Ekeus, "The United Nations Special Commission on Iraq: Activities in 1992," in *SIPRI Yearbook 1993*, 691–702.

33. Anthony Lake, "Confronting Backlash States," *Foreign Affairs*, March/April 1994, 45–53. A good review of publicly available information on Iran's WMD and missile programs is given in Cordesman, *Iran and Iraq*, 41–55.

34. Cordesman, *Iran and Iraq*, 41–55.

35. National Security Council memorandum from Daniel Poneman, special assistant to the president and senior director for nonproliferation and export controls, to Robert Gallucci, assistant secretary for political-military affairs, Department of State, and Ashton Carter, assistant secretary for nuclear security and counterproliferation, Department of Defense, 18 February 1994.

36. Note that good intelligence is necessary for the effectiveness of many nonproliferation tools—for example, providing information to the IAEA on possible undeclared nuclear facilities in NPT non-nuclear-weapons states in order to justify special inspections of such facilities and closing loopholes in various export regimes by detecting illicit transactions.

37. Egypt and Syria have also done so.

38. Israeli support for a nuclear-weapons-free zone was recently reiterated by Prime Minister Yitzhak Rabin. Speaking before the National Press Club in Washington, D.C., on 16 November 1993, he stated: "Israel's policy was and is that we will not be the first to introduce nuclear weapons to the context of the Arab-Israeli, Islamic-Israeli conflict. Today, we are ready to sign on a bilateral basis agreement about a nuclear-free zone in the Middle East with all the Arab and Islamic countries who are relevant to the issue to have a bilateral supervision that will be decided by agreement between them and us."

39. Cohen and Miller, "Facing the Unavoidable."

40. *Nonproliferation and Export Control Policy*, Fact Sheet (Washington, D.C.: The White House, 27 September 1993).

41. See F. Berkhout, O. Bukharin, H. Feiveson, and M. Miller, "A Cutoff in the Production of Fissile Material, *International Security* 19, no. 3 (winter 1994/1995): 167–202.

42. In fact, it is opposed by some nonproliferation analysts principally on these grounds. See, for example, David Fischer, "Some Aspects of a Cut-off Convention" (undated draft paper for United Nations Institute for Disarmament Research, London, spring 1994).

43. For an excellent summary of the history of the CWC and its provisions, see J. P. Perry Robinson, Thomas Stock, and Ronald G. Sutherland, "The Chemical Weapon Convention: The Success of Chemical Disarmament Negotiations," in *SIPRI Yearbook 1993*, 705–732.

44. R. Hooper, "IAEA Development Program for a Strengthened and More Cost-Effective Safeguards System," draft for the Department of Safeguards, IAEA, Vienna, Austria, March 1994.

45. For more details about these export control regimes, see *ATR*, 86–90, and Office of Technology Assessment, *Export Controls and Nonproliferation Policy*, OTA-ISS-596 (Washington, D.C.: Office of Technology Assessment, May 1994).

46. In addition, all state parties to the NPT agree not to transfer nuclear technology or related equipment to any non-nuclear-weapons state unless the latter will accept IAEA safeguards over these materials. Most of the states in the Middle East, except Israel, are parties to the NPT; on the other hand, none are potential suppliers of nuclear technology, again with the exception of Israel.

47. See "Students in Germ Weapons Alert," *The Independent*, London, 16 March 1993, 1; "Security Row over Foreign Scientists," *The Independent*, London, 25 April 1994, 2; and "Universities Act on Fear of Nuclear Proliferation," *The Independent*, London, 22 July 1994, 9.

48. *ATR*, 16; see also Shahram Chubin, "Southern Perspectives on World Order," *The Washington Quarterly*, autumn 1993, 96–97.

49. During the Iran-Iraq War, Iraq bombed two partially-completed, German-built nuclear power reactors at Bushehr in Iran seven times between March 1984 and July 1988, causing heavy damage, and, according to Tehran radio, killing thirteen people. According to an Iraqi defense strategist cited by Leonard Spector, Iraq's primary motivation for these attacks was "to take advantage of the 'cover of war' to thwart Iran's nuclear capabilities, recognizing that once the conflict ended, preventive attacks on the nuclear site would carry far greater political costs and could potentially reignite the war between the two states." See Leonard Spector, *Nuclear Ambitions* (Boulder, Colo.: Westview Press, 1990) 190.

There are several reasons why the Iraqi attacks on the Bushehr reactors did not arouse as much controversy as the Israeli bombing of the Osiraq reactor. In the first place, the "cover of war" *was* effective in blunting international criticism, especially in the United States, where there was little sympathy for the Iranian government in any case. In addition, since the reactors were unfinished and there was no nuclear material on site, the International Atomic Energy Agency had not become involved in applying safeguards. This was in contrast to the situation at Osiraq, where the Israeli attack was widely perceived as a vote of no confidence in the International Atomic Energy Agency safeguards system, and precipitated a heated debate on the efficacy of such safeguards in deterring diversion of nuclear materials in peaceful use to nuclear weapons. In the Arab world especially, the attack on Osiraq was also seen as an example of Israeli arrogance and lack of respect for international norms.

50. Article X permits withdrawal by a party on three months' advance notice "if it decides that extraordinary events, related to the subject matter of this Treaty, have jeopardized the supreme interests of its country."

51. See Michael M. May and Roger D. Speed, "The Role of US Nuclear Weapons in Regional Conflicts" (Livermore, Calif.: Lawrence Livermore National Laboratory, June 1993).

Seth Cropsy, "The Only Credible Nuclear Deterrent," *Foreign Affairs*, March/April 1994, 14–20; and Eric H. Arnett, "Deterrence after Nuclear Proliferation: Implications for Nuclear Forces and Defense Spending," *The Nonproliferation Review*, winter 1994, 10–17.

52. Statement by U.S. secretary of state Cyrus Vance: "US Assurance on Non-Use of Nuclear Weapons, June 12, 1978," in *Documents on Disarmament*, United States Arms Control and Disarmament Agency, Publication #107 (Washington, D.C.: U.S. Government Printing Office, 1978), 384.

53. "Nuclear Weapons: A No-First-Use Doctrine Exists for All Non-Nuclear States," *F.A.S. Public Interest Report*, September/October 1994, 1–2.

54. May and Speed, "The Role of US Nuclear Weapons in Regional Conflicts"; Cropsy, "The Only Credibly Nuclear Deterrent"; and Arnett, "Deterrence after Nuclear Proliferation."

55. For a recent discussion, see Barry M. Blechman and Cathleen S. Fisher, "Phase Out the Bomb," *Foreign Policy*, winter 1994–95, 79–96.

12

SOURCES OF POTENTIAL CONFLICT IN THE PERSIAN GULF: THE WATER FACTOR

Thomas Naff

Even in the earliest sources of antiquity, water was consistently a key factor of security and conflict among the inhabitants of the Euphrates River basin. Hammurabi, in his code of laws, made what was perhaps the first known attempt to set legal rules for the ownership and use of water in order to avoid strife among the basin's polities. Later, very early in the Muslim era (at the battle of Siffin [657 A.D.] on the lower Euphrates, which pitted the fourth caliph Ali against the insurgent Mu'awiyya—a conflict whose outcome changed the course of Islamic history) water played an important strategic role for both sides.[1]

Today water continues to be an issue of serious contention in the Euphrates basin and in other parts of the Persian Gulf region. But the cause of most current tension is not an actual shortage of water. The Euphrates basin does not yet suffer from scarcity—although it looms— except in a few highly localized situations, and southward the states of the Arabian Peninsula have so far been able to produce enough desalinated water to supplement their dwindling groundwater resources, at least for the short term. Rather, potential water-related conflict in the Persian Gulf region lies in an intricate web of problems: maldistribution, mismanagement, poor planning, unsustainable population growth, overexploitation, pollution, serious inadequacies of supply projected for the near future, and the complicated hydropolitics among the Euphrates' riparians—Turkey, Syria, and Iraq—that not only share the river but mutual hostility as well.

Further complicating the picture is Turkey's recently acquired ability to exercise complete control over the Euphrates, 96 percent of which rises in the Anatolian Peninsula and whose total average annual flow is about 30 billion cubic meters (bcm) per year. Ankara demonstrated this power in January 1990 when, for the first time in history, it cut off the entire flow of the river for two months during the first phase of filling the reservoir behind the Ataturk Dam. Despite Turkey's assurances that it would not abuse its superior hydrogeological position, its downstream neighbors remain troubled, especially Iraq, which was acutely aware that during the Gulf War Turkey came under pressure to cut the flow of Euphrates water to force Iraq into quick submission. Nor were the strategic implications of this power lost on Syria.

Compounding Iraq's vulnerability is the extent to which the Turks and Iranians have potential control of the Tigris River as well: over 60 percent of that watercourse, whose annual average flow is about 32–33 bcm, originates in the mountains of eastern Anatolia, while another 10 percent of its source rises in Iran. Both Turkey and Iran clearly possess the capacity to reduce the flow of the Tigris River into Iraq. In these circumstances, without some kind of negotiated agreement with Turkey, Syria, and Iran, Iraq cannot safely rely on utilizing the waters of the Tigris to mitigate anticipated losses from the Euphrates, nor can Syria, in the absence of a firm agreement with Turkey, be assured of its supply of Euphrates water.

Thus far, the aquifers that Iraq shares with Saudi Arabia and Jordan have not been a source of friction but could become so very quickly (Amman has for some years complained informally that the Disi aquifer in southern Jordan, which is shared with Saudi Arabia, is being harmed and diminished on the Jordanian side through overpumping by the Saudis). Should water supplies from the two rivers be decreased significantly, then Iraq will have to exploit all possible groundwater resources as fully as possible. That development could bring competition from those neighbors with whom it shares aquifers, who are themselves already facing imminent water shortages.

The climate of the Arabian Peninsula is for the most part arid to hyperarid. The great bulk of its natural, undesalinated fresh water comes from very limited underground sources—many of which are nonrenewable—with very little more from precipitation in areas of higher elevation. The average annual rainfall for the seven nations of the peninsula is only 81 mm, ranging from a low of 70 mm in Kuwait and Bahrain to 122 mm in Yemen. The average annual rate of evaporation for all the peninsula's countries is 43 times the rate of precipitation.[2]

Relative to its demographic growth rate—plus the pace and patterns of water consumption, certain unsound policies, and the current limits of desalination technology—the Arabian Peninsula may well be at the threshold of chronic shortages that will only grow more acute unless these patterns of usage are altered. Although it will become necessary for those peninsular states who desalinate their water to invest even more in the technology, it will not suffice simply to put more money into desalination in order to solve their water problems (almost 50 percent of the world's total desalination capacity is already centered in the peninsula). For the technology to produce enough additional fresh water fast enough to keep abreast of the increasing demand and to make cost effective the very large investment required, an affordable major scientific breakthrough in desalination processes and engineering would have to occur in the near future. Presently, no such technological advances are projected in the next decade.[3] It is possible that such dramatic progress could be made, but in a highly arid climate, it is an extremely risky gamble to formulate water policies on the basis of anything but current reality. Even if the needed technological advances were made, the lead time it would take to reap their benefits on the required scale would probably be too long to avoid a crisis if present trends of consumption and management are not radically changed.

Except for the Caspian littoral and a few parts of the northwest, all of Iran's 1,650,000 square kilometers of land are semiarid, arid, or extremely arid. Only 5 percent of this area is cultivated, requiring large amounts of water for irrigation. Most of Iran is in a constant process of desertification. Thus, exploitation of its arid lands by dryland farming and other means is of great importance to Iran, particularly since the production of its qanats has been declining steadily.[4]

Toward the end of the 1950s, specialized departments were formed in Iran's Ministry of Agriculture and at Tehran University for the development of programs of watershed management, conservation, and desert research. It was not until 1967 that the country's water resources were nationalized, and this was followed in 1974 by the establishment of a Department of the Environment in the Prime Minister's Office.[5] Iran, which is environmentally similar to Iraq, faces water problems that are on the whole probably a little more serious, though of a different nature.

While Iran is a potentially important player in the hydropolitics of the Persian Gulf, two factors mitigate against including Iran significantly in this analysis. First, the mullahs have tended to neglect Iran's water problems. Iran's hydrological infrastructure, like most of its economic bases, has suffered badly since the revolution, particularly in the wake of the war with Iraq.

In April 1995, domestic water shortages became so severe that thousands of Iranians in Islamshahr, a working-class district south of Tehran, took to the streets to demand adequate supplies of fresh water. The demonstrations grew so large and violent that the Revolutionary Guard was called out to quell them by force, resulting, it was reported, in hundreds of dead and wounded.[6] It would take considerable expenditure to improve the water sector to the point where it could serve the needs of a population that is expected to double by 2010, numbering some 100 million. Given such urgent domestic needs, the deteriorating state of the economy, and the high loss of professional human resources in the war with Iraq, it is unlikely that Iran would choose to initiate a policy of aggressive hydropolitics against Iraq. Iran is not dependent on any Iraqi sources of water, would have no legitimate claims on Iraq's surface waters, and so far as is known, does not share aquifers with Iraq.

But Iraq is dependent to a degree on waters that originate in Iran. For the past few years there has apparently been serious discussion in Tehran about developing the Lesser Zab for irrigation and hydroelectric energy. The Lesser Zab provides 17 percent of the Tigris's flow in Iraq. Should Iran's development plans for the Lesser Zab be fully implemented— depending on Turkish and Syrian activities on the Euphrates and upper Tigris—tensions with Iraq could be engendered by possible reductions in the flow of the Tigris into Iraq. There may be an element of malice toward Iraq in this scheme, but if there is, it must be secondary; plans for hydrologically developing the Lesser Zab preceded the revolution by some years. Otherwise, there is no clear evidence that water has played a significant role in Iran's strategic planning or relations with its Arab neighbors. Reinforcing this conclusion is the fact that during the war with Iraq, Iran made no effort to cut off water from either the Lesser Zab or the Diyala River, which also feeds the Tigris. The second reason for giving Iran only limited attention in this chapter is that it has been not been possible to collect reliable data on hydrological conditions and other water-related issues in Iran since the revolution, making any authoritative statements all but impossible.[7]

Water has become a factor in an interesting security relationship that is evolving between Iran and Qatar, one of Tehran's smaller Arab neighbors. Should Qatar's approach succeed, it might presage a general strategy that could be profitably employed with local adaptations by other smaller peninsular actors who are proximate to Iran. Since early spring of 1994, the Qataris and Iranians have been holding serious talks about the possibility of Iran selling Qatar water from the Karoun (or al-Karun) River, which originates in Iran and flows into the Shatt al-Arab with a flow of 27 bcm—not an insignificant body of water. The water sought by the Qataris would be delivered by means of a pipeline that would serve a dual purpose. It would be run along the southern Iranian littoral deliberately routed through a string of impoverished, water-short villages, and then over into Qatar, thus benefitting needy Iranians and simultaneously providing a source of hard currency from water sales to Qatar. Qatari authorities stress that this water would not be used for such "strategic" purposes as drinking or for industry, which would tie Qatar's water security to Iran. Rather, it would be used to recharge fossil aquifers whose water would then be used for such nonstrategic functions as gardening or recreation.

This is only one of many overtures that Doha, for the sake of its security, has made to Tehran in quest of positive ways to engage its powerful, bellicose neighbor. Qatar prefers cooperation and friendship to confrontation. The underlying assumption of this policy is that given the issues of potential dispute that could erupt between the two neighbors—e.g., possible expansion of Iranian claims to the northern segment of the oil field that lies along the median Qatari-Iranian oil line in the Gulf—the best strategic option is to base relations with Iran on friendship and good neighborliness. Water, a resource even more vital than oil but presently less controversial, is perceived as a positive link. While such a policy is fraught with risks, it is believed to be less dangerous than any other approach that could antagonize the Iranians. Qatar is sensitive to the fact that it has very little sympathetic standing in American or European public opinion and therefore cannot count on being defended by the West from Iranian aggression.[8]

Irrespective of region or conditions, solutions to water problems must always be commensurate with the complex nature of water—that is, solutions must necessarily involve several simultaneous approaches on many linked salients: technological (including biotechnology), economic, managerial (including demand management), political, demographic, educational, and ideological. The parched nations of the Persian Gulf are particularly susceptible to this dictum. With a sharper focus on the major issues of water, security, and conflict in the Persian Gulf region, the picture becomes at once clearer and more troubling. For purposes of analysis, a distinction needs to be made between the hydropolitical situations in Iraq and the Arabian Peninsula. Although the two cannot be disaggregated in geopolitical and strategic terms, their hydrological conditions are sufficiently different to warrant separate treatment.

The Arabian Peninsula

Despite shortages, there is not yet a water crisis either collectively or singly among the nations of the Arabian Peninsula serious enough to create conditions that could erupt in water-related conflict. The problems that exist are more hydropolitical than purely hydrological, but serious nonetheless. There are among all the actors of the Peninsula shortsighted policy and behavioral trends that are moving them in the direction of possible water-based conflict. What makes this situation disturbing is that in the arid climate of the region, where fresh-water supplies receive so little replenishment and consumption is rising so rapidly, crisis conditions could develop very quickly, before effective means for managing them could be mobilized. In those circumstances, water scarcity could combine with other factors to contribute significantly to political and economic dislocations, which could, in turn, lead to state weakness and potential conflict.

Although there are no surface river systems among the nations of the Arabian Peninsula, they are not entirely free from possible transboundary water disputes. Border oases, for example, have a long history of contention, and some states, such as Saudi Arabia, Yemen, Iraq, and the United Arab Emirates, share aquifers. Several countries have in recent years undertaken systematic audits of their water supplies—e.g., Saudi Arabia, Oman, and Qatar. Despite some very good individual national hydrological surveys, there has been no comprehensive, integrated, accurate mapping and analysis of all the peninsula's underground water resources to determine not only quantities, quality, and systemic and hydrogeological interconnections, but how much is renewable or non-renewable (i.e., fossil). These data are essential for effective management, especially demand-management, of water and for determining the safe-yield of groundwater sources. Aquifers are of a certain delicacy. Because the effects of misuse are hydrologically cumulative, aquifers can be seriously harmed or destroyed in a relatively short time, especially in the absence of good data for managing them; most aquifers cannot be recovered once they are ruined.

Consumption Trends Among the GCC Nations

It is apparent from some available data[9] that the nations of the GCC are using up their fresh-water resources at a rate that, if unaltered, will place them on the precipice of a very serious crisis within a generation. For instance, Qatar's groundwater reserves are under extreme pressure because of overexploitation: withdrawals of water exceed by five times the natural annual recharge of the aquifers. Between 1972 and 1993 Qatar accumulated a water deficit of about 850 million cubic meters (mcm), which amounts to one-third its total estimated supply. Water levels have been dropping between 0.05–1.0 meters each year, with a commensurate rise in salinity and deterioration of quality. Given Qatar's climate, geology, and environment, such depletion rates are simply unsustainable. Unsalinated Saudi groundwater reserves are estimated to be between 300 and 500 bcm. This estimate is almost certainly too high, as the Saudi kingdom is known to have increased its consumption of water for agriculture alone more than tenfold in the past fifteen years.[10] The aquifers underlying the Khuff Formation in central Saudi Arabia have been drawn down by about 14 meters in the last 15 years.

In 1965, inhabitants of the GCC states used water for domestic purposes at the rate of 165 litres per capita per day (lcd). In the decade of the 1980s, that figure increased to 300 lcd and presently stands at 400 lcd, a rate of consumption comparable to Israel's and some smaller industrialized states of Europe who have exponentially more water. By far, the largest consumer of water for all the peninsular countries is the agricultural sector, which was collectively using some 3.1 bcm/yr in 1980. That rate is projected to rise by the year 2000 to 24.8 bcm/yr. The largest single country increase for the same period will occur in Saudi Arabia, where the agricultural sector's share of water will surge from 1.8 bcm/yr in 1980 to 20 bcm/yr by the turn of the century. Bahrain's consumption in the same period will have almost doubled, from 70 mcm/yr to 130 mcm/yr, while Qatar's will have quadrupled, from 40 mcm/yr to 160 mcm/yr. The projected total water requirements of the peninsula in the year 2000 are expected to be 31.6 bcm rising to 35.4 bcm by 2010. Of those amounts, agriculture is expected to consume 27 bcm in 2000 and 29 bcm in 2010, leaving only 4.5 bcm and 6 bcm respectively for all other purposes. Compounding these figures is the fact that between 25 percent and 30 percent of water used in GCC agriculture is lost every year to waste and inefficiency.[11]

Such consumption trends make it easier to understand why desalination alone, particularly in light of present technical limitations, cannot within the foreseeable future solve the peninsula's looming water scarcity problems. Underlying this situation like a grumbling volcano is the collective rate of population growth among the GCC nations, one of the highest in the world. Between 1970 and 1990, the total peninsular population increased from 18 million to 31 million.[12] At an overall average growth of 3.6 percent per annum, the current number of inhabitants of the peninsula will double in about 25 years. This is a region, it should be recalled, that is already the largest importer of food per capita on earth.

Water and Oil

In nature, water and oil are geomorphologically closely affiliated; technologically, water plays a key role in the production of oil. This relationship raises a weighty question: Do these natural and technological connections mean that the shortage of fresh water in the Persian Gulf area and the growing demand on it for human consumption ultimately constitute a serious limitation on the continued high level of oil production, with the obvious concomitant socioeconomic and political implications? If the comprehensive role of water in oil production is taken at face value, the short answer would be an apparent yes; closer scrutiny of the facts, however, yields a more complicated no. Oil and water, as we shall see, do (metaphorically) mix in the Middle East.

The production of oil, and all other forms of energy from fossil fuels and nuclear power, requires the use of relatively substantial amounts of water—preferably, but not always necessarily, fresh water. Reciprocally, the movement of water necessitates the expenditure of significant quantities of energy in the form of oil or gas. Israel, for example, uses about one-fifth of its total national energy supply just to move water. While the oil resources among the GCC countries are collectively huge, they are finite and unevenly distributed. More to the point, their water resources are only a fraction of their petroleum-based energy supply, which, considering the role of water in oil production, gives the appearance of being a limiting factor in the production of that vital commodity.

Water is necessary for almost all of the processes of oil production—for the exploration and drilling of oil and gas (which requires far less water than oil) and, for the extraction of oil, including drilling, flooding, and treatment. For example, in the United States, where oil reserves are all but exhausted and wells need to be flooded or injected with water to build enough pressure to pump up the remaining oil, the production of 500 million tonnes of oil per year requires about 45 mcm of water—that is more than three times the useful water available from the Jordan River.[13] A by-product of oil production is saline water, which is brought up simultaneously with the oil and must somehow be eliminated safely. Ways for pumping oil out of nearly used-up or low-pressure wells have had to be devised. The most common techniques for secondary and tertiary recovery of residues involve a significant input of water by flooding under pressure or the injection of steam. Most of the water used for the various means of producing oil is completely consumed or is unusable for other purposes. Once the oil is extracted, its refinement entails large volumes of water too, 96 percent of which is entirely used up. The generation of energy by the burning of oil or gas (or the production of nuclear power) also involves large amounts of water for cooling purposes.[14]

Given the essential role water plays in the extraction and refinement of oil, it would seem that the continued high rate of exploitation and production of the region's enormous oil reserves (Saudi Arabia alone pumps eight million barrels a day) could simply overwhelm the Gulf's meager water supplies, or, the very slightness of the latter vital resource could severely limit the production of oil. Either way the result would be water-based problems that could cause conflict, most probably if combined with other destablizing issues. However, that scenario is very unlikely to occur.

Generally speaking, it takes a barrel of water to produce a barrel of oil.[15] However, because each reservoir has its own peculiarities, each has its own water-to-oil ratio. Moreover, if a faster rate of production is desired, then the ratio changes to more water per barrel of oil, whatever the features of the reservoir. In most of the Middle East, especially the Persian Gulf region (except for the Neutral Zone between Saudi Arabia and Kuwait), oil is free flowing. That is, there is enough natural hydrogeological pressure to keep the oil flowing once it is tapped, obviating the need for constant insertions of water at each well or field. There is so much oil that the draw-down rate to the point of requiring water is not inordinately high. But the rate of production is high enough to require the injection of water around the edges of the fields to keep the wells free flowing. In Saudi Arabia if an oil well produces fewer than 5,000 barrels per day, it is shut down to preserve the pressure.

Oil in the Persian Gulf region was originally formed in an environment of water. It is found in the same rocks that also captured water. In fact, most of the oil in the region is of that type; it is underlaid by huge reservoirs of very deep, highly saline water that provides much of the pressure that makes the oil free flowing. The Wassiyya aquifer that underlies eastern Saudi Arabia, Kuwait, and Iraq is estimated to be over 4,000 feet deep and to contain between 800 bcm and 1,600 bcm (or five to ten trillion barrels) of very saline water. At its shallowest end as it approaches Riyadh in the west, it gradually becomes fresh water, only a small fraction of the total.

Fresh water is preferred for use in oil operations. However, salt water will perform the same function in drilling, though the resulting saline muddy slush must be disposed of, which adds to the cost. Water is used in this function to enable the drill to move faster and to make it easier to pull the drill up. When an oil field is drilled without the use of water, the usual average yield is about 25 percent of the actual supply in the rock. The gas that is produced with the oil can be compressed and reinjected to increase the yield, but it is not as effective or as cheap as water, which produces a 30 to 35 percent recovery rate. Because saline water from sea or ground sources can be used in the drilling and pumping stages of oil production, water is therefore not a limiting but rather an efficiency and cost factor. In other stages of refinement, modification, and transformation into other products, it is mostly fresh water that is needed—some of which can be reused—but not as yet in such great quantities as to be a limitation. Enough desalinated water is presently being produced to satisfy the fresh water needs of industries in the peninsula associated with oil without cost to the other economic sectors. That situation is expected to continue without serious problems in the short term.

Other Persistent Factors of Potential Conflict

Nevertheless, a superordinate reality remains: The fresh water reserves of the peninsula are being consumed at a faster rate than they can presently be replenished. Those peninsular nations presently desalinating water have been driven by need to increase production significantly within the next decade. For example, Saudi Arabia, which desalinates the most water at 800 million gallons a day, plans to lift the daily volume to one billion gallons over the next five to ten years. Unless there is a significant breakthrough in purification technology soon, however, even the oil-rich nations of the Gulf, which have the necessary cash and surplus energy, cannot rely on desalination alone to keep abreast of their projected water demand in the short run, and perhaps into the intermediate future.

Salinated and desalinated water can probably provide the oil industry with its needs, but for the other economic sectors, the prognosis is less certain owing to several factors already adumbrated: foremost, a population growth rate unsustainable in relation to rising demand for decreasing supplies of water, unacceptable levels of inefficiency and waste, and defective planning and policy decisions. The persistence of these circumstances could rapidly create destablizing, conflict-prone hydropolitical conditions. Any significant domestic conflict in any of the key actors in the peninsula could have large regional and international repercussions.

An obvious prerequisite for conflict avoidance in those circumstances is far better planning and management of water resources. The problem lies not so much with the technocrats as with the decision makers. Unnecessarily (some critics say wantonly) wasteful policies continue in the face of alarming shortages. Some actors in the peninsula persist in water mining—i.e. withdrawals from a depletable, nonrenewable reserve of water such as a fossil aquifer. This practice is often carried on in order to grow water-guzzling, highly subsidized crops in the hopeless pursuit of food security, Bedouin demands, or worse, to demonstrate for reasons of prestige that despite the aridity of their environment, governments can export agriculture—paying no heed to the fact that the export of agriculture is tantamount to the export of water. As one expert has argued, ". . . crops produced with mined water contribute to a false sense of food security, since the harvest cannot be sustained over the long term."[16] That same wheat grown in certain parts of the peninsula can be purchased from abroad for one-tenth its price in subsidies and water. There is not a single peninsular nation (with perhaps the exception of Yemen) that cannot afford to import all of its agricultural needs at far lower cost in money, water, and energy than its own irrigated food crops.

Saudi Arabia is a good example. Three-quarters of Saudi Arabia's water supply sits in groundwater reserves, most of which are fossil. Saudis have been pumping that water at a rate more than five times the estimated recharge. By 2010, the nation's aquifers are projected to hold 42 percent less water than they did in 1985.[17] Some of that water is used for oil-related purposes, but large quantities are drawn for growing irrigated crops like wheat, which is then subsidized and exported. Saudi Arabia, it is reported, continues to use vital water reserves in a hopeless endeavor to become self-sufficient in certain food types. The only way that could be done even on a relatively small scale (and for the short term only) is through intensive irrigation at great cost to the nation's very limited supplies of water and with very high subsidies to the farmers.

For climatic reasons, Saudi Arabia will always be dependent on food imports, which will perforce grow steadily as the population increases. (Reports from the Saudi Kingdom indicate that water policies are being reassessed with a view to greater conservation and efficiency.) As stated, the nations of the Gulf region already import more food proportionately per capita than any other part of the world. Climate and hydrogeology dictate that the nations of the Arabian Peninsula cannot simultaneously carry on irrigated agriculture on any significant scale and oil production with its related industries for very long without ruining their vital water resources. The consequences would be unbearable.

But these problems are not without possible solutions. The most difficult and longest term approaches would be to stabilize population growth at sustainable levels, cease irrigated agriculture except in those very few areas where renewable water resources can be sufficiently recharged, invest heavily in water technology (including purification and conservation technology), and improve water planning and management, including a shift to demand management. There are indications that progress along these lines is in the making. Demand management is receiving serious attention among policy makers, more water experts are being trained, and their advice is being heeded more often. Conservation measures have begun, as in the United Arab Emirates, where a series of water harvesting dams was built with a total storage capacity of some 70 mm to supplement the recharge of groundwater aquifers that receive an inadequate 120 mcm of annual rainfall. Water supplies and quality are being more closely monitored. The public is being educated (with varying degrees of effort) about the need for conservation. The recycling of waste water is being studied, and members of the Gulf Cooperation Council (GCC) are calling for cooperative endeavors in attacking the peninsula's water problems.[18] Various proposed alternative sources of water and technological solutions are also receiving consideration.

Other than desalination, the most prominent among the bruited technological solutions to the peninsula's water problems is water importation. Proposals range from icebergs towed from the antarctic to "medusa bags" (huge nylon or polyester bags capable of carrying hundreds of thousands of cubic meters of water towed by ocean-going tugs) to long-range pipelines. While it is hypothetically possible to tow an iceberg from Antarctica to, say, Saudi Arabia, it would have to be of enormous dimensions for a sufficient portion of it to survive the trip to be useful. But because of its immensity and the consequent slowness of its movement, it would have to circumnavigate the lower latitudes of the Earth about four times to escape the strong ocean currents of that region, leaving very little of its original volume by the time it reaches its destination. Medusa bags, on the other hand, are a practical possibility—they would not constitute a solution per se, but could provide an important marginal supply of fresh water especially in emergency situations. Presently, successful experiments have been conducted with bags that hold about a quarter of a million cubic meters of water. These bags are still too small to be cost effective, but there are bags with a 1.5–2 mcm capacity in the planning stages. They can be used in conjunction with pipelines. It has been calculated that medusa bags would cost more than one-third less for the transport of water than using converted oil tankers.[19]

The most publicized proposal for water transfer is the "Peace Pipeline," vigorously promoted by the late Turkish prime minister, Turgut Özal in the 1980s.[20] The original proposal called for the construction of dual 1,600-mile pipelines. These pipes would carry fresh commercial water from two rivers in Turkey, the Seyhan and Ceyhan, presumed to have some 16 mcm surplus per day that flows into the Mediterranean. The delivery of this water would be intended as a supplementary rather than a primary source. The "western" conduit would deliver water to Syria, Jordan, and the western coast of Saudi Arabia, while the "Gulf" pipeline would provide water to Kuwait, Qatar, Bahrain, the United Arab Emirates, and Oman. Preliminary feasibility studies paid for by Turkey were completed in 1987; on the basis of those studies, Turkey received, in 1989, $1.9 billion in loans from the United States and Britain to complete the necessary studies preparatory to building the pipeline. The final plans produced an estimated cost of about $13 billion for the Persian Gulf pipeline and about $9 billion for the western pipeline, with a completion time of about a decade. The pipes would be buried two meters below the ground except for mountainous stretches, where they would be run through tunnels.

The proposal has not yet advanced beyond the planning and discussion phase and is, in fact, dormant. The reasons for its dormancy are not technical—in that respect, the project is quite feasible—rather they stem from a combination of security and economic considerations. The chief constituents of the main target, the Gulf nations, have not bought into the plan, nor have other key actors such a Syria. All fear dependency on Turkish water and all believe the pipeline would be easily susceptible to sabotage and the cost of the water would be very high. The countries through whose territories the pipelines must pass, especially Syria, have not responded enthusiastically. Because the negotiations required must involve so many actors, these states believe the discussions will be complex, long, and difficult with no assurance of success. Another serious potential problem that acts as a brake on the project is the belief that Turkey's own increasing water needs over the next half century will require the use of all of its water resources, leaving no surplus for the pipelines.[21] Although quiescent for the present, the idea has not yet been rejected outright by the Persian Gulf states, and in conditions of extreme shortage, could be revived. Moreover, such states as Saudi Arabia and Kuwait could use a piped supply to recharge some of their fossil aquifers annually to create a strategic reserve of water.

Prognosis for Water Conflict in the Peninsula

In sum, under the prevailing hydrological and political circumstances among the states of the Arabian Peninsula, it is unlikely that water, in and of itself, will be the source of acute international conflict in the near future, although the longer term is less assured. Several influences combine to reduce the probability that a single factor—even one as significant as water scarcity—will precipitate serious conflict in the short run. Such influences include the existence of the GCC, which serves as a matrix for common policy among the most important peninsular actors; the friendly relations among most of the peninsular states; the strategic and economic importance of their collective oil reserves to themselves and to the rest of the industrialized world; their shared fear of the military and ideological designs of Iraq and Iran; and their collective wealth, which will allow at least a marginal increase of supplies from desalination. In addition, policy makers are, incipiently, taking a more rational view of their nations' water problems, which is beginning to translate into positive actions.

But it should be stressed that the states of the Arabian Peninsula are not altogether immune from water-related conflict, particularly of the domestic genre. Given the demographic growth rates in the peninsula, increasing water scarcity, if unmitigated, could be a cause of domestic economic, social, or political destablization. This is true especially if water shortage combines with other factors of conflict, which often occurs in arid regions. The repercussions of water-related conflict could quickly become international. For example, assume hypothetically that a major oil producer—e.g., Saudi Arabia—suffers a severe, prolonged water shortage in combination with serious civil unrest stemming from the agitations of a radical religiopolitical group, or from poor leadership. Each causal factor of unrest, including water, would tend to intensify reciprocally all of the other factors of potential conflict, and the probability of strife would rise accordingly.

The Euphrates Basin

There exist many historical, hydropolitical, and ideological reasons for conflict among the riparians of the Euphrates basin where the consequent possibilities of dissension are much higher. Animosity and mistrust have tainted Turkish-Syrian relations since June 1939, when Turkey, with French collusion, annexed the Syrian district of Alexandretta, renaming it Hatay. On the other hand, Turkish-Iraqi relations have been largely cordial since the establishment of the Turkish Republic, even though Turkey cooperated with the UN coalition in the Gulf War of 1990. The Turks are anxious, for economic reasons, to reestablish good relations with Iraq. Between Iraq and Syria, there is a deep ideological divide that appears to be unbridgeable so long as presidents Hafiz al-Assad and Saddam Hussein remain ensconced as heads of their respective regimes. The chasm was created by several forces: a power rivalry between the two presidents, each perceiving himself and his nation as the natural leader of the Arab world and, until recently, the most uncompromising anti-Israeli rejectionist; an angry ideological split between the Syrian and Iraqi branches of the Baath Party; and, not least, by a personal contempt and hatred that each leader harbors toward the other. However, in arid lands, water is a superordinate interest and has often overridden many divisions between neighbors for the sake of survival. As will be evidenced shortly, Syria and Iraq for precisely this reason have held technical talks—albeit infrequently—about sharing water and even discussed specifics of allocating the Euphrates' flow after it leaves Turkey.

But there is one significant common ground on which Iraq and Syria stand—that is, their mutual concern over whether there will be sufficient flow in the Euphrates to satisfy their long-term needs when Turkey fully implements the Greater Anatolia Project (GAP). As indicated, about 96 percent of the flow of the Euphrates rises in Turkey and about 65 percent of the waters of the Tigris originate there as well. GAP encompasses both river basins, though, because of insufficient finances, work has been undertaken only on the Euphrates. When completed and fully operational, the projected cost of GAP will have been upward of $32 billion (up from earlier estimates of $20 to $24 billion), and the project is expected to account for 22 percent of Turkey's total hydroelectric energy production and 19 percent of the country's irrigable land (about 1,500,000 new hectares).[22] It is clearly a huge undertaking that will consume enormous amounts of water. Furthermore, unless Turkey is persuaded to clean up the water it sends downstream, Syria and Iraq will have to contend with water polluted by salts and chemical residues from fertilizers and insecticides carried back to the main river channel by return flows from the massive irrigation involved.

Although Syria and Iraq share common concerns, the field is not level. Syria is an upper riparian to Iraq. Some reputable analysts (e.g., Kolars) have estimated that once GAP is completely implemented on the Euphrates, Syria could lose about 40 percent of its supply of Euphrates water, and Iraq as much as 70 percent. Unlike Iraq, Syria does not have the current advantage of Tigris waters flowing over its territory and thus depends more heavily on the Euphrates. But if and when Turkey develops the Tigris on its side of the border—and if Iran decides to use more of the feeder streams that supply the Tigris after it leaves Turkey—Iraq could face a hydrological crisis of very large dimensions, losing up to 75 percent to 80 percent of its supply from surface waters. Furthermore, Iraq's demographic growth rate will double its population within about 25 years (so will that of Syria), and Iraq does not have a considerable sea coast from which to derive any substantial amounts of desalinated water.

It is improbable that Iraq's groundwater sources could make up enough of the prospective losses from surface flows to allow Iraq to avert a crisis—should those losses transpire. What is presently known about Iraq's aquifers—most of which have been located but are incompletely mapped, unevaluated, and known to be fossil—indicates that groundwater could supply no more than 30 to 40 percent of Iraq's needs. This would still leave a 60- to 70-percent potential shortfall in total supply, even when reckoned only on the basis of usage projected for the next decade. The shortfall could be larger, depending on population growth and whether Iraq adequately improves management and usage efficiency and conservation. (These conservative estimates are subject to error, because it has not been possible at this stage to determine the safe yields of most of the aquifers.)

There are other serious deficiencies in the groundwaters of Iraq that limit their usefulness. They lie very deep and are generally of poor quality; they are very brackish and would require desalination. The necessary technology for extraction and purification would require considerable on-going expenditures. In addition, most of Iraq's soil is of such poor quality that the cost of drainage and reclamation to leech out the salts would be another persistent high expenditure of money and water. Because of the poor grade of Iraq's soil, great amounts of irrigation water are needed to grow crops. Thus, farming such land would require continuing water and agricultural subsidies to farmers to make the cost of the food produced affordable.

There is a certain historical irony in the present situation. Iraq was rich in soil, irrigation, canals, and agricultural production, as late as the 1950s. At times in this century, Iraq was producing enough food—especially wheat and rice—to feed a population of some 35 million people. But the effects of long-term natural changes in the river channels, soil erosion, and salination of irrigated land has caused a steady reduction in per capita agricultural production in Iraq. Since 1958, Iraq has changed from being mainly an agricultural nation that exported wheat, rice, and other foodstuffs to being an oil-producing, semi-industrial country that imports most of it food. Neglect of proper drainage and irrigation practices, worsened by the migration of farmers to the oil fields and cities, led to increased salinity of the soil. The problems of poor-quality water and soil have been compounded by the government's policy of making agriculture and water a matter of military security. Between 1974 and 1984, public investment in the water sector was 15 percent of the agriculture budget; in the decade between 1980 and 1990, that investment dropped to 5 percent when 85 percent of the agricultural budget was transferred to the military sector, reflecting Saddam Hussein's aggressive policies toward Iran and Kuwait.

Some steps have been taken to mitigate these conditions through the construction of irrigation projects equipped with controlled intakes, concrete canals, sluice gates, syphons, and a network of drainage pipes and canals laid down as preventive measures against the further salinization of the soil. The entire drainage network is connected to a single main drain canal that runs between the two rivers for the collection of irrigation wastes that are discharged into the Gulf.[23] But as important and impressive as these technical improvements are, they have been applied to only a small part of the agricultural sector; they will amount to little more than stop-gap measures unless they are introduced nationwide. Presently, most of the nation's irrigation system remains in unsatisfactory condition: water withdrawal is uncontrolled; the distribution system, structures, and canals are inefficient and insufficient; field drainage facilities are lacking; and field irrigation is poorly executed. Endemic water-quality problems have already been exacerbated by the economic embargo imposed on Iraq after the Gulf War, which has caused a severe shortage of chemicals needed for water treatment. This situation has affected the safety of the drinking-water supply, which has produced concomitant health problems. Most importantly, the larger underlying issue of basinwide cooperation on allocation and usage must be successfully engaged if there is to be sufficient water for drinking, industry, and the maintenance of a significant agricultural sector.

An added political and security complication for Baghdad is the fact that most of the Tigris watershed inside Iraq lies entirely within Kurdistan, the northern area where there is presently an autonomous Kurdish area under UN protection. In the unlikely event there were to be a permanent autonomous or independent Kurdish entity established in the north, Iraq's water supply from the Tigris would be vulnerable to manipulation by the Kurds. Ironically, the Iraqis themselves demonstrated the strategic uses of water in that area by using it as a weapon against the Kurds. Baghdad deliberately located most of Iraq's small dams in the Kurdish north to create a barrier of water to prevent Kurdish rebels from advancing southward against Iraqi forces during anti-Kurdish operations. Before the Gulf War, there were plans for constructing a cascade of 13 dams on the Rawandoz River for just that objective.[24]

If the worst-case scenario of a 70- to 80-percent loss of total water supply were to occur, among the most serious consequences would be a decline in Iraq's ability to produce oil and a loss of the authorities' capacity to deliver vital public services. Unlike the oil producers of the GCC, Iraq does not have a long sea coast where large quantities of water could be desalinated or pumped for use in oil production. Were Iraq to lose that much water, or even 50 to 60 percent (which is quite possible), in a relatively short time span, the socioeconomic and political impact would be devastating. In those circumstances, Iraq would become vulnerable to a mixture of destablizing security hazards: domestic political and sectarian factionalism, civil strife, or dismemberment by civil war or by aggressive neighbors. Alternatively, depending on the nature of Iraq's leadership and other local regional relationships, Iraq could again become aggressive toward its Arab neighbors north or south with the object of gaining more of the flow of the Euphrates and Tigris Rivers or acquiring a longer sea front for the purpose of increasing the supply of water for desalination. If hostilities over water were to develop, the conflict would be international. Moreover, if the cause were presented as water deprivation, the Iraqi public (judging by the results of interviews conducted by the author) would most probably view the issue as a national, patriotic war and give its full support. However, water is infrequently the sole cause of large-scale conflict, rather it is almost always an important element in a combination of factors that contribute to the conflict.

Although it is possible for these conditions to develop fairly quickly from a combination of factors such as prolonged drought (which occurs relatively often in the area), together with resource mismanagement and failure among the basin riparians to arrive at cooperative arrangements for equitable apportionment, the present situation affords all the basin actors time to avert a crisis if there is a will to do so. This window of opportunity exists because the prospects that Turkey will acquire the financing necessary for completing all the stages of GAP within the foreseeable future are dim. The bases for a successful negotiation are in place, albeit dormant. Much depends on how water plays out in the foreign relations of the Euphrates basin riparians, most particularly in our case, the hydropolitics of Iraq.

International Dimensions of Iraqi Water Problems

Because Iraq's two main rivers both originate outside its boundaries, water for Iraq is an important strategic and international issue involving Turkey and Syria on the Euphrates, Turkey and Iran on the Tigris, and Iran over the Shatt al-Arab, although the last is more of a boundary than a water issue. The aquifers that Iraq shares with Saudi Arabia and Jordan have not as yet caused friction (the flow of these aquifers is northwest to northeast, thus favoring Iraq). Reinforcing the perception of Iraqi authorities that water is an issue of paramount importance in foreign relations is their awareness that the nation's oil resources will be eventually depleted or that other cheaper, more secure energy sources will be developed as substitutes, but that there is no alternative to water for domestic and agricultural use.[25]

Despite the absence of formal international apportionment and usage agreements among the riparians of the Euphrates and Tigris Rivers, they have yet to resort to military action over water, though in a few instances hostilities have been only narrowly averted. The chief reasons for the successful avoidance of violent conflict have been that none of the principals involved has wanted a war over their shared water supplies; Turkey has been a member of NATO, which meant that an attack on Turkey could involve NATO forces; and, since the Gulf War, the military balance of power has shifted decisively to Turkey (which, of course, is still a member of NATO). The dispute between Iraq and Iran over the Shatt al-Arab has been rooted not in water supply but in control and right of use. Over the past century, there have been several negotiations about the Shatt al-Arab, but in most cases the agreements reached have been unilaterally abrogated by one side or the other. The last accord was reached in 1975 when Iraq agreed to cede half of the Shatt to Iran if the latter would cease its support of the Iraqi Kurds. Saddam Hussein disavowed the agreement when he invaded Iran. After 1979, the issue was not discussed until 1990, when Saddam Hussein gave up his claim to sole control as a concession to get a quick settlement from Iran in order to free up troops for use against the United States and its allies in Kuwait.

The absence of enduring agreements is not due to the failure of the parties to negotiate. Considering the record of animosity among the three riparians, there have been a surprising number of exchanges aimed at developing at least an interim working arrangement during the last thirty years. Negotiations over that time have produced bilateral agreements between Turkey and Iraq and between Iraq and Syria and a Joint Technical Regional Rivers Committee, but as yet no tripartite treaty for equitable sharing. The Turkish-Iraqi accord is an annex to their 1946 Treaty of Friendship and Good Neighbourly Relations and governed the flow regulations of the Euphrates and Tigris Rivers. The annex concerning the Euphrates amounted to little more than a statement of good intentions, because without the participation of Syria, nothing of import could be accomplished. In April 1990, before the Iraqi invasion of Kuwait, Iraq and Syria are reported to have negotiated a tentative apportionment arrangement for Euphrates water. The agreement would give Syria 42 percent and Iraq 52 percent of the flow downstream of Turkey, and would establish a joint technical committee to resolve details of the monthly division of water. If such an accord formally exists, it has obviously been set aside for the time being, although there is no evidence that either party has discarded the agreement since the Gulf War. In 1983, Syria accepted an invitation to participate in the Joint Technical Committee that was formed by Turkey and Iraq in 1980, turning it into the only trilateral body where common water problems are discussed by representatives of all three riparians.[26] But since the trilateral committee's first meeting in November 1983, it has met only sporadically with few productive results. The representatives have been given only restricted authority to agree to anything beyond technical matters—for example, the Iraqi delegate, who had the least amount of authority, never held a rank higher than that of a director-general.[27]

Neither Iraq nor Syria has resorted to litigation under international riparian law as a means of insuring its fair share of water. While they have not gone to court, they have buttressed their claims with a combination of judicial principles that include those of no significant harm, equitable utilization (rational sharing based on real need, economic development, size of population, etc.), and historical or prior use. For their part, the Turks have adopted the legal stance assumed by most upper riparians—absolute sovereignty over all resources within their borders. That is, Turkey asserts the right to do or not to do whatever it pleases with waters originating in its territory. Turkey has paid a serious price for its reticence to adhere to the established law that obliges nations that undertake activities harmful to other riparians to notify and consult with them prior to initiating such projects. The World Bank has rejected Turkey's requests for GAP loans because of its rule, based on that law, that where development of water resources could affect other users, all the concerned parties must agree to the loan. Thus Syria has successfully blocked Turkey's loan application for years and has made it more difficult for Turkey to obtain capital from other sources. Ankara has been effective in finding alternative resources, but now the failure to obtain large loans from either the World Bank or others in the current restricted international financial market has significantly slowed progress on GAP. An unintended salutary consequence has been the creation of more lead-time for negotiating an apportionment agreement.

Iraq and Syria recognize that because Turkey has invested so much political and financial capital in GAP—which, if successful, would transform the economy of Turkey with commensurate social and political rewards—Ankara cannot be expected either to retreat or make significant changes in its determination to carry through on GAP. They have, accordingly, focused their efforts on the quantity and quality of water sent down from Turkey. The natural flow of the Euphrates River is estimated to be over 900 cubic meters per second (cm/s). The long-term adjusted rate is somewhat less than that figure, about 750–800 cm/s. But because the river's flow varies so much from year to year, and even within seasons of a single year, it has been possible for each party to argue with some justification for its own calculations of the rate. Turkey has guaranteed a minimum flow of 500 cm/s to Syria and Iraq, which in turn have rejected that figure as inadequate, countering with a demand of at least 700 cm/s. This occurred most recently at a ministerial-level meeting in June 1990.

At the same time, Turkish authorities have made strenuous efforts to reassure their riparian neighbors that Turkey would not use water as an instrument of coercion or as a strategic weapon against Iraq and Syria. In 1989, however, then-prime minister Turgut Özal threatened to cut off the Euphrates if Syria and Iraq did not stop the aid he accused them of giving to the Kurdish Workers' Party (PKK) insurgents. Likewise in 1990, the Turkish Minister of State, Kamran Inan, was reported to have stated that Turkey was under no obligation to conform to international stipulations regarding the Euphrates and Tigris Rivers.[28] On the other hand, Turkey has fairly consistently fulfilled its pledge to send down 500 cm/s and during the Gulf War resisted all suggestions that it cut off the Euphrates to force Iraq into submission.

The Prospects for Water-Related Conflict in the Persian Gulf

It would appear that factors of scarcity, security, and conflict combine to produce a higher probability of water-related strife for Iraq and the other riparians in the Euphrates-Tigris basins than do the same factors operating in the Arabian Peninsula. In Iraq, Saddam Hussein's leadership and the effects of the Gulf War are additional destabilizing factors. Warfare and other types of acute conflict among the Euphrates and Tigris basin actors, however, are unlikely in the foreseeable future, if for no other reason than Iraq is debilitated from the Gulf War. Domestic conflict, in which water plays a supporting role to other causes, is a more likely scenario.

Essential to Iraq's economic recovery and stability is the improvement of its water infrastructure, the introduction of advanced water technology, a program of strict conservation, and efficient water management, all of which will require an infusion of foreign capital. Iraq's international credit status was destroyed by the Gulf War but should recover slowly once the economic embargo is lifted and oil sales resume. But financial and technical support from abroad will continue to be difficult for some time owing to prevailing conditions of political and economic instability, Iraq's refusal to provide information necessary to obtain help from the World Bank, and the shrinkage of the international financial market. This situation will have to improve relatively quickly if Iraq is to position itself to avoid the real possibility of a water crisis.

GAP does pose a threat to Iraq and Syria; but since mutual animosity has inhibited cooperation in persuading Turkey to agree to a firm, long-term commitment on an adequate amount of water to be released downstream, each has responded differently to the perceived menace. Syria, the more hostile, has done all it can to block access to financial assistance for GAP, while Iraq, hoping to capitalize on traditional friendship with Turkey, has offered oil and hydroelectric power from its northern dams as part of a negotiated settlement.[29] But little in the way of a sustainable, long-term settlement on apportionment and usage can be accomplished without the full engagement of all three parties in the negotiating process and agreement on the final arrangements. That is unlikely to happen in the short term unless Saddam Hussein is removed or Iraq is able to undertake a full-scale recovery program. Then, because water is such an overriding issue for both Iraq and Syria (and because Hafiz al-Assad is nothing if not a pragmatist), even with Saddam Hussein in office, Syria and Iraq might be able to act in concert if such cooperation appears to promise concessions from Turkey or can avert a serious water crisis.

The most likely short-term scenario for the Euphrates basin is that little progress will be made toward a negotiated settlement as long as Saddam Hussein remains in power and the situation created by the aftermath of the Gulf War continues. The situation will fester until sustained, sharp shortages are experienced downstream, at which time tensions could erupt dramatically and lead to a regional (and therefore international) crisis. In the meantime, water issues compound other factors that promote domestic conflict in Iraq, intensifying and broadening their impact and contributing to internal instability.

Water crises and conflict are avoidable in the Euphrates basin, and water security is achievable. Scarcity as a determinant of possible conflict in the basin stems not from a dearth of water, but from maldistribution and mismanagement of that water. Though the effects of maldistribution are little different from real shortage, the former type of problem yields to solutions more readily. Despite poor distribution, there is enough water in the Euphrates and Tigris Rivers for all users, provided that there is cooperation in its management, preferably a single, representative, basinwide body with sufficient authority, expertise, and funds to oversee allocation and usage and provided that efficiency and conservation are practiced in all water activities and that the demographic growth rate is aligned with the limits of the water resources. These are very difficult goals to achieve in the best of circumstances but almost impossible without political stability and harmony among the concerned riparians. Nevertheless, they must somehow be attained if conflict is to be avoided.

Notes

1. E. de Vaumas, "Le contrôle et l'utilization des eaux du Tigre et de l'Euphrate," *Revue de Géographique Alpine* 46 (1958): 235–55; J.B. Pritchard, ed., *Ancient Near Eastern Texts Relating to the Old Testament*, 3rd ed. (Princeton: Princeton University Press, 1969), 168; on Siffin: Al-Ya^{c}qubi, Tarikh al-Ya^{c}qubi, 2 vols., (Beirut: Dar Sadir, 1977), vol. II, 187–88.

2. Jamil Al-Alawi and Mohammad Abdulrazzak, "Water in the Arabian Peninsula: Problems and Prospects," in P. Rogers and P. Lydon, *Water in the Arab World* (Cambridge: Harvard University Press, 1994), 176–178.

3. John Keenan, *The Potential and Limitation of Water Technology*, AMER Middle East Water Reports, Parts I and II, Philadelphia, (1986, 1989).

4. A qanat is an underground channel by which water is brought from various sources by means of gravity flow to where it is needed for irrigation. A qanat is built and maintained by a series of wells that give access to the channel every 10 to 50 meters along its course. Qanats take years, sometimes generations, to construct and require considerable, long-term investment.

5. Department of the Environment, Office of the Prime Minister, Case Study on Desertification in Iran: Turan, Tehran, May 1977, 97 pp.

6. *Washington Times*, 5 April 1995, A13.

7. The author has just become aware of a statistical abstract of Iran published in Tehran in 1992 and of a report that the Iranian authorities have published a recent volume on water in Iran. He has not been able to locate copies as of this writing. Depending on the contents of these two volumes, the statement concerning sources might have to be altered.

8. Information on the Qatari-Iranian water talks and their context were provided in a personal communication by Dr. John Duke Anthony, president of the National Council on U.S.-Arab Relations, based on recent discussions Dr. Anthony had with the foreign minister of Qatar. The author wishes to thank Dr. Anthony for sharing his information and insights.

9. Some of the data used in this section are drawn from summaries of unpublished papers delivered at the second Gulf Water Conference (hereafter Gulf Water II), whose theme was "Water in the Gulf: Towards Integrated Management," held in Manama, Bahrain, November 5–8, 1994, under the auspices of the Bahrain-based Water Sciences and Technology Association (WSTA) and the GCC General Secretariat. The summaries are published by the *Gulf Daily News*, Nov. 6, 1994. Other data are drawn from the AMER Middle East Water Database in Philadelphia.

10. Al-mahmoud Abdulrahman et al., Qatari Ministry of Municipal Affairs and Agriculture, and Abdul Latif Al-Mugrin, deputy assistant secretary-general, GCC Secretariat, Gulf Water II.

11. Al-Mugrin, Gulf II; see also Al-Alawi and Abdulrazzak, "Water in the Arabian Peninsula," 177, 186–191.

12. Al-Alawi and Abdulrazzak, "Water in the Arabian Peninsula," 172.

13. One tonne = one long ton = 2,240 pounds or 1.016 metric tons.

14. For an excellent brief treatment of this topic with supporting data, see P. Gleick, "Water and Energy," in Gleick, ed., *Water in Crisis*, (New York and Oxford: Oxford University Press, 1993), 66–79.

15. Some of the information and data contained in the following section was provided in personal communications by various geologists and hydrologists formerly with the ARAMCO Oil Company, for which the author expresses his thanks.

16. Postel, S., "Water and Agriculture," in Gleick, ed., *Water in Crisis*, 59.

17. Ibid., 59.

18. *Gulf Daily News*, Nov. 6, 7, 1994.

19. Water Commission of Israel, Assessment of Medusa Bag technology undertaken by Tahal, 1991; also data provided to the author by James Cran, President of Medusa Corporation, November 1994.

20. Mention has already been made of a proposed transfer of water by pipeline from Iran to Qatar.

21. Turkey's economic development plans are among the most ambitious in the region and its population is growing at about 3.6 percent per annum.

22. The best source in English on the GAP project is J. Kolars and W. Mitchell, *The Euphrates River and the Southeast Anatolia Development Project* (Carbondale, Ill.: Southern Illinois Press, 1991); for a picture of how GAP affects the hydropolitics among the Euphrates riparians, see the respective articles by a Turkish, Syrian, and Iraqi specialist in *Research & Exploration* (A Scholarly Publication of the National Geographic), November 1993, vol. 9, pp. 50–79; see also Naff & Matson, *Water in the Middle East*, 83–110.

23. The information on water-sector investments and water and soil conditions in Iraq is drawn from an analysis of Iraq's water situation in *Water Issues in Iraq*, by A. Hardan and T. Naff, prepared for Associates for Middle East Research (AMER), August 1991, 70 pp., unpublished; the data used is from the AMER Database on Middle East Water.

24. Hardan and Naff, *Water Issues in Iraq*, 40.

25. Hardan and Naff, *Water Issues in Iraq*, 56–60.

26. S. McCaffrey, "Water, Politics, and Conflict," in Gleick, *Water in Crisis*, 95, 100–101; Hardan and Naff, *Water Issues in Iraq*, 57–8.

27. Ibid., 57.

28. McCaffrey, *Water, Politics, and International Law*, 93.

29. Hardan and Naff, *Water Issues in Iraq*, 58

30. This statement is based on private communications to the author by very well-placed authorities in both Iraq and Syria who are involved with the shaping of hydropolitical policies.

Part IV.
SECURITY ARRANGEMENTS AND
IMPLICATIONS FOR U.S. POLICY

13

SECURITY ARRANGEMENTS IN THE PERSIAN GULF

William B. Quandt

The security dilemma in and around the Persian Gulf can be easily stated: there is no set of purely local arrangements that holds much promise of providing security for all of the states and peoples of the region. If the recent past is any guide, security will be achieved, if at all, through a balance of power between large regional states that seek to establish a degree of hegemony and states outside the Persian Gulf that aim to prevent domination of the area and its resources by any single dominant power. In the absence of some such balance, at least in the near term, the Gulf seems fated to experience prolonged periods of conflict and warfare.

Prospects for a "Security Community"

In theory, the choices for the Gulf region need not be so stark. One could imagine the emergence of a "security community" based on shared values and common rules of the game of interstate relations. To some extent, this is what the Gulf Cooperation Council (GCC) aspires to be. But the two largest states in the region, Iran and Iraq, are distinctly outside the framework of this embryonic security community. Were they to join it, their size and their distinctive political agendas would radically transform the GCC into a wholly different type of organization.

Still, over time it might be possible to imagine that regional security could be the result of fundamental changes in the nature of relations among the states of the region. For now, however, this does not seem likely for several reasons.

First, there is the problem of regime incompatibility. For a security community to emerge, a wide range of shared values needs to be present.

To say the least, this is not the case among the Islamic Republic of Iran, Baathist Iraq, and the petro-monarchies of the GCC. At least at the level of regime interests, differences are profound.

Second, ideological competition is compounded by the uneven distribution of population, power, and resources. Iran dwarfs all the other states in terms of population, but ranks well behind Saudi Arabia and Iraq in terms of known oil reserves. Iraq, with enormous reserves of oil, has had great difficulty in reaching international markets, either because of its near-landlocked position or because of internationally imposed boycotts. The weakest states militarily are often extremely rich, making them tempting targets for extortion and pressure, if not outright invasion.

Third, the presence of so much oil, and hence potential wealth, combined with its maldistribution, provides an obvious source of conflict within the region, as well as a rationale for external intervention. Were the Gulf an impoverished backwater, its security problems would look considerably less daunting. Even if conflict were rife, as it was among Arabian tribes in the pre-oil era, it could be limited by some sort of regional balance. Even Abd al-Aziz Al Saud (Ibn Saud) was unable to conquer the entire Arabian peninsula, although he came remarkably close to unifying the feuding tribes by conquest—and intermarriage.

Fourth, with the emergence of the modern state, and with access to petro-dollars and therefore modern arms, large-scale offensive warfare has become a possibility, as demonstrated during the 1980s by the Iran-Iraq War, and then in 1990 by the Iraqi invasion of Kuwait. This type of warfare bears faint resemblance to the patterns of traditional—and limited—conflict that prevailed in the region prior to the oil era. Warfare has become much more lethal. Civilian populations are targeted and weapons of mass destruction have been used. As the invasion of Kuwait showed, some of the small states, no matter how much they may spend on their defense, cannot stand up to the onslaught of modern tanks backed by airpower and huge manpower reserves.

Problems with a Regional Balance of Power

If a security community consisting of the states within the region is a distant prospect at best, then some variant of balance-of-power is the only way of providing for the security of the region. The problem here is that the requirements for a workable local balance do not seem to exist at present. First, there are only two big powers in the immediate region, Iran and Iraq. A balance of power system works more smoothly with at least three participants. In theory, Saudi Arabia or the GCC might be seen as such a third party, but there are serious limits on the military potential of regimes that have relatively small populations and are reluctant to contemplate conscription. At best, the GCC states have some modest self-defense capabilities, plus the means to buy large insurance premiums with their oil revenues.

Since a regional balance of power in the Gulf remains elusive, the smaller powers in particular have been tempted by a variant of balance-of-power politics whereby Iran and Iraq are encouraged to compete with one another, while the GCC seeks support from outside the region, especially from the United States. This was the model followed during the 1980s, with the GCC providing significant support to Iraq to keep it from collapsing in the face of superior Iranian manpower resources. While the GCC states managed to survive as Iran and Iraq bled, one could hardly say that regional security was enhanced. And once Iran was forced to sue for peace in 1988, Iraq soon presented an unmanageable threat to Kuwait.

Some might argue that the Iraqi threat could have been handled if only the United States had been more attentive or the Kuwaitis less provocative. Even if that is true, one can hardly design a stable security system that depends on a country thousands of miles away reading the warning signals more accurately than those on the front line—or on small powers always appeasing larger neighbors. In short, the externally supported balance-of-power system seems adequate for preventing the emergence of a hegemonic power; but it may not do very well at deterring aggression in the first place.

After Saddam's Defeat

In the aftermath of the defeat of Saddam Hussein's aggression against Kuwait, Gulf security became internationalized to an unprecedented degree. Iraq was weakened on the battlefield, subjected to U.N.-enforced sanctions, and disarmed of most of its weapons of mass destruction. In addition, a Kurdish self-governing area emerged under Western protection in northern Iraq, and Iraqi aircraft were also excluded from flying in the south. The net effect of these constraints was to ensure that Iraq would not be able to threaten its immediate neighbors, or to repress its Kurdish minority, as long as the external intervention continued. Still, the Iraqi regime remained in power; Iraq retained a large conventional military that could easily threaten the Kurds and Kuwait if external protection were lifted; and the regime carried out an aggressive policy of subduing the Shiite majority in the south despite the "no-fly" zone. In short, Iraq was crippled by the outcome of the war and the imposition of sanctions, but Iraq could emerge again as a powerful country threatening the smaller states of the Gulf.

If Iraq paid a very high price for Saddam's folly of invading Kuwait, Iran was, by contrast, a clear beneficiary. Its prime rival for regional influence was weakened; Iraqi oil was taken off the market and Iran was able to begin the process of rebuilding its shattered economy and military forces, following the chaos spawned by a decade of war and revolution in the 1980s. In regional terms, Iran was clearly on its way to becoming the dominant power, although its capacity to project military power was severely limited by its own modest capabilities and the presence of outside forces in and around the region. Still, compared to the other states in the vicinity, Iran has the makings of a major power—population, oil, water, an educated citizenry, trading partners, an experienced military, and a degree of stability. Although the economy is still quite weak, it seems only a matter of time before sustained recovery could begin.[1]

In order to get some sense for how future security arrangements in the region might evolve, let us look at several different scenarios involving Iran and Iraq, since they are the most likely powers to try to challenge the regional status quo.

Iraq and Gulf Security: Alternative Futures

Rehabilitating Saddam

With the passage of time and the growing strength of Iran, some in the region and beyond will doubtless make the case that the time has come to rehabilitate Iraq under Saddam's leadership. Those who favor this course point to the fact that Iraq represents something of a bulwark against Iran and its Islamist revolutionary agenda; Saddam, whatever his faults, can keep Iraq together as a unified state; Saddam will be eager to export oil and to trade with the West; and his desire for rehabilitation will mean that he can be pressured into making concessions as the price for the lifting of sanctions.

The most likely state to promote this line is Turkey, which is uneasy with the emerging Kurdish state in northern Iraq; which could benefit from Iraqi oil exports; and which worries about unchecked Iranian influence, not so much in the Gulf but in Central Asia and the Azerbaijan-Armenian arena. Turkey is also beginning to experience a growth in Islamist political movements, and therefore any step that might check Iran's regional influence would be welcome. Others who might lend support to the lifting of sanctions on Iraq would be Egypt and Jordan, both of whom might see a reformed Saddam as the least bad alternative for Iraq. Some might even argue that he could be persuaded to lend his weight to the Arab-Israeli peace process, which would help to undercut the Islamist opponents of a settlement with Israel. In the Gulf, Qatar and

Oman seem somewhat open-minded about dealing with Iraq in more positive ways, and Yemen, especially if Ali Abdallah Salih succeeds in subduing the south, might follow suit as a way of striking back at the Gulf states that favored the southern secessionists in the mid-1994 crisis.

Russia, France, and China might also favor the lifting of sanctions against Iraq. In each case the motives would be somewhat different. France hopes to develop the rich oil areas of southern Iraq once the sanctions are lifted; Iraq would also be a plausible customer for French products and arms. For the Russians, the issues are almost entirely financial, with an added touch of concern for the rise of Islamic polities to the south. Iraq owes Russia billions of dollars and could be a customer for billions more of exports, including arms. Iraq is seen by some on the right-wing of Russian politics as an ally against Islamic radicalism. China's stance toward Iraq will be influenced by economic prospects and a certain distaste for the idea that the international community should interfere in the internal affairs of other countries because of human rights violations, for example.

The moment of truth for those hoping to rehabilitate Saddam will come periodically when the U.N. Security Council is asked to extend the sanctions regime now in place. Those favoring a lifting of sanctions point out that Saddam has complied with the terms of U.N. Security Council Resolution 687 calling for destruction of weapons of mass destruction; the regime has shown that it is here to stay; the Iraqi people, not the regime, are suffering; and continuation of the sanctions will lead to the collapse of Iraq and the creation of an independent Kurdish state, with all the unpredictable consequences that would follow from that. Some Arab nationalists argue that the pressures on Iraq are simply designed to keep the Arabs weak and divided; some Islamists argue that sanctions against Iraq provide a pretext for a Western military presence in the Persian Gulf region.

So far the debate over lifting sanctions on Iraq has not been openly influenced by considerations of oil. But Iraqi oil is the unacknowledged key to how the debate will unfold. Those who are adamantly opposed to lifting sanctions—Kuwait and Saudi Arabia, for example—also stand to lose the most if Iraqi oil were to reenter the market in the near term. Most western oil companies are also uneasy about the reentry of Iraqi oil. No one doubts, however, that there will be a time in the not-so-distant future when Iraqi oil will be more welcome in the marketplace, as demand rises, prices inch higher, and available spare capacity dries up. In a sense, then, a waiting game has begun. Can Saddam remain in power long enough for the pressures on oil supplies to lead to a demand for allowing Iraqi oil into the market?

In the near term, this scenario of rehabilitating Iraq seems to have little chance of success for one simple reason: the United States is deeply opposed to lifting sanctions on Iraq as long as Saddam Hussein is in power. If necessary, Washington will use the veto in the U.N. Security Council to prevent the lifting of sanctions; or will work to insure that any easing of pressure on Iraq is very slight. But the more time passes, the greater will be the pressure to accommodate the partisans of rehabilitation, for the simple reason that Iraqi oil will be needed, and Iraqi strength may be required to offset Iran's growing power. Washington may now prefer to speak of "dual containment" instead of returning to the old "balance of power" game in the Gulf,[2] but a combination of isolationism, demand for Iraqi oil, and the erosion of the anti-Iraqi alliance may bring the United States, and others, to a grudging acceptance of a rehabilitated Iraq. This clearly is Saddam's dream—and Kuwait's nightmare.

Gamble on Saddam Junior

Most of the arguments in favor of rehabilitating Saddam Hussein would be heard even more loudly if he were to be replaced by another, less aggressive Sunni Baathist military officer. Indeed, many have thought that a "Saddam Junior," more beholden to the GCC and the West, is the best outcome that one could hope for. This time, however, the West would presumably be more vigilant in watching for signs that a new leader might have ambitions that were not so different from his predecessor. Such a leader would almost certainly find it difficult to accept the newly demarcated border with Kuwait; he would resist the demands for reparations and debt repayment; he would seek to rebuild Iraq's military potential and to export oil to pay for these programs. In short, the new regime might be almost as difficult to deal with as a crippled Saddam. The chance that such a regime would be seen in Washington as eligible for full rehabilitation seems slight.

Long-Term Containment

If Iraq is not to be rehabilitated and integrated into the security arrangements for the region, and if it continues to be sufficiently powerful to constitute a threat, then the most obvious means for dealing with the present regime is some form of long-term containment. This seems to be the policy adopted by the Clinton administration and supported by the governments of Kuwait and Saudi Arabia.[3] As long as sanctions against Iraq are maintained and Iraqi oil is kept off the international market, containment is a viable strategy. Iraq will not be able to threaten its neighbors (although it is quite capable of threatening its own citizens and of carrying out various types of destabilizing acts—subversion, terrorism, hostile propaganda—against states in the region).

The problem with the containment strategy is not its short-term effectiveness. Rather, the questions involve the viability and desirability of such an approach over the longer run. As demand for Iraqi oil rises later in the decade, there will be increasing difficulty in keeping the sanctions regime in place. Saddam's near compliance with the disarmament provisions of U.N. Resolution 687 already raises questions about how long sanctions can be maintained with any shred of international legality. So, at some point the consensus needed to maintain a policy of containment could evaporate, and Saddam could begin to rebuild his power. The first victims of such a development might be the Kurds in northern Iraq, especially if they revert to internal factionalism.

An alternative outcome of a containment policy might be the disintegration of the Iraqi state. Already the Kurdish zone in the north is acquiring habits of independence; the south might conceivably follow suit if the containment policy were aggressively pursued. In time, the realm of the Iraqi state might be reduced to Baghdad and the surrounding countryside. It is hard to imagine that such a development would not have profound consequences for regional security.

Disintegration

No one concerned with Gulf security has openly advocated the fragmentation of the Iraqi state as a way of enhancing the region's well-being. But the lack of such an avowed goal does not mean that some parties might not see advantages in Iraq's demise. One can easily imagine Iraq's neighbors rushing to win control and influence over the oil-rich areas of the country, or over geographically contiguous zones. Some would no doubt discover that Iraq was the product of colonial map-making in the first place, and that a redrawing of the map along new lines was a proper postcolonial response. The problem, of course, is that it would be impossible to find any agreement within the region or beyond on how Iraq should be repartitioned. However artificial the present Iraqi state may be, it is hard to imagine other arrangements that would be more widely accepted. In terms of the overall balance of power in the region, a division of Iraq would, of course, further strengthen the position of Iran as regional hegemon.

Democratization and Reintegration

The only prospect other than containment, dismemberment, or some form of balance of power for ensuring that Iraq will not threaten the security of the Gulf in the foreseeable future would entail far-reaching changes in the nature of the regime in Baghdad, coupled with conscious efforts to reintegrate Iraq into the regional framework of security. To some extent, this seems to be the other face of American policy toward Iraq—beyond containment of the Saddam regime lies the prospect of its replacement by a democratic opposition that would rehabilitate Iraq as a peaceful partner committed to new security arrangements. While some lip-service is paid to this scenario, it is hard to find much evidence that anyone in the region, or anyone in Washington for that matter, is putting much weight behind it. The Iraqi democratic opposition is still treated as a questionable alternative to the Baghdad regime. Its Kurdish component had won considerable respect prior to the factional fighting in mid-1994, but many perceive that the Kurdish agenda is more focused on Kurdish independence than on creating a democratic Iraq; the Sunni component of the democratic opposition seems feeble; and the Shiites seem narrowly sectarian in outlook. For the moment, the leadership of a future democratic Iraq is in doubt.

Some would go so far as to argue that the structure of Iraqi society precludes any real democratic openings, at least for the foreseeable future.[4] This view is rooted in the belief that Iraq is fated to be ruled by the Sunni minority centered in Baghdad; rule by the Sunnis will never be fully accepted by the more numerous Shiites or the independence-minded Kurds. Thus, the minority regime will have to depend on coercion to hold onto power, while playing divide-and-rule politics with other elements of Iraqi society. Already some observers see Saddam strengthening his rule by building up the role of the traditional tribal leaders in the south at the expense of the Shiite religious establishment and more secular elements in Shiite society. In this view, even when Saddam passes from the scene there is little hope for a democratic Iraq.

Still, once Saddam has lost power, there will be some chance of a reshuffling of the deck and possibly a different distribution of power, even if not full democracy. In any event, there will be the question of how to deal with a successor regime, whether it is of the "Saddam junior" variety or consists of some combination of today's opposition elements. The most obvious flaw in the current policies of those who are calling for the overthrow of the Saddam regime is that they have said very little about how a successor regime would be treated. For example, will a successor regime, provided that it abides by U.N. resolutions, still be required to pay reparations to the victims of Saddam's wars? Will a successor regime be held responsible for the debts incurred by Saddam's regime prior to 1990?

If the answer to these questions is yes, a new regime could be burdened from the outset with enormous claims on its financial resources, claims that could easily run as high as $200 billion. At today's oil prices, it would take nearly twenty years for Iraq to pay off such claims if Iraq produced at full capacity and spent all of its oil revenues to meet its foreign obligations, leaving nothing to spend on domestic development. Obviously, no regime that hoped to win legitimacy in the eyes of its own people could be expected to meet these obligations.

This raises the policy issue of whether the United States, Russia, Kuwait, Iran, Saudi Arabia, and Israel, all of whom have major claims against Iraq, could be persuaded to agree to waive their claims if a new Iraqi regime were to adopt policies that were compatible with internal democratization, power sharing, or decentralization, and were to commit itself to new regional security arrangements. Were they to do so, and were sanctions to be lifted, at least in part, as soon as Saddam left the scene, opposition forces might have a clearer incentive to take the risks entailed in challenging Saddam. And the international community would have considerable leverage with a new regime to oblige it to keep to its commitments. This would require, however, a high degree of prior coordination among all of those most concerned with Iraq's future, and with Iraqi opposition figures. It would require that Turkey be satisfied with the way in which an autonomous Kurdistan would fit into a democratic Iraq; that the GCC states would accept the importance of allowing the Shiites of Iraq to play a political role more commensurate with their numbers; and that Iran would not see the rehabilitation of Iraq as aimed primarily against its interests. In short, this most promising of scenarios for dealing with Iraq is also the most complex.[5] But if regional security is ever to be achieved primarily through the creation of a security community instead of an unsteady balance of power, some such transformation within Iraq seems necessary.

Iran and Gulf Security: Alternative Futures

Iran represents a quite different problem for Gulf security compared to Iraq. At various times in the past, it has sought to undermine the legitimacy of regional governments, has engaged in harsh propaganda campaigns, has sponsored terrorism and coup attempts, notably in Kuwait and Bahrain, and has flexed its military muscle. But with few exceptions, military force has not been deployed beyond Iran's international borders. (The exceptions, of course, involve Iraq, which had sent its own forces into Iranian territory in September 1980; and the use of Iranian force to occupy the Tunbs and Abu Musa in the lower Gulf). During the long Iran-Iraq war of the 1980s, Iran's only direct military threat to those GCC countries supporting Iraq took the form of ineffectual air sorties against Saudi Arabia, which were easily repulsed.

Despite this record of relative restraint in the overt use of force, Iran is seen by many in the region as harboring hegemonic ambitions and seeking to challenge the status quo. Nonetheless, most regional countries maintain some form of relationship with Iran, and political dialogue is a normal part of their dealings with Tehran. In addition, a growing number of other powers—notably Germany, Russia and Japan—are expanding their relations with Iran.

Two quite distinct approaches to Iran can be identified:

Containment

The United States is the leading advocate of a policy of trying to limit Iran's power through containment. The practical application of this policy is sometimes hard to discern, since even the United States is expanding its commercial contacts with Iran, and most other countries make no pretense of using economic pressure to influence the Islamic Republic.

Containment does, clearly, entail a continued American military presence in and around the Gulf to deter any overt acts of Iranian aggression against GCC states. In addition, the United States and European countries vie with one another to sell military equipment to GCC states, ostensibly to contribute to a balance of power against both Iraq and Iran (although the primary motive is probably just as much to advance commercial interests).

The most recent U.S. interpretation of containment[6] contains several qualifications that are noteworthy. First, Washington does not challenge the legitimacy of the regime in Tehran; it relates its efforts at containment to specific areas of Iranian policy; and it invites a political dialogue to discuss differences.

The list of policy concerns that lie behind the U.S. containment policy include possible Iranian development of nuclear weapons and other weapons of mass destruction; support for radical Islamic movements in Egypt, Algeria, Lebanon, and among the Palestinians; support for terrorism; and opposition to the Arab-Israeli peace process. In an effort to persuade Tehran to change its ways, the Clinton administration has been trying to reach agreement with other countries on tight export controls on dual-use technology and has been arguing (unsuccessfully) for tight limits on credits to Iran until changes take place in these areas of policy dispute.

Most of Iran's main trading partners are willing to pay at least lip service to the U.S. objective of restricting the transfer of technology that might enhance Iran's capacity to develop weapons of mass destruction, but no one seems much interested in withholding trade or credits to try to force change in other areas of Iran's behavior. As a result, containment as a policy designed in Washington can only be seen as working in a very narrow sphere—namely, slowing Iran's acquisition of some military capabilities and providing a degree of protection for the GCC from any Iranian effort at direct military intimidation.

Normalization

The alternative policy that seems to be favored by most Europeans, Russia, and Japan, as well as some regional parties, is based on a normalization of relations with Iran. The argument in favor of this policy is that Iran cannot be isolated; that its policies will become more moderate as it becomes more economically interdependent; that its early revolutionary fervor is burning out and its efforts at economic reform show a growing pragmatism that should be rewarded; that Iran is too weak at present to constitute much of a threat to anyone; and that President Rafsanjani represents a moderate tendency that should be supported against the more radical elements.[7]

This school of thought would argue that it does not matter a great deal if Tehran opposes the Arab-Israeli peace process; that its involvement with Islamic movements elsewhere is marginal to their influence; that Iran's military capabilities are exaggerated; and that Iranian support for terrorism has declined since the release of Western hostages in Lebanon. Many would agree that efforts should be made to prevent Iran from acquiring weapons of mass destruction, but they would find it understandable that Iran would seek to rebuild its military strength in light of its defeat in the war with Iraq and Iraq's use of chemical weapons.[8] On the nuclear issue, no one seems quite sure where things stand or what to do about Iran's possible ambitions in this regard.

Those who pursue a policy of normalization with Iran do not really have an answer for dealing with the possibility that Iran will seek to assert its hegemony in the Gulf, or perhaps they see that outcome as inevitable and tolerable. They argue that Iran can be constrained by the web of economic and diplomatic ties that are being forged. In a reprise of the old Nixon-Kissinger view, some outside the region do not see much of a problem in letting Iran play the role of regional policeman. After all, Iran will probably want to see the Strait of Hormuz open; it will want to see oil flowing; and it will need customers and trading partners.

The unstated part of the policy of normalization, at least on the part of some of its adherents, is that the United States is stuck with a policy of protecting the GCC countries for reasons of its own, and that therefore Iran will not really be in a position to throw its weight around. In short, the United States should continue to adopt a policy of defiance toward Iran, leaving others free to normalize relations. This somewhat cynical posture helps to explain why Europeans and Japanese are quite content to go separate ways with the United States with regard to policy on Iran.

Some signs are beginning to emerge that Americans are questioning the wisdom of maintaining a policy of undifferentiated hostility toward Iran.[9] While the concern over nuclear capabilities is likely to remain acute in Washington, most of the other grievances against the Tehran regime are not incompatible with some measure of normalization of relations. The major reason for the policy of nondialogue in both Washington and Tehran has more to do with perceived domestic public opinion than with a clear articulation of national policy. No leader in either capital wants to be seen as "soft" on the other. Iranian authorities are probably even more reluctant to be seen as engaged in dialogue than are their American counterparts.

Possible Outcomes

Pure "Dual Containment"

If Iran were to adopt a harshly revolutionary stance and Iraq were to remain under Saddam's rule, then an approximation of the "dual containment" policy might be pursued by the United States with considerable support from the status quo powers of the region and with the cooperation of key Western powers. The policy may seem wrong-headed to many because it offers no positive incentives for improved behavior, but such a policy could be maintained if two conditions were met: the world felt little need for Iraqi oil; and Iran was more feared than its market was coveted. This outcome also assumes that Iran and Iraq will not join forces to challenge the containment regime. Were they to do so—an unlikely but not impossible prospect, at least for a short time—the policy of dual containment could be challenged if Iran agreed to help Iraq circumvent the sanctions regime by agreeing to export some of its oil and to import goods on Baghdad's behalf. In brief, a number of conditions could make it difficult to maintain this policy over the medium to long term.[10]

Containment Plus

This outcome describes a situation in which Iran in particular would be offered a mixture of positive and negative incentives to play a more cooperative role in regional security. Some degree of Western military presence would be retained in and around the Gulf for deterrence, but most other efforts to contain Iran would be dropped, and normal relations would be entered into, as a quid pro quo for Iran accepting the legitimacy of the existing regional order and refraining from developing weapons of mass destruction. In short, the one specific demand made of the Tehran authorities would be that they not develop nuclear weapons;

other policy disagreements would be dealt with through normal channels. Iran would be included in regional discussions of security issues and arms control.

In this scenario, Iraq might continue under some form of sanctions regime while Iran is reintegrated into the region. Apart from the difficulty of believing that Saddam's regime can be changed, this "Iran first" policy recognizes the greater strategic weight of Iran and the nonviability of a pure containment policy toward Tehran. It starts from the assumption that Iran might become a status quo power more readily than Iraq if it were given some positive incentives to cooperate with the regional order.

Rehabilitate a Democratic Iraq as Part of an Emerging Regional Security Community

This outcome assumes that Iran is mellowing and Saddam is gone. In such circumstances, there would be a strong interest in bringing Iraq back into the regional system as a cooperative player. To do so would almost certainly require a fundamental change in the nature of the regime. As long as the Kurds and Shiites are excluded from power, it is hard to imagine a regime in Baghdad that will not rely heavily on force and therefore constitute a potential threat to others in the region. By contrast, a more representative regime might be more easily held accountable by the international community, which would have considerable influence over how it was reintegrated into the region and how claims against the regime were handled.

In this most optimistic of scenarios, the United States would be able to consider some reduction of its military presence in and around the Gulf. But it would be many years before one could be confident that a stable regional order had emerged; the smaller states are bound to feel vulnerable; and therefore some degree of outside power would almost certainly have to remain as a part of the regional balance. But such a U.S. military presence need not be highly visible or particularly costly. As such, it could be acceptable to the Iranians, who are most likely to resent it; and to the small states, who will want some insurance.[11]

Pipelines, Politics, and Security

If Iran and Iraq are eventually to be brought into the security architecture of the Gulf region as stable partners, economic interests will provide at least part of the incentive for them to cooperate in seeking stability. One prospect that is not too far over the horizon envisages the construction of oil and gas pipelines that would possibly add to their incentives to work for regional peace.

For Iran, South Asia may emerge as a growing market for its oil and for oil carried by pipeline from the Caspian Sea to the Indian Ocean. If India succeeds in sustaining rapid growth in coming years, its need for imported energy could grow very rapidly, and a pipeline through Iran to the Gulf of Oman-Arabian Sea would be attractive to Indian importers. As Indonesian output declines, which is now expected, markets throughout Asia would find oil through an Iranian-based network to be most attractive. Iranian officials are already speaking of South and East Asia as special areas of interest.[12] Virtually all experts agree that this pipeline makes economic sense, but Western firms will not participate in its construction as long as the United States is strongly opposed. At some point in the future, Washington may have to weigh the arguments in favor of such a project as part of its overall strategy for regional security.

As Iraq reenters the oil market, the issue will again arise of how best to reach those markets. Pipelines across Turkey are one obvious possibility, as are the existing pipelines across Saudi Arabia. But Iraq might also be tempted by the idea of a pipeline to the Eastern Mediterranean, perhaps with its outlet in Gaza. In conditions of peace between Israel and the Arabs, the taboo on using such a port would fade.

Assuming such projects were to materialize, how might they affect regional security? At best, they might create conditions in which each of the major power centers in the Persian Gulf region would have its own network for exporting oil to different parts of the international market, thereby reducing some of the competitive pressures that otherwise tend to arise; each of the major oil producers would have a certain interest in regional stability; and each would have the means to promote domestic development. If Iraq's interests could be turned away from the Gulf, where it will always be frustrated by its narrow outlet to the sea and its potential vulnerability to closure of the Strait of Hormuz or dependence on Saudi Arabia for transit of its oil, toward the Eastern Mediterranean, that might reduce the incentives for Iraq to seek hegemony in the Gulf. Similarly, if Iran had an outlet for its oil, and for oil from the Caspian region, that bypassed the Gulf, Iran also might be less insistent on seeking hegemony in the Gulf per se.

Needless to say, these scenarios are quite speculative and may never come close to materializing. But decisions on building future pipelines will be far more than just technical matters; they could have far-reaching consequences for Gulf security as well. The basic point here is that making the Gulf less crucial to the economic futures of both Iran and Iraq might be a step along the way of moving from an externally dominated balance of power system toward a stable security community of the future. There would still, no doubt, be a great deal of competition among Gulf powers, but hopefully less incentive for war than in the recent past.

Notes

1. See Jahangir Amuzegar, *Iran's Economy Under the Islamic Republic* (New York: I. B. Tauris, 1994), esp. p. 330. By 1991–92, real per capita income was about 60 percent of the prerevolution level. At high rates of growth, it might take another twenty years to return to the levels of the late 1970s.

2. See Anthony Lake, "Confronting Backlash States," *Foreign Affairs* 73, no. 2 (March–April 1994): 45–55.

3. Warren Christopher, "Wobbly on Iraq," *The New York Times*, 29 April 1994, p. A27.

4. This point has been argued forcefully by Charles Tripp in "The Future of Iraq and of Regional Security," elsewhere in this volume.

5. Consider the analogy of how the allied powers treated Germany after World Wars I and II. The punitive conditions, including reparations, after World War I were easy to agree upon but had disastrous consequences; the policy of rehabilitating a democratic Germany after World War II was much more difficult to carry out, but has proved to be a great success for the stability of Europe.

6. Lake, "Confronting Backlash States."

7. Shireen Hunter, *Iran after Khomeini* (New York: Praeger, 1992), argues that Iranian nationalism has become a strong force under the relatively moderate leadership of President Rafsanjani. See also "Iran's Difficulties Lead Some in U.S. to Doubt Threat," *The New York Times*, 5 July 1994, p. A1.

8. Shahram Chubin, *Iran's National Security Policy: Intentions, Capabilities, and Impact* (Washington, D.C.: The Carnegie Endowment for International Peace, 1994), 29–55.

9. See Geoffrey Kemp, *Forever Enemies? American Policy and the Islamic Republic of Iran* (Washington, D.C.: The Carnegie Endowment for International Peace, 1994), makes the case for a cautious effort to improve relations through dialogue.

10. Gregory Gause III, "The Illogic of Dual Containment," *Foreign Affairs* 73, no. 2 (March–April 1994): 56–66. Rejecting Lake's arguments, Gause foresees a possibility that Iran and Iraq will be pushed toward cooperation. To prevent this, he maintains that the U.S. economic embargo of Iran should be lifted and a dialogue should begin.

11. An analogy might be found in the continued American military presence in Asia, where a stable regional balance of power has also remained elusive. China campaigned for years against the American presence, but, as its own relations with Washington improved, the American presence ceased to be much of an issue. Over time, it simply became part of the security architecture of the region, and no one was eager to see it removed. By the same token, no one felt very threatened by it either. One could do much worse than look at recent East Asian history for examples of how to address regional security when the local balance of power has not proved to be viable. The key there has been rapid economic development; a measure of external power for purposes of containment and reassurance; and diplomatic efforts to resolve conflicts.

12. See the interview with Iranian Foreign Minister Ali Akbar Velayati, *Al-Wasat* (London), 3 March 1994, no. 111, 22–24.

14

ARMS SALES AND ARMS EMBARGOES IN THE PERSIAN GULF: THE REAL DILEMMAS OF DUAL CONTAINMENT

Thomas L. McNaugher

No one cares much for "dual containment," the U.S. strategy toward the Persian Gulf. Even the State Department wanted to drop the phrase for a time, although in recent months consensus within the U.S. government has been restored, at least outwardly. Critics rightly see it as reducing to cant two different policies toward two very different countries. U.S. officials understandably do not like the personalities or the policies of either Iran or Iraq. But against Iraq they have used military force, and they maintain an international embargo aimed at toppling the country's leader. By contrast, they hold Iran's revolutionary government to be legitimate, if unsavory, and seek merely to isolate it until it behaves in a fashion that U.S. officials find acceptable.

Dual containment makes more sense if seen less as a policy for dealing *with* the Persian Gulf's two larger powers than as a policy of protecting U.S. interests in the Gulf *without* the engagement of Iran and Iraq. The strategy captures the frustration of U.S. policymakers, who can find no reliable way to deal constructively with either one—having tried in both cases, with embarrassing results. U.S. policy thus seeks to suppress the strength of both, presumably in hopes that more constructive options will emerge later. Until that happy day, U.S. military forces will continue to carry the burden of containment when diplomacy fails. They have performed well in that role, both at the end of the Iran-Iraq War, when U.S. naval vessels protected reflagged Kuwaiti tankers and otherwise suppressed Iranian harassment of Gulf shipping, and more recently, in ejecting Iraqi forces from Kuwait.

The other side of dual containment is the effort both to shore up military forces on the Arabian Peninsula and to ensure that U.S. forces can enter the peninsula quickly to contain the two larger Persian Gulf powers. Here too, U.S. policy appears to have been a great success. By most measures, Saudi Arabia now fields the most sophisticated and effective air force around the Gulf. Meanwhile, despite the absence of formal bases in the Gulf, the United States has clearly demonstrated its ability to ship large forces to the region very quickly.

Yet there is tension between the twin goals of U.S. policy toward the Arabian Peninsula. In the past, enhancing Saudi military strength also increased U.S. deployability; selling F-15s to the Saudis meant that F-15 spare parts and basing gear were already available in the kingdom when the crisis came. With oil income down and public expenses up, however, Riyadh can no longer increase its military strength without cutting social services—a politically difficult choice under any circumstances. A shift in the balance of U.S. cooperation with Saudi Arabia away from the sale of expensive weaponry and toward less visible preparations for U.S. crisis deployment would reduce this dilemma. Given the amount of equipment and infrastructure already available in the kingdom, such a shift would incur little strategic risk, yet U.S. preferences seem to be moving in the other direction, mainly to preserve the United States' defense industrial base.

As this chapter surveys the military situation around the Persian Gulf, it suggests that U.S. arms sales may cause problems with other elements of dual containment. Obviously the United States is not arming Iran or Iraq. Suppressing Iranian and Iraqi strength depends instead on pressuring China and Russia to reduce their arms sales to these countries. This would be difficult enough to do under any circumstances, but it looks hypocritical indeed when the United States is working hard to flood the global arms market with its own products. Thus, while the Gulf offers no easy policy alternatives, the one the United States could adopt at its own initiative—containing its arms sales—is the one that is getting no attention.

Living with Iraq

U.S. policymakers have aimed at eliminating Saddam Hussein at least since March 1991, when President George Bush called on the Iraqi people to "rise up and overthrow the dictator Saddam." Yet when Iraqis sought to answer Bush's call, he chose order—evidently even Saddam's order—

over the prospect of chaos in Iraq. But that policy failed as well, as Saddam's inimitable way of imposing order on his diverse constituents forced Bush and his coalition partners to create a safe haven in northern Iraq to protect Iraq's Kurds. That safe haven still exists, as do the underlying contradictions of a policy that wants Saddam gone but order maintained.

To resolve this contradiction the United States has helped bring together elements of an alternative government-in-exile, the Iraqi National Congress, which promises from bases in Iraqi Kurdistan as well as abroad to construct a more democratic Iraq on the ashes of Saddam's regime. This adds a political dimension to U.S. strategy that was missing in the immediate aftermath of Operation Desert Storm. But it takes a massive leap of faith to assume that the Iraqi National Congress could bring order to Iraq's diverse and unruly population. Thus it is worth considering fallback strategies in the likely case that U.S. policy toward Iraq fails.

Living with Saddam Hussein

The most likely failure is the one currently before us. Saddam remains in power after four years of sanctions, not to mention inglorious defeat. Increasingly, his longevity is forcing U.S. policymakers to contend with centrifugal pressures within the Operation Desert Storm coalition. The continuing misery of the Iraqi people, Iraq's "good behavior" strategy, and above all the lure of financial gain have led France and Russia to assert that Iraq should be given some reward for "substantial compliance" with U.N. resolutions. Thus far the United States has been able to contain any real erosion in its U.N. position, and Saddam's recent belligerence—moving two Republican Guard divisions toward Kuwait in October 1994—may help the United States stave off erosion still longer. But it is doubtful that even recent Iraqi provocations will glue France and Russia back into the international coalition for long. U.S. strategists must consider the increasingly likely prospect that Saddam will outlive the coalition that defeated him.

It is not impossible to contain a Saddam who is once again receiving an oil income and is thus able to pursue his nuclear ambitions (albeit under the U.N.'s lingering inspection regime) and terrorize his neighbors. Iraq's military is roughly half what it was before Operation Desert Storm. It may get no larger even if the U.N. sanctions regime fails, since Saddam's political base has narrowed considerably since 1990, making it dangerous for him to organize and arm the million-man force he once maintained.[1] Lacking spare parts, Iraq's weaponry is deteriorating, as is morale among its troops, save perhaps those pampered souls who protect Saddam. A postsanctions Iraq will be able to refurbish its arsenal, though probably mostly with Russian and Chinese weaponry. Saddam's forces will probably always be technologically inferior to U.S. forces.

Such an army can easily threaten the Kuwaitis, but no one else. To the east Iraq faces Iran, a country even the impetuous Saddam may refrain from attacking again, given what happened the last time he did so. To the north lies Turkey, with its large and reasonably well-trained military. To the west lies Syria and then Israel, another country Iraq has attacked in the past with embarrassing results. Iraq's dismal access to coastline sharply limits its naval ambitions. The "easy" victims lie to the south, which is the direction Saddam faced in 1990—and evidently still faces today.

Saddam will presumably continue to employ terrorism, but here as elsewhere, his lack of subtlety simplifies life for his adversaries. The assassination attempt on George Bush was so ham-handed that one is tempted to dismiss Kuwaiti claims that it was masterminded by Saddam. But more recent mischief, clearly traceable to Iraq, has been similarly clumsy. The assassination in Beirut of an Iraqi dissident in March of 1994 unraveled within days, as Lebanon's government identified the responsible Iraqi diplomats and severed relations with Iraq to deprive them of diplomatic immunity. Terrorism will always be a bother, but Saddam's kind of terrorism is likely to be easier to track than most. Moreover, as the Lebanon case suggests, this is the kind of Iraqi threat local governments can handle with limited U.S. support.

Iraq's clandestine nuclear and missile programs will be hard to track, despite the overlay of inspectors now covering the country. Saddam has demonstrated unusual subtlety and technical finesse in this area, perhaps because conspiracy is his forte and the work itself is left to scientists and engineers trained abroad. The breakup of the Soviet Union has opened an additional path to nuclear statehood. Small amounts of bomb-grade nuclear material have been confiscated by German police over the past six months; one shudders to imagine the material that might be traveling south, where police nets are more porous and governments genuinely seek the material.[2]

The good news is that the prospects for stalling Iraq's nuclear program, in particular, are better now than they would have been in the absence of the Kuwait crisis. U.N. teams have destroyed some portion of the original program. Their inspections have given the world a clearer idea of the full scope of Iraq's unconventional-weapons program and its supplier network, although evidently some important gaps remain in this information.[3] Nonetheless, outsiders have a much better grip on what to target among Iraq's imports than they enjoyed before 1991. And so long as Saddam remains in power it will probably remain easier than is usually the case to marshal international concern. (Those most concerned about proliferation might even prefer having Saddam around for this reason.)

In the near term, at least, the real challenge of living with Saddam will be less the threat he poses to neighbors than the absolutely certain threat he will pose to Iraq's Kurds. Past experience suggests that Saddam's revenge will come almost immediately after the Kurds lose their U.N. protection, and it will be brutal in the extreme. There will be no CNN cameras to record the tragedy, and the Turks, whose call for help with Kurdish refugees helped spark Operation Provide Comfort in 1991, are more likely this time to cooperate tacitly with Saddam by sealing their border with Iraq.

The *realpolitik* solution to this dilemma—also, unfortunately, a very likely one—would be to leave the Kurds to their fate, something the United States has done before and many Kurds expect it to do again. Yet the moral obligation here, born of Bush's incendiary rhetoric during and just after Operation Desert Storm, is not easily set aside. Arguably there is a practical challenge as well, since it is not clear that allowing Saddam to crush the Kurds will "solve" the Kurdish problem even in the real-politik way. Turkey's recent efforts to repress its Kurds have helped *increase* the size of Turkey's Kurdish People's Party (PKK) and the level of Kurd-related violence across Turkey.[4] Repression seems to aggravate rather than alleviate the Kurdish problem.

Whether festering violence in Turkey and northern Iraq would affect the United States depends partly on the role U.S. policymakers see for Turkey in U.S. policy toward the Middle East and Central Asia. As Henri Barkey has put it:

> The persistence of a violent domestic conflict will undermine Turkey's role as a stabilizing influence in the regions in which its interest and those of its Western allies coincide. As long as the Kurdish conflict continues, Turkey will remain vulnerable to the manipulations of Syria, Iraq and Iran. . . . As a result, the potential for conflict between Turkey and these other regional powers cannot be ruled out. In addition, civil violence will not only deter foreign companies from investing in Turkey, but will also affect Turkey's commercial and diplomatic relations with the West. . . .[5]

An alternative policy would be to protect Iraq's Kurds in the context of a moderated Turkish policy toward its own Kurds. Such a policy would encourage federalism and a degree of regional autonomy for Turkey's Kurds, while maintaining coalition bases in eastern Turkey from which to deter Saddam's aggression in northern Iraq. Arriving at such a solution would require a much broader debate about the Kurdish issue in Turkey than is presently occurring; indeed, the Turks have been unwilling even to lift the embargo on Iraqi Kurdistan for fear that doing so would promote the establishment of an independent Kurdish state in Iraq.[6] The United States might help prompt such a debate, however—a long shot, perhaps, but better than leaving the Kurds to their usual fate in Iraq.

Living with Saddam's Fall

The goal of U.S. strategy towards Iraq evokes the old Chinese curse, "May you get what you desire." The United States wants to topple Saddam, but it has no believable strategy for dealing with the success of that effort. Iraq's inventors complicated the problem of political succession in Iraq by enclosing Arabs and Kurds, Shiites and Sunnis within Iraq's borders. No doubt Saddam has made things worse by killing many of the state's effective politicians while sharpening and deepening suspicions among those left alive. Against these impediments to civil society and political order, the U.S.-backed, Kurdish-dominated Iraqi National Congress is the slenderest of reeds.

A vast majority of concerned onlookers no doubt prefer the emergence of another authoritarian regime, which is probably more likely now than in the immediate aftermath of Operation Desert Storm, when Iraq's army was routed and in disarray. The Saudis and Kuwaitis cannot relish the prospect of an emerging democracy in Iraq, setting an uncomfortable precedent and giving U.S. policymakers a strategic as well as a political alternative to protecting their monarchies. U.S. policymakers might welcome democracy, but only if it were to emerge quickly amid relative stability—an almost unimaginable possibility—to prevent intrigue or intervention by neighbors, especially Iran. No authoritarian regime can be worse than Saddam. Lacking Saddam's special stake in resisting U.N. appeals, a successor regime is likely to be amenable to the array of carrots the U.N. will be able to offer Iraq once Saddam is gone.

This is a plausible outcome, but so is turmoil, lasting perhaps a very long time. One danger in this case is that the U.N. will fritter away the leverage implicit in its control over sanctions by currying the favor of an emerging government only to find a new government in power soon thereafter; it will be difficult to reimpose sanctions once they have been removed. Another danger is that competing factions in Baghdad will seek support from outsiders—such as the United States, Iran, Russia, France— making it impossible to maintain coalition discipline and sucking outsiders into Iraq's brand of internecine warfare. Distant outsiders like the United States may retreat, leaving the action to Iraq's immediate neighbors.

The most worrisome of these is Iran. Indeed, the prospect of Iranian intrigue in an unstable Iraq must rank among the worst-case scenarios for U.S. military planners. It cannot be effectively countered by U.S. military forces, nor is talking to Iran, as Gregory Gause has suggested, likely to be very helpful.[7] It is doubtful that Iran will fully control activities along its border with Iraq; money, arms, and people will flow across that border spontaneously, as evidently happened in the weeks just after Iraq's defeat in 1991. Meanwhile, surely talks with the United States are as likely to inflame as to pacify the Iranian political scene. In the end, neither the U.S. government nor the Iranian government is likely to trust the other sufficiently to believe in words. Both will examine actions, and actions on both sides will probably be ambiguous enough to undo even a carefully elaborated diplomatic framework.

Surely the most serious underlying contradiction of dual containment is that its success in Iraq's case will make it harder to contain Iran. What U.S. policymakers cannot bring themselves to recognize is that this contradiction is serious enough to warrant coming to terms with Saddam. Their refusal to do so may be understandable, given Saddam's egregious behavior, but the embargo itself is having egregious effects on the people of Iraq. In the end, of course, it will be less the misery of ordinary Iraqis than the lure of money that will fracture international support for the embargo. Chances are, the United States will have to come to terms with Saddam. Fortunately, containing him within his borders presents few difficulties to military planners.

Containing Iran

Iran violates all the standards the United States now applies to Iraq, and then some. Like Iraq, Iran represses minorities, especially the Baha'is. Like Iraq, Iran seems bent on acquiring nuclear, biological, and chemical munitions, along with missiles to deliver them. Like Iraq, Iran rejects peace with Israel, and Iran is in a position to do more about it, through support to Hamas and what is left of Hezbollah in Lebanon. Unlike Iraq, and very worrisome to U.S. strategists, Iran supports Islamic movements elsewhere, notably in Sudan and Algeria. Its agents assassinate Iranian dissidents abroad; presumably they would assassinate author Salman Rushdie if they could find him. Finally, Iran is engaged in a military buildup that Iraq cannot match, at least for the moment. Surely Iran needs to be contained every bit as much as Iraq.

But Iran's government has not incurred global wrath by invading a neighbor, and while it certainly deserves the wrath of some of its constituents, overall it seems to be reasonably legitimate. Thus "dual containment" implies different treatment for Iran than it does for Iraq. Rather than call for the ouster of Iran's present regime, U.S. strategy seeks merely to penalize bad behavior, while holding out rewards for good behavior.

There is a general desire to slow the pace of Iran's economic and military growth. The United States has tried to organize an international embargo on the sale of weapons and so-called dual-use technology to Iran. It also opposes the extension of financial credits to Iran. It is willing to talk to authorized representatives of the Iranian regime, but so far has encountered no takers.

The Iranian Military Build-Up

U.S. diplomats had to work hard to isolate Iran late in the Iran-Iraq War, when Iran threatened Persian Gulf shipping as well as Iraq, yet Operation Staunch, as it was called, barely succeeded—and then only very late in the war, when the international consensus against Iran peaked. Today, U.S. policymakers are not seeking the near complete isolation they sought with Staunch years ago; in some commercial areas, for example, U.S. trade with Iran is on the rise.[8] But they also have much less to work with today, with the Iran-Iraq War virtually forgotten, Iraq the main enemy, and a "pragmatist" like Hashemi Rafsanjani the elected president of Iran. Most Western countries refuse to sell weapons to Iran and avoid commerce in nuclear technology, but their definition of "dual use" is quite narrow; they will happily supply commercial aircraft to Iran, for example, if U.S. administrations deny their own firms export licenses.[9] Ultimately they resisted U.S. efforts in the spring of 1994 to prevent a major rescheduling of Iran's debts.[10] Overall, Japan and the Europeans see hope in Rafsanjani's pragmatism and his effort to impart market reform. The United States is more skeptical.

Tensions between the United States and its friends would be greater, perhaps, were Iran not rendering moot the underlying military issues by making a mess of its economy. Much of the economic reform President Rafsanjani promised during his campaign has been blocked by conservatives in Iran's *Majlis* who favor state control of the economy. In fact, the clergy still controls much of Iran's economy through its ownership of land and assets confiscated from private owners early in the revolution. It runs its own economy in limbo between the public and the private sectors, adding an element of uncertainty to Iran's economic management that scares off private and foreign investment. Meanwhile, after avoiding debt during most of the Iran-Iraq War, Iran ran up an external debt of some $29 billion by 1993, and it has been late in paying on letters of credit.[11]

The high cost of debt servicing and relatively low income from oil sales constrained Iran's defense spending to the $4 billion to $6 billion range in 1991 and 1992.[12] This represented a significant portion of Iran's gross domestic product—roughly 8 to 9 percent—yet the amount remains vastly smaller than the $14.5 billion that Saudi Arabia budgeted for defense that year.[13] Even suspicious U.S. government officials assume that Iran has been spending no more than $2 billion a year on military equipment, and recently those estimates have shrunk to a mere $800 million.[14] Iran can now buy Russian and Chinese weapons at bargain-basement prices, and these two countries have become its dominant arms suppliers. But the amounts involved have been small so far. Between 1989 and 1992 Iran spent $2.2 billion on arms from Russia and $1.1 billion on arms from China[15]—for several hundred Soviet-made tanks, twenty Su-24 Fencer long-range strike aircraft, and thirty MiG-29 fighters. Iran has also purchased two Kilo-class submarines and may have two more on order.[16]

Two billion dollars a year does not make an arms race, or even much of an arms buildup. Moreover, the numbers overstate the military significance of Iran's purchases, since they cannot capture the operational costs of converting from a Western to a Russian-Chinese force posture. Iran's air force is scarcely larger than Saudi Arabia's, and it lacks the latter's sophistication and elaborate command and control. Indeed, Iran's mixture of aging, often inoperable U.S. aircraft and newer Russian equipment guarantees command, control, maintenance, and training problems for some years to come. At the moment, Iran's navy is also roughly equal to Saudi Arabia's, although the Saudis split their fleet between the Persian Gulf and the Red Sea. Again, Iran's is a hodgepodge force of U.S., United Kingdom, Russian, and South and North Korean ships, whereas Saudi Arabia has purchased its two fleets, mostly from the United States and France.[17]

It is not the present reality that scaremongers have in mind when they worry in public about Iran's military buildup, but rather the trend. Recent reports of a $15 billion Iranian-Russian arms deal are probably false, but they may nonetheless indicate Iran's goals.[18] The deal reportedly includes three more submarines, 12 Backfire long-range bombers and associated AS-6 antiship missiles, and the latest MiG-31 and Su-35 fighters. If Iran ultimately buys such equipment, it will field a formidable and very long-range air force, but at current spending rates, it will be years before the Iranians can amass this force, if in fact the deal is ever consummated.

The Kilo-class submarines do, of course, represent a qualitative change in armaments around the Persian Gulf, and they have started a mini-arms race insofar as the Gulf sheikhdoms have begun searching for antisubmarine warfare equipment for their coastal patrol craft. These will give Iran the capability to threaten a vital sea-lane, but their use in that way would provoke a global reaction. Such is the importance of the Strait of Hormuz in particular—and freedom of the seas in general—that when Iran's Revolutionary Guard Navy laid mines near the Strait of Hormuz in 1987, five European navies joined the U.S. and Soviet navies in patrolling these waters. The submarines are more likely to be used to complicate the military planning of navies that might threaten Iran's long coast. Despite their sophisticated antisubmarine warfare equipment, U.S. admirals worry about the presence of diesel submarines patrolling the warm and noisy waters around the Gulf.

Iran has the population, the resources, the coastline, and the strategic depth to be the dominant Persian Gulf power, and it would seem to be committed to realizing that potential over the long haul. Whether or not Rafsanjani is a pragmatist, his country still protests the status quo, and even pragmatic Iranians can be expected to throw their country's weight around as it grows more powerful. At $6 billion a year for defense, however, and against a backdrop of logistics and technological impediments, it will be some years before Iran realizes its goal.

Iran's Unconventional Build-Up

Having been pummelled by Iraqi missiles in 1988 and today facing Israeli missiles presumably armed with nuclear warheads, it would be strange indeed if Iran were not pursuing the development of its own unconventional weapons and missile delivery systems. Fortunately, the most worrisome of these—nuclear weapons—seem to be relatively low on Iran's present list of priorities. Former Central Intelligence Agency director James Woolsey does not see Iran acquiring nuclear weapons in less than eight to ten years, unless it receives foreign assistance.[19] Iran has been at pains to disavow any such intention. It signed the Nuclear Nonproliferation Treaty years ago, and in 1992 it allowed inspectors from the International Atomic Energy Agency full access to its nuclear facilities, even encouraging them to examine additional sites. They found nothing of concern,[20] but then they didn't find much in Iraq, either, until after Operation Desert Storm. At the very least, through its commercial and research nuclear programs Iran seeks to acquire the option to acquire nuclear weapons in the future.

There is less uncertainty about Iran's missile purchases. Iran's first major Scud purchase was from North Korea during the Iran-Iraq War, and it purchased still more Scud-Cs from North Korea three years ago. Evidently North Korea remains Iran's chief missile supplier, in part because U.S. pressure has prevented China from entering the Iranian market.[21] Reports suggest a more recent deal for North Korea's new, longer-range and reportedly more accurate Nodong I, and possibly the still longer-range Nodong II.[22] The Nodong I was first tested (at less than maximum range[23]) in May 1993, and it is not yet in production; it will be a few years before North Korea can deliver it in quantity, and much could happen to that beleaguered country in the meantime. Still, if or when these missiles enter Iran's inventory, they will substantially improve

Iran's missile force, bringing Israel as well as Iraq into range. Iran will not be caught short, as it was in 1988, in another missile duel with Iraq—or perhaps with Israel.

Nor, one suspects, will it be caught short in a chemical-weapons battle with Iraq, after Iraqi chemical attacks scattered Iran's troops in 1988 and the mere rumor of chemical warheads atop Iraq's incoming Scuds panicked the citizens of Tehran, helping to bring Iran to the negotiating table. The supply link here may be China, although the U.S. effort to substantiate this link by pressuring a Chinese commercial vessel, the *Yin He*, on the high seas proved an embarrassment when inspections turned up nothing.[24] Iran already has the capacity to make chemical weapons[25] (and probably biological weapons as well[26]). It seeks through imports to improve this arsenal, and those improvements could be significant. Iran's quest for chemical weapons cannot be stopped entirely.

Still, the United States might slow the process—hoping, perhaps, for more constructive options to emerge via change in Iraq or through international arms sale controls. One lesson from Operation Staunch was that if technology embargoes are to work at all, they must be focused on a relatively short list of truly critical technologies. Nuclear technologies unquestionably lie at the top of this list. Even more critical than missile components are technologies that provide accuracy, since inaccurate missiles are generally less effective than strike aircraft. Chemical-weapon precursors can be added to the list, although these fall well short of nuclear weapons in their effects.[27] Bioweapon technologies probably deserve to be on the list, but these technologies remain so highly classified that little can be said about them here.

Iran has been trying to buy or to develop internally most of these technologies; only its nuclear ambitions are uncertain. Meanwhile, it has had very little trouble buying conventional arms from Russia and China or getting financial help from Western Europe and Japan. The experience of Operation Staunch suggests that the degree of isolation the United States now seeks to impose on Iran may be counterproductive, since it risks diluting U.S. efforts to stop the flow of what is really important.

The United States and the Iran-Iraq Balance

No matter how enfeebled their militaries and how slow the Persian Gulf military buildup, clearly Iran and Iraq maintain capabilities that can threaten the smaller states of the Arabian Peninsula. Dual containment implies a continued U.S. obligation to handle these threats. At the moment, with Iran weak and Iraq in the hands of the unpredictable Saddam Hussein, the military demands of dual containment derive mostly from Iraqi behavior, and Saddam's recent troop movements gave the United States a chance to show that it is still capable of at least containing Iraq's external behavior.

If and as Iran pieces together its military forces, however, the containment problem is likely to shift back toward Iran, where it lay in the 1980s. The Persian Gulf "balance" is not really a balance; population and geostrategic position give Iran a natural advantage over Iraq. In the 1980s the logic of the situation led Saddam to moderate his behavior; Iraq could not face Iran without Arab (and, indirectly, U.S.) support for strategic depth, financial support, and (in the U.S. case) military pressure. In 1990, that logic became one of Saddam's excuses for invading Kuwait. Iraqi diplomats have been touting the Iranian threat among the Gulf sheikhdoms over the past year or two—a line of argument the sheikhdoms would find appealing had they the slightest trust in Saddam. A more reasonable Iraqi leadership might see in Iran's growing strength the basis for an accommodation with the Gulf sheikhdoms, however, and even Saddam might succumb to that logic in the long run.

Geography alone dictates that Iraq will absorb the brunt of any Iranian ground force attack toward the Arabian Peninsula, as it claims to have done from 1982 to 1988. So long as Iraq does so successfully, Iran's direct challenge to the sheikhdoms will be complicated by the water of the Persian Gulf. Although Saudi Arabia's elaborate air defense network and growing navy could probably handle Iran's cross-Gulf threat at the moment, the Saudis are unlikely to take on Iran without U.S. backing. Fortunately, air and naval warfare are U.S. strengths as well, and they are likely to remain so even if ground forces are decimated by post-Cold War budget cuts. As we saw in 1987 and 1988, water clarifies even guerrilla warfare. The Iranian threat will grow, and the purchase of submarines in particular will complicate U.S. military planning. But unless the United States turns totally inward, the interdiction of Iranian action across the Gulf will not strain U.S. forces for some years to come.

Thus far, however, the United States has not turned inward, either in its foreign policy or in its defense spending. The U.S. defense budget has come down with the end of the Cold War far more slowly that in earlier postwar periods, in large part because a broad public consensus exists on the need to defend U.S. interests in the Persian Gulf and on the Korean peninsula—sites of the two "major regional contingencies" that dominate post-Cold War U.S. defense planning. Indeed, Saddam can take personal responsibility for this, since the U.S. defense budget was in virtual "free fall" until his invasion of Kuwait provided the United States with a sense of danger to replace the defunct Soviet threat. Saddam's use of Scud missiles during that crisis shored up support for spending on missile defenses as well.[28]

If U.S. defense reductions sound large, it is because the size of the reduction is exaggerated by the size of the Reagan administration defense buildup that preceded it. Budget authority for national defense in fiscal year 1994 (FY1994) was $266.7 billion in 1995 dollars, down roughly a third from the FY1985 high of $401.2 billion (again in constant 1995 dollars), yet FY1994 budget authority remained well above national defense budget authority in the mid-1970s; even the planning figure for FY1998 is above the 1975 low of $236.7 billion, and it is on a rough par with budget authority in the early 1960s. Despite the end of the Cold War, the U.S. defense budget is only just reaching the low end of the Cold War range for defense spending.[29]

To be sure, hard choices lie ahead. Without denying the relatively gentle decline in U.S. defense spending, the fact remains that the Defense Department has been living off the largesse of Reagan-era procurement spending, which purchased an impressive array of new weapons coming out of development at the end of the 1970s. This has permitted both the Bush and the Clinton administrations to cut defense spending largely by cutting procurement and, to a lesser extent, force structure. This cannot go on forever; aging weaponry will have to be replaced. In Clinton's defense plan, procurement spending turns gently upward starting in FY1996. Yet few observers expect this turnaround actually to occur, and even if it does, it will be too small to keep pace with the needs of U.S. forces.[30] As a rule, weapons last longer than the services predict, although aging weapons cost more to maintain, and that can undermine readiness. The United States can probably defer a procurement spending surge until 1998 or 1999, but at that point the services and the nation's defense industrial base will be approaching a minor crisis.[31]

By then, however, the United States should have a better sense of its role in the post-Cold War world. The world too will have changed. There might be a friendlier regime in Baghdad, and no regime at all in Pyongyang, the result of war or North Korea's collapse. Or both situations could be much worse, prompting major adjustments in U.S. defense spending. One could wish for a more rational and forward-looking defense planning process, but, by historical standards, the present planning process has been uncommonly rational and outward looking.

Saving the Saudis?

Ironically, where we find a hint of dangerous irrationality in U.S. planning for the Persian Gulf is in U.S. policy toward its friends—notably Saudi Arabia—and it stems largely from an attempt to forestall the defense industrial "crunch" alluded to above by increasing arms sales abroad. Although the danger is difficult to gauge, U.S. arms transfers to

Saudi Arabia have reached a point where they cause more trouble than they are worth, both within Saudi Arabia and among other arms suppliers.

Alone in Front

If anyone is racing in the Persian Gulf's arms market, it is Saudi Arabia. Between 1986 and 1993 the Saudis took delivery of $55.6 billion in arms.[32] This was roughly 23 percent (by value) of all arms delivered worldwide during that period, and over twice the value of weapons delivered to Iraq—which, at $22.7 billion in arms imports, was the runner-up in this race. Yet while arms shipments to Iraq fell to near zero after 1990, Saudi Arabia's imports rose from $25.8 billion in 1986 to 1989 to $29.8 billion in 1990 to 1993. Saudi orders for new arms also rose between the two periods, from $32.6 billion in 1986 to 1989 to $35.1 billion in 1990 to 1993. Strikingly, while virtually every other arms trade statistic is falling—the size of the global market, sales and deliveries to other Middle East states, and so forth—the numbers that describe Saudi Arabia's arms purchases continue to rise.

As with Iran, however, large Saudi orders do not mean large Saudi deliveries. Saudi Arabia may have a much smaller population than Iran and its oil income may be considerably higher, but it also has the cost of previous weapons orders and the bulk of Operation Desert Storm to finance. Saudi Arabia had to set up a $4.5 billion line of credit with J. P. Morgan, for example, to cover part of its $55 billion share of the cost of Desert Storm,[33] and they have been forced to stretch delivery schedules, reschedule payments, and borrow billions of dollars to finance their arms purchases.[34]

When it is finally assembled, the Royal Saudi Air Force, already more technologically sophisticated and operationally coherent than those around it (save Israel's), will be larger and also more offensive in character than ever before. It now has roughly one hundred strike aircraft, but half of these are aging F-5Es that will be replaced or complemented by the very advanced F-15Es it ordered in the aftermath of Operation Desert Storm.[35] Its fighter force of seventy-eight F-15C/Ds and twenty-four British Tornadoes will acquire more of each aircraft. All will be tied together through the five airborne warning and control system aircraft the Royal Saudi Air Force purchased in the early 1980s. Add to this the fact that Saudi pilots are the best trained of the major Persian Gulf air forces, and the result is the best air force in the Gulf.

Saudi Arabia placed its first order for U.S. M1A2 tanks in 1989, and Iraq's attack on Kuwait prompted them (as well as the Kuwaitis) to buy still more. The Royal Saudi Land Forces now have thirty of these tanks.

Recruitment problems and the relative unpopularity of ground force service have always limited the effectiveness of the Saudi ground forces, and these liabilities plus their relatively small size in comparison even to post-Desert Storm Iraq suggest that they will serve at best as a screening or delaying force, buying time while U.S. and perhaps other allied forces enter the Arabian Peninsula.

There is operational logic to the shape of Saudi forces. Saudi ground forces probably cannot hope to take on the larger forces of Iraq, or in the worst case Iran. But the al-Saud probably feel an obligation to put up some kind of a fight to sustain their legitimacy. Hence, they buy sophisticated ground equipment, but at a lower level of priority than equipment for their air forces. The latter should be able to defend the kingdom's airspace quite handily if Riyadh chooses to do so. In any large-scale confrontation—a replay of Iraq's 1990 invasion, for example—securing airspace will be crucial not only for defense but also for protecting ports and infrastructure essential for bringing U.S. forces into the kingdom quickly.

Clearly, Saudi arms purchases from the United States also help pave the way for the rapid insertion of U.S. forces in a crisis. Long before the Kuwait crisis, the Saudis began building infrastructure and buying spare parts, ammunition, and maintenance facilities with an eye as much to use by U.S. forces as to use by their own. The effort paid off in 1990, when U.S. aircraft landed at Saudi airfields stocked with U.S.-made munitions, spare parts, and maintenance test equipment. The purchase of M-1 tanks will extend this capability to the realm of ground warfare.

In fact, it makes little sense to speak of Saudi forces apart from U.S. forces and support. The kingdom's airborne warning and control system aircraft, for example, are still manned and maintained mostly by U.S. crews, tank maintenance is contracted to U.S. companies, and much of the country's infrastructure has been shaped with U.S. military requirements partly in mind. In the aftermath of Operation Desert Storm, still more U.S. hardware was left in the Persian Gulf region. As the recent deployment of U.S. forces to the Gulf demonstrated, between ground force equipment stored in Kuwait and on ships afloat, the United States can move the better part of a mechanized division to the Gulf in roughly two weeks.

This raises questions about the urgency with which the kingdom is modernizing its own forces. Size disparities between Saudi Arabia and its neighbors make it unlikely that the Saudis will ever be able to defend themselves, especially on the ground. Even if they wanted to try—and that seems doubtful—the slow pace of neighboring buildups presents little to worry about, and in the end the United States has repeatedly demonstrated the capacity to move quickly to defend the kingdom as well as Kuwait. Indeed, it is hard to imagine a more credible U.S. security commitment than this one, which originated in promises to King Abd' al-Aziz ibn Saud during World War II, and thus predates the formation of NATO. Given tight financial constraints, it would seem logical to slow the purchase of expensive end items, such as F-15s and M1A1s, and focus instead on purchasing ammunition and spare parts. Why do the Saudis insist on going into debt to purchase big-ticket items that they do not really need?

The solution to this puzzle may lie in a new rationale that has crept into the kingdom's justification for its arms purchases since 1990—namely, that such purchases help to sustain the U.S. defense industrial base. Saudi Arabia's ambassador to the United States, Prince Bandar bin-Sultan, stated this rationale most clearly when he announced the kingdom's decision to upgrade its commercial aircraft fleet with a split buy of Boeing and McDonnell-Douglas airliners: Riyadh was, he stated, "ready to share the burden of maintaining the United States aerospace industry."[36]

In fact, Saudi Arabia is the major participant in a conscious U.S. effort to use arms sales to preserve jobs and excess capacity in the U.S. defense industrial base while it sorts out post-Cold War priorities. Both the Bush and the Clinton administrations have instructed ambassadors and embassy staffs to take a more active role in promoting the sale of U.S. weaponry in the countries in which they serve. Helped by terrific advertising—Operation Desert Storm—and by the fact that many of the weapons used in the Gulf War are at the relatively inexpensive end of long production runs, U.S. arms makers have come to dominate the global arms market.

Indeed, the figures are impressive. While in 1991 U.S. defense firms contracted for some $9 billion in overseas sales, in 1993 the total value of U.S. arms sales agreements (not deliveries) had risen to $32 billion.[37] In 1992 the United States for the first time supplied over half of the conventional arms sold or delivered to the Third World. Although the value of arms agreements signed with Third World countries has dropped steadily since the end of the Cold War, the value of U.S. arms agreements signed from 1990 to 1992 outpaced the value of contracts signed in the late 1980s.[38] The trends have prompted one analyst to suggest seriously that the United States is in the process of driving the rest of the world's arms producers out of business.[39]

As impressive as the overall U.S. standing in the global arms bazaar is Saudi Arabia's role in the undertaking. The $30.4 billion in U.S. arms contracts that the Saudis signed between 1990 and 1993 came to more than half of all U.S. arms contracts, just over half of all Middle East arms contracts, and roughly 28 percent of *all* arms contracts signed with all vendors in all regions during that period.[40] The kingdom's purchase of commercial U.S. aircraft, which came after intensive lobbying by President Clinton, is expected to "temporarily resuscitate the aerospace industry,"[41] while no doubt helping McDonnell-Douglas through difficult times with its ailing C-17 military transport program. Saudi F-15 purchases, combined with production of F-15s offered to Israel in compensation for the Saudi sale, have also single-handedly kept the McDonnell-Douglas F-15 line operational. Likewise Saudi and Kuwaiti M1A1 purchases have added significantly to business at General Dynamics' Land Systems Division in Michigan.

In terms of its motivating logic, this policy has been a great success. The U.S. defense industrial base has seen its share of the mergers and acquisitions that one would expect to accompany the post-Cold War drawdown of defense. Overall, however, the industry remains profitable. The number of independent aircraft assembly lines has slowly fallen, as Northrop has purchased Grumman and Lockheed has bought General Dynamics' F-16 line, but the number remains well above the level of one or two, where monopoly concerns begin to mount.

As well served as U.S. economic interests may be by current arms sales policy, however, the question remains of whether they serve U.S. security interests in the Persian Gulf. The latest round with Saddam Hussein prompted a spate of articles in the Western press concerning Saudi Arabia's financial problems, raising the question of whether "Saudi spending on U.S. weapons has actually made the kingdom less secure by saddling it with new financial obligations."[42] To be sure, many countries would love to have the kingdom's financial "problems." The Saudis still have $15 billion in government assets, down from over $120 billion in the mid-1980s, but still more than many countries can boast, vast oil reserves give them an excellent credit rating if they wish to borrow internationally, and they continue to supply most social services to citizens free of charge.

But in politics everything is relative, and the Saudis are no longer nearly as well-off as they once were. They have to cut somewhere, and that, as Washington well knows, can be politically painful. The situation inevitably creates tension between social spending and defense spending. The latter now consumes a third of Saudi government spending, but pressures in this sector are upward, not only to finance new weaponry, but also to cover some portion of the cost of deploying U.S. troops to the Persian Gulf for the latest confrontation with Saddam.

Meanwhile, the kingdom is not getting easier to govern. Since Operation Desert Storm, the religious militants have demanded greater say in the kingdom's governance; so have Western-educated modernizing elites. We know little about what goes on behind the closed doors of the ruling family. But one senses that the crucial balancing act between tradition and modernity, militant religious and essentially Western values, is getting harder to maintain.

This is not to suggest that Saudi stability now hinges on the issue of buying more F-15s or M1A1s. We know very little about the deeper sources of Saudi stability. Surely, however, money accounts for at least part of the kingdom's remarkable ability to weather the stresses generated by events and trends around the Persian Gulf over the past two decades: Iran's revolution, the Iran-Iraq War, the dramatic decline in oil revenues after 1981, and Iraq's invasion of Kuwait and the subsequent deployment of several hundred thousand foreign troops to Saudi soil for Operation Desert Storm. Given that Saudi Arabia is the single pillar on which U.S. Gulf strategy rests, it would make sense to rethink the balance between U.S. domestic economic and political needs and those of Saudi Arabia.

Arms Sales and Arms Control

Criticism of U.S. arms sale policy would be fairly weak if it were framed strictly in terms of Saudi stability. Arguably, however, that policy also undermines the international dimension of dual containment—namely, the effort to curb arms sales to Iran and Iraq. The challenge in this case lies principally with Russia and China, whose arms sales have fallen since the end of the Cold War but remain a problem. The United States faces the daunting task of asking these states (and others) to curb their arms sales while the United States floods the world with its arms. It seeks to help them with "conversion" of defense industries to commercial undertakings, yet uses arms sales to slow precisely that process at home.

All might be well if aggressive U.S. arms sales were indeed driving other arms manufacturers out of business, as Ethan Kapstein has suggested. And Kapstein may be right in the case of Europe's defense industries, which have always suffered from relatively small national markets and short production runs. These circumstances forced European defense establishments to begin collaborating in the development of tactical and commercial aircraft in the 1960s, when Cold War demand was still running high. Russia and China, by contrast, have large internal markets and equally large "objective" defense requirements. Neither is doing very well in the global arms bazaar, albeit less for lack of trying than as a result of the relatively antiquated weapons they (especially China) have to offer. But it would be surprising indeed if these defense industries disappeared. More likely, they will tap into the advanced technologies of neighbors and the United States and slowly develop better products.

Not surprisingly, given the obsolescence of most of its weapons technologies, China services markets the United States will not service: "backlash" states, such as Iran and Libya. In the late 1980s China became Iran's chief source of arms, the largest violator of Operation Staunch.[43] Competition from Russian arms has cut into China's market, forcing China to offer technologies the United States will not supply: nuclear and missile technologies and chemical precursors. The United States has had some success in curbing China's worrisome sales, save perhaps to Pakistan. In October 1994 China finally agreed to observe the technical details of the Missile Technology Control Regime, suggesting that even sales to Pakistan may now be curbed—although that remains to be seen.

Yet clearly China is not happy with the prevailing balance of arms sales. China withdrew from the conventional arms trade talks in 1992 to protest the Bush administration's decision to sell 150 F-16s to Taiwan. Thereafter it scarcely denied accusations that it was selling missile components to Pakistan, despite its verbal commitment (offered in November 1991) to observe the restraints of the Missile Technology Control Regime. Instead, it expressed its willingness to discuss compliance with the Missile Technology Control Regime when the United States agreed to discuss *its* compliance with the 1982 United States-China Communiqué on Taiwan, which imposed limits on U.S. arms sales to Taiwan. Subtly, it sought to forge a link between U.S. conventional arms sales and its own sale of unconventional weapons.

The United States agreed to such a dialogue late in 1993,[44] although in doing so it intended to do no more than listen politely to Chinese protests. Evidently that is what has happened; when China formally agreed to abide by the technical details of the Missile Technology Control Regime in October 1994, no mention was made of arms sales to Taiwan, nor did the Taiwan issue arise during Defense Secretary William Perry's visit to China that same month.

If China continues to grow, however, it can be expected again to link its arms sales to those of the United States. Its immediate goal in doing so may be to acquire the technological "gifts" with which the United States has purchased China's compliance with arms control agreements. Over the long run, however, its goal appears to be to achieve some control over the content of such agreements—to become a rule maker rather than a rule taker.[45] In the realm of conventional arms transfers, that is likely to mean either letting China export more, or reducing the size of U.S. arms exports.

Conclusions

The United States faces fairly risky times ahead in the Persian Gulf. The two largest Gulf regimes are unremittingly hostile to it, and one—Iraq—still poses a threat to Kuwait. Meanwhile, the base from which the United States operates is narrower than ever. Even while peace breaks out, painfully, in the Levant, the Gulf stands apart, mired in the politics of repression and militant Islam, stuck largely outside the emerging global economy save as a supplier of its primary fuel. It faces change only of the most ominous sort—namely, the possible emergence of missiles armed with nuclear and chemical warheads.

With its interest in oil likely to be compelling for years to come, the United States has little choice but to deal with the Persian Gulf as best it can. In fact, it has been remarkably successful in weathering military crises both subtle (reflagging) and stark (Operation Desert Storm). The military scenarios the region has created thus far have been amenable to U.S. military action, and U.S. public support has been sufficiently strong to permit the use of military force. Obviously no one is anxious to continue using force in this or any other part of the world, but until the United States confronts more reasonable states in the region, it will at least have to plan seriously on doing so.

Alas, the one state with which it can reason, and on which it depends for entrée to the Persian Gulf, is the one its arms sales policy treats virtually as a cash cow: Saudi Arabia. Clearly the Saudis no longer have the cash, and although they are a long way from destitution, their current financial situation is forcing them to confront thorny political issues. Whether this will produce instability is anyone's guess, but such is the importance of Saudi Arabia to U.S. strategy that the United States has good reason indeed to avoid discovering the limits of Saudi stability the hard way. Clearly, the United States is prepared to contain Iraq and Iraq; arms sales serve no overpowering strategic purpose. The source of inflexibility lies largely in domestic U.S. politics.

Like questions about Saudi stability, questions about the relationship between arms sales by the United States and those by other suppliers have no immediate answers. In the absence of arms sale control agreements, any reduction in U.S. arms sales would merely open the market to others. The real question is whether U.S. willingness to reduce its arms sales might open opportunities in the conventional arms talks for overall controls on such sales. No one is currently trying to answer that question. To make the attempt, the United States will have to contain itself—which evidently is much harder than containing Iraq and Iran.

Notes

1. On the various maladies of Iraq's military and questions about its political loyalty, see Michael Eisenstadt, *Like a Phoenix from the Ashes? The Future of Iraqi Military Power* (Washington, D.C.: Washington Institute for New East Policy, 1993), esp. pp. 43–66.

2. U.S. officials believe that Iraq could have a nuclear device within "three to six months" if it were able to obtain bomb-grade material from Russia. See Philip Finnegan, Theresa Hitchens, and Barbara Opall, "Nuclear Bomb Is within Iraq's Reach," *Defense News*, 12–18 September 1994, 3, 24.

3. Evidently U.S. intelligence agencies have been unable fully to unravel Iraq's nuclear supplier network, and they worry that Iran as well as Iraq may plug into it again when international pressure eases. Steve Coll, "U.S. Halted Nuclear Bid by Iran: China, Argentina Agreed to Cancel Technology Transfers," *Washington Post*, 17 November 1992, A1.

4. See Henri J. Barkey, "Turkey's Kurdish Dilemma," *Survival*, winter 1993–94, 52–54.

5. Ibid., 66.

6. Turkey has even opposed U.S. talk of lifting U.N. sanctions on the Kurdish areas of Iraq in order to help the Kurdish economy while keeping pressure on Saddam. See the discussion in House Subcommittee on Europe and the Middle East, *Developments in the Middle East, March 1994*, 1 March 1994 (Washington, D.C.: Government Printing Office, 1994), 26–27.

7. F. Gregory Gause III, "The Illogic of Dual Containment," *Foreign Affairs* 73, no. 2 (March/April 1994): 60–63.

8. Geoffrey Kemp points out that U.S. exports to Iran went from zero in 1989 to a projected $1 billion in 1993, and this overlooks the $3.5 billion that U.S. oil firms have returned to Iran by buying Iranian oil and refining it outside the United States. See his *Forever Enemies? American Policy and the Islamic Republic of Iran* (Washington D.C.: Carnegie Endowment for International Peace, 1994), 6. Because Iran was forced to change its internal fiscal policies, actual U.S. exports in 1993 were just over $600 million.

9. Steve Coll, "Technology from West Floods Iran: Equipment Intended for Civilian Projects Has Military Uses," *Washington Post*, 10 November 1992, p. A1.

10. See "Agreements on Debt Rescheduling Signed," FBIS-NES-94-074, 18 April 1994, 69.

11. See International Institute for Strategic Studies, *The Military Balance, 1993–1994* (1993), 115, and Vahe Petrossian, "Iran: Rafsanjani Seeks Way Out of Embarrassment," *Middle East Economic Digest*, 27 August 1993, 18.

12. Uncertainties are due to exchange rate problems. See Shlomo Gazit et al., *The Middle East Military Balance, 1992–1993* (Boulder, Colo.: Westview Press, 1993), 234, and Anoushiravan Ehteshami, "Iran's National Strategy: Striving for Regional Parity or Supremacy?" *International Defense Review*, 4 (1994): 29.

13. International Institute for Strategic Studies, *The Military Balance, 1993–1994*, 127. Adding in money spent on arms purchased abroad and defense construction

projects, the institute estimates that Saudi defense spending in 1992 may have been as high as $35 billion.

14. Elain Sciolino, "Iran's Difficulties Lead Some in U.S. to Doubt Threat," *New York Times*, 5 July 1994, p. A1.

15. Between 1989 and 1992, Russia accounted for 49 percent of all arms deliveries to Iran and for 64 percent of all arms contracts. China accounted for 24 percent of the arms deliveries and 16 percent of all contracts. See Richard F. Grimmett, *Conventional Arms Transfers to the Third World, 1985–1992*, Report 93-656F (Washington, D.C.: Congressional Research Service, July 1993), 32, 42, 44.

16. International Institute for Strategic Studies, *The Military Balance, 1993–1994*, 114–115; Ehteshami, "Iran's National Strategy," 33–34.

17. General information on Saudi and Iranian forces comes from the International Institute for Strategic Studies, *The Military Balance 1994–1995* (London: Brassey's, 1994), 128–29, 137–38.

18. See Malcolm R. Davis, "Russia's Big Arms Sales Drive," *Asia-Pacific Defence Reporter*, August–September 1994, 11–12. Doubt about the validity of such reports stems mainly from Iran's penury, but also from U.S. pressure on Russia to curb arms sales specifically to Iran.

19. Sciolino, "Iran's Difficulties."

20. Ehteshami, "Iran's National Strategy," 36. Note the official U.S. reaction to the inspections: "Iran has tried to incorrectly characterize the results of the visit as a clean bill of health for its nuclear program. The International Atomic Energy Agency has made clear that it could not vouch for facilities and sites visited, nor could it preclude the possibility that the facilities and sites visited would be used for other activities in the future." U.S. Arms Control and Disarmament Agency, "Adherence to and Compliance with Arms Control Agreements and the President's Report to Congress on Soviet Noncompliance with Arms Control Agreements," 14 January 1993, 17–18.

21. Douglas Jehl, "Iran Is Reported Acquiring Missiles," *New York Times*, 8 April 1993, p. A9.

22. Ibid.

23. Evidently the North Koreans could not test the missile at full range without sending it over Japanese airspace, something they were loathe to do, especially during the tense negotiations then under way over their nuclear weapons program. Reports indicate that North Korea may try to test the missile at full range from Iran. See Martin Sieff, "N. Korean Missiles May Be Tested in Iran This Year," *Washington Times*, 16 June 1994, p. A13.

24. Warren Strobel and Martin Sieff, "Blunder at Sea Embarrasses U.S.," *Washington Times*, 8 September 1993, 1.

25. As former CIA director Robert Gates put it, "Iran has an active chemical weapons programme. . . . It has produced at least several hundred tons of blister, choking and blood agents . . . at steadily increasing rate since 1984." Quoted in *Chemical Weapons Convention Bulletin*, March 1993, 13.

26. "The United States has determined that Iran probably has produced biological warfare agents and apparently has weaponized a small quantity of those agents."

U.S. Arms Control and Disarmament Agency, "Adherence to and Compliance with Arms Control Agreements," 14.

27. For an elaboration of these arguments, see Thomas L. McNaugher, "Ballistic Missiles and Chemical Weapons: The Legacy of the Iran-Iraq War," *International Security* 15, no. 2 (fall 1990): 5–34.

28. The Clinton five-year plan also allocates $17 billion for missile defenses. In its fiscal year 1994 submission, the Clinton administration shifted the focus of earlier ballistic-missile defense programs from national defense against long-range missiles to theater defense against shorter-range rockets, such as the Scud and the Nodong I. See Steven Kosiak, "Analysis of the Fiscal Year 1995 Defense Budget Request" (Washington D.C.: Defense Budget Project, 25 February 1995), 5.

29. Kosiak, "Analysis of the Fiscal Year 1995 Defense Budget Request," table 3. The national defense account (050) includes defense-related spending from other departments—notably the Department of Energy, which handles nuclear weaponry. It is thus higher than the Defense Department's budget authority (the 051 account). Budget authority includes money authorized (mainly for weapons and research and development) but not necessarily spent in the same year (as opposed to "outlays," which represent the amount actually spent in a given year).

30. See Congressional Budget Office, "Planning for Defense: Affordability and Capability of the Administration's Program," (Washington, D.C.: Congressional Budget Office, March 1994), 11–12. The office computes nominal replacement rates for modernizing U.S. forces based on the age of existing inventories and the expected size of the force. In the case of ships, fighter aircraft, and tanks, "steady state" replacement rates are substantially larger than those envisioned in current plans.

31. Indeed, at that point the Cold War defense establishment may well be in complete crisis. The defense industry, long familiar with the "boom and bust" of Cold War U.S. defense spending, will be looking for production contracts that will "get it well" after a lean decade of research and development, but if the weapons coming out of the industry are still more expensive to buy and maintain than those they replace, as has been largely the case in the past, the procurement surge, if it comes at all, will only expose the deeper problems in the nation's procurement process. Arguably, large procurement budgets in the 1980s allowed the Department of Defense to defer facing the toughest issues associated with the end of the Cold War, but only until the next generation of weapons comes along.

32. Unless otherwise specified, figures here are from Grimmett, "Conventional Arms Transfers to the Third World."

33. Clay Chandler, "Desert Shock: Saudis Are Cash-Poor," *The Washington Post*, 28 October 1994, A1, A30.

34. In January 1994, for example, the Saudis and the five major U.S. defense suppliers to the kingdom reached agreement to reschedule $9.2 billion in payments due, originally, in 1994 and 1995. The Saudis have raised some of the money from local banks and the Gulf International Bank. See *Middle East Economic Digest*, 29 April 1994, 10.

35. Force levels are from International Institute for Strategic Studies, *The Military Balance 1994–1995*, 138.

36. Thomas L. Friedman, "Saudi Air to Buy $6 Billion in Jets Built in the U.S.," *New York Times*, 17 February 1994, p. A1.

37. Natalie J. Goldring, "In Search of Arms Trade Control: Breaking the Cycle of Regional Arms Races" (paper presented before the International Studies Association, 28 March–1 April 1994), 3.

38. Grimmett, "Conventional Arms Transfers to the Third World," 18, 20, 37.

39. Ethan B. Kapstein, "America's Arms-Trade Monopoly," *Foreign Affairs* 73, no. 3 (May/June 1994): 13–19.

40. Computed from table 1C in Grimmett, "Conventional Arms Transfers to the Third World," 52.

41. Friedman, "Saudi Air to Buy $6 Billion in Jets."

42. Chandler, "Desert Shock: Saudis Are Cash-Poor," p. A30. See also Geraldine Brooks, "Saudi Arabia Is Facing Debts and Defections that Test U.S. Ties," *Wall Street Journal*, 25 October 1994, 1.

43. Although for the most part the number of Chinese weapons flowing to Iran was small, China's sale of Silkworm missiles to Iran became a serious issue in United States-China relations in 1987, when U.S. naval vessels began protecting Kuwaiti tankers journeying up the Persian Gulf. By threatening to withhold export licenses for key technologies Beijing was seeking, the United States was able to gain China's commitment to stop selling Silkworms. See Robert S. Greenburger, "U.S. Retaliates against Chinese for Sales to Iran," *Wall Street Journal*, 22 October 1987, 35; and Dilip Hiro, "Iran's Home-Made Arms Industry," *The Middle East*, April 1988, 18–19.

44. Henry Sokolski, "US Satellites to China," *International Defense Review*, April 1994, 24.

45. For a deeper discussion, see Thomas L. McNaugher, "A Strong China: Is the U.S. Ready?" *The Brookings Review* 12, no. 4 (fall 1994): 14–19.

15

REGIONAL SECURITY IN THE PERSIAN GULF: OBSTACLES AND OPTIONS

Richard K. Herrmann

Competing national ambitions, uncertain power differentials, and pent-up demands for domestic political change have made peace and security difficult objectives to achieve in the Middle East. Beyond these three factors, the systemic linkages between various conflicts in the region complicate matters significantly. For instance, twice in the recent past, unexpected developments in the Persian Gulf have badly disrupted progress in creating a process of change toward settlement in the Arab-Israeli conflict. The Iranian revolution diminished the achievement of the Camp David Accords, and Iraq's invasion of Kuwait put an end to the Bush administration's unilateral efforts to organize Israeli-Jordanian-Palestinian pre-election talks in Cairo. The multilateral Madrid process and the Gaza-Jericho agreement promise new achievements, perhaps possible because of the defeat of Iraq and the end of the Cold War. It is still unclear, however, whether this process of change in Arab-Israeli relations will promote peaceful adjustments in the Persian Gulf or will, once again, be vulnerable to unexpected threats spilling over from un-resolved Gulf animosities. This chapter examines the prospects for regional security in the Persian Gulf, but it assumes at the outset that just as in the Arab-Israeli conflict, progress in managing the conflicts in the Gulf must be thought of in dynamic terms within a regional and global system.

What is necessary in the long run for stable peace in the Persian Gulf is not possible today. The conflicts between Iran and Iraq, Iraq and Saudi Arabia, Iran or Iraq and the United States, and both Iran and Iraq with Israel are not amenable to short-term solutions. A host of other conflicts further complicates matters, as do internal opposition movements in Iran, Iraq, and Saudi Arabia, all of whose prospects for achieving radical political change are hard to assess. This chapter, consequently, concentrates on the objectives for regional security without implying that they are achievable in the short run.

The Objectives of Regional Security

At an abstract level, regional security would be achieved in a situation in which all of the governments in the region put the highest priority on the tasks of domestic economic development, saw little reason to attack or subvert others, and faced overwhelming costs if they tried. In this situation, imperial ambitions and defensive preoccupations would be set aside in favor of mutual economic gain and improvement in the quality of life. At the same time, both interdependent economic levers and military forces of countries in the region and outside of it would limit perceived opportunities for exploitation. Under these conditions, players in the region might be ready to accept something like the principles of the Helsinki Final Act, which included, among other things, respect for equal sovereignty, nonresort to the use or threat of force, inviolability of frontiers and territorial integrity, nonintervention, the peaceful settlement of disputes, equal rights and the self-determination of peoples, and respect for human rights and fundamental freedoms. As these political conditions were reached, arms control arrangements would become increasingly achievable, as they were in the U.S.-Soviet relationship. Of course, some military confidence-building measures may help to achieve the political conditions, but, judging from both the Cold War and other regional conflicts, it seems unlikely that unilateral military options will be surrendered independent of political reconciliation.

At a practical level, there is little agreement in the region regarding what must change in order to enhance regional security. To U.S. officials it appears that Iraq and Iran are the main obstacles, representing potential revisionist states that will forgo domestic priorities in order to pursue international expansion. To contain them, Washington concludes that it must preserve the current asymmetry in regional power that resulted from the collapse of the Soviet Union, Iran's setbacks in the Iran-Iraq War, and Iraq's defeat in the Gulf War. Beyond freezing the power asymmetries, the Clinton administration's policy of dual containment envisions a change in political regime in Iraq and at least a change in behavior in Iran. The conviction among leaders in Washington that Saddam Hussein still harbors revisionist ambitions and that the clerics in Iran might return to a messianic agenda provides sufficient reason to push for change inside both regimes and perhaps even to engage in "preventive war" should either "rogue" regime threaten to break out of containment, perhaps by acquiring nuclear weapons.

Meantime, in Saudi Arabia, the incentives to bring down the regime in Baghdad are strong and the costs of trying to do so are uncertain. Many Saudis complain that Washington's reluctance to topple the regime in Baghdad reflects Washington's interest in preserving Saudi dependence on U.S. protection. This dependence, of course, complicates Saudi efforts to deal with Arab nationalist or Islamic populist movements at home. Both the foreign military threats and the domestic pressure only incline the kingdom to push harder for preservation of the existing asymmetric power relationships. This involves containing Iranian military acquisition and Iran's economic recovery. With regard to Iraq, it involves bringing down the regime of Saddam Hussein and perhaps even dismembering Iraq.

Inside Iraq, of course, security is a rare commodity. It is not clear that the security of the people in Iraq would be assured even if the regime in Baghdad did give top priority to domestic reconstruction. The regime rules by coercion and faces opposition from Kurdish independence movements and Shia factions in the south, and, reportedly, it also faces desires for change within the Sunni Arab core. The U.N. sanctions have taken a heavy toll on the Iraqi economy and standard of living. Also, especially with regard to the Kurds, the sanctions put the territorial integrity of Iraq at risk. At this point, the Iraqi regime has many reasons to challenge the current regional status quo through subversion, terrorism, or whatever other means it can muster. While Saddam Hussein's ambitions may be temporarily constrained by overwhelming external power, they are unlikely to have entirely dissipated, and even if they have, the Iraqi internal security dilemma will provide incentives that work against Helsinki-type objectives.

Finally, in Iran the obstacles to regional security appear particularly formidable. The clerical regime faces serious disaffection at home, soft oil prices that make its economic mismanagement only more painful, and substantial U.S. efforts to constrain its economic and military development. For revolutionary leaders like Ayatollah Khamenei, the collapse of support for revolutionary objectives at home, including support among the technocrats inside the bureaucracy of the state, is exacerbated by external U.S. pressure applied to compel a retreat from the politics of revolutionary Islam. For the current Iranian government, accepting the power asymmetries of today as a permanent condition only ensures the capitulation of populist Islam to U.S. and Israeli preferences. Not accepting these asymmetries, on the other hand, may risk provoking a preventive war against Iran. Seeing overwhelming U.S. power as a threat to the interests of the Islamic republic, the regime in Tehran has strong incentives to pursue compensatory balancing options in the international system with Russia, China, and the new industrial states of South and Southeast Asia. It also may try to acquire nuclear weapons and promote anti-American political change in the Muslim world.

From nearly all points of view, the most serious obstacle to achieving regional security in the Persian Gulf is the revisionist ambition of the other actors. There is little agreement, however, on who the revisionists are. Most regional players would prefer a peace through strength approach as long as their strength is preponderant. To some degree, the classic elements of a spiral conflict are in place and are driving a regional arms race. At the same time, it is not only perceptions of threat that inhibit movement toward a regional security system. Incompatible political objectives and uncertainty about the power relationships of the future complicate the situation. They allow politicians on all sides to see opportunities to exploit current or future options and to resist accepting the existing political status quo as a starting point, as was necessary in the Helsinki process. The mix of threats and opportunities in the region has resulted in at least three major trends working against the achievement of regional security. The first is the unresolved status of Iraq and its future role in the region, the second is the spiral conflict between the United States and Iran, and the third is the regional arms race toward weapons of mass destruction.

Three Trends Running against Regional Security

The Unresolved Status of Iraq

Although Iraq was defeated in the Gulf War, neither its potential power base nor its political leadership was transformed. Saddam Hussein may have been surprised by his pan-Arab popularity during the crisis over Kuwait; after all, he had never ruled as a charismatic or populist leader. His message in 1990 excited many Arabs and promised a future with a powerful Arab state that mobilized the resources of the Arab world and took its place as a great power in the next century.[1] The image of an Arab peace-through-strength strategy may have promised dignity and international respect to an Arab mass base hungry for both, but it frightened the Persian Gulf Arab regimes that would be its first victims and certainly alarmed Israel and the United States. Iraq was soundly defeated, but for many Arabs the crime of Saddam was to push the crisis all the way to war and thus risk, and then lose, the Arab bargaining leverage. Invading Kuwait may have been seen as inappropriate, but the popular Arab attitudes on this point were far from reassuring for either the conservative Arab oil exporters on the Gulf or security-conscious Israelis.

For them, the aspirations of Saddam Hussein and many Arab nationalists were clear and could only be contained by superior power. How to achieve this in the long run, however, remained controversial.

Although a number of analysts advocated positive U.S.-Iraqi relations before the Gulf War,[2] arguing that Saddam Hussein had changed his attitudes about the West and had relaxed his Arab nationalist ambitions, after the Gulf War there appeared to be almost universal consensus about Saddam's aspirations. He was seen as an aggressive leader who aspired to play the role of an Arab Bismarck with the tactics of Genghis Khan. Most American analysts assumed that he wanted to dominate the Persian Gulf, use its financial resources to acquire a major military capability, and then move toward hegemony in the Arab world and perhaps the Middle East overall. Moreover, it appeared that Saddam calculated relative power in psychological rather than strictly material terms, putting heavy emphasis on willpower and a determination to make the impossible possible.[3] Therefore, even though he might be deterred or, if necessary, defeated, this could be accomplished only at substantial cost and with persistent vigilance.

Many Persian Gulf Arabs, Israelis, and Americans complain in hindsight that President Bush did not continue the Gulf War until Saddam Hussein had been toppled and the Iraqi military had been more thoroughly destroyed. Faced with the persistence of the current Iraqi regime, they see no solution to their long-term security dilemma. Iraq can be contained with sanctions and intrusive U.N. inspection regimes, but for how long? The costs of the status quo are terrible for the Iraqis and heartbreaking for many other Arabs. Saddam's ambitions may not be as likely to wane as is the international consensus containing Iraq. Arab nationalists will empathize with the suffering of the Iraqi people, and financial considerations will bring Russian, French, and German interests back to Iraq. Because the Arab agenda voiced by Saddam is much less threatening to European audiences than it is to Gulf Arab, Israeli, and U.S. audiences, Washington is likely to find it increasingly difficult to sustain U.N. support for the sanctions regime that Iraq faces. The Iraqi government certainly calculates this way.[4] If the sanctions regime does not lead to political change in Iraq before the sanctions wither, then over time Saddam's government will rebuild the Iraqi power base and return to its revisionist agenda.[5] Recent Iraqi statements about the vulnerability of Arab Persian Gulf states only reinforce this interpretation.[6]

With the return of U.S. troops to Kuwait in the fall of 1994, the pressure to either dispense with Saddam Hussein or accept his eventual international rehabilitation increased. Preserving the post-Gulf War status quo of a weak and isolated Iraq ruled by Saddam Hussein would be increasingly expensive and perhaps politically untenable. At the same time, a revitalized Iraq still ruled by Saddam would frighten the Persian Gulf states and their allies and perhaps touch off a preventive war. Iraq without Saddam Hussein, however, was also no panacea for regional security. Although reports of assassination attempts, military arrests, and other plots appear regularly, it is impossible to predict how a transition in Iraq would unfold or what it would unleash.[7] An Iraq that was led by a Baath Party freed from Saddam's dictatorship might align with Syria and seek its support for Iraq's territorial claims against Turkey and Iran. Such a development could affect Syrian calculations about the possible long-term power options in the region and, in turn, affect its policies toward Israel. A more Islamic Iraq, on the other hand, might find a way to join the Economic Cooperation Organization with Iran, Turkey, and Pakistan and strengthen the political pressures facing conservative Gulf states. Presumably, without Saddam Hussein and the Takriti-dominated elite, Iraq would be able to build international support for lifting the U.N. sanctions and, in reasonably short order, recoup the international leverage associated with its population, military, and resource bases. Given the general popularity of the ideas voiced by Saddam in 1990, these alternative scenarios for Iraqi recovery are hardly more reassuring to conservative Gulf states and Israel than the gradual recovery of Saddam Hussein's Iraq.

The vision of a democratic Iraq, representing a voluntary confederation of the peoples living in Iraq, is attractive in Washington. There is a hope that such an Iraq would provide domestic security for its people and, as a democracy, be constrained from foreign aggression. No one, however, thinks that creating such an Iraq will be an easy or short-term task. Many analysts in Washington and in the region fear that the vision is naive. They argue that it overestimates the unique effects of Saddam Hussein's personality and underestimates how much the nature of the Iraqi state and the divisions among the potential opposition groups require authoritarian leadership and will be moved by widespread Arab nationalist sentiments.[8] In their view, Iraq as a unit is a "failed state," and the only real solution for regional security is its dissolution. This might involve creating an independent Kurdish state, allowing the Sunni minority to integrate with Syria, and letting the Shia follow their own course either with the Sunni Arabs, perhaps with Iran, or maybe as a small state themselves. The Kurdish state would most likely receive support from Israel and the United States, whereas the Sunni might get help from Saudi Arabia.

New state structures in the territory currently ruled by Baghdad might address the various fears of a resurgent Iraq, but would at the same time fuel other anxieties. These might include Turkish and Iranian fears of Kurdish secession, Saudi fears of a more powerful Shia Iranian base, and Israeli fears of both a more powerful Iran and a more powerful Syria. The transition to a new state structure could touch off a regional war as Turkey, Iran, Syria, Saudi Arabia, and Israel all move to influence the direction of change. At this point, the foreign minsters of Turkey, Iran, and Syria have met at least six times to discuss the future of Iraq and to insist on the preservation of its territorial integrity. The various Kurdish factions and Shia opposition groups, in contrast, have sought support from abroad while fighting among themselves.[9] The persisting, if not escalating, hostility between the United States and Iran (and populist Islam, more generally) only increases the fears in Washington about the unresolved situation in Iraq and complicates efforts to enhance regional security.

U.S.-Iranian Spiral

The notion of a spiral conflict implies that some of the escalation in the hostility is due to mutual perceptions of threat that could be reduced if the two sides understood better each other's security dilemmas. However, in the U.S.-Iranian case, leaders on both sides insist emphatically that this is not true of their hostile relationship. It is based, they argue, on fundamentally incompatible interests and ambitions. Leaders in both Washington and Tehran insist that the tension is a result of the imperial and immoral aspirations of the other. In their view, it can be contained only by mobilizing sufficient countervailing power and can be resolved only if the countervailing power compels a fundamental transformation in the political system of the adversary.[10] How much of the relationship is a spiral and how much is a deterrence situation based on immutable incompatible interests is difficult to decipher. It is necessary to do so, however, before examining competing strategies for trying to convince both sides to focus on domestic concerns, confident in their security and deterred from seeking exploitative opportunities.

It is clear to most Americans that President Clinton was elected on a promise to give primary attention to domestic priorities. The same is true for most Iranians with regard to President Rafsanjani. While some leaders on both sides recognize the importance of the domestic pressures facing their counterparts, the prevailing views conclude that even if the leaders themselves wanted to concentrate on domestic issues, thereby making regional security more possible, they would be unable to do so because of the decisive weight of the fundamentalist clerics in Iran, according to the U.S. view, and the Zionist and military vested interests in the United States, according to the Iranian perspective. At this point, the national security arguments carry the day on both sides. Washington pursues "dual containment" and tries to mobilize European and Japanese pressure against Iran and Iraq; Iran, meantime, tries to construct a regional and Asian answer to containment, based on Islamic ties to Pakistan, Turkey, the newly independent countries of Central Asia, the countries of the Association of Southeast Asian Nations, and China.

President Rafsanjani is not anxious to become an Iranian Gorbachev—that is, a leader who initiates reform within the system and engineers a process of change that destroys the regime. He appears, however, to identify strongly with the Iranian nation and, while loyal to the transnational Islamic ummah, is less ready than prominent revolutionary clerical leaders are to sacrifice Iranian interests for the broader ummah agenda.[11] This, along with his interest in economic development, leads him to avoid direct confrontations with the United States. He appears determined to meet the United States with countervailing power if necessary but is also prepared to pursue de-escalatory moves and détente. In the fall of 1993, this latter idea was advanced by Rafsanjani's former representative to the United Nations, Raja'i-Khorasani, touching off an intense debate in Tehran.

Khorasani wrote a letter to Ayatollah Khamenei reportedly advancing the idea that Iranian relations with the United States were necessary. He argued that U.S. power was a fact of life in the Persian Gulf and that the hostility between the United States and Iran, while partly based on conflicting interests, could be defused in important ways.[12] Washington and Tehran, for instance, had a common interest in not allowing change in Iraq to spark a regional war, and both needed to play a role in any Persian Gulf security system. Moreover, Iran could help the United States and Russia find a solution in Afghanistan, and the United States could help Iran deal with potential Turkish-Iranian tensions and obviously make it easier for Iran to acquire foreign capital. Needless to say, the argument provoked a storm of criticism from within the regime, including a direct denunciation by Ayatollah Khamenei, who equated it with capitulation.[13] Rafsanjani did not endorse the Khorasani line, but the newspaper he controls argued that the United States needed and wanted a relationship with Iran and that with certain adjustments in both U.S. policy and Iranian policy this was possible.[14] One unconfirmed report in April 1994 suggested that after months of fighting over the issue, Khamenei had asked Rafsanjani to study the question of relations with the United States and include Khorasani in the deliberations.[15]

Iranian opposition to a U.S. presence in the Persian Gulf, Tehran's terror and assassination operations against Iranian dissidents abroad, and its condemnation of the Gaza-Jericho settlement work against any rapprochement in U.S.-Iranian relations. So does Iranian sympathy for populist Islamic change in Egypt and Saudi Arabia. Iran's support for Hezbollah and Hamas and the violence that these groups direct against Israeli and U.S. targets also fuels escalation and reinforces stereotypes on all sides. Although the United States and Iran still do between $4 billion and $5 billion of business with each other each year related to the oil trade, popular images on both sides present a picture of unmitigated and total hostility. Few issues play a bigger role in supporting these conclusions than the Iranian opposition to the Gaza-Jericho peace process, a process that the Clinton administration sees as its greatest foreign-policy achievement.

Ayatollah Khamenei, like other revolutionary clerics, condemned the Gaza-Jericho settlement and reaffirmed Muslim claims to the Islamic holy sites in Jerusalem.[16] He publicly received Fathi al-Saqaqi of the Palestinian Islamic Jihad in Tehran while promising more than $10 million to Hamas.[17] Rafsanjani has also been critical of the accord, but, according to revolutionary clerics, the president has met with Arafat and has not raised concerns about his "capitulation" with enough vigor.[18]

Although Iran is opposed to the Gaza-Jericho plan, it is less clear what its bottom line is with regard to Israel. Iranian leaders all agree that the current accord does not go far enough in addressing the aspirations of the Palestinians and in protecting Muslim claims to Jerusalem. They also agree that it has been negotiated from a position of Arab weakness and Islamic disunity.[19] Some leaders call into question the existence of Israel, but most feel that the Palestinians should have a state that includes some arrangement with regard to Jerusalem, and they argue that Israel will agree to this only if it is compelled to do so by countervailing power.[20] Whether they would accept a two-state solution is not clear, but Rafsanjani has not questioned the position of President Assad, who evidently accepts a two-state solution. The Foreign Ministry is clear in its confidence in Syrian policy,[21] while even more hard-line voices, such as the Deputy Speaker of the Majlis, Hasan Rowhani, continue to travel to Damascus, meet Assad, and express their confidence in him, despite their criticism of the Palestine Liberation Organization-Israeli peace process.[22]

It is important to note that Israel and Iran were traditional allies and that even in the 1980s they continued to find reasons to cooperate against Iraq. Islamic clerics, of course, identify with Jerusalem in ways that complicate Iranian-Israeli relations, but Iranian nationalists are more flexible in this regard. For leaders like Rafsanjani, who identify strongly with both Islam and the Iranian nation, the situation is unclear. No confident judgments can be made about what is possible in the future. In Israel, of course, Iranian power is seen not in simple bargaining terms, but rather as a potentially serious long-term threat. For Iran, on the other hand, Israel remains the main spearhead of Washington's imperial aspirations in the region and a serious enemy of Islam.[23] In both cases, fears about future power relationships, as much as imperial ambitions, drive the arms race.

Regional Arms Race

Oil revenues have made it possible for states in the Persian Gulf to acquire ever more sophisticated weapons. The persisting political conflicts in the area have given them the incentive to do so. The net result has been a steady escalation in the acquisition of weapons, the levels of weapons deployed against one another, the levels of threatened violence backing up deterrent threats, and the determination to seek weapons of mass destruction.

Weapons Acquisition. The rate of weapons acquisition has been uneven across the key states in the region. In the early 1980s, Iraq led the way, with Saudi Arabia not far behind (Table 15.1). Iran trailed substantially behind as much of the world tilted toward Iraq. Deliveries to Iraq dropped noticeably after the 1988 cease-fire with Iran, and they continued to decline into 1990. Since the Gulf War, U.N. sanctions have prevented Iraq from rejoining the race, and few, if any, weapons deliveries have been reported. Deliveries to Iran, meantime, have continued, although quantities have dropped

Table 15.1. Trends in weapon acquisition (in billions of dollars).

	Iran	Iraq	Saudi Arabia
1982–1985	6.99	27.7	23.25
1986–1989	8.12	18.0	23.48
1989–1992	4.50	5.0	25.50

Source: Richard F. Grimmett, *CRS Report for Congress: Conventional Arms Transfers to the Third World, 1985–1992* (Washington, D.C.: Congressional Research Service, 19 July 1993).

to under $5 billion from 1989 to 1992, less than one-fifth of the value of the weapons delivered to Saudi Arabia in the same period. In 1992, for instance, Iran received $300 million in deliveries, making it the tenth-largest recipient in the world, while $4.5 billion worth of arms were delivered to Saudi Arabia, which made it the largest recipient in the world.[24] In terms of defense expenditures, the Saudis and Iranians were more similar: in 1992, Saudi Arabia spent $14.5 billion, or 13 percent of its gross national product, and Iran spent $13 billion, or nearly 15 percent of its gross national product.[25] In Saudi Arabia's case, the United States and Western European states have been the main suppliers throughout the past decade. In Iran's case, China was the main supplier from 1986 to 1989, but Russia became by far its largest supplier in the more recent period.[26]

Weapons Deployment. The uneven trends in weapons acquisition and the losses suffered by Iran and Iraq in the two recent Persian Gulf wars have not entirely overcome the leads that Iran and Iraq had over Saudi Arabia. They have, however, gone a long way toward reducing military imbalances that might have previously encouraged one side to attack. Today Saudi Arabia's army remains much smaller than Iran's, but its air force has better planes, with pilots who train more often (Table 15.2). Iraq still enjoys a sizable advantage in tanks over Saudi Arabia or Iran but has a comparable number of aircraft and pilots, neither of which per-formed well in the war for Kuwait. Perfor-mance, training, coor-dination among units, reconnaissance, com-mand and control, and the host of other fac-

Table 15.2. Selected military capabilities, 1994–95.			
	Iran	Iraq	Saudi Arabia
Army troops	305,000	350,000	73,000
Tanks	700	2,300	700
Combat aircraft	262	316	293

Source: International Institute for Strategic Studies, *The Military Balance, 1994–95* (London: International Institute for Strategic Studies, 1994).

tors that go into a serious study of the military balance are not reflected in the crude figures displayed in Table 15.2. The Gulf Cooperation Coun-cil forces suffer weaknesses in many of these areas, as do the armed forces of Iran and Iraq. The balance is complicated further by logistic and naval limitations. While the balance is difficult to assess in detail, there is no obvious opportunity for any single regional player to establish decisive superiority. Foreign support for regional actors makes the situation more complex still, but for the most part it heavily favors the GCC. Although China and Pakistan provide matériel to Iran and Iraq, their ability and willingness to do so is rather small compared with the U.S. commitment to the GCC states.

Threats. The dangers in the arms race are that it may upset the balance in the future, and it makes estimating relative power a more difficult and uncertain enterprise. Both change and uncertainty in relative power have led to war before, and the escalation ensures that if war comes, it will be fought with more destructive weapons.[27] To some extent, the destabiliz-ing effects of the current arms race may be offset by the enhanced deterrent power it lends to Saudi Arabia and the GCC states. After all, the GCC states have not traditionally challenged either Iran or Iraq, and they still cannot match either state in terms of troops under arms. The GCC connection to the United States, however, communicates more to Iran and Iraq than simply deterrence. The memory of Operation Desert

Storm and the United States' support for Israeli nuclear superiority and Israel's compellent policy toward the Palestinians convinces many Iranian and Iraqi leaders that recent trends may portend threat in the future. Certainly in Iran these trends have contributed to the search for missiles and weapons of mass destruction.

Weapons of Mass Destruction. Few possible developments frighten U.S. and Israeli leaders more than nuclear proliferation in the Persian Gulf. In both Washington and Tel Aviv, nonproliferation is high among foreign-policy priorities, with the U.S. policy of dual containment taking special aim at Iran and Iraq. In Iran there is also talk of nonproliferation; Iran, after all, has signed the Nuclear Nonproliferation Treaty and agrees to regular International Atomic Energy Agency inspections. Iran's focus of concern is Israeli nuclear forces, the U.S. display of firepower in Operation Desert Storm, and recent arms deliveries to the GCC. Iranian leaders speak often about U.S. and Israeli hostility toward Islam, and Iran in particular, and have no trouble imagining scenarios in which Iran will be in conflict with a nuclear-capable power. In this circumstance, Iran does not enjoy a deterrent nuclear umbrella, nor can it expect Russia, China, or any other nuclear-capable state to extend deterrence. The logic pushing Iran toward the development of its own nuclear device and missile delivery system is powerful. Iranian leaders deny a nuclear ambition, but few in Washington or Tel Aviv believe them. While the United States works to prohibit Iranian progress in the nuclear arena, the options for acquisition of materials and help with internal development expand as Iranian relations with China, Kazakhstan, North Korea, Pakistan, and Russia improve.

To date, both the evidence of and the arguments over Iran's progress towards developing and acquiring nuclear weapons are mixed. To some extent, the debate over this issue follows predictable political lines: Israeli and U.S. officials assert that Iran is actively attempting to develop nuclear weapons or to acquire them from elsewhere, while Iranian and, to some extent, Russian and European statements argue that Iran is not seeking such capabilities and that the Iranian nuclear program is directed toward peaceful civilian energy uses. Evidence about Iran's intentions and actions to date is thin. Probably the most consistent source of such evidence is the International Atomic Energy Agency, which regularly inspects Iranian nuclear facilities under the terms of the Nuclear Nonproliferation Treaty. Hans Blix, the agency's secretary-general, has asserted repeatedly that Iran "is using nuclear energy in a peaceful way" and does not intend to do otherwise.[28] Such assertions are contradicted by U.S. and Israeli claims that Iran is seeking to acquire nuclear weapons, backed by observations of Iranian-North Korean technical cooperation over the past decade and some evidence that nuclear scientists from the former Soviet Union have gone to work for Iran and other countries in the region.[29] These assertions have been weak on hard evidence, however, and Western claims about Iranian activities sometimes contradict one another: while the Central Intelligence Agency believes that Iran lacks a program to develop long-range missiles, Israel's intelligence agency has asserted that Iran is a year away from such a capability.[30]

There are strong disincentives and substantial obstacles working against the Iranian development of nuclear weapons and other weapons of mass destruction, but the current trends in the conventional arms race in the Persian Gulf are not among these. To the contrary, they push in the opposite direction, and Rafsanjani makes no secret of the active missile industry in Iran.[31] Because of the U.N. sanctions, Iraqi programs have been stalled, but the effort there provoked an Israeli attack in the early 1980s and was part of the Bush administration's calculation to prosecute the Gulf War the way it did.[32] Israeli leaders have traditionally felt that their nuclear capability gives them an escalatory option that can short-circuit a drawn-out war and deter Arab hopes for success in a war of attrition. Washington, likewise, might act preemptively against an Iranian nuclear program. Even if Iran did make the transition to a mutual nuclear deterrent relationship vis-à-vis Israel, there is no assurance this would be stable. It might only encourage Israeli planning for preemptive strikes and promote an Iranian and Arab notion that escalation in a conventional war could be kept limited and that war, therefore, might be a viable option.

In the early 1970s, U.S. arms control advocates tried to persuade the Nixon administration not to deploy missiles equipped with multiple independently targeted reentry vehicle (MIRV) warheads. The temptation to exploit the Western technological lead over the Soviet Union, however, was too great. Eventually, both sides deployed the systems, adding to the security of neither. In the 1980s, the Reagan administration decided to pursue the Strategic Defense Initiative, evidently hoping that competition in the technological high frontier would bankrupt Moscow and convince Soviet leaders that they could no longer compete. Many U.S. leaders believe that the Strategic Defense Initiative and Reagan's "peace through strength" policies helped to end the Cold War and that—although arms races can turn out as the MIRV experience did— they can also lead to unilateral victory. I will pursue this argument further below, but at this point suffice it to say that the arms race in the Persian Gulf continues to ensure that national-security elites prevail internally in most countries and that foreign threats continue to command high priority over domestic concerns. Whether the United States should step up the pressure unilaterally in the hope of breaking the backs of the current regimes in Iran and Iraq and compelling inward-looking leaders to take power or whether the United States and other players important to the region should look for alternative paths along which to pursue the objectives of regional security is a question pursued in the next two sections.

The Role for U.S. Power: Dual Containment?

At the beginning of the Cold War, George Kennan argued for a strategy of containment.[33] The logic was straightforward. He felt the Soviet Union, like Nazi Germany before it, was expansionist and ruled by a mass-based populist party playing on the symbols of greatness and world leadership. A frontal confrontation from outside the state would strengthen the popular patriotic support for the regime, legitimate its domestic mobilization on a war footing, and risk unacceptable levels of violence. A better strategy would be to deny the regime success in foreign policy and take away its ability to legitimate its claim to worldwide vanguard status. In this situation, the regime would be compelled to establish its legitimacy by attending to domestic and quality-of-life issues at home and thus be forced internally to moderate its foreign ambitions. The Clinton administration has borrowed the label of Kennan's strategy in its policy of dual containment toward Iran and Iraq.[34] The essence of the strategy is to isolate and sufficiently pressure the regimes in Tehran and Baghdad, hoping that such containment will produce either internal revolt and regime change or a fundamental transformation of the regimes from within.[35]

Because of the enormous military advantage that the United States enjoys vis-à-vis Iraq and Iran, dual containment may work. The record with this sort of coercive diplomacy is mixed, but in theory it can be successful.[36] In practice, its prospects in the specific circumstances of the Persian Gulf and the costs, both direct and in lost opportunities, that it will generate must be considered.

Containing Iraq

Although the Iraqi regime enjoys neither the mass base support nor the global potential power that Stalinist Russia did, it does aspire to change the state structure in the Persian Gulf. U.S. power plays a central role in containing Iraqi revisionist ambitions, but it is not sufficient to achieve the objectives of regional security. Iraq is contained by U.N. restrictions on both military acquisition and commercial behavior. Even if the international consensus in favor of continuing to apply the commercial sanctions weakens, as it appears to be doing, the consensus on long-term monitoring and U.N. imposed restrictions on Iraqi military acquisition is firm. A U.N. inspection system is in place, and it will make the rebuilding of Iraqi military assets difficult. At a minimum, it will provide early warning and lengthen the time frame of any future Iraqi buildup.

Moreover, Iraq's neighbors in Saudi Arabia, Turkey, and Iran are all opposed to the reemergence of Iraqi power. Although Iran and Iraq have engaged in bilateral talks, they continue to be unlikely allies as long as Saddam Hussein remains in power.[37] Turkey, meantime, is interested in commercial relations with Iraq, but not in the revival of a militarist Iraqi state. In both Turkey's and Iran's cases, substantial regional power could be brought to bear against Iraq, as could countervailing forces from Saudi Arabia, Syria, and even Egypt.

There are a number of viable military options for containing Iraq. Some of them revolve around U.S. power, but others mobilize European and regional states to play a role as well. During the Gulf War, the U.N. coalition coordinated multilateral power, especially at sea. After the war, there was talk of a GCC alliance with Egypt and Syria.[38] The "GCC plus two" idea was short-lived and not popular in Saudi Arabia and other GCC states. The Persian Gulf states preferred a defense relationship with the United States that promised better weapons and greater freedom of political maneuver within the arena of intra-Arab politics.

The availability of the U.S. option in many ways drove out consideration of more regionally based plans. It allowed the sheikdoms of the Persian Gulf to assert a notion of Gulf-state nationalism and to deny their connection to Arab nationalism. Whether the publics in the Gulf agree with their rulers' hopes that state nationalism now supersedes Arab nationalism is unclear, but the exclusive reliance of the Gulf states on Washington has frustrated the leaders in Cairo and Damascus. Both after the Gulf War and in the fall of 1994, the gulf states turned to the United States for troops and defense, ignoring Arab options for dealing with the Iraqi threat. The resulting U.S.-GCC alliance has contained Iraq, but it has not helped to secure the political acceptance in the region of the city-state sheikdoms that now claim to be nations. Gulf-state nationalism may replace Arab nationalism, but if it does not, the sheikdoms' exclusive reliance on Washington will complicate future regional plans and leave Washington with the unenviable choice of either increasing its permanent military presence to preserve political control or accepting the risks of political change in the midst of populist alienation and dislike for the United States and its presence in the region.

Containing Iran

U.N. sanctions and broad regional opposition to Saddam Hussein create options for dealing with Iraq that do not exist for dealing with Iran. The avenues for change in Iran, however, are different. Unlike in Iraq, where the prospects for change within the regime are unlikely, in Iran transformation within the regime is possible and, some say, already under way. The German government, for instance, appears to envision a process of economic engagement with Iran, like the détente it had with the Soviet Union in the 1970s.[39] This, it hopes, would strengthen Rafsanjani and the technical class in Iran and lead to a process of change similar to what it saw in Moscow in the 1980s, with revolutionary institutions losing their grip under the pressure of economic development and global interdependence. The United States, on the other hand, appears to prefer a more radical scenario. Rather than working for change within the system, at the risk of strengthening and legitimating Rafsanjani and his cohort, the United States would prefer to isolate the entire regime and push it toward collapse or capitulation.

To make the U.S. scenario work, Washington needs to persuade Berlin to forgo its détente strategy. It also needs to isolate Iran effectively and contain the dangers of the military-political spiral that will result until a threshold is reached and the regime capitulates or collapses. There are significant obstacles to achieving U.S. objectives in this way. First, Iran is not isolated, and it plays an important role in the Persian Gulf, the Caucasus, South Asia, and Central Asia. It is active geopolitically, working to counter U.S. pressure. It has worked hard to revive the Economic Cooperation Organization, connect the Economic Cooperation Organization to the Association of Southeast Asian Nations and court relations with Muslim Southeast Asians in Indonesia.[40] Iran continues to be an important oil exporter and promises to be an important source of natural gas well into the next century. Recently, Iran and Turkmenistan agreed to build pipelines connecting their enormous gas reserves to the expanding markets in South Asia and Southeast Asia.[41] There also is substantial European interest in pipelines running to the West as well.[42]

Iran's military and economic relations with Pakistan continue to expand, as do its relations with China.[43] Tehran has also had success in developing an arms relationship with Russia, and while Russian leaders fear Islamic radicalism in Central Asia and blame Iran for some of their troubles, they also appreciate the mediating role that Iran has played in the Tajik and Afghan civil wars and agree with the Germans regarding the best strategy for change.[44] Iran has also managed to open a serious dialogue and commercial relationship with India, despite Iran's growing ties with Pakistan and its open support for Muslims in Kashmir. Finally, many Europeans agree with the German assessment of Iran and, despite U.S. pressure, have agreed to negotiate the extension of financial credits to Iran. In the spring of 1994, talks were under way between Iran and Italy, Spain, France, Belgium, and the Netherlands. Japan in early 1994 extended $2 billion in credit to Iran, while Germany extended $2.6 billion.[45] Iran's total foreign debt is around $30 billion—a substantial figure, according to clerics who fear dependence, but manageable (assuming oil prices do not stay soft forever), given the potential of Iran's economy.

Western European, Russian, and Asian decisions not to isolate Iran not only work against the success of the U.S. scenario for change but also reinforce the view in Washington that without allied support, there is no choice but for Washington to go it alone and extend its military influence to the Persian Gulf. Central to this conclusion, of course, is an assumption that Iran needs to accommodate Washington's demands with regard to a nonproliferation nuclear policy, renunciation of terrorism, and acceptance of the Gaza-Jericho process. Although many leaders in Europe, Russia, and Asia would like Iran to accept these conditions as well, there is much less consensus on these matters than there is the United States. This may be especially true for the Gaza-Jericho process, where Asian and Russian leaders and even many Western Europeans see Iranian opposition to the process as best dealt with by further and faster Israeli concessions to the Palestinians, and not only by more U.S. and Israeli pressure on Iran, Hamas, and Hezbollah.

Perhaps the biggest risk in the unilateral strategy of U.S. preponderance is that it does not allow for an easy transition to an alternative regime in the future. In fact, it relies so heavily on coercive diplomacy and military instruments—what Joseph Nye calls hard power—that it establishes a security regime that will last only as long as the preponderant power is exercised.[46] In this situation, Washington could face a situation in the Person Gulf analogous to what Mikhail Gorbachev faced in Eastern Europe. The Gulf will be important to U.S. interests, but a burden to dominate and impossible to withdraw from without facing nationalist and revolutionary change, much of which will be anti-American. This may not be a compelling argument against the role Washington wants to play militarily today, but it is a powerful reason to look beyond unilateral U.S. options and explore strategies of regional inclusion and change.

Alternative Regional Options

At this point, strategies for security in the Persian Gulf are competitive. The GCC states turn to the United States for arms transfers and either on-the-ground or over-the-horizon military commitments. The Iranians, meantime, construct a countervailing Asian or Muslim axis that might facilitate the proliferation of missiles and weapons of mass destruction. Washington traditionally enhanced the security of its allies in the GCC by arms transfers, and it only accelerated the trend in this regard after the Gulf War. Neither Iran nor Iraq has been able to keep up in the arms race in the 1990s, but both will surely try their best if the momentum continues. No doubt, the globalization of the weapons industry and the downturn in the domestic demand for arms in the United States, Russia, and Europe has intensified the commercial competition for the Persian Gulf arms market.[47] Despite several rounds of talks among supplier countries about coordinating and limiting arms transfers to the Gulf, business is still booming. The escalation may appear to buy unilateral security for the GCC states in the short run, but it risks pushing the confrontation to ever higher levels of potential violence. It keeps external security at the top of everyone's agenda and works against a turn toward domestic preoccupations that would enhance regional security. At a moment when offensive options are limited on all sides, there are at least four alternatives worth pursuing.

First, the rapprochements between Saudi Arabia and Iran and between other GCC states and Iran that began in 1993 and 1994 should be encouraged. The movement in these relationships is very tentative and preliminary, but it is positive just the same. At this point, even the reported telephone calls between King Fahd and President Rafsanjani serve a useful function, as would the further resolution of the Iran-United Arab Emirates dispute over Abu Musa.[48] No doubt, serious differences and fears remain. The royal family, for instance, has decided to make concessions to the Shia Arabs in the Eastern Province of Saudi Arabia in ways never before considered, possibly as a way to defuse the Iranian political threat or perhaps as a gesture to Iran. The decision may serve both functions, as has Iran's pursuit of pragmatic cooperative relations with Qatar and Kuwait.[49] Foreign Minister Velayati's emphasis on state-to-state relations also provides the logic for a new dialogue, as does the debate among the Saudi elite concerning the spiral nature of their current confrontation with Tehran.[50]

Second, a new security dialogue in the Persian Gulf should be promoted, perhaps leading to an institutionalized conference, such as the Conference on Security and Cooperation in Europe became in the 1970s. At present, this idea may seem farfetched, but it could be a compromise outcome between the two opposing conceptions that Washington and Tehran are pushing. The United States and Russia are committed to the multilateral security talks connected to the Madrid process. These talks, although they have been ongoing for some time, have made only limited headway in the Levant and have hardly begun in the Persian Gulf. Saudi

Arabia and the GCC states have been reluctant participants, if participants at all, and Syria has boycotted the entire formal procedure. The problem is that the multilateral talks are burdened by the weight of Arab-Israeli political differences and the Arab reluctance to engage in creeping normalization of relations with Israel prior to political settlement.

While the United States has tied multilateral talks to the Arab-Israeli process initiated in Madrid, Iran has been promoting a regional conception of a new security regime. Upon his return from Central Asia in late 1993, President Rafsanjani began to speak of a regional Asian security arrangement.[51] In early 1994, the Iranian foreign ministry developed the idea further. Foreign Minster Velayati, after meeting with Chinese, Russian, Indian, and Pakistani leaders in March 1994, suggested there should be a regional Asian security force able to help solve and prevent conflicts between countries in the region.[52] Deputy Foreign Minister Javad Zarif expanded on the idea in April, calling for the establishment of new security and cooperation arrangements in the Persian Gulf, coordinated limits on military expenditures, ceilings on arms transfers, and the establishment of a zone free from weapons of mass destruction in the Gulf and the Middle East.[53] Predictably, the Iranians drew attention to Israeli nuclear forces in their discussion of a zone free from weapons of mass destruction, but by doing so they only reaffirmed the obvious need to find a way to eventually merge the Madrid multilateral arms control talks and the Iranian proposals. Obviously, even if there is progress on Arab-Israeli issues and the multilateral security talks bear fruit in terms of confidence-building measures and arms control, these cannot go very far if they do not involve Iraq and Iran. Neither Syrian nor Israeli security can be assured independent of the arms race in the Gulf.

What is needed is a regional process of security talks that focus on the Persian Gulf and are cut free from the Madrid process. These talks should not be sponsored by the United States and Russia, although both need to attend. Perhaps the Islamic Conference Organization and the Economic Cooperation Organization, or Pakistan and Turkey, can host the meeting and determine the participants. At minimum, it needs to include Saudi Arabia, Turkey, Iran, the GCC states, and the non-Persian Gulf states that these countries think are essential: perhaps Egypt, Syria, the United States, Russia, and China. In the long run, this process would need to connect to the Madrid agenda, including normalization with Israel, but it is premature to seek this long-term objective now. Insisting that the final status of Jerusalem be included at the beginning of the Madrid process would doom the enterprise. Insisting that the Gulf players accept the process of normalization with Israel within the Madrid formula would likewise ensure that security talks in the Gulf are stillborn.

A separate process is necessary now that would promote a Persian Gulf-wide discussion of coordinated limits on weapons acquisition, deployments, confidence-building measures, the future of Iraq, and peacekeeping forces (some of which may not come from countries in the region), which might help to secure mutual deterrent relationships. There might also be agreement in this forum on issues related to political noninterference, and someday even agreement on principles like those outlined at Helsinki. That, of course, like the connection to the Madrid agenda, would need to be the result of a process, not the precondition for its initiation. Syria could be a direct participant in both the Gulf and the Madrid multilateral processes; Egypt might be as well, and thus serve as a conduit for future coordination. Achievements in the Gulf forum could promote progress in the Madrid process and be a stabilizing factor should Gaza-Jericho and Golan negotiations not proceed smoothly.

Third, the regional forum must deal with the future of Iraq. Many of the players will want to see the regime in Baghdad collapse. Possibly in concert, some of them can make this happen. The regional adversaries certainly have more stake in breaking the stalemated status quo than the United States or Russia does. If the decision made by the local players is to leave the internal scene in Iraq alone, then the major concern is that any normalization of relations with Iraq be tied to Iraq's pursuit of domestic concerns and its abandonment of heavy investment in military programs. The best way to accomplish this is to enforce Iraqi compliance with the U.N. accords that ended the Gulf War. These include both economic sanctions and long-term monitoring. While there is some European and Arab interest in identifying an end point for economic sanctions, there is no disagreement regarding the implementation of long-term monitoring and lasting military restrictions.

If the decision is not to move decisively against the Iraqi regime and not to tolerate the stalemate and its effect on innocent Iraqis, then there are a number of options, assuming that in all cases the long-term U.N. monitoring and military limitations will be strictly enforced. One possibility is a regional agreement with the U.N. to lift, probably gradually, parts of the economic sanctions contingent upon Iraq's full compliance. Another avenue would be to leave the U.N. sanctions in place, but change the mechanism for Iraqi oil sales and revenue distribution. Currently, under U.N. resolutions 706 and 712, any revenues from Iraqi oil sales go into a U.N.-managed escrow account, from which the U.N. pays reparations to Kuwait and Saudi Arabia, among others, and buys consumer and humanitarian goods for Iraqi citizens. The regime in Baghdad refuses to sell oil under these conditions and insists that some of the revenues should come back to the Iraqi regime for it to spend and distribute. Rather than lifting the sanctions, the U.N. and the regional forum discussed here could adjust the percentage of revenue that Iraq's government could control and spend, thus encouraging Iraq to reenter the market and alleviate the suffering of its people while retaining international leverage over Iraq's future compliance with long-term monitoring and military limits. There are other tactical options for partial normalization that countries in the region could pursue, but the most essential requirement is that they pursue the task of change in Iraq with a common front and with active coordination among themselves. The danger of competitive interference must be reduced.

Currently, all the governments of the Persian Gulf express a preference for a unified Iraq within its present boundaries. Even the Kurdish leaders, such as Talabani and Barzani, agree that in the short run Iraq's territorial integrity should be preserved and some sort of federated and democratic government should be created. The struggle within Iraq appears to be much more a struggle against Saddam Hussein's regime than it is a separatist struggle of Kurds, Sunni, and Shia. As we have seen in Yugoslavia, of course, this can change quickly, and civil wars even without foreign intervention can consume tens of thousands of lives. In the Persian Gulf, it is essential that transition in Iraq not touch off a regional war and that neighboring countries do their best to limit their competitive interference and dampen rather than inflame potential civil war.

At present, there are Turkish ground troops in northern Iraq pursuing Kurdish guerrillas in the PKK. Presumably, they will not stay long, but the temptations for Iraq's neighbors to intervene unilaterally are real. In this case, the government in Ankara may have only domestic security in mind, but oil and land may appear to others as considerations in the background. The United States, the United Kingdom, and France provide air cover from Turkey over northern Kurdish areas of Iraq. These air forces also fly through southern Iraqi airspace, operating out of Saudi Arabia and Kuwait. In both cases, this aerial activity is justified under the U.S., United Kingdom, and French interpretation of U.N. resolution 688 concerning humanitarian resistance to Iraqi repression. Within the parameters of a regional forum, it may be possible to obtain broader support for these missions as well as reduce unnecessary collateral perceived threats. Moreover, even though there may not be appropriate regional forces ready to take over these missions, it may make sense to begin the cross-regional coordination of the process to minimize competitive fears. Neither Iran, Turkey, nor Saudi Arabia shows much interest in dividing or conquering Iraq, but each would be nervous if it appeared that others were pursuing a competitive advantage there. Israel might be in a similar situation, alarmed by a unilateral Syrian role in Iraq. Again, a regional forum would not solve the problem of Iraq, but it would mitigate the more dangerous possibilities inherent in scenarios for change.

Fourth, the United States and Iran should move away from their confrontational rhetoric. Neither nation wants a full-scale confrontation with the other, and they continue to carry on sizable and active commercial relations with each other. They may have sharply different policy objectives, but some of the tension is a product of unnecessary spiral behavior. Participation in the regional forum could defuse some of this as long as each side recognizes that it is not going to eliminate the other from the region. It is not necessary that Washington and Tehran have normal relations—neither government is ready for this—but movement in this direction might be possible through the progress of the regional security conference. The United States, meantime, could relax its containment effort in the economic and financial realm if Iran agreed to the Persian Gulf security agenda that it has recently proposed and that has been partly modified in the proposal above. The regional agreements on acquisition limits, defense expenditures, and deployments, along with the Nuclear Nonproliferation Treaty and International Atomic Energy Agency procedures already in place, would restrict Iran's military potential and limit the danger in Iranian economic recovery.

Economic progress may strengthen the current regime in Iran, but if the majority of the population is as alienated from this regime as most reports contend, then no one will confuse this progress with truly greater regime legitimacy. To the contrary, the economic agenda is more likely to create its own momentum, empowering technical and middle-class business people and weakening the control of clerical and ideological zealots. It is difficult to predict how far this will lead and whether Rafsanjani would survive, would be swept aside by hard-line opponents, or would be swept aside by reform elements who see him as part of the hard-line revolutionary regime. In any case, the economic agenda will lead to greater interdependence and generate new interests that would be jeopardized by a return to a revolutionary foreign policy. It would also focus attention on domestic satisfaction, growth, and the priorities defined as consistent with regional security at the beginning of this chapter.

Finally, it is important to close this argument where it began, that is, with a clear recognition that the objectives of regional security in the Persian Gulf are not within reach in the short run. The states in the area are preoccupied with external threats and foreign opportunities, and while domestic demands press them, they nevertheless retain their outward-looking priorities. The differences and hostility between them are great, and the confrontational rhetoric among them is fierce indeed. To make matters still more complicated, the conflicts in the Gulf are connected to surrounding contests between Arabs and Israelis, Pakistanis and Indians, Russians and Central Asians, and Armenians and Azerbaijanis in ways that compound tensions in the Gulf and facilitate the importation of ever more sophisticated and destructive weapons. What I propose in this chapter is not a panacea or a recipe for near-term peace. Instead, the four options discussed above are designed simply to promote a process of change from which new political conditions and relationships might emerge. After all, one task of strategic analysis is to identify why the objectives we seek today are impossible to reach and to identify what needs to be changed so that we have a better chance tomorrow.

Notes

1. Saddam Hussein, "Speech to ACC Summit," Amman Television, 24 February 1990, Foreign Broadcast Information Service, Near East and South Asia 90-039, pp. 1-5, and Saddam Hussein, "Speech to Arab Summit in Baghdad," Baghdad Domestic Service, 28 May 1990, FBIS-NES-90-103, pp. 2–7.

2. See, for example, Laurie Mylroie, "After the Guns Fell Silent: Iraq in the Middle East," *Middle East Journal* 43 (1989): 51–67.

3. Speech by Saddam Hussein, Baghdad Republic of Iraq Radio Network, in FBIS-NES-94-012, pp. 34–40.

4. "Interview with Vice President Taha Yasin Ramadan," *Al-Jumhuriyah*, 6 February 1994, pp. 4–5, in FBIS-NES-94-030, pp. 29–30; "Interview with Foreign Minister Muhammad Sa'id al-Sahhaf," Dohar Qatar Television Service, 18 February 1994, in FBIS-NES-94-037, pp. 21–25; Sa'id al-Sahhaf, "Resolution 706 Contains Traps and Snares to Shackle Iraq and to Continue Imposing the Blockade; There Is a Treacherous Game in Applying the Resolutions Aimed at Avoiding Fulfillment Obligations," *Al-Thawrah*, 16 March 1994, in FBIS-NES-94-059, pp. 42–50.

5. Salah al-Mukhtar, "The Success and Failure of U.S. Plans in Light of the Leader's Speech," *Al-Jumhuriyah*, April 1994, pp. 1–2, in FBIS-NES-94-084, pp. 66–68. See also Baath Party statement, Baghdad Republic of Iraq Radio, 6 April 1994, in FBIS-NES-94-068, pp. 23–28.

6. Speech by Saddam Hussein, in FBIS-NES-94-012; speech by Saddam Hussein, Baghdad Republic of Iraq Radio Network, 13 March 1994, in FBIS-NES-94-049, pp. 31–32; and "Statement by the National Command of the Arab Socialist Ba'th Party," 3 March 1994, in FBIS-NES-94-043, pp. 36–37.

7. Reportedly, a military coup attempt failed in July 1993, as did an assassination attempt in January 1994. *Akhir Khabar*, 13 November 1993, p. 1, in FBIS-NES-93-218, p. 44; also see Gerald Butt, "Saddam Survives Attack," *The Daily Telegraph*, 18 January 1994, p. 12, in FBIS-NES-94-012, pp. 40–41.

8. In the fall of 1993, the Islamic al-Da'wah withdrew from the Unified Iraqi National Congress. Other key opposition leaders also debated suspending participation, deeply divided over the wisdom of endorsing continued U.N. sanctions on Iraq, among other things. "Major Changes in Iraqi Opposition Movements' Ranks Abroad," *Al-Ouds al-'Arabi*, 28 November 1993, p. 3, in FBIS-NES-93-229, pp. 21–22.

9. Mas'ud Barzani's Democratic Party of Kurdistan declared the Turkey-based Kurdish Worker's Party the most serious threat to the Kurdish nation, and a

terrorist organization, see "Interview with Mas'ud Barzani," *Al-Hayah*, 19 December 1993, p. 6, in FBIS-NES-93-245, pp. 27–29, and message addressed to the people of Iraqi Kurdistan by Mas'ud Barzani, leader of the Democratic Party of Kurdistan, on 27 December, Voice of Iraqi Kurdistan, 27 December 1993, in FBIS-NES-93-247, p. 26. Meantime, Jalal Talabani's Patriotic Union of Kurdistan attacked Islamic organizers in Kurdistan. See *A Collection of Documents Accusing the Missionary and Terrorist Wing in the Kurdish Islamic Movement and its Conspiracy towards the Federal Government in the Iraqi Kurdish Region* (Damascus: National Kurdish Union, 1993).

10. See speech by Ayatollah Ali Hoseyni Khamenei, Tehran Voice of the Islamic Republic of Iran First Program Network, 3 November 1993, in FBIS-NES-93-212, pp. 58–61; FBIS-NES-93-212; speech by Ayatollah Ali Khamenei, Tehran Voice of the Islamic Revolution, 13 April 1994, in FBIS-NES-94-072, pp. 47–48. Also see Anthony Lake, "Confronting Backlash States: A Debate," *Foreign Affairs* 73, no. 2 (March/April 1994): 45–55.

11. Rafsanjani said several times in 1993, that Iran should curtail foreign adventures, put national interests ahead of revolutionary ideology, and contain excessive religious zeal at home. See James A. Bill, "The United States and Iran: Mutual Mythologies," *Middle East Policy*, 2 no. 3 (1993): 101–102.

12. Translation of excerpts from an analytical statement issued by the Mojahedin of the Islamic Revolution Organization on relations with the United States, in *Tehran Kayhan International* (in English), 23 September 1993, in FBIS-NES-93-212, pp. 63–72, and interview with Tehran Majlis Deputy Sai'd Raja'i-Khorasani in Beirut *Al-Safir* (in Arabic), 29 November 1993, in FBIS-NES-93-238, pp. 65–67.

13. Speech by Khamenei, in FBIS-NES-93-212.

14. "Relations, Negotiations," *Tehran Times* (in English), 6 November 1993, in FBIS-NES-93-219, p. 74, and "Conciliatory Overtures," *Tehran Times* (in English), 8 March 1994, in FBIS-NES-94-047, p. 39.

15. "Tehran Preparing to Open New Page in Relations with Washington," *Al-Sharq al-Awsat*, 17 April 1994, p. 4, in FBIS-NES-94-076, p. 65.

16. See speech by Khamenei, in FBIS-NES-93-212, and speech by Khamenei, in FBIS-NES-94-072. Also, see Lake, "Confronting Backlash States," and statement by Ayatollah Khamenei in Tehran Voice of the Islamic Republic of Iran, 25 February 1994, in FBIS-NES-94-039, pp. 94–95. Also, see interview with Hojjat ol-Eslam val Moslemin 'Ali Akbar Mohtashemi, *Jahan-e Eslam*, 17 October 1993, p. 8, in FBIS-NES-93-213, pp. 45–49.

17. On support for Hamas, see *Al-Shira'*, 13 December 1993, p. 9, in FBIS-NES-93-239, p. 41. For Khamenei's views on Gaza-Jericho, see *Al-Sharq al-Awsat*, 24 October 1993, p. 3, in FBIS-NES-93-205, pp. 49–50.

18. Interview with Hojjat ol-Eslam val Moslemin 'Ali Akbar Mohtashemi, *Jahan-e Eslam*, 18 October 1993, p. 9, in FBIS-NES-93-216, pp. 47–50, and in FBIS-NES-93-215, pp. 50–52.

19. "Open Dialogue" with President 'Ali Akbar Hashemi-Rafsanjani, Beirut Tele-Liban Television Network, 28 November 1993, in FBIS-NES-93-231, pp. 47–55, and report of a speech by President Rafsanjani, Tehran Voice of the Islamic Republic of Iran (in Persian), 11 March 1994, in FBIS-NES-94-048, p. 40.

20. "Open Dialogue" with Rafsanjani, in FBIS-NES-93-231, and report of speech by Rafsanjani, in FBIS-NES-94-048.

21. "Interview with Foreign Minister Ali Akbar Velayati," *Al-Diyar* (in Arabic), 17 December 1993, p. 27, in FBIS-NES-93-244, p. 50, and "Interview with Foreign Minister Dr. Ali Akbar Velayati," *Al-Awsat* (in Arabic), 14–20 March 1994, pp. 22–24, in FBIS-NES-94-054, 63–66.

22. See coverage of Rowhani's trip to Damascus, Tehran Voice of the Islamic Republic of Iran, 8 April 1994, in FBIS-NES-94-068, 46.

23. Statement by Khamenei in FBIS-NES-94-039.

24. Richard F. Grimmett, 1985–1992," *CRS Report for Congress: Conventional Arms Transfers to the Third World* (Washington, D.C.: Congressional Research Service, 19 July 1993), 70.

25. Central Intelligence Agency, *The World Fact Book 1992*, 160–162, 300–301.

26. Grimmett, 41–47.

27. Wayne H. Ferris, *The Power Capabilities of Nation-States: International Conflict and War* (Lexington, Mass.: Lexington Books, 1973). See also Robert Gilpin, *Change and War in World Politics* (New York: Cambridge University Press, 1981).

28. Reuters News Agency, 20 April 1994; Iranian News Agency, 19 April 1994.

29. Former Central Intelligence Agency Director James Woolsey claimed before a Senate Select Intelligence Committee hearing in January 1994 that Iran, left to its own devices, will probably take at least eight to ten years to construct a nuclear bomb, although he expects the Iranian government to try to shortcut the process by purchasing nuclear material, warheads, or missiles. See also statements by Lynn Davis, undersecretary of state, quoted by Reuters News Agency, 10 December 1993, and reports on KBS Radio, Seoul, 24 February 1994 and 11 April 1994. Davis admitted that, while the United States has reports of former Soviet scientists travelling to Iran and other potential proliferators, it is difficult to determine exactly what these scientists are doing, "because we don't have very good intelligence in these countries."

30. See statements by the Israeli chief of Air Force intelligence in *Bit'On Heyl Ha'Avir*, 20 December 1993, and Central Intelligence Agency statements reported by the World Press News Agency, 24 December 1993. To some extent, the differences are technical; the Central Intelligence Agency's reports were aimed primarily at assessing the near-term ability of Iran to threaten the United States directly (presumably with intercontinental-ballistic-missile technology), while Israeli reports were directed at estimating Iran's theater missile capability. Reports have indicated that Iran and North Korea may be jointly constructing a facility to build the Korean-designed Nodong-1 missile in Iran; see KBS Radio, Seoul, 11 April 1994, and the discussion below on Iranian missile programs.

31. "Open Dialogue" with President Rafsanjani, in FBIS-NES-93-231.

32. See testimony by Secretary of Defense Richard Cheney before the Senate Armed Services Committee, U.S. Congress, Senate, Committee on Armed Services, *Crisis in the Persian Gulf Region: U.S. Policy options and Implications*, 101st Cong., 2nd sess., 3 December 1990, (Washington D.C.,: Government Printing Office, 1991), 649–55.

33. See George Kennan, "Moscow Embassy Telegram #511: The Long Telegram," in *Containment: Documents on American Policy and Strategy, 1945–1950*, eds. Thomas Etzold and John Lewis Gaddis (New York: Columbia University Press, 1978), 50–63.

34. Lake, "Confronting Backlash States."

35. See Warren Christopher, "Interview," *The New York Times*, 31 March 1993, A3, and Martin Indyk, "Address to the Soref Symposium" (The Washington Institute for Near East Policy, Washington, D.C., 18 May 1993).

36. See Alexander George and William Simmons, eds., *The Limits of Coercive Diplomacy* (Boulder, Colo.: Westview, 1994).

37. In October 1993, the first high-level talks since the war for Kuwait opened between Iran and Iraq when Iranian deputy foreign minister Mohammad Javid Zarif arrived in Baghdad. Issues related to U.N. resolution 598, especially remaining prisoners of war were discussed, as were the Iraqi airplanes flown to Iran during the war over Kuwait. Iran has said it that will not return these planes until all U.N. sanctions on Iraq have been lifted. In February 1994, Iraqi Foreign Ministry undersecretary Sa'd Abd-al Majid al-Faysal was in Tehran to continue the talks. Although both sides agreed that the groundwork had been laid for a ministerial-level meeting, none of the central political disagreements had been resolved. Zarif expressed interest in developing more normal relations with Iraq to stabilize the region and to forestall great-power intervention. Just the same, Iranian newspapers continued to condemn Saddam's rule and Iraq's spring offensive in the marshlands populated by Shia Arabs and accused Iraq of still harboring aggressive ambitions while currying favor with Washington. Iraqi first deputy prime minster Taha Yasin Ramadan, meantime, said that normal relations with Iran would be impossible without settlement on both the prisoner-of-war and the Iraqi airplane issues and, like the Iraqi press, implied that Washington was working through Iran to divide and conquer Iraq. On Iran-Iraq talks, see Voice of the Islamic Republic of Iran, 18 October 1993, in FBIS-NES-93-200, p. 75; *Al-Wasat*, March 1994, in FBIS-NES-94-042, pp. 38–39; and interview with deputy foreign minister Mohammad Javad Zarif, *Al-Wasat*, 21–27 March 1994, in FBIS-NES-94-059, pp. 80–82. On Ramadan's views, see interview with Vice President Taha Yasin Ramadan in al-Sha'b, 1 April 1994, in FBIS-NES-94-068, pp. 28–31. For general press coverage, see commentary, Voice of the Islamic Republic of Iran, 18 October 1993, in FBIS-NES-93-200, pp. 74–75; "Normalizing Ties with Baghdad," Kayhan International (in English), in FBIS-NES-93-241, p. 52; and Makil Mansur, "Iranian Rulers Are Treacherous Revanchists in the Service of Washington," *Al-Thawrah*, 2 March 1994, in FBIS-NES-94-047, pp. 16–17.

38. See "Damascus Declaration," 6 March 1991, FBIS-NES-91-045, 7 March 1991, pp. 1–2.

39. Robert Greenberger, "Clinton Administration Accuses Bonn of Blocking Its Efforts to Isolate Iran," *Wall Street Journal*, 14 October 1993, p. 18, and Elaine Sciolino, "US and Germany at Odds on Isolating Iran," *New York Times*, 2 December 1993, p. A13.

40. Voice of the Islamic Republic of Iran (in Persian), 24 November 1993, in FBIS-NES-93-226, pp. 60–61, and Iranian News Agency, in FBIS-NES-93-228, pp. 79–80.

41. The pipeline between Iran and Pakistan would stretch 1,100 miles and cost $4.5 billion. It could bring 1.6 billion cubic feet of gas per day to Pakistan. United Press International, 13 December 1993. Iran and Pakistan signed a memorandum of understanding initiating the project in April. Reuters, 13 April 1994. Iran, meantime, concluded an oil deal with Turkey and agreed to consider a new gas pipeline as well. Reuters, 22 December 1993. Iran has also been negotiating with India regarding the laying of a pipeline for gas from Qeshm Island to India. OPEC News Agency, 3 March 1994.

42. Hashemi Rafsanjani's son is part of the Iranian-Turkmen working group planning the $1.9 billion pipeline (Reuters, 25 January 1994). Construction of the gas pipeline to Europe through Iran and Turkey reportedly began in the spring of 1994. ITAR, 21 March 1994. Turkmenistan's government reportedly approved both the gas and the oil pipeline projects in April. Reuters, 6 April 1994.

43. "Pakistan toward Stability," *Salam* (in Persian), 12 October 1993, in FBIS-NES-93-205, p. 51; interview with Mohammad Javad Larijani, *Keyhan*, 5 October 1993, in FBIS-NES-93-206, pp. 63–67; Voice of the Islamic Republic of Iran (in Persian), 8 December 1993, in FBIS-NES-93-234, p. 47; address by Iranian Parliament Speaker 'Ali Akbar Nateq-Nuri, Islamabad PTV Television Network, 11 April 1994, in FBIS-NES-94-072, pp. 52–53; and on relations with China, see IRIB Television Network, 4 March 1994, in FBIS-NES-94-044, p. 53.

44. See interview with President Rafsanjani, Voice of the Islamic Republic of Iran in Persian, 29 October 1993, in FBIS-NES-93-208, pp. 53–56, and Friday prayer sermon by President Rafsanjani, Voice of the Islamic Republic of Iran (in Persian), 5 November 1993, in FBIS-NES-93-214, pp. 65–69. Also see Richard K. Herrmann, "Russian Policy in the Middle East: Strategic Change and Tactical Contradictions," *Middle East Journal* 48, no. 3 (summer 1994): 455–474.

45. "A Failure for Containment," *Kayhan International*, 18 April 1994, in FBIS-NES-94-078, pp. 49–50.

46. Joseph Nye, *Bound to Lead: The Changing Nature of American Power* (New York: Basic Books, 1990).

47. Richard A. Bitzinger, *The Globalization of Arms Markets in Transition* (Washington, D.C.: Defense Budget Project, 1993), and Erik Kiefel and Richard Bitzinger, *The Globalization of the Defense Industry: Roles and Responsibilities of the Federal Government* (Washington, D.C.: Defense Budget Project, 1994).

48. IRNA, 13 October 1993, in FBIS-NES-93-197, p. 50; see also interview with Foreign Minister 'Ali Akbar Velayati, *Al-Safir* (in Arabic), 27 November 1993, in FBIS-NES-93-228, pp. 73–77.

49. Interviews with Velayati, in FBIS-NES-93-228, FBIS-NES-93-244.

50. Interview with Velayati, in FBIS-NES-94-054. While Saudi officials continue to warn about the danger of Iran, there appears to be a debate regarding how best to proceed. Some Saudis favor a modified German strategy; others prefer to stick entirely with dual containment. Personal interviews, Riyadh, April 1994.

51. Friday prayer sermon by Rafsanjani, in FBIS-NES-93-214.

52. Interview with Velayati, FBIS-NES-94-054.

53. IRNA, 20 April 1994, in FBIS-NES-94-076, pp. 64–65.

INDEX

Shia Muslims: grievances in Gulf
states, 196–197; Iranian support
for uprising in Iraq, 90; primary
axis of identity of most, 47; potential conflict with, 29; viewed as
heretics in Saudi Arabia, 197

Shurish, Sami, 234

Sibila, battle of, 69

Siffin, battle of, 295

Silkworm anti ship missiles, 204, 257;
prevention of the sale of, 360

Simko, Kurdish chief attempting to
control West Azerbaijan, 236

Sims, Nicholas, 265

Somalia: civil war within, 25; cost of
intrastate conflict, 46; legitimacy
of ruling military elite in question, 57; war with Ethiopia of, 58

Sorani Kurdish, 217

"Sources of Conflict in the Middle
East," ix

South East Anatolia Development
Project, 229

South Ossetia, 23

South Yemen. *See* Yemen

South East Anatolia Development
Project. *See* Greater Anatolia
Project

Soysal, Mümtaz, 172, 177

Stanley, Linn, x

Stein, Janice Gross, ix, xi, 187; essay
of, x

Strait of Hormuz, Iran desire to keep
open, 331

Strategic Defense Initiative, value in
ending Cold War, 373

"strategic committee," 221

Styx missile, 259

Su-24 Fencer long-range strike
aircraft, bought by Iran, 204, 345

subidentities as a cause of death in the
Arab world, 54

Sudan: armed insurrection in, 62; cost
of intrastate conflict, 46; growing
factor of Iran in, 203; involved in

ethnic affairs of Ethiopia; Iranian
support of Islamic movements in,
343; Iranian support of Islamic
regime in, 91, 95, 111; Israel involved in ethnic affairs of, 59;
legitimacy of ruling military elite
in question, 57; marked ethnic
heterogeneities in, 48; problems
with Egypt of, 26; ruling military
elite from Khartoum province, 57;
source of water for, 17; types of
minorities in, 47

Sudanese civil war, loss in lives from,
45

Sudanese Liberation Army, goals of,
61

sulfur mustard, 255

Supreme Council for the Islamic
Revolution, 139, 145

Sykes-Picot agreement, 56, 232

Syria: acute conflicts over water, 17;
Alawite military regime rules, 57;
bad relations of Turkey with, 168;
biological warfare capability, 270;
chemical warfare capability, 270;
cost of intrastate conflict, 46;
could lose about 40 percent of its
supply of Euphrates water, 309;
crude manipulation of Arab
nationalism 77; dependent upon
Russia as main arms supplier, 33;
involved in ethnic affairs of Iraq
and Lebanon, 59; Israel peace accord effect on Turkey, 185;
legitimacy of ruling military elite
in question, 57; marked ethnic
heterogeneities in, 48; need for
peace treaty with Israel, 80; nonsignatory to Chemical Weapons
Convention, 278; not part of
working group on Arms Control
and Regional Security, 279; officers conference at Homs in 1962,
158; possible military support for
Iran by, 114; probably possess offensive chemical-warfare capability, 266; quasi liberal system of
governance in past of, 56; relies on
waters of the Euphrates, 16;

About the Authors

Shaul Bakhash is a Robinson Professor of history at George Mason University and was educated at Harvard and Oxford Universities. He worked for many years as a journalist in his native country of Iran, where he was a correspondent and an editor for *Kayhan* newspapers and reported on Iran for such publications as the *Economist*, the *London Times*, *Financial Times*, and *Newsweek* magazine. He taught history at Tehran University, and in 1977 joined the faculty of Iran's Reza Shah Kabir University. Since 1980, he has taught at Princeton University, held fellowships at the Institute for Advanced Study at Princeton and the Woodrow Wilson International Center for Scholars in Washington, DC, and was a Guggenheim Fellow in 1985-86. His articles have appeared in *New York Review of Books*, the *New Republic*, the *Washington Post*, the *New York Times*, the *Los Angeles Times*, and the *Boston Globe*. He is author of *Iran: Monarchy, Bureaucracy and Reform Under the Qajars* and, most recently, *The Reign of the Ayatollahs: Iran and the Islamic Revolution*.

Shahram Chubin has taught at the Graduate School of International Studies in Geneva since 1981. Formerly he was director of regional security studies at the International Institute of International Studies in London from 1977 to 1981. His publications include *Iran's National Security Policies: Motivations, Capabilities, Impact; Germany and the Middle East: Problems and Prospects;* and *Iran and Iraq at War.* He has contributed chapters most recently to *International Perspectives on the Gulf Conflict 1990-91, Nuclear Proliferation After the Cold War,* and "Iran and the Lessons of the War with Iraq" in *Arms Control and Weapons Proliferation in the Middle East.* Dr. Chubin has published articles in *Daedalus, Foreign Affairs, Foreign Policy, International Security, Washington Quarterly, Survival, The World Today,* and *Adelphi Papers.* He received his doctorate from Columbia University and did his undergraduate work at Oberlin College. Dr. Chubin has been a consultant to the U.S. Department of Defense, the Hudson Institute, and the United Nations. His current research interests include weapons proliferation, and regional security with an emphasis on the Persian Gulf.

Richard K. Herrmann is the director of the Foreign Policy Analysis Program at the Mershon Center and is an associate professor of political science at The Ohio State University. He holds a Ph.D. and M.P.I.A. from the University of Pittsburgh and a B.A. from Miami University, Oxford, Ohio. Dr. Herrmann served on the secretary of state's Policy Planning Staff at the U.S. Department of State from 1989 to 1991. He is currently the co-editor of *International Studies Quarterly*, which is the flagship journal of the International Studies Association. Dr. Herrmann has written extensively on U.S. and Soviet foreign policy and the politics of the Middle East. His first book was entitled *Perceptions and Behavior in Soviet*

Foreign Policy. He has published articles in *International Security, World Politics, American Journal of Political Science, Political Science Quarterly, International Organization,* and *Political Psychology.*

Saad Eddin Ibrahim is chairman of the board of the Ibn Khaldoun Center for Developmental Studies. He was formerly director of the Center for Arab Unity Studies in Cairo and secretary general of the Arab Organization for Human Rights. Dr. Ibrahim has taught at the American University of Cairo, Cairo University, the American University of Beirut, Purdue University, DePauw University, the University of California, Los Angeles, and the University of Washington. His publications include *Sociology of the Arab-Israeli Conflict, Kissinger and the Middle East Conflict,* and *The Great Arab Sedition in the Gulf.* He has also published numerous articles in scholarly journals in both Arabic and English. Dr. Ibrahim received his B.A. from Cairo University and his Ph.D. from the University of Washington.

Geoffrey Kemp is a senior associate at the Carnegie Endowment for International Peace and the director of the Middle East Arms Control Project. He served in the White House during the first Reagan administration and was special assistant to the president for national security affairs and senior director for Near East and South Asian affairs on the National Security Council Staff. From 1970 to 1980, he was on the faculty of the Fletcher School of Law and Diplomacy, Tufts University. Dr. Kemp is the author of *The Control of the Middle East Arms Race,* co-editor of *Arms Control and Weapons Proliferation in the Middle East and South Asia,* and co-author of *India and America After the Cold War* and *Forever Enemies?: American Policy and the Islamic Republic of Iran.* He received his Ph.D. in political science at M.I.T. and his M.A. and B.A. degrees from Oxford University.

David McDowall served in the British Army in the United Kingdom and the Far East before studying Islamic and modern Middle East history at Oxford University. Subsequently he worked with the British Council in India and Iraq, and with UNRWA and Oxfam in the Near East. He has travelled extensively in the region and is now an independent writer and specialist on Middle East affairs. He is author of several publications for the Minority Rights Group including *Lebanon: A Conflict of Minorities, The Kurds, The Palestines, The Kurds: A Nation Denied,* and *The Palestinians: The Road to Nationhood.* He is also the author of *Palestine and Israel: The Uprising and Beyond, Europe and the Arabs: Discord or Symbiosis?* and *A Modern History of the Kurds.* He has also written on Britain, *An Illustrated History of Britain,* and is the author of several books for children. Mr. McDowall is currently writing the Middle East section of a *World Directory of Minorities* for the Minority Rights Group.

Thomas L. McNaugher was a senior fellow in the Foreign Policy Studies Division of the Brookings Institution when he wrote this chapter. He is now the director of the Army Strategy and Doctrine Program at the RAND Corporation. He is the author of *Arms and Oil: U.S. Military Strategy and the Persian Gulf* and numerous articles on the Persian Gulf and other national security issues. Dr. McNaugher is a U.S. Military Academy graduate with a Ph.D. in government from Harvard.

Marvin M. Miller is a senior research scientist with the Department of Nuclear Engineering and the Defense and Arms Control Program at M.I.T. Previously, he was on the faculty of Purdue University from 1967 to 1974, conducting research in laser theory and applications. At M.I.T. his research and teaching focus on arms control, particularly nuclear proliferation, and the environmental impacts of energy production and use. From 1984 to 1986, Dr. Miller was a Foster Fellow with the Nuclear Weapons and Control Bureau of the U.S. Arms Control & Disarmament Agency with whom he continues to maintain a consulting relationship. His writings have appeared in such publications as the *New York Times,* the *Washington Post, International Security, Scientific American, Washington Quarterly,* and the *Bulletin of the Atomic Scientists.*

Thomas Naff is a professor of Asian and Middle Eastern Studies at the University of Pennsylvania. He earned doctorates from the School of Oriental and African Studies at the University of London and the University of California, Berkeley. He was director of the University of Pennsylvania Middle East Center from 1967 to 1985 and the founder and director of the Middle East Research Institute from 1979 to 1985. Since 1984, Dr. Naff has directed an international research project on water issues in the Middle East. The results are being published by State University of New York Press in thirteen volumes. Dr. Naff is director of the Associates for Middle East Research Middle East Water Database and in 1994 he was elected to a three-year term as executive director of the Middle East Water Information Network. Dr. Naff has taught, published, and lectured on a wide range of Middle Eastern subjects.

Soli Özel is an assistant professor of Middle East Studies at the Johns Hopkins University School of Advanced International Studies. He is the executive editor of the bi-monthly journal *Gorus,* and the co-editor in chief of *Turkey Almanac,* both published in Istanbul, Turkey. From 1993 to 1994 he was a columnist for International Affairs in the Turkish weekly *Nokta.* He is currently working on a project about the economic and political dynamics of Turkey's newly emerging provinces tentatively entitled "Turkey's Tigers."

William B. Quandt assumed the Byrd Chair in Government and Foreign Affairs at the University of Virginia in the fall of 1994, where he teaches on the Middle East and American Foreign Policy. Prior to this appointment, he was a senior fellow in the Foreign Policy Studies Program at the Brookings Institution. Dr. Quandt has served as a staff member on the National Security Council, worked at the RAND Corporation in the Department of Social Science, and taught at the University of Pennsylvania, U.C.L.A., and M.I.T. Dr. Quandt has written numerous books, including *Peace Process: American Diplomacy and the Arab-Israeli Conflict Since 1967; The United States and Egypt: An Essay on Policy for the 1990s; Camp David: Peacemaking and Politics; Saudi Arabia in the 1980s: Foreign Policy, Security, and Oil; Decade of Decisions: American Foreign Policy Toward the Arab-Israeli Conflict, 1967-1976;* and *Revolution and Political Leadership: Algeria, 1954-1968.* He also edited *The Middle East: Ten Years After Camp David.* His articles have appeared in a wide variety of publications. Dr. Quandt received his B.A. in international relations from Stanford University and his Ph.D. in Political Science from M.I.T.

Abdel Monem Said Aly is director of the Al-Ahram Center for Political and Strategic Studies in Cairo. He obtained his B.A. from Cairo University and his M.A. and Ph.D. in political science from Northern Illinois University. He has worked at the Al-Ahram Center since 1975 as a researcher, senior researcher and head of the international relations research unit, and as deputy director for research and publishing. Dr. Said Aly was a research fellow at the Brookings Institution in 1987 and worked as a political adviser in the Amiri Diwan of the State of Qatar between 1990 and 1993. In Arabic, he has published books, articles, and chapters on the world system, Arab relations with the regional and global orders, European integration, and the Arab-Israeli conflict. In English, he has contributed papers, published articles and chapters in the United States, France, Sweden, and Singapore on Middle East regional security, Egypt's political system, national security, and arms control policies.

Ghassan Salamé is director of studies at the Centre national de la recherche scientifique and professor of international relations at the Institut d'études politiques in Paris. He has taught international relations at the American University and at St. Joseph University, both in Beirut. Professor Salamé has written and edited a number of books on Middle East politics, the latest being *Democracies without Democrats* and *Proche-Orient: les exigences de la paix.*

Hassan Saleh is the head of research and publication at the Amiri Diwan in the State of Qatar and a part-time assistant professor of modern Middle East history at the University of Qatar. He obtained his B.A. from Cairo University, his M.A. in history from Eastern Michigan University, and his Ph.D. in modern Middle Eastern history from the University of Michigan. He has contributed articles on the Persian Gulf and Middle East history, regional security, and policies to various publications.

Barham A. Salih is the representative of the Kurdish Regional Government in the United States. Since April 1991, he has been acting as a liaison between the Iraqi Kurdish movement and the U.S. Government. Prior to his Washington tenure, Mr. Salih served as a spokesman for the Patriotic Union of Kurdistan and was active in promoting the Kurdish issue in various European countries. He is a member of the Leadership Council of the Patriotic Union of Kurdistan and a senior foreign policy advisor to Mr. Jalal Talabani. Mr. Salih is widely published in the Kurdish press and is a frequent speaker at conferences and seminars convened to discuss the Kurdish and Iraqi issues. Mr. Salih, a native of Iraqi Kudistan, was educated in the United Kingdom, where he received his B.A. in civil engineering and a Ph.D. in statistics and computer modeling. He worked as an engineering consultant with major UK companies before his appointment to the Kurdish representation in United States. Mr. Salih serves on the boards of many Kurdish and Iraqi educational, cultural, and humanitarian organizations.

Janice Gross Stein is the Harrowston Professor of conflict management and negotiation at the University of Toronto and a fellow of the Royal Society of Canada. She was project director of CANADA 21, a private sector commission preparing recommendations for Canadian foreign and defense security from 1993-1994 and has been on the advisory boards of numerous other organizations. Dr. Stein co-authored *Rational Decision-Making: Israel's Security Choices, 1967, Psychology and Deterrence,* and has just completed *We All Lost the Cold War.* She has co-edited *Getting to the Table: Processes of International Prenegotiation* and *Choosing to Cooperate: How States Avoid Loss.* Her special area of interest is conflict management and conflict resolution.

Charles Tripp is presently senior lecturer in politics with reference to the Near and Middle East in the Department of Political Studies at the School of Oriental and African Studies, London University, and is also chairman of the Centre of Near and Middle Eastern Studies at SOAS. After gaining his doctorate in Egyptian politics, he worked at the International Institute for Strategic Studies, London and at the Graduate Institute for International Studies, Geneva before returning to London in 1986 to take up his present position.